LABOUR LAWS AND GLOBAL TRADE

The focus of globalisation studies is on how global processes can be better regulated in order to deliver both economic growth and social justice. Labour laws provide an excellent case study of the creation of a new framework to reconcile free trade and investment with social objectives.

This book, written by a leading authority on international and comparative labour law, provides a thoughtful and comprehensive analysis of the new methods of transnational labour regulation that are emerging in response to globalisation. The author reassesses orthodox views, from the viewpoint of a theory of comparative institutional advantage, and suggests ways in which transnational regulation can be re-invented in the new global economy.

This will be of interest to students of law, human rights, industrial relations, globalisation, international trade and development, as well as policy-makers in international and regional organisations, governments, employers' bodies, trade unions and NGOs.

D1281607

Labour Laws and Global Trade

BOB HEPPLE

·HART·
PUBLISHING

OXFORD AND PORTLAND, OREGON
2005

Hart Publishing
Oxford and Portland, Oregon

Published in North America (US and Canada) by
Hart Publishing c/o
International Specialized Book Services
5804 NE Hassalo Street
Portland, Oregon
97213-3644
USA

Hart Publishing is a specialist legal publisher based in Oxford, England.
To order further copies of this book or to request a list of other
publications please write to:

Hart Publishing, Salter's Boatyard, Folly Bridge,
Abingdon Road, Oxford OX1 4LB
Telephone: +44 (0)1865 245533 or Fax: +44 (0)1865 794882
e-mail: mail@hartpub.co.uk
WEBSITE: http//www.hartpub.co.uk

British Library Cataloguing in Publication Data
Data Available
ISBN 1–84113–160–1 (hardback)
1–84113–187–3 (paperback)

Typeset by Hope Services (Abingdon) Ltd.
Printed and bound in Great Britain by
TJ International Ltd, Padstow, Cornwall

To Mary

CONTENTS

BOXES

TABLES

PREFACE

The focus of globalisation studies has been shifting towards the question of how global processes can be better regulated in order to deliver both economic growth and social justice embedded in the rule of law.[1] There is a rapidly expanding body of literature on the subject, mainly written by economists, political theorists and trade specialists. Why has a scholar and practitioner of labour law ventured into this controversial area? The first reason is a belief that the rules and practices governing productive work are as essential as property rights for the functioning of the market economy. Labour laws also have an important moral dimension. They thus provide an excellent case study of the possibilities for creating a legal framework within which economic integration in a globalised market economy can be reconciled with the ideals of social justice.

In order to understand the legal process we must, as Kahn-Freund famously said, recognise that law is 'neither a professional tool nor an academic toy, and…it has higher purposes than the convenience of the legal profession or the training of the minds of law students'.[2] Those 'who seek to penetrate the process of legal policy making as well as deductive reasoning must seek to penetrate the social objectives pursued by legislatures, judges and administrators, and… must seek to do so whether or not they have been made explicit by those who make the decisions.'[3] I have tried to provide an analysis of transnational labour regulation and to penetrate its objectives in the new global economy. I hope this will help all sides of the debate to argue on the basis of knowledge and reason, instead of simply voicing the stereotypes and dogmas of pro- and anti-globalisation ideologies. Since my readers will have varying degrees of legal knowledge I have, wherever possible, inserted boxes in the text which briefly explain terminology and legal institutions, and provide examples.

The second reason for this book is more personal. My intense interest in international and comparative labour law began in the 1950s when I was a voluntary adviser to the South African Congress of Trade Unions (SACTU), then heavily persecuted by the apartheid government because it was the only multiracial union federation and was closely allied to the ANC. On behalf of the organisation, I drafted petitions to credentials committees of successive

---

[1] Held (2004) at xv.
[2] Kahn-Freund (1978) at 293.
[3] Kahn-Freund (1978) at 278.

International Labour Conferences, challenging the Government's exclusive choice of workers' delegates from the all-white racist unions. To my astonishment, the ILO whose Constitution and conventions oppose all forms of discrimination, repeatedly rejected our petitions. Ultimately, however, international pressure forced the apartheid regime to withdraw from the ILO in 1964.[4] This was the beginning of a campaign that led to international sanctions and contributed to the fall of apartheid. This experience predisposed me to the idea that trade sanctions should be used against countries that violate basic labour standards. My research for this book, over the past decade, has led me to modify that belief, and to argue that only in the case of pariah states (*hostis humani generis*) such as apartheid South Africa and the military junta in Myanmar will the advantages of trade sanctions outweigh the undoubted benefits of free trade in promoting economic growth, democracy and impoved labour standards.

My views about the possibilities and limits of transposing international and regional labour standards into national systems of labour law have been affected by my experiences, since 1974, as an independent expert for the European Commission on projects such as the directive on the protection of acquired rights of workers on the transfer of undertakings and the implementation of EC labour law by the UK. By 1986, I had become convinced that the methods of negative and positive harmonisation of labour laws being pursued by the EC were inadequate, sometimes even counter-productive, as a means of reconciling economic integration and social policy. In meetings of experts under various presidencies from 1989, I was one of those who advocated a framework of fundamental human rights, in place of partial harmonisation.[5] Although far from perfect, the EU Charter of Fundamental Rights, now incorporated in the EU Constitution signed on 29 October 2004, has enormous potential. One of my concerns in this book is how the new framework of rights can provide a floor on which the 'soft law' of the Open Method of Co-Ordination and Social Dialogue can function effectively.

My work as an ILO expert in the 1990s taught me about both the dangers and possibilities of using foreign experts in the law reform process in developing countries and emerging market economies. In Namibia I was asked to draft a Labour Code for the newly independent state in a very short period. I encountered inter-departmental disputes, stand-offs between civil servants who had served the old colonial regime and the new inexperienced Ministers and their staffs, a weak and divided trade union movement and powerful mining and farming interests, as well as some lawyers who wanted the quick-fix of importing inappropriate models from the US. The experience was quite different in my native South Africa, as an ILO expert on the Cheadle Committee which drafted the South African Labour Relations Act in 1994. Here I found a committed Ministry of Labour, outstanding labour law specialists, strong trade unions which had been forged in the long struggle against apartheid and were close to the political leadership, and employers who were ready and willing to engage in constructive social dialogue. The Act that was produced was the product of intense consultation and discussion, blending foreign experience with the organic development of the country's labour laws. In Russia, sent by the ILO to advise the Government on labour relations, I witnessed the struggles of the new 'alternative' unions to establish their independence in the face of chaotic liberalisation, and without effective legal guarantees, while the 'official' unions and enterprise management retained the mindsets of the Soviet period.[6] My conclusion was that labour rights need to start at home, and to be fashioned so as to improve, not diminish, the comparative advantages of each country in the new global economy. This led me to study the new scholarship on comparative institutional advantage, and to seek to develop it in respect of labour laws (chapter 10, below).

I owe many intellectual debts. Paul O'Higgins, who was my teacher, supervisor and later teaching and research colleague at Cambridge from 1964, impressed upon me the importance and relevance of international labour law. Otto Kahn-Freund and Bill Wedderburn showed me the enormous contribution that comparative law can make to understanding the social purposes of law. Kurt Lipstein sparked my interest in EU law even before the UK had joined the Community, and has continued to inspire and encourage me, and to guide me through the mysteries of the conflict of laws. Many of my ideas developed in the course of working with colleagues in the European Labour Law Group which produced *The Making of Labour Law in Europe* (1986),[7] contributing to Roger Blanpain's *International Encyclopedia for Labour Law and Industrial Relations* and many of his other comparative projects, editing contributions in my role as Chief Editor of volume XV of the *International Encyclopedia of Comparative Law* (Max-Planck Institute, Hamburg), undertaking research projects for the International Institute for Labour Studies and the UN Conference on Trade and Development, serving as a member of an ILO expert group on standards-related activities and decent work, participating in numerous international seminars and conferences, and teaching with colleagues in courses on International and Comparative Labour Law in London, Cambridge and Cape Town Universities, and on Civil and Political Rights in the EU in Cambridge. It would be invidious to attempt to name all these colleagues and students—to echo Montaigne, I have 'gathered a posy of [their] flowers, and nothing but the thread that binds them is my own.'

---

[4] The story is told by Luckhardt and Wall (1980) at 388-93.

[5] This work was undertaken with my friends and colleagues Roger Blanpain, Silvana Sciarra and Manfred Weiss, and won the support of over 100 labour law specialists: see Blanpain *et al* (1996).

[6] For these reflections, see Hepple (1994).

[7] Hepple (1986a).

I am especially grateful to those colleagues who read and commented on draft chapters of this book, in particular Catherine Barnard, Lance Compa, Simon Deakin, Sandy Fredman, Jo Scott, Katherine Stone, and Erika Szyszczak. The usual disclaimers apply. Daniel Bethlehem and Jo Scott kindly allowed me to absorb the basics of International Economic Law in their Cambridge classes. Jean-Claude Javillier and the Standards Branch of the ILO provided me with extensive information and analysis of the work of the ILO. I had excellent research assistance from Claire da Silva, Sarah Fraser, James Hawkins and Nicola Thompson. Keith Ewing, Francis Maupain, and Katherine Stone kindly permitted me to see their papers which are awaiting publication, and I had the good fortune to be able to consult proof copies of Neville Rubin's comprehensive *Code of International Labour Law*. The Leverhulme Trust generously awarded me an Emeritus Fellowship which has covered my research expenses. The Master and Fellows of Clare College, and the Faculty of Law in the University of Cambridge, provided me with the space, facilities, and stimulating environment in which to work. Finally, but ultimately crucial, I pay tribute to the enormous patience and encouragement of my publisher, Richard Hart.

This is a project which has developed over many years and, inevitably, I have drawn on and cannibalised a number of my published articles, listed in the References, with due acknowledgment to their publishers.[8] Most of the book consists of previously unpublished material.

Clare College
Cambridge
30 September 2004

---

[8] In particular, Hepple (1993), (1997), (1999a), (1999b), (2002a), (2002b),(2002c), (2003).

TABLE OF ABBREVIATIONS

AB   Appellate Body (WTO)
AFL-CIO   American Federation of Labor-Congress of Industrial
                  Organisations
APEC   Asia Pacific Economic Co-operation Agreement
ATCA   Alien Tort Claims Act (US)
BIAC   Business and Industry Advisory Group (OECD)
C   Convention (ILO)
CBERA   Caribbean Basin Economic Recovery Act (US)
CBI   Caribbean Basin Initiative
CAFTA   Central American Free Trade Agreement
CCALC   Canada-Chile Agreement on Labor Co-operation
CCAS   Conference Committee on the Application of Standards (ILO)
CEACR   Committee of Experts on the Application of Conventions and
                  Recommendations (ILO)
CEEP   Centre Européen des Enterprises Publiques
CFI   Court of First Instance (EU)
CFA   Committee on Freedom of Association (ILO)
CIME   Committee on Investment and Multinational Enterprises
                  (OECD)
CME   Co-ordinated Market Economy
DGV   Directorate-General on Employment, Industrial Relations and
                  Social Affairs (EU)
DSU   Understanding on the Rules and Procedures Governing the
                  Settlement of Disputes (WTO)
DSB   Disputes Settlement Body (WTO)
EC   European Communities (see p 195)
ECE   Evaluation Committee of Experts (NAALC)
ECHR   European Convention for the Protection of Human Rights
ECJ   European Court of Justice
ECOSOC   Economic and Social Committee (EU)
ECR   European Court Reports
EES   European Employment Strategy
EMU   European Monetary Union
ESC   European Social Charter (Council of Europe)
ETI   Ethical Trading Initiative

ETUC	European Trade Union Confederation
EPZ	Export Processing Zone
ERA	Employment Rights Act (UK)
EU	European Union (see p 195)
EWC	European Works Council
FDI	Foreign Direct Investment
FFC	Fact-Finding and Conciliation Commission (ILO)
FTAA	Free Trade Agreement of the Americas
GATS	General Agreement on Trade in Services (WTO)
GATT	General Agreement on Tariffs and Trade
GB	Governing Body (ILO)
GSP	Guaranteed System of Preferences
ICFTU	International Confederation of Free Trade Unions
ICJ	International Court of Justice
ILC	International Labour Conference
ILO	International Labour Organisation
ILS	International Labour Standards
IMF	International Monetary Fund
ITF	International Transport Workers Organisation
ITGLWF	International Textile, Garment and Leather Workers' Federation
ITO	International Trade Organisation
LME	Liberal Market Economy
MAI	Multilateral Agreement on Investment
MERCOSUR	Mercado Commun del Sur
NAALC	North American Agreement on Labor Co-operation
NAFTA	North American Free Trade Agreement
NCP	National Contact Points (OECD)
NGO	Non-governmental organisation
NLRA	National Labor Relations Act (US)
NLRB	National Labor Relations Board (US)
OCSE	Organisation for Co-operation and Security in Europe
OEDC	Organisation for Economic Co-operation and Development
OMC	Open Method of Co-ordination
OPIC	Overseas Private Investment Corporation (US)
OTCA	Omnibus Trade and Competitiveness Act (US)
SACU	Southern African Customs Union
SADC	Southern African Development Community
SE	Societas Europea (European company)
SEA	Single European Act
SNB	Special Negotiating Body (EU)
SRI	Socially Responsible Investment

TBT	Agreement on Technical Barriers to Trade (WTO)
TCM	Technical Co-operation Mission (ILO)
TEU	Treaty of European Union
TNC	Transnational corporation
TUAC	Trade Union Advisory Committee (OECD)
TULRCA	Trade Union and Labour Relations (Consolidation) Act (UK)
UEAPME	International Association of Crafts and Small and Medium Enterprises
UNCTAD	UN Conference on Trade and Development
UNDP	UN Development Programme
UNICE	Union of Industrial and Employers' Confederations of Europe
USCIB	US Council for International Business
USTR	US Trade Representative
VCLT	Vienna Convention on the Law of Treaties
WB	World Bank (International Bank for Reconstruction and Development)
WFTU	World Federation of Trade Unions
WTO	World Trade Organisation

TABLE OF CASES

EUROPEAN CASES

AUSTRALIA

CANADA

MEXICO

SOUTH AFRICA

SCOTLAND

UNITED KINGDOM

UNITED STATES OF AMERICA

WTO CASES

1

Does Transnational Labour Regulation Matter?

1. Aim and scope of this book
2. Labour in the new global economy
3. Dilemmas of labour laws
4. The case for transnational regulation

1. Aim and scope of this book

This aim of this book is to examine the new methods of *transnational labour regulation*[1] that are emerging in response to economic globalisation.

For the past two centuries the need for labour regulation across national boundaries has been fiercely contested. For extreme free trade advocates who favour the removal of all barriers on trade and investment accompanied by the deregulation of labour markets, the issue is simple. Transnational labour standards, at least if they are effectively enforced, undermine the comparative advantage of countries. According to this view, *domestic labour laws* are as much a determinant of comparative advantage as natural endowments, resources and preferences. At the other extreme, protectionists argue for the safeguarding of national markets and *domestic labour laws* against external regulation. For them too, the issue is straightforward. In the 1880s, the German economist Friedrich List, arguing for the protection of infant industries against British competition wrote: 'in order to allow freedom of trade to operate naturally, the less advanced nations must first be raised to that stage [to which] the English nation has been artificially elevated.'[2] Today some economists contend that fast economic growth in the developing countries will automatically lead to the improvement of *domestic labour laws*. Many politicians in developing countries believe that transnational regulation is a cynical

[1] See Box 1.1 for terminology.
[2] List (1885).

form of 'social imperialism' through which developed nations seek to exclude competition by imposing standards that they themselves ignored in the process of industrialisation.[3] They say that pressure for free trade is often a case of 'do as I say, not as I do.' This can be illustrated by President George W. Bush's imposition of tariff increases to protect the uncompetitive US steel industry, a measure declared unlawful by the WTO in 2003. The revenues from the tariffs were not being transferred to protect the pensions and healthcare of the most vulnerable US workers; indeed, attempts in the US Congress to expand protection for workers displaced by trade agreements have met with resistance by the Bush Administration.[4] This affected competition from countries like South Korea, Japan and Europe; the protection this gave US steel workers was both short-lived and illusory.

Most governments and policy makers, however, are neither pure free trade advocates nor pure protectionists. They do not think there is a simple choice between more jobs (free trade) and better jobs (protection). They do not want to enter a 'race to the bottom', the memorable phrase used by Mr Justice Brandeis in 1933 to describe the competition between states to reduce regulatory requirements so as to attract business.[5] They are striving to achieve a balance between free trade and investment, on the one hand, and employment growth and the raising of social and labour standards, on the other hand. The South African Minister for Trade and Industry, for instance, said the only way for his country to achieve sustainable employment 'is to change the structural base of its economy, which had for too long relied on tariff protection and state subsidies.'[6] The ANC Government in South Africa has accepted the need for 'flexible' labour markets in response to global competition. The burning question, contested with its trade union allies, is whether and how this can be reconciled with the hard-won labour standards embodied in South African legislation since 1995. Similar choices face governments, employers and unions in other countries. We are left, in Sciarra's words, with 'a hybrid labour law, torn between its old protective function and the new aspiration towards flexibility.'[7]

These issues are not only at the heart of controversies about employment and social policy within states. They are also reflected on an international scale, within the World Trade Organisation (WTO), the International Labour Organisation (ILO), the International Monetary Fund (IMF) and World Bank (WB), and also within regional groupings such as the European Union (EU), North American Free Trade Agreement (NAFTA), the *Mercado del Sur*

---

[3] Anderson (1996) at 452.
[4] Gould (2001) at 735.
[5] *Liggatt v Lee*, 218 US 517 per Barndeis J dissenting at 559; see generally Barnard (2000a).
[6] *Labour News* [South Africa], 13 May 1998.
[7] Sciarra (1996) at 13.

(MERCOSUR) in South America, the Asian Pacific Economic Co-operation Agreement (APEC) and the Southern African Development Community (SADC).

The questions with which this book is concerned should be of interest to all those who seek a path between the extreme versions of free trade and pro-tectionism, irrespective of their political affiliation. It will be argued that the reconciliation of global trade and labour rights will not come from relocating labour law within the sphere of international trade law (chapters 4, 5 and 6, below). Instead, efforts should be directed at shaping the many new strands of transnational labour regulation that are emerging so as to spread the benefits of growing trade and investment to the poorest, to protect basic human rights, and to contribute to social justice and democracy. This is a complex and difficult process, to which there is no single solution.

Any study such as this must begin with the International Labour Organisation (ILO) which since 1919 has adopted *international labour standards* (ILS). The ILO is unique among international institutions both in its tripartite structure (governments, employers and unions), and in its super-visory system. The effectiveness of this structure, the content of the standards produced, and their implementation have been criticised from many perspec-tives. Can an early 20th century institution survive in the 21st century global economy, and, if so, how does it need to change? (chapter 2, below.) The methods of transnational regulation have multiplied in response to modern economic globalisation. These include corporate codes and labels, transna-tional collective agreements, and guidelines from international organisations (chapter 3, below), unilateral social clauses (chapter 4, below) and bilateral and regional agreements making trade conditional upon observance of specified labour standards (chapter 5, below). Some governments, notably that of the US with support from American unions and many NGOs, want the multilateral WTO trading system to link *internationally recognised worker rights* to free trade (chapter 6, below). There is an increasing number of dis-putes in national courts and tribunals involving a transnational element, for example when a claim is made against a transnational corporation (TNC) for wrongs committed in another country where it operates (chapter 7, below). The process of integrating free movement of goods, services and capital with a social dimension has gone furthest in the EU; a number of general lessons about successfully combining economic and social integration emerge from this experience (chapters 8 and 9, below).

A spider's web of *hard* and *soft* transnational regulation is being weaved around domestic labour laws and is profoundly influencing them. In the light of the developments analysed in the earlier chapters, the final chapter offers a reassessment of the orthodox views on the effects of globalisation on labour laws, in particular from the viewpoint of the theory of comparative institutional advantage, and suggests ways in which transnational labour regulation can be re-invented for the modern global economy.

A necessary preliminary, in this chapter, is to outline the nature of the new global economy and the dilemmas it poses for labour laws, and then to take a fresh look at the economic and moral case for transnational labour regulation.

Box 1.1

TERMINOLOGY

Domestic labour laws: These apply within a defined national territory or locality where work is performed, although in some cases (discussed in chapter 7) they may have extra-territorial effect or be applied to workers posted by their employer to another country. The term 'laws' is used broadly to refer to legislation, judge-made common law, collective agreements, and other formal and informal rules and procedures including custom and practice. Some of these are *hard* law, legally enforceable through courts, while others are *soft* operating only as guidelines, but the line is difficult to draw because courts and tribunals may take account of these practices or recommendations when interpreting and applying hard law.

International labour standards: These are embodied in conventions and recommendations of the ILO. Conventions are *hard* standards legally binding on ILO Member States which ratify them, subject to international supervision. Recommendations cannot create legal obligations and are usually described as *soft* standards, although in practice they may differ little from conventions. Eight 'core' conventions (on freedom of association, the right to collective bargaining, discrimination, and the elimination of forced labour and child labour) are binding on all ILO member states (chapter 2, below). The standards are usually directed at states rather than corporations or individuals. These standards must be distinguished from '*internationally recognised worker rights*', a term of different scope used in US trade legislation (chapter 5, Table 5.A, below).

Transnational labour regulation: This term is used compendiously to refer to both *hard* and *soft* rules and procedures which apply across national boundaries, that is in more than one jurisdiction. They may be *unilateral*, applied by one country to another without agreement, or *bilateral* as a matter of treaty between two countries, or *regional* by treaty between a number of states within a particular region of the world, or *multilateral* such as the WTO agreements. These rules may be directed at states, or corporations or individuals.

2. Labour in the new global economy

What is 'globalisation'?

The term 'globalisation' is a tag attached to 'often very different cultural, economic and social processes.'[8] 'Economic globalisation' describes 'the integration of economic activities across borders through markets.'[9] Laws play an essential role in this process by either ensuring the free movement of goods, services and capital, or by erecting barriers against them. The words 'global trade' are used as short-hand to denote these essential features of the world-wide market economy. In theory, globalisation should also encompass free movement of labour. An obvious solution to the inequalities between poor and rich countries would be free migration. But labour has remained relatively immobile for a number of reasons. These include political opposition to immigration, sometimes fuelled by racism, the reluctance of people to be uprooted, the lack of demand for unskilled labour in developed countries, and difficulties experienced by migrants such as language differences, lack of skills, and the costs of legal migration.[10]

The extent of modern globalisation, how it differs from earlier processes, and whether it is likely to increase or decrease are all contested issues in the voluminous literature on the subject.[11] What is undisputed is that revolutionary technological changes, in communication and information, are giving rise to a network society that creates unprecedented opportunities for trade and investment. Economic integration is advancing rapidly. Goods are produced where costs are lowest and consumers in virtually all countries can choose from the same range of branded products.

Much of the dramatic increase in world trade over the past two decades reflects the growth of global production systems. 'Products that might 20 years ago have been produced in one country are now made up of components that have crossed dozens of borders before final assembly.'[12] Developing countries increasingly export manufactured goods and services instead of concentrating on primary goods and raw materials. These new growing economies are competing with the developed countries who also compete with each other.

In this new globally competitive economy, the exploited human beings with whose dignity and welfare the founders of labour laws were concerned, are

---

[8] Hirst and Thompson (1999) at xiii.
[9] Wolf (2004) at 14.
[10] Bhagwati (2004) at 208–18; Wolf (2004) at 85–87.
[11] For an excellent overview see the essays in Michie (2003).
[12] Oxfam (2002) at 39.

now most likely to be found in sweatshops[13] in South Asia or the Caribbean producing clothes for supermarkets in Europe and America; or in slum factories in East Asia assembling circuit boards for transnational IT companies. Or they might be independent coffee producers in Kenya or Guatemala facing ruin because of the plummeting prices at which they have to sell their crops to TNCs that control the market. Meanwhile, manufacturing industries in Europe, once reliant on the unionised labour of full-time men, have been greatly reduced, especially in the UK, and standardised terms of employment have been eroded. They have been replaced by an increasingly feminised and non-unionised labour force of part-time, temporary, and self-employed 'flexible' workers mainly engaged in service industries. 'As low-wage economies in the developing world become more integrated with high-wage economies in the industrialised world, there is downward pressure on the latter.'[14] Read your daily newspaper and you will find stories of workers in the older EU countries being made redundant as their employers relocate to Eastern Europe, Vietnam or Bangladesh. One is no longer surprised to make one's airline booking via a call centre in India. The growing phenomenon of 'offshoring' indicates that it is not only in manufacturing that global competition is taking place, and that not all workplaces in developing countries are sweatshops (see Box 1.2). Equity analysts, medical specialists, architects, even lawyers, in Europe and the US are facing competition from far cheaper skilled professionals in Asia and other countries such as South Africa.

The role of transnational corporations

The role of TNCs in the globalisation process is also contested.[15] What is clear is that TNCs have been the driving force in technological innovation in communications, transport and information.[16] Three-quarters of world trade originates with TNCs, one-third of which takes place between subsidiaries of the same TNC.[17] In 1976, there were 11,000 TNCs with 82,600 foreign affiliates; by 2002, there were 64,592 TNCs with 851,167 foreign affiliates. TNCs have also been responsible for new forms of investment and business organisation that have transformed the world of work. These include licensing agreements and franchising, strategic alliances and joint ventures, sub-contracting and

---

[13] The term 'sweatshop' was coined in the 19th century in Britain to describe establishments in unorganised trades where wages and conditions were considered exploitative ('sweated labour' was often home work).

[14] Oxfam (2002) at 90–91.

[15] Wolf (2004) at 220–48.

[16] Ietto-Gillies (2003) at 141.

[17] Ietto-Gillies (2003) at 141.

Box 1.2

OFFSHORE OUTSOURCING[18]

'Office Tiger, an outsourcing company with offices on the sixth floor of a pink stone shopping mall in Chennai—formerly known as Madras—is emerging as a virtual research arm of Wall Street. The company employs postgraduates, financial analysts and business planners. Their average age is 26 . . . With six of the top 12 [US] investment banks as clients, Office Tiger is doubling its capacity in the Chennai arcade. . . . US banks have led the way in outsourcing to India procedures such as information techno-logy systems, management and data transactions. They have saved $8bn in the past four years, according to Nasscom, India's IT lobby group . . . They are paid high salaries by Indian standards ($1000 per month), but this is only one-eighth of the salary of a similarly qualified worker in Manhattan.'[19]

'It is not just India that is an attractive outsourcing—or offshoring—des-tination. HSBC is transferring staff to China and Malaysia, while Eastern Europe is also popular . . . The trend has drawn sharp criticism from trade unions. Amicus [a British trade union] reiterated its warning that the UK could lose 200,000 jobs in financial service by 2008 . . .'[20]

'The combination of low wages and relative flexibility of an almost wholly non-unionised and youthful labour force enables investors to undertake tasks that were previously ignored. For example wage costs amount to about 30 percent of a typical call centre in India, compared with 70 percent in the US or UK. This gives an Indian call centre the latitude to add extra functions and continue operations around the clock.'[21]

'While researchers had estimated that 2m to 5m jobs could move offshore over the next 5 to 10 years, the number could be far greater, UNCTAD suggested . . . Offshoring opens the possibility of reaping all the benefits associated with the international division of labour in the production of services . . . [A]ny country seeking to prevent offshoring would run the risk of declining competitiveness.'[22]

---

[18] 'Outsourcing' has been going on for centuries. It occurs both within and beyond borders. 'Offshoring' indicates the export of jobs. This can be inside the same organisation or outside it.

[19] *Financial Times*, 20 August 2003, at 11.

[20] *Financial Times*, 3 December 2003, at 3.

[21] *Financial Times*, 28 January 2004, at 19.

[22] *Financial Times*, 23 September 2004, at 9.

offshoring. The networks formed by TNCs 'transcend national boundaries, identities and interests.'[23]

The very concept of a 'transnational' as a corporation which is strongly linked to a nation-state where its headquarters is based has been questioned.[24] The TNCs have been described as 'the power-holders of wealth and technology in the global economy'[25] because of their ability to shift production around the globe, to bypass national governments, and to account only to themselves for intra-firm trade and transfers (see Box 1.3). Others argue that the claim that companies are stronger than national governments is both factually wrong and misconceived.[26] Whatever view one takes about the merits of the rival arguments, there can be no doubt that national labour laws have to take account of the fact that the operations of TNCs are increasingly decentralised and specialised and are dependent upon complex, interlocking, cross-border networks. This has both positive and negative implications. Local specialised subsidiaries may be able to serve other firms in a national or regional market and to create jobs. On the other hand, these specialised branch plants enjoy little autonomy and even routine decisions may be made centrally and communicated electronically to relatively junior local representatives in another country. Access to the real decision-makers by local union representatives is problematic.

Box 1.3

TNCs ON THE MOVE IN EUROPE

In 1996, the Hoover company decided to close its plant near Dijon in France, with the loss of 600 jobs, and transfer its activities to Cambuslang near Glasgow in Scotland, where 400 new short-term jobs were created. This followed the conclusion of a collective agreement between management and the British Amalagamated Engineering and Electrical Union (AEEU), which provided for flexible use of labour, new working patterns, a no-strike deal and pay freeze.

Martine Aubry, the French Minister of Labour, and her Prime Minister, attacked Hoover's relocation as 'social dumping'.[27] The British Prime Minister, John Major, responded: 'If investors and business choose to come to Britain rather than pay the costs of socialism in France, let them call it "social dumping". I call it dumping socialism.'[28] The French state was powerless to prevent the relocation.

---

[23] Catsells (1996) at 192.

[24] Ghoshal and Bartlett (1993).

[25] Catsells (1996) at 192.

[26] Wolf (2004) at 221–30.

[27] *European Industrial Relations Review and Report* 230, at 16.

[28] *Financial Times,* 6 March 1996. At the same time Rowntree, the confectioner, was quietly moving part of its activities from Glasgow to Dijon!

Not long afterwards, Renault, the French company, announced the closure of its plant at Vilvoorde in Belgium as part of a global restructuring plan. A Belgian labour tribunal declared Renault's decision unlawful on grounds that Belgian law and collective agreements on consultations with workers' representatives had been flouted. A French labour tribunal at Nanterre went even further, declaring Renault's decision to be null and void. Notwithstanding these rulings, Renault was eventually able to go ahead with the closure. The workers had to be content with a social plan mitigating the effects of redundancy.[29]

3. The dilemmas of labour laws

The view from the developed countries

These features of the new economy mean that labour law is now inevitably global law and not just the concern of a particular nation-state. There are, however, different perspectives from the developed and developing countries about the impact of global trade. Understandably, workers and their unions in the developed countries threatened by cheap imports complain that competition from 'cheap labour' standards in developing countries and also in the emerging market economies of Central and Eastern Europe is unfair. They see this as a threat to their own employment, wage levels and bargaining strength.[30] An unemployed US software applications developer is reported to have said: 'when our laws allow US corporations systematically to replace our workers with cheaper-waged [foreign] workers there is something wrong with our laws'.[31] On the other hand, the President of Germany's largest employers' organisation has commented: 'In the old days, employers asked themselves "how bad is the wage agreement for me?". Today they say "I don't care about the agreement any more, because I have four or five excellent exit routes. I may simply relocate 10,000 jobs in the Czech Republic. Or I may outsource." '[32] The mere threat of a strike by capital (the 'exit route') is likely to secure concessions.

Such threats of relocation by TNCs are greatly facilitated by the new mobility of international capital and by the legal guarantees in regional and international agreements of free movement of capital, goods and services (Box 1.3, above). The freedom of movement of individual workers across borders is

---

[29] *European Industrial Relations Review and Report*, 279, 282, and 289.
[30] Castells (1996) at 192; Wolf (2004) at 5.
[31] *Financial Times*, 24 September 2003.
[32] *Financial Times*, 21 August 1996.

severely limited, and in any event is no counterpart to the free movement of investors. Transnational industrial action, as a countervailing power to cross-border management decision-making in TNCs, has been a rarity. It is subject to severe legal restrictions, sometimes outright prohibition, in almost every country and these restrictions have increased over recent decades (chapter 7, below). This has compounded the problems for weak international unions representing an increasingly fragmented workforce. More generally the decline of organised labour's political strength is reflected not only in the policies pursued by right-wing neo-liberal governments, such as the Republicans in the US, but also in those of the centre-left such as the Democrats in the United States, New Labour in the UK, the Social Democrats in Germany and Sweden and the Socialists in France, who have, to a greater or lesser extent, accepted the need for 'flexible' labour markets in response to the forces of global competition.

These developments have put national labour laws in the developed countries under irresistible pressures. The coverage of labour legislation has shrunk as the fragmentation of labour markets and the trends to more insecure, irregular, non-unionised forms of employment have increased, with about a third of all employed workers in most developed countries now being in non-regular, non-full time work.[33] Union membership, collective representation, and collective bargaining have also declined. Bargaining in all industrial countries increasingly takes place under the shadow of threats to relocate or to merge with foreign corporations: domestic labour laws rarely offer rights to bargain about strategic corporate-level decisions such as these.

The view from the developing countries

There is a different perspective from the poorer developing countries. These states are under immense pressure to compete among themselves for access to world markets and investment. This is particularly the case in those export zones (EPZs) in which labour standards have been abandoned, and basic labour rights to freedom of association and effective collective bargaining are denied. In some cases (eg Myanmar, Sudan) there has been brutal repression.

However, most developing countries want to enhance and improve living and working conditions; in particular they are paying increasing attention to workers in the vast, heterogeneous, and still growing informal sector. This, as the ILO has repeatedly noted, 'constitutes an important, if not central, aspect of the economic and social dynamics' of these countries.[34] The informal sector includes a wide variety of activities ranging from petty trade, service repairs and domestic work to transport, construction and manufacturing. It rarely

[33] Standing (1997) at 19–21.
[34] ILO (1997c) at 176; Schlyter (2003).

involves a clear-cut employer-employee relationship. The diversity of jobs and employment status make it difficult for informal sector workers to organise themselves into unions; moreover patriarchal family and ethnic loyalties may count for more than solidarity between workers. The ILO points out that informal sector units 'operate on the fringe, if not outside, the legal and administrative framework', with many ignoring or paying scant attention to regulations concerning safety, health, and working conditions.

In the past few years a number of trade unions and NGOs around the world have supported initiatives to help informal sector workers. The state has a major role to play in helping informal sector workers overcome their disadvantages. This makes it a priority of national policy to establish and enforce a regulatory framework in which 'the right of informal sector workers to join or create representative associations of their choosing, as well as state recognition of their role as interlocutors and/or partners in policy-making or programme implementation are . . . key enabling factors'.[35]

A threat to these essential national policies comes from the neo-liberal creed espoused by the IMF and World Bank. Stiglitz, former chief economist at the World Bank, has commented: '[A]s hard as workers have fought for "decent jobs", the IMF has fought for what is euphemistically called "labour market flexibility", which sounds like little more than making the labour market work better but as applied has simply been a code name for lower wages and less job protection.'[36] The aim of these financial institutions is to encourage growth, but they have underestimated the effect of their actions in enriching political and military elites at the top while destroying those kinds of solidarity between states, communities and workers which might increase these countries' bargaining power with investors. In recent years, the financial institutions have tried to redress the balance to some extent by making their funding conditional on the recipient country recognising basic labour standards. The familiar story is that a developing country seeking World Bank or IMF support or tariff preferences from the US or EU, is asked to produce what amounts to paper evidence that the country is observing basic labour standards. This leads to the employment of an 'expert' who rapidly drafts a Labour Code for the state in question. Aid or loans then flow, or trade preferences are granted, but the Labour Code remains unenforced. Behind the paper tigers of laws and codes of conduct, is the thriving jungle of the market. Where there is mass unemployment, difficult trade-offs have to be made between employers' demands for 'flexibility' and workers' demands for decent jobs. Unions, where they exist, may have little option but to accept worse employment conditions, and those workers who dissent have few if any rights (Box 1.4, below).

---

[35] ILO (1997c) at 176.
[36] Stiglitz (2002) at 84.

Box 1.4

FLEXIBILITY AND THE RIGHT TO STRIKE IN SOUTH AFRICA

VWSA, a subsidiary of the transnational Volkswagen corporation, invested during the apartheid era in a plant in Uitenhage, one of the 'Bantustan' areas of cheap labour. In 1998, after the newly democratic South Africa re-entered the world economy, VWSA made a multi-billion Rand agreement to export 68,000 Golf vehicles to the UK. This required more cars to be produced in a shorter time, with the resultant introduction of round-the-clock working 6 days a week. The National Union of Metal Workers of South Africa (NUMSA) signed a collective agreement implementing these changes. About 1300 workers at the plant went on strike protesting at their union's decision to suspend 13 shop stewards who had rebelled against the agreement. They were dismissed. It was reported that 'droves of unemployed youth file into Volkswagen to fill the jobs vacated by the dismissed workers. In Port Elizabeth, 50km south, people queue in the hope of a few hours' work at the company.'[37]

The unofficial strikers were condemned by President Thabo Mbeki for damaging their country's image in the eyes of foreign investors. At the same time, plans were announced to make South Africa's Basic Conditions of Employment Act more 'flexible'. The workers who were dismissed suffered tremendous hardship; no less than 5 committed suicide. The dismissed workers lost their claims for unfair dismissal. The strike was characterised as an 'internal union dispute' and not a protected strike. The Constitutional Court ruled that the individual's 'right to strike' enshrined in the Constitution did not protect unauthorised strikes.[38] The Constitution was unable to protect the dignity of those whose working conditions were undermined because the corporate strategy of a TNC, accepted by an exclusive bargaining agent, required them to produce more cars in a shorter time. One of the dismissed workers, a 55-year old man with 18 years' service, blamed the officials of his union for being 'co-opted into the globalisation process.'[39]

---

[37] *Sunday Independent* [South Africa], 5 March 2000; *Mail and Guardian*, 18–24 February, 2000.

[38] *Xinwa v Volkswagen of SA (Pty) Ltd* (2003) 32 *Industrial Law Journal* [South Africa] 1077 (CC); for earlier proceedings see *Mzeku v Volkswagen SA* (2001) 23 *Industrial Law Journal* [South Africa] 771 (CCMA); 993 (LC), 1575 (LAC); comment by Hepple (2004b).

[39] Hepple (2004b) at 18.

4. The case for transnational regulation

Labour laws serve vital *economic* functions. The employment relationship provides one of the essential foundations of the business enterprise. Labour laws determine the rights and obligations of the parties to that relationship. These affect the efficiency of the firm in a competitive market, and the redistribution of benefits and risks between employers and workers and between groups of workers. These laws may also provide incentives or disincentives for improving skills and productivity. Equally important, labour laws have *moral* functions, upholding human dignity and the notion that 'labour is not a commodity or article of commerce'.[40] Since people work not only to earn a living, but also to achieve personal fulfilment labour laws affect both their physical and psychological well-being. Labour laws uphold human rights in the workplace, such as the rights to equality, to associate in trade unions and to assemble peacefully, to privacy and free speech.

The case for transnational labour regulation rests on similar economic and moral grounds, but with the important qualification that locating regulation at supranational level may sometimes have adverse consequences that may not arise from domestic labour laws. There is relatively little empirical evidence because of the absence of comparable cross-country studies of the enforcement of transnational standards. So many of the arguments remain speculative.

Social dumping: a race to the bottom?

The oldest argument for transnational regulation is that world trade is between countries with different levels of labour rights and labour costs. This can lead to 'social dumping', that is the export of products that owe their competitiveness to low labour standards. It may also encourage a 'race to the bottom'. The frequently expressed fear is that low-wage imports from newly industrialising countries are causing rising unemployment and falling relative wages among unskilled workers, and that outflows of foreign direct investment (FDI) to these countries is destroying jobs in the industrialised countries.

A general definition of 'social dumping' is suggested by Grossmann and Koopman[41]:

> Unlike conventional dumping which means selling abroad below cost or at lower prices than charged in the home market, 'social dumping' refers to costs that are for their part depressed below a 'natural' level by means of 'social oppression' facilitating unfair

[40] The words used in Art 427 Treaty of Versailles (1919), and in the Declaration of Philadelphia (1944).

[41] Grossmann and Koopman (1996) at 116.

pricing strategies against foreign competitors. Remedial action would either consist of the offending firms consenting to raise their prices accordingly or failing that, imposing equivalent import restrictions.

This approach depends on identifying those measures of 'social oppression' which cause wage costs and labour standards to be unfairly depressed. Put in economic terms, the 'social dumping' case for transnational labour regulation is that it is necessary to remove those distortions on competition which are not related to productivity. Such distortions occur when firms are able to utilise undervalued labour. By undervaluation is meant paying workers with comparable skills and productivity different wages simply by shifting demand for labour to a more disadvantaged group of workers who are unable to resist. Firms that can undervalue labour in this way can avoid more radical solutions to their competitive problems, such as by restructuring or investment in new technologies. Indeed, the availability of undervalued labour discourages innovation, and firms which are innovative face unfair competition from firms which are inefficient technically and managerially but are able to be profitable in the short-term by employing undervalued labour.[42] This argument was the justification given for including in the Treaty of Rome of 1957 a provision requiring equal remuneration for men and women doing the same work (chapter 8 below). There are obviously greater opportunities for using undervalued labour in a system which discriminates on grounds of sex, race, or any other arbitrary basis. A similar argument justifies measures against other forms of social oppression such as forced and child labour.

It is doubtful, however, whether the notion of social dumping is adequate in itself to form the theoretical basis for a new approach to transnational labour regulation. First, it over-emphasises the role of labour costs in decisions about relocation. Enterprises are not likely to relocate to another state with lower *nominal* labour costs if those costs simply reflect lower productivity of workers in that state. This would mean that there is no net difference in unit labour costs. The basic point is that what matters is not the *nominal* level of wage costs in a firm or industry but the net unit labour costs, that is the costs of labour for each unit of production after taking productivity into account. If labour costs do not reflect the relative productivity in a particular state and enterprises relocate to that state, the result would be to increase demand for labour, with the likelihood of rising wage levels. This would, in due course, cancel out the advantages of a relocation which was based purely on low labour costs. The *World Investment Report 1994*, concluded that 'despite a few notable cases, TNCs do not often close down, on account of low labour cost considerations alone, production facilities in one country to re-establish them in another country . . . Broader and more important macroeconomic and cyclical factors,

---

[42] Deakin and Wilkinson (1994); and Deakin and Wilkinson (forthcoming).

technological change and labour market inflexibilities are the principal influences on the growth and distribution of employment.'[43]

Secondly, there is little empirical evidence to support the claim that comparative advantage does in fact flow from social dumping, whether this is through the violation of core labour standards or simply because of the comparative advantage of cheap labour.[44] An OECD study in 1996 (revised in 2000) argued persuasively that patterns of specialisation are mainly determined by relative factor endowments, technology and economies of scale. The study pointed to empirical research which indicates that there is no correlation between aggregate real wage growth and the level of observance of core labour rights, such as freedom of association. The balance of evidence suggests that trade and investment flows are only minor factors in the rise in unemployment and wage inequality in the industrialised countries, and that the benefits from increased exports of skill-intensive goods and services outweigh the disadvantages of liberal trading regimes.[45] Moreover, aggregate data on FDI suggests that the presence or absence of core labour standards are not important determinants. Host states that observe core standards are not significantly worse in attracting FDI than those which systematically abuse these standards. Similar conclusions were reached by a report on labour standards in the Asia-Pacific region.[46] This is not to deny that there are abuses of labour standards linked to export sectors (especially in Export Processing Zones, EPZs). The ILO has reported that many obstacles are placed in the way of enforcing labour laws in EPZs. For example, until 2004, in Bangladesh freedom of association was not recognised for workers in EPZs, and this was publicised as a 'non-fiscal' incentive to investment. When the Government lifted the ban, it faced a court challenge by 22 companies.[47] Even worse abuses are usually found in domestic, non-trade sectors which do not rely on FDI.

This critique of the theory and practice of social dumping leads one to reject as inadequate, and ultimately illusory, the notion that transnational standards can or should provide a level playing field in respect of labour costs.

Improving economic performance

The argument about the race to the bottom can be turned on its head to contend that raising labour standards may raise productivity and so encourage FDI.[48] Although the developing countries enjoy the comparative advantage of

---

[43] UNCTAD (1994) at xxvii.
[44] Erickson and Mitchell (1998) at 170–71.
[45] OECD (1996, revised 2000); Lee (1996) at 485.
[46] Commonwealth of Australia (1996).
[47] ILO (2004b) at 38.
[48] OECD (1996, revised 2000).

low labour costs, high labour standards are conducive to high levels of labour productivity and hence long-term competitive advantage.[49] A study by the International Institute for Labour Studies found a positive, though weak, correlation between the core labour rights of freedom of association and collective bargaining with FDI.[50] Another study by the Institute, in 2003, based on data from 162 countries concluded that in general higher manufacturing exports occurred when there was democracy, freedom of association and collective bargaining rights.[51] However, this conclusion has to be qualified in respect of labour-intensive exports, where the higher wages associated with collective bargaining can reduce exports; against this must be balanced the predictability of wage costs which may result from bargaining.[52] High standards promote better labour relations, co-operation and sharing of information, all of which tend to enhance productivity.[53]

However, it has to be conceded that even if the implementation of core international labour standards in developing countries does not necessarily affect the costs and patterns of production directly, there may be adverse indirect consequences in the short- or medium-term.[54] In most developing countries only a small proportion of the labour force (on average 15 percent) is employed in the formal sector. Informal work is predominant, and there is a surplus of labour.[55] Introducing international labour standards may raise wages in the formal sector, but at the cost of increasing economic segmentation of the labour market. A small elite of labour in some sectors of the formal economy (particularly in export industries) can extract rents while the informal sector and small producers continue to decline. International standards will not be effective without macroeconomic growth and structural changes. Formalising the informal sector is not within reach. For labour standards to be relevant to the majority of the world's workers they have to be able to reach the informal sector. This means that the main goal of transnational regulation should be the reduction of poverty and inequality.

Reducing poverty and inequality

Can transnational labour regulation contribute significantly to the reduction of global poverty and inequality?[56] The starting point is to recognise that

---

[49] Deakin and Wilkinson (1994) at 307–9.
[50] Kucera (2004).
[51] Kucera and Sarna (forthcoming).
[52] ILO (2004b) at 15.
[53] Palley (2003).
[54] Singh and Zammit (2003) at 191–204.
[55] World Bank (1995).
[56] DFID (2003) sees this as the main aim of transnational standards.

increased participation in world trade can lead to dramatic reductions in poverty in developing countries. Compared with foreign aid, it has far more potential to help the poor; but aid and trade must go hand in hand, so as to give the poor capabilities which will help them to work in export industries. It has been suggested that a one percent increase in the world-export share for each developing country could reduce world poverty by 12 percent. Labour-intensive manufacture of exports can generate income and employment for the poor which will reduce poverty. There is convincing evidence from East Asia that export-led growth can have a dramatic effect on poverty. In the 1970s 6 out of 10 people in that region lived in extreme poverty; by the end of the 1990s fewer than 2 out of 10 were in that position.

However, the crucial point from the perspective of labour laws is that the benefits from trade to the poor are never automatic. For example, in Latin America despite a rapid growth in exports there has been rising unemployment and even before the Argentinian crisis, a disastrous drop in real incomes. In Latin America the pay gap between college-educated workers and unskilled workers increased by 18–25 percent in the 1990s. In China, income inequality and unemployment have also grown dramatically as that country has been integrating into world markets. In many developing countries, growth has been achieved at the price of deplorable working and living conditions.

Deregulation of labour markets has involved the dismantling or non-enforcement of minimum wage laws and wage protection. The entry of more women into the labour market—what has been called 'global feminisation'—has been driven by their use as cheap labour, earning only about three-quarters of the average male salaries in manufacturing industries.[57] There is much evidence of excessive working hours, poor levels of employment protection and weak trade union rights in those industries in which women are concentrated. In many countries women suffer the double disadvantage of poor working conditions and wages, and also being compelled by social norms to transfer their income to men.

Moreover, concentration on labour-intensive export industries can leave countries 'trapped in low-wage, low-skill sections of the global economy'.[58] An example is Bangladesh where foreign investors have been attracted by the combination of low wages ($1 to $1.50 per day, less than half that in India) and quotas imposed under the Multi-Fibre Agreement on more competitive suppliers such as India and China. As Europe and the USA phase out these quotas by 2005 under a WTO agreement, Bangladesh will lose markets and with them foreign investors.

---

[57] Heintz (2003) at 219–22.
[58] Oxfam (2002) at 75.

These examples reinforce the arguments made by some economists that national labour laws, such as a minimum wage and equal pay for women, are necessary in order to promote longer-term productivity and competitiveness. Under-valued labour leads to productive inefficiency, hampers innovation and results in short-term strategies and destructive competition. Basic labour rights are necessary in order to correct this market failure.[59]

There is much debate among economists about the consequences of globalisation on both poverty and inequality. These concepts are often used together but they are distinct. Poverty refers to those who fall below a certain minimum standard. It can be measured first on an absolute basis, referring to people whose income is insufficient to cover basic needs; or it may be defined on a relative basis by referring to those people whose income does not allow them to function properly in their particular social environment.[60] Sen argues persuasively that poverty should be seen as a deprivation of basic capabilities, rather than merely as low income. Although the system of social security in European countries may make up some of the deficiency in income of those who are unemployed, loss of work can have 'far-reaching debilitating effects on individual freedom, initiative, and skills'. It contributes to 'social exclusion' by reducing self-reliance, self-confidence as well as harming psychological and physical health.[61]

Relative poverty within the world's richer countries is put into the shade by the gap between rich and poor countries. The average income in the richest twenty countries is 37 times the average in the poorest twenty, a gap that has doubled in the past forty years. The increasing prosperity of an elite in the developed countries has 'gone hand in hand with mass poverty and the widening of already obscene inequalities between rich and poor.'[62] According to the World Bank, in 1998 almost half the world's population were living on less than $2 a day and a fifth on less than $1 a day, the same figure as in the mid-1980s.[63] Human development indicators, such as infant mortality, undernourishment, adult illiteracy and access to clean water, reveal extremely high levels of deprivation in South Asia and sub-Saharan Africa. 'The wealth that flows from liberalised trade is not pouring down to the poorest, contrary to the claims of the enthusiasts for globalisation.'[64]

The concept of equality is elusive. Equality of what? This may refer to equality of income or resources, or it may be what Sen calls the 'equality of capabilities', such as education and training, human rights and democratic

---

[59] Deakin and Wilkinson (2000) at 56–61.
[60] Atkinson (2001).
[61] Sen (1999) at 20–21.
[62] Oxfam (2002) at 5.
[63] World Bank (2001) at 3.
[64] World Bank (2001) at 65.

freedoms. There is, of course, an overlap because lack of income may make it impossible to acquire capabilities and lack of capabilities affects the capacity to earn a living. Equality for whom? Some groups, such as women, disabled people and ethnic minorities are at a particular disadvantage and are victims of discrimination in respect of both income and capabilities. There is also general inequality of incomes. One way of measuring this is to consider separately the top and bottom income distribution (the top 10 percent expressed as a percentage of the median, and the median expressed as a percentage of the bottom decile). If we do this, then we find that since the 1970s there has been a rise in inequality in the top 10 percent in the USA, a rise in inequality in both in the top and bottom deciles in the UK, and relatively little change in other OECD countries such as Germany, Sweden and Canada.[65]

Another way of measuring inequality in the EU—focusing on those with the lowest incomes—is through an indicator of social cohesion used by Eurostat, the so-called S80/S20 ratio—the ratio of total income received by the 20 percent in the country's population with the highest income to that received by the 20 percent of the country's population receiving the lowest income (so that if the share of the top 20 percent in total income is 45 percent, and that of the bottom 20 percent is 9 percent, then the ratio is 5.) By 1997 and 1998, this ratio was around 5.4 for the 15 Member States, but with considerable variations ranging form 2.7 in Denmark to 4.4 in the Netherlands, 5.7 in the UK and 7.2 in Portugal.[66] In a much earlier age, Plato proposed that the maximum limits between poverty and wealth in the citizen body should be set at 4 to 1 in order to avoid civil disintegration.[67]

If our concern is with equality of capabilities, then our measures of inequality will relate not simply to income, but more broadly to opportunities to pursue an occupation or career of one's own choosing, to freedom of association including the right to form and join trade unions, and to participate in economic and political decision-making that affect one's life, as well as other rights now enumerated, for example, in the EU's Charter of Fundamental Rights (chapter 9, below). A central task of transnational labour law in the era of modern globalisation must be to facilitate equality of capabilities. This involves designing an optimal system of regulation to reduce inequality by promoting fair representation and eliminating exclusion and institutional barriers to full participation (chapter 10, below).[68]

[65] Atkinson (2001).
[66] Eurostat website http//epp.eurostat.cec.eu.int/.
[67] Cited by Cowell (1977) at 26.
[68] Hepple (2001) at 14.

A race to the top?

A further argument for transnational labour regulation is to harness the processes *within* the market activities of TNCs which favour the raising of labour standards, that is a 'race to the top'.[69] This has been called an 'instrumental' approach.[70] The internal labour markets of TNCs usually provide better wages, conditions of work and social security benefits than those prevailing in domestic firms, due to the fact that they tend to be concentrated in industries which utilise high skills, are capital-intensive, and have superior managerial and organisational techniques. Indirectly, there may be a spillover of the best practices of these TNCs to domestic firms.[71]

A great many consumer goods and other products are now produced through global commodity chains. Workplaces in different countries are connected by contractual or ownership links between enterprises that form a transnational 'chain' of production and distribution. For example, in 1961 only four percent of the clothes sold in the United States were imported; today imports account for over 60 per cent. Although often labelled as products of US TNCs, these clothes are mainly produced in developing countries either by a subsidiary of the TNC or by an outside contractor. The market is dominated by a few large retailers who set not only the price but also the design and quality of the goods, and this in turn affects the wages and conditions of workers who produce them.

On the one hand, these global commodity chains enable TNCs to dominate international markets. On the other hand, these very links provide new opportunities for solidarity between workers in different countries, and between workers and consumers. This provides a social basis for new forms of labour regulation. The legal sources for such regulation are to be found in the mechanisms for interpreting and enforcing contracts between enterprises in different countries. This type of production entails a distinct form of internationalised labour market, dominated by TNCs. These corporate giants can choose where to locate their sources of supply, as well as opting between outside contractors or setting up subsidiaries in which the TNC has an ownership stake. In both cases the different producers operate under various national systems of labour law. Even if the central management of a TNC lays down employment rules or codes of conduct, these have to be interpreted and enforced under the multiple national systems in which the TNC or its contractual suppliers operate. Thus, if a TNC decides to observe multinational codes of conduct, it will have to find managerial means of ensuring compliance

---

[69] Hepple (1999b).
[70] Chin (1998) at 47.
[71] UNCTAD (1994) at 196–97.

with these labour standards within the affiliates of the TNC, and contractual means in relation to its suppliers. However, in both cases, it has no means of influencing entirely independent enterprises in the same country.

The global commodity chains dominated by TNCs generate employment through various linkages with enterprises in home and host countries. The *World Investment Report 1994* reported that 'as a general rule, for each job directly generated by a TNC, one or two may result indirectly from backward and forward linkages.'[72] Lall points out:

> The attraction of developing countries is no longer the presence of large protected markets, cheap unskilled labour and exploitable natural resources. Increasingly, FDI flows into competitive and higher technology activities which require disciplined and productive labour, high skill levels, world-class infrastructure and a supportive network of suppliers.[73]

Whether or not the quality of employment is raised throughout the global chain of production and distribution depends largely on corporate integration strategies. In the emerging model of complex integration—that is regionally or globally integrated production and distribution networks within function, product or process specialisation—there is likely to be a degree of convergence in the employment conditions of parent and foreign affiliates in order to maximise the global efficiency of the TNC. The TNC will increasingly rely on workforce quality in the host country, and this can be encouraged in order to generate positive effects on labour conditions throughout the global commodity chain, and hopefully also into the informal sector.

The task, therefore, is to create a transnational regulatory framework which encourages and develops the potential of TNCs to raise the labour standards of economically and socially disadvantaged groups of workers and producers, particularly in the informal sector. At national level, the application and elaboration of this framework has to take account of specific local cultural, social and economic features. We must, therefore, evaluate the emerging methods of transnational labour regulation according to their potential for the dissemination of 'best practices' and for developing solidarity between workers employed by TNCs in different countries.

Human rights and democracy

The international human rights movement has, until recently, paid relatively little attention to workers' rights. As Leary says, 'the human rights movement and the labour movement run on tracks that are sometimes parallel and rarely

[72] UNCTAD (1994) at 192.
[73] Lall (1995) at 521.

meet.'[74] This is surprising because lists of human rights include many rights relevant to work, such as the right to form and join trade unions, the right to free choice of employment, the right to equal treatment, rights which prohibit forced labour and child labour. The extent of workers' rights in a country is a sign of the status of human rights in general. Repressive regimes outlaw independent trade unions, arrest and murder trade unionists.

There are many reasons for the parallel tracks of workers' rights and human rights. The first is the abiding disagreement as to whether workers' rights are human rights at all. At one extreme, there are those who contrast legal rights with socially accepted principles of justice. They argue that treating the latter as 'rights' does not make sense. One cannot have a 'right' to something which is impossible to deliver, such as holidays with pay for everyone. Social rights generally require positive action by the state and others. To provide a meaningful 'right to work' or 'right to social protection' requires resoures which a poor state does not have under its control. Nor are all these rights, for example to paid leave, moral rights. Although they are desirable social goals, to call them human rights is to devalue the importance of basic civil and political rights.

Against this extreme position, Sen[75] has argued that rights-based reasoning and goal-based programming are not necessarily antithetical. He suggests that it is only if we make the fulfilment of each right a matter of absolute adherence (with no room for give and take and no possibility of acceptable trade-offs), as some libertarians do, that there is a real conflict. He says that it is possible to formulate rights in a way which allows them to be integrated within the same overall framework as objectives and goals, such as those encapsulated in the ILO's notion of 'decent work' (see chapter 2, below). For example, the rights of those at work can be considered along with—and not instead of—the interests of the unemployed. Sen points out that there is no 'right' against dying of hunger, but that legal rights of ownership and contract can go hand-in-hand with some people failing to get enough to food to survive. For this reason it is natural to promote the right to work and the right to social protection in order to provide a minimum guarantee of survival. The right to property—the primary legal foundation of the market economy—has to be balanced against 'rights' such as these.

A second reason for the differences in trajectories of workers' rights and human rights has been the tendency, until fairly recently, of human rights organisations to give priority to civil and political rights, and, on the other hand, the focus of labour advocates is on local and economic issues. At the international level, the conventions and recommendations of the ILO were not

[74] Leary (1996b) at 22.
[75] Sen (2000) at 123–24.

originally conceived as statements of human rights. The ILO's official compilation includes only three sets of instruments under the heading 'basic human rights'. These relate to freedom of association, forced labour and equality of opportunity and treatment. The ILO's 1998 Declaration of Fundamental Principles and Rights at Work (chapter 2, below) added the elimination of child labour to these categories.

Although the vast bulk of international labour standards are not classified as human rights, it is rights such as freedom of association that are crucial to the sustainability of economic development. In the words of the UK's Department for International Development:

> [Core labour standards] reduce the risk of social and political instability by enhancing equity and social justice. Strengthening workers' rights also increases the ability of people to withstand the impact of shocks which often affect developing countries whether at macro level, such as financial crises, or household level such as illness. Freedom of association has been critical to the development of improved social protection of workers through political campaigning and other action by labour movements. Core labour standards provide a framework of rights and responsibilities—for firms, governments and workers—to underpin production processes which assures the dignity and well-being of all parties.[76]

Conclusion

The ghost of David Ricardo's theory of comparative advantage continues to haunt debates about free trade and transnational labour regulation. The theory, based on a simple numerical model of the manufacture of English cloth and Portuguese wine, holds that free trade does not impoverish nations by driving their production abroad but makes them richer by allowing each to specialise in the goods it makes more efficiently and to trade them for even more goods that it needs from other countries. Modern adherents of free trade view all restrictions on trade—including transnational labour regulation—as an attempt to protect private interests against the economic welfare of the public. The flaw in this argument, which becomes apparent if one revisits Ricardo's own text, is that the model is a static one based upon trading partners with a fixed mix of endowments. Moreover, Ricardo's model is expressly based on the assumption that capital is not mobile with 'most men of property [being] satisfied with a low rate of profits in their own country, rather than seek[ing] a more advantageous employment for their wealth in foreign nations'.[77] A modern theory of comparative advantage has to take account not only of the fact that capital is global and a growing share of trade takes place within TNCs.

---

[76] DFID (2003) at 9.
[77] Ricardo (1817, 1971 ed) at 155.

It also has to consider the comparative advantages of the variety of national labour laws. Such a theory challenges the orthodox assumptions about the effects of labour laws on global trade, and points the way towards a modern re-invention of transnational labour regulation (chapter 10, below).

Transnational labour regulation does matter. This is not because there is a serious risk of 'social dumping'; in any event, it would be impossible to achieve a level playing field in respect of labour costs. Transnational measures, if effective, may promote better economic performance, but it has to be recognised that, so far as the developing countries are concerned, these measures have to be carefully framed and targeted towards the informal sector, and to the reduction of poverty and inequality. The new methods of transnational regulation can be used to develop a 'race to the top' by spreading the best practices of TNCs, and by promoting sustainable development through fundamental human rights at work. These interventions have to be shaped in ways that not only fulfil these objectives but also maximise the comparative institutional advantages which countries enjoy as a result of their domestic labour law systems. How this can be done—and how it cannot be—forms the subject of this book.

2

The Effectiveness of International Labour Standards

1. Origins 1818–1919

The issue whether labour relations remain governable within nation states under a system of free trade is not new. Robert Owen, the idealistic British mill owner, advocated that all countries should protect the new working classes from 'the causes which perpetually generate misery in human society'.[1] Owen imagined a world filled with model communities like his own New Lanark.[2] In 1818, he presented two Memorials to the Congress of the Concert of Europe meeting at Aix-la-Chapelle inviting the Congress to appoint a Commission to visit New Lanark, 'to investigate the whole of the new arrangements, which, under modifications, he has to propose for adoption in all countries.'[3] His mission in Europe failed, but he was successful in securing the enactment in 1819 of a British Bill limiting the hours of children in cotton factories—'the real beginning of industrial legislation'.[4]

---

[1] Owen (1818). I am grateful to Professor Stanley Engerman for his help with information concerning Owen's Memorials. These documents make it clear that, contrary to common belief, Owen did not submit a plan for international labour legislation: Engerman (2001).

[2] Owen (1813).

[3] Owen (1818).

[4] Follows (1951) at 2. The 1819 Act was very much watered down from Owen's draft: see Hutchins and Harrison (1926) at 24, and generally on early legislation chs 1 and 2.

Owen's purpose—like that of a number of other enlightened entrepreneurs and public health physicians in the early stages of the industrial revolution—was humanitarian. He was not prompted by the belief that social problems require an international solution, nor that free trade was making nations interdependent. Those ideas are usually attributed to Jacques Necker, a Swiss banker, who argued in 1788 that if France abolished the Sunday rest day its competitive position would be improved only if other countries did not follow suit, and that, therefore, the workers' rest day could be maintained only if it was observed by all countries. Necker did not propose international labour legislation, but he appreciated that the question of workers' protection was an international one.[5] Daniel Legrand, an Alsatian manufacturer, addressed appeals to European statesmen between 1840 and 1848 arguing that the international regulation of labour was a practical way of overcoming the dilemma faced by industrialising countries which might expose themselves to destructive foreign competition if they adopted humanitarian measures to protect their own workers. Legrand was also one of the few early protagonists of international labour standards to link the economic and political case: international standards would forestall the social upheavals that would occur once the working masses refused to tolerate their degrading conditions.[6]

The validity of Legrand's basic premise, that the competitive position of socially advanced nations would be jeopardised, was not challenged. The orthodox belief of *laissez-faire* economic liberalism was that in a world of perfect competition and free trade a reduction in working hours and prohibition of child labour would raise the price of domestic goods. Cheaper foreign goods produced without those restrictions would be imported so undermining national prosperity. Protectionist barriers were ruled out, and the modern idea that competition could be offset by technological advances was not accepted. One way out of this dilemma, while leaving the theory of comparative advantage intact, was to create a minimum international standard below which workers should not be allowed to fall. Another, advocated by Marx and his followers in the First and Second Internationals was international working-class action for the 8-hours' day and restrictions on juvenile and child labour. This action would provide 'schools of class struggle' directed towards the winning of political power and the establishment of socialism. Nothing less would 'do away with the miseries of the industrious masses.'[7]

It was neither international labour legislation, nor socialism which prevailed prior to the First World War. Labour laws were almost entirely national, established by sovereign states. The development in European countries stood

---

[5] Alcock (1971) at n6.
[6] Ghebali (1989) at 3.
[7] Marx (1864) at 77; and on the Ten Hours Act, Marx and Engels (1848) at 76.

'for about seventy years in the shadow of the British legislation . . . Britain was the first country of the industrial revolution and it had practised free trade on a world scale (based on its colonies) and it was the leading proponent of the economic theory of liberalism.'[8] By the end of the 19th century most European countries and some of their overseas dominions had protective legislation for children and women in factories and mines, based on British models, although there were important differences in coverage. The protection of children was seen as compatible with freedom of contract because children lack capacity to make their own decisions. They are wards of their parents and the state. The protection of women was more controversial. Classical economists, like Nassau Senior and John Stuart Mill, as well as the Women's Rights Movement in Britain, thought it was indefensible to treat them differently from men. But for male trade unionists, unable to secure universal protection by collective bargaining or legislation, it was natural 'to fight the battle from behind women's petticoats' in order to benefit themselves.[9] Legislation in favour of all workers was partial, covering specific abuses such as the truck system, and some aspects of health and safety.

In federal states, such as the USA, Switzerland, Australia and Canada, there were often differences between constituent states, cantons or provinces. Sometimes federal legislation could be more extensive, for example US President van Buren's 1840 law applying the 10-hour day to all federal employees on public works, reduced to 8 hours in 1868. Legislation in European and North American industrial countries preceded that in most of Africa, Asia and South America by at least half a century. Although European nations had colonies, so-called 'native labour' was generally considered to be outside the standards set for the metropolis.[10]

The Industrial Revolution was thus a Babel from which a confusion of labour laws emerged. The peculiarities of these laws sprang from a variety of factors, including the stage of economic development, the extent of liberal democracy, the character of national employers' and trade union movements, as well as the dominant ideology in each country.[11] But there were parallel developments. As countries achieved universal adult male suffrage the ruling parties sought the allegiance of the electorate by enacting protective legislation. One example is Bismarck's social insurance system (1881) copied even in technical details in Austria, and inspiring welfare legislation in Britain (1908) and elsewhere. Another example is the 8-hour working day—a demand of international workers' demonstrations every May Day from 1890—promulgated by the Council of Peoples' Commissioners in Germany in 1918, soon

---

[8] Ramm (1986) at 76.
[9] Creighton (1979) at 19–37.
[10] Engerman (2001).
[11] Hepple (1986a) at 12–30.

followed in Luxembourg (1918), Denmark (1919), France (1919), the Netherlands (1919), Belgium (1921) and Italy (1923). Even then, labour legislation on subjects such as the working time of adult men and paid holidays, tended to be introduced only where the industrial power of trade unions was too weak to achieve satisfactory conditions by collective agreement.

At the same time as these national developments, attempts were being made within Europe to achieve labour standards by international agreement. Some entrepreneurs echoed Legrand's argument that domestic laws put them at a disadvantage compared with manufacturers in countries with less protective legislation. The French decree of 1848 promulgating a 10-hour day for all workers was abrogated after only five months on the ground that it would be impossible to conclude an international treaty on this question.[12] Not surprisingly, it was the richer nations with the most advanced labour standards that were the first advocates of international labour standards.[13] In 1889 the Swiss Government proposed an international conference in Berne to secure an international agreement on work in factories. Kaiser Wilhelm II, wanting to emphasise his own innovations in social matters, pre-empted the Swiss by convening a conference in Berlin in 1890. Fourteen states participated. The results were modest, but the conference managed to agree a series of principles of international law reflecting the European model, including minimum ages for child employment, maximum hours and prohibition of night work for children, young persons, and women, and provision for labour inspection.[14]

In 1901 an International Association for Workers' Statutory Protection was formed in Basle. Its main aim was the encouragement of state intervention. This led to the creation of a scientific institute, called the International Labour Office based in Basle, which was politically neutral and gave information on workers' protection. By 1913, three-quarters of its budget came from European governments and the USA. In 1905–06 a conference was held in Berne resulting in the first two international treaties, one prohibiting the use of white phosphorous in the manufacture of matches (accepted by fourteen nations), and the other prohibiting the employment of women on night work in industry (accepted by seven nations). Between 1904 and 1915 there were also more than twenty bilateral agreements between European nations on labour matters (in one case the USA was involved).[15] These agreements most frequently covered insurance compensation for workers of one country injured in another. Only the French-Italian treaty of 1904 included a statement of intent by one country (Italy) to change laws on hours of work and minimum age for entry to the labour market, to reach the level in another country

---

[12] Ramm (1986) at 279.
[13] Engerman (2001).
[14] Ramm (1986) at 279–80.
[15] In the late 19th century there were several bilateral labour migration agreements.

(France). Thus, by 1914 the movement for international standards had made very little progress, was exclusively between industrial countries without great disparities in their standards, and lacked any mechanism for effective enforcement.

2. Foundation and Formative Years of the ILO: 1919–46

This situation was transformed by the establishment of the International Labour Organisation (ILO) in 1919. The First World War had led to a split in the international socialist and trade union movements between revolutionaries who advocated international class struggle to overthrow capitalism, and reformers who favoured the gradual introduction of democratic socialism or simply an extension of workers' rights under capitalism. The shock caused by the October 1917 Revolution in Russia convinced industrialists and most conservative, liberal and democratic socialist politicans that class collaboration was essential. Labour leaders such as George Barnes in Britain and Albert Thomas in France were co-opted into government. They, together with Edward Phelan and Harold Butler, British civil servants, were key figures in setting up the ILO. Thomas and Butler were successively Directors of the International Labour Office during the inter-war years. Phelan, the 'father' of the ILO's unique tripartite structure, became Director of the Office during World War II and was co-draftsman[16] of the 1944 Declaration of Philadelphia which redefined the ILO's objectives (below). Men such as these were highly influential in securing an integral role for the trade unions in drawing up the social clauses of the peace settlement, which made provision for an international labour code backed by supervisory machinery, and for the tripartite (governments-employers-workers) composition of the new Organisation.[17]

What emerged was, however, a disappointment for the trade unions. A series of international trade union conferences culminating in Berne in 1917 had agreed a far-reaching programme of demands for the Peace Treaty. These included an International Parliament of Labour which would 'not produce international conventions without legal effect but international statutes which should have the same effect as national statutes on their ratification.'[18] Defeated Germany adopted the ideas of the Berne conference in its draft of international labour law for the Peace Treaty, but this was rejected by the Entente Powers.

---

[16] With CW Jenks, another British public servant who later became Director-General.
[17] Ghebali (1989) at 6–7.
[18] Ramm (1986) at 283.

Instead, Part XIII of the Treaty of Versailles, establishing the ILO, provides that drafts of conventions and recommendations require the approval of two-thirds of the delegates at the annual International Labour Conference. The trade unions had proposed that half the delegates should be trade union representatives, but the Treaty provides that the Conference is to be composed of two government delegates, one employers' delegate and one workers' delegate from each Member State. Conventions and recommendations do not have automatic effects, but must be submitted by governments to their 'competent authority' (usually the legislature) to consider whether or not to accept them. Only when ratified without reservation does a convention become internationally binding on the Member State. Whether the convention also becomes binding as part of the law of the land depends on national constitutions. For example, under the US Constitution a treaty approved by the Senate is the supreme law of the land, while under the British Constitution an Act of Parliament is required.

A weak form of supervision through complaints to the International Labour Office (the permanent secretariat of the ILO) was introduced. Any dispute relating to the ILO Constitution or ratified conventions can be referred to the Permanent Court of International Justice (now called the International Court of Justice) in The Hague. In practice this provision has been used only on four occasions all between 1923 and 1932. Although Member States have the obligation to observe the basic principles of the constitution, to submit conventions to the 'competent authority', and to make reports to the International Labour Office, national sovereignty is fully respected. The International Labour Conference is a kind of legislative body, but a convention retains the characteristics of a traditional multilateral treaty. It is binding only on a State which ratifies it and it requires a minimum number of ratifications before entering into force.[19]

Instead of creating binding rules of international law, as the unions had wanted, Article 427 of the Versailles Treaty simply declared nine 'methods and principles' to be of 'special and urgent importance.' These were—

1. Labour should not be regarded as a commodity or article of commerce.
2. The right of association for all lawful purposes by the employed as well as the employers.
3. The payment to the employed of a wage adequate to maintain a reasonable standard of life, as this is understood in their time and country.
4. The adoption of an 8-hour day and of a 48-hour week as the standard to be aimed at where it has not already been attained.
5. The adoption of a weekly rest period of at least 24 hours, which should include Sunday wherever practicable.

---

[19] Valticos and von Potobsky (1994) at paras 80–81.

6. The abolition of child labour and the imposition of such limitations on the labour of young persons as shall permit the continuance of their education and ensure their proper physical development.

7. The principle that men and women should receive equal remuneration for work of equal value.

8. The standard set by law in each country with respect to the conditions of labour should have due regard to the equitable economic treatment of all workers lawfully resident therein.

9. Each state should make provision for a system of inspection in which women should tke part, in order to ensure the enforcement of the laws and regulations for the protection of the employed.

Although the Treaty stated that this enumeration was neither complete nor final, the International Federation of Trade Unions was critical of the absence of many of their demands.

Despite all these constitutional weaknesses, the ILO was considerably more successful in attracting members in the inter-war years than the League of Nations to which it was linked through the Treaty of Versailles. While three dictatorships (Germany, Italy and Japan) withdrew, there were other countries which remained in the ILO after withdrawing from the League. The United States (not a member of the League) and the Soviet Union both joined in the 1930s. In the early years the Organisation was dominated by European powers, who with the 'white' British dominions constituted nearly 50 per cent of the membership.

In the period up to World War II, the International Labour Conference adopted 67 conventions and 66 recommendations. These were published together in 1939 as the International Labour Code. The Code included not only subjects already familiar in European and North American labour laws, such as hours of work, minimum age, employment of women, and health and safety, but also transnational problems such as maritime work, migrant workers, and forced labour. Perhaps the most successful aspect of the ILO's activities was the collection and dissemination of a mass of social information by the Office, making it a 'laboratory of the art of social policy'.[20]

In the economic depression and national political turmoil of the 1930s, the ILO's ratification process slowed down, falling from 79 ratifications in 1929 to 28 in 1932 and rising only slightly to 43 in 1938. Member States were more interested in reducing domestic unemployment than in implementing international standards. However, the Second World War provided an impetus for the renewal of the ILO and international labour law.

The ILO became a specialised agency under Article 57 of the United Nations Charter, preserving its independence and tripartite structure. The

---

[20] Ghebali (1989) at 13 quoting Georges Scelle.

standard-setting system was made more flexible and efficient. There was clarification of the nature of a recommendation (defined as a measure adopted by the Conference 'where the subject, or an aspect of it, dealt with is not considered suitable or appropriate at that time for a convention'[21]); it was declared that no ILO standard may affect national provisions which ensure more favourable conditions for the workers concerned;[22] and a system of reporting on unratified conventions and on recommendations was introduced. Proposals for tilting representation in favour of workers 2-1-2 (government, employers, workers) or for equal representation (2-2-2) were rejected.

Perhaps the most important change was the broadening of the objectives of the ILO through the Declaration of Philadelphia, adopted at the 26th Annual Conference in 1944, which was appended to the ILO's revised Constitution in substitution for the general 'methods and principles' of Article 427 of the Versailles Treaty. The 1919 Constitution set out three objectives of international standards: social justice, international peace and the regulation of international competition. The 1944 Declaration reaffirmed the 'fundamental principles' on which the ILO is based, in particular that—

- Labour is not a commodity;
- Freedom of expression and of association are essential to sustained progress;[23]
- Poverty anywhere constitutes a danger to prosperity everywhere.

In the inter-war years, Albert Thomas, the first ILO Director, had regarded the idea of social justice as inseparable from the objective of lasting peace. The 1944 Declaration reaffirmed this link, but also recognised social justice as a distinct objective in its own right. This was in effect a reassertion of the Owenite belief in global human welfare, expressed in Article V of the Declaration as 'fully applicable to all peoples everywhere', significantly not limited to workers. This was spelt out in Article II(a) as a right of all human beings, irrespective of race, creed or sex, 'to pursue both their material well-being and their spiritual development in conditions of freedom and dignity, of economic security and of equal opportunity.' The Declaration stressed that the 'attainment of the conditions in which this shall be possible must constitute the central aim of national and international policy' and that policies and measures 'should be judged in this light and accepted only in so far as they may be held to promote and not to hinder the achievement of this fundamental objective.' Thus not only were social rights and other human rights inextricably

---

[21] ILO Constitution, 19(1).

[22] Art 19(8).

[23] Ghebali (1989) at 62, comments that 'while the framers of the Declaration could take freedom of association for granted, the case for freedom of expression was less obvious. It was included deliberately to make clear the connection between freedom of association and civil liberties generally.'

linked, but social and human objectives were seen to be paramount aims of economic development.

The argument for international standards as a means of regulating competition received no explicit mention in the 1944 Declaration. The Preamble of the 1919 Constitution had stated in its third paragraph that 'the failure of any nation to adopt humane conditions of labour is an obstacle in the way of other nations which desire to improve the conditions in their own countries', but in the inter-war years, little attention was paid by the ILO to this issue. The regulation of international competition is perhaps implicit in the reaffirmation in 1944 of the principle that 'labour is not a commodity',[24] but it was only in the 1970s that there was renewed debate about the role and impact of international standards in preventing destructive competition, and 'concurrently, eliciting and promoting *constructive competition* by ensuring rights of collective organisation and worker participation in decision-making, improving the productivity and motivation of workers, raising aggregate demand by increasing labour incomes, and promoting employment creation, active labour market policy and socially desirable forms of adjustment.'[25]

3. Decolonisation and the Cold War

The renewed ILO which emerged at the end of the Second World War was predicated, in Cooney's words, on 'rising unionism, standardised employment relations, direct state involvement in a wide range of economic activities and various forms of societal corporatism'.[26] The Declaration of Philadephia reflects 'the even more specific Keynesian phase in economic history characterised by a policy emphasis on full employment and social welfare.'[27] This was, in retrospect, a unique period in which organised labour and its political allies enjoyed unprecedented power in western countries. There was a widespread political consensus to avoid a return to the economic depression of capitalism in the 1930s, and there was a commitment to guarantee human rights. Politicians were pledged to provide a broad range of social and economic rights as well as the more traditional civil liberties. These rights were seen as being collective and substantive, not merely individual or procedural.

This post-war model was exposed to a series of challenges which threatened the survival of the ILO. The first was decolonisation, which had barely begun

---

[24] Ghebali (1989) at 66.
[25] Sengenberger (1994b) at 3.
[26] Cooney (1999) at 369.
[27] Cooney (1999) at 369.

when the War ended. From an elite of 52 mainly western industrial states in 1946, the ILO's membership grew to 80 in 1958 and 177 in 2003, thus more than trebling in just over half a century. In 1960 alone 15 new African countries joined the Organisation. This mass admission of developing countries had profound repercussions. Their main preoccupation was with technical co-operation, such as assistance with the drafting of labour codes, which would help them to claim compliance with international standards, alhough the reality was often much different. These new nations demanded greater representation in the ILO bodies. The great disparities in economic and political conditions between the new developing states and older industrial states led to pressure for greater flexibility in standard-setting. The presence of these countries also resulted in a new form of politicisation within the ILO, aimed at the activities of transnational corporations and also at states which were seen to have colonial-type policies, such as the apartheid regime in South Africa[28] and Israel in respect of the occupied territories.[29]

A second challenge was the Cold War. The Soviet Union, which had lost its ILO membership when it was excluded from the League of Nations in 1939, was readmitted in 1954, and it was followed by other communist states.[30] This revived the pre-War dispute as to how tripartism, based on the idea of independent employers' and workers' representatives, could operate in the case of a country where there was no distinction between state, government, and employer. This issue was never satisfactorily resolved.[31] Other features of the communist systems, such as the trade union monopoly, the lack of independence of the official trade unions, and rules concerning social 'parasitism', were held by ILO committees to be incompatible with ILO conventions on freedom of association and forced labour. These countries accused the ILO supervisory bodies of partiality and tried to make fundamental changes in the way they operated. On the other hand, it seems likely that the dialogue between the ILO and the communist governments in the 1970s and 1980s (for example about the Polish *Solidarity* movement) helped the process of liberalisation.[32] More generally, 'the ILO's area of interest made it an ideal forum for political and ideological conflicts between communism and capitalism.'[33] This was exacerbated by the split between the western-leaning International Confederation of Free Trade Unions (ICFTU), which enjoyed close relations with the ILO, and

[28] This led in 1964 to the withdrawal of South Africa from the ILO: see Alcock (1971) at 318–37.

[29] The condemnation of Israel in 1974 was one of the reasons provoking the withdrawal of the USA from the ILO from 1975–1980: see Ghebali (1989) at 114, and generally at 48–49.

[30] The Peoples' Republic of China resumed participation in 1983.

[31] Alcock (1971) at 284–317.

[32] Héthy (1994) at 276.

[33] Myrdal (1994) at 340, who claims that 'the communist countries were keen for the rules to cause problems for companies and governments in market economies' (at 341).

the communist-led World Federation of Trade Unions (WFTU). Since the collapse of communism in the Soviet Union and Central and Eastern Europe, these ideological divisions have been replaced by common concerns as to how to meet the major new challenges of globalisation.

4. Challenges to universality

Is it possible to confront the globalisation of markets with a globalisation of workers' rights? In the ILO's logic, the globalisation of rights involves the adoption of international labour standards (ILS), and their ratification and implementation by Member States who thereby undertake to submit to the ILO's unique supervisory system.

Declining standard-setting and uneven ratification

Judged by the criterion of adoption of ILS, there has been a marked decline in ILO standard-setting (see Box 2.1). In the first two decades of the ILO (1919–39), an average of just over 3 conventions were adopted each year; and in the period 1946–66, an average of 2.6 per year. In the next two decades (1967–86) this fell to 1.6 per year, and in the decade 1987–1996, 1.9 per year. From 1997–2004 only 5 conventions have been adopted, with none in 1998, 2002 and 2004.[34]

At first sight the picture is more optimistic in relation to ratification. By September 2004, there had been 7235 ratifications of 185 conventions. The potential is close to 27,000. Although this represents an increase of nearly 20 per cent over the past decade, three-fifths of ILO Member States have ratified fewer than one-quarter of ILO conventions open for ratification, and more than one-fifth have ratified fewer than 20 conventions.

The causes: overproduction or irrelevance?

Far from decrying the declining rate of new conventions and the uneven spread of ratifications, the employers' group within the ILO and other critics have focused their attention on the 'overproduction' of ILO instruments.[35]

---

[34] Up-to-date information on ILS can be found on the ILO website www.ilo.org. For a comprehensive code combining the texts of all conventions and recommendations with the interpretations by the ILO committees, see Rubin (forthcoming).

[35] Córdova (1993) at 138; and see Myrdal (1994) for the similar views of a prominent member of the Employers' group.

Box 2.1

ILO MACHINERY FOR THE FORMULATION OF INTERNATIONAL LABOUR STANDARDS (ILS)

The choice of subject for ILS is generally the responsibility of the tripartite Governing Body (GB), which decides upon its inclusion on the agenda of the International Labour Conference (ILC). In making its choice, the GB uses studies prepared by the technical branches.

Once the subject has been selected, a cycle of discussions begins and is spread over 40 months. This cycle is divided into two distinct phases: (1) consultations based on sending a questionnaire to governments which must consult the most representative national bodies of workers and employers; and (2) examination of the texts, following which the tripartite ILC adopts a convention and/or recommendation. In practice only half the Member States reply to questionnaires and less than one-third communicate comments from employers' and workers' organisations.[36] The report and proposed conclusions based on the consultation are discussed by a special technical committee, and then in plenary session by the ILC. Based on this first discussion, the Office prepares a draft instrument(s) to be sent to governments for their comments and those of workers' and employers' bodies. In the light of these comments, the Office prepares a revised draft which forms the basis for the second discussion in a tripartite technical committee and then by the ILC in plenary session. Once approved, the ILC's drafting committee prepares a definitive text which is formally adopted by the ILC. The ILC has adopted 185 conventions and 194 recommendations.

Ratified conventions create legally-binding obligations on Member States, subject to ILO supervision. Recommendations cannot create international legal obligations. Both conventions and recommendations are drawn up by the same process and are subject to the same follow-up procedures, apart from those recommendations designed to monitor the application of ratified convention. A Member State has to report on how effect could be given to an unratified convention; it need not do so in the case of a recommendation, but it must specify modifications which may be necessary to adopt or apply a recommendation.

---

[36] ILO, Doc.GB286/LILS/1/1 (Mar.2003), para14.

Córdova calculated that in 1990 there were over 2,100 substantive labour standards in the then 170 conventions and a further 2,500 guidelines in the 180 recommendations. There were about 10,000 sections in the whole corpus of conventions. He concluded that 'not even in the most regulatory-prone countries is it possible to find such an extensive number of norms.'[37] He attributed this principally to the broadening of the ILO's remit since the Declaration of Philadelphia to include broad areas of social policy going far beyond the pre-War concentration on basic conditions of work. Alongside this is a tendency to deal with minute sectoral questions such as the certification of ships' cooks, crew accommodation and anthrax prevention. The effect of this 'overproduction' of standards was to undermine the ILO's supervisory system which could not properly examine national reports on the application of conventions and recommendations, nor deal thoroughly with complaints of violations.

Córdova argued that the root causes for the growth of labour standards were threefold: the lack of responsibility of delegates at the International Labour Conferences for ratification which presents itself as a problem to national governments only after adoption by the Conference; the constant pressure of European trade union delegates who have been the most vigorous initiators and supporters of international standards; and the International Labour Office's institutional interest in maintaining the production of standards. These and similar views were influential in the ILO's decision to concentrate on 'core' standards after 1997 (below). Underlying the whole debate was the decline in trade unionism and collective bargaining and deregulatory trend in the developed countries, as illustrated by the British Conservative Government's refusal to accept rulings by the ILO supervisory bodies (see Box 2.2). In the developing and emerging market economies, as well, the process of liberalisation did not sit comfortably with ILO standards.

The subject matter of the declining number of ILO conventions and recommendations differs from those adopted in the early years following the Declaration of Philadelphia until 1981. The emphasis in that period was the promotion of freedom of association, collective bargaining and tripartism.[38] These pro-collective standards now have to fight for survival in an increasingly individualistic climate. The last convention specifically to promote collective

---

[37] Above, at 146, 147.

[38] Notably C87, Freedom of Association and the Right to Organise, 1948; C98, Application of the Principles of the Right to Bargain Collectively, 1949; C135, Protection and Facilities to be Afforded to Workers' Representatives in the Undertaking, 1970; C141, Organisations of Rural Workers and their Role in Economic and Social Development, 1975; C144, Tripartite Consultations to Promote the Implementation of International Labour Standards, 1976; C151, Protection of the Right to Organise and Procedures for Determining Conditions of Employment in the Public Services, 1978.

Box 2.2

BRITAIN AND THE ILO

In Britain, after 1979, ILS were seen as an obstacle to the neo-liberal agenda of weakening trade unions and 'deregulating' labour markets. The Thatcher and Major governments ratified only one of the 25 new ILO conventions adopted by the International Labour Conference between 1979 and 1996, and denounced a significant number of conventions which earlier British governments had ratified, in order to pave the way for domestic legislation abolishing wages councils, revoking the fair wages resolution, and altering the protection of wages and night work provisions.[39] A significant number of complaints were taken to the supervisory bodies in Geneva, particularly in relation to the 'core' freedom of association and right to organise. These included the withdrawal of union membership rights at the Government Communications Headquarters, the termination of collective bargaining rights for teachers, the abolition of the Civil Service Arbitration Agreement, the dismissal of striking seafarers, the blacklisting of trade unionists by the Economic League, and the comprehensive complaints against the employment laws of the 1980s.[40] The adverse rulings of the supervisory bodies had little impact on the Conservative administrations: there are no effective sanctions against regimes which believe that downscaling is necessary in order to remain competitive and attractive to domestic and multi-national investors.[41] Although the New Labour Government, elected in 1997, has ratified five conventions, Britain's strike laws remain inconsistent with ratified ILO conventions.[42]

---

bargaining was adopted in 1981.[43] The absence of new international standards on workers' participation is the glaring gap of the past two decades in which serious attacks have been made in many countries on trade unionism and collective bargaining. Of the 31 new conventions and 2 protocols to existing conventions adopted from 1981–2003, 10 related to safety, health and social

[39] See Ewing (1994) at 53.
[40] See Creighton (1994) ch 1.
[41] Brown and McColgan (1992) at 279.
[42] Ewing and Hendy (2004). The 5 ratified conventions are C111, Discrimination (Employment and Occupation), 1958; C138, Minimum Age, 1973; C178, Labour Inspection (Seafarers), 1996; C180, Seafarers' Hours of Work and Manning of Ships, 1996; C182, Worst Forms of Child Labour, 1999. The UK is yet to ratify C181, Private Employment Agencies, 1997; C183, Maternity Protection, 2000; C184, Safety and Health in Agriculture, 2001; and C185, Seafarers' Identity Documents, 2003.
[43] C154, Collective Bargaining, 1981.

security,[44] 9 to individual employment protection,[45] 9 to seafarers,[46] and the rest were on miscellaneous topics including labour statistics,[47] labour inspection,[48] employment promotion,[49] and a relaxation in controls over private employment agencies.[50] The great majority of these new conventions were adopted by close voting margins, indicating a lack of consensus even on these non-collective topics.

The real question posed by globalisation, however, is not whether there are too many international standards, but whether or not the standards set are the ones that are needed to counteract the effects of globalisation on the majority of the world's workers, and whether these standards are being effectively implemented. The issue is qualitative not quantitative. One indication that there is something seriously wrong is the failure of most developing countries to ratify ILO conventions and to implement them. From this the inference may be drawn that the standards are not appropriate to the real needs of those countries.

The scale and nature of the problem

In order to show the scale of this problem, it is useful to analyse two separate elements: the number of ratified conventions and the number of 'observations' made by the Committee of Experts on the Application of Conventions and Recommendations (CEACR). Ratification alone is not a satisfactory measure

[44] C155, Occupational Safety and Health and the Working Environment, 1981; C157, Establishment of an International System for the Maintenance of Rights in Social Security, 1982; C159, Vocational Rehabilitation and Employment (Disabled Persons), 1983; C161, Occupational Health Services, 1985; C162, Safety in the Use of Asbestos, 1986; C167, Safety and Health in Construction 1988; C170, Safety in the Use of Chemical at Work, 1990; C174, Prevention of Major Industrial Accidents, 1993; C176, Safety and Health in Mines, 1995; C184, Safety and Health in Agriculture, 2001.

[45] C156, Equal Opportunities and Equal Treatment for Men and Women Workers with Family Responsibilities, 1981; C158, Termination of Employment at the Initiative of the Employer, 1982; C171, Night Work 1990; C172, Working Conditions in Hotels, Restaurants and Similar Establishments, 1991; C173, Protection of Workers' Claims in the Event of Insolvency of their Employer, 1992; C175, Part-Time Work, 1994; C177, Home Work, 1996; C182, Worst Forms of Child Labour, 1999; C183, Maternity Protection, 2000.

[46] C163, Seafarers' Welfare at Sea and in Port, 1987; C164, Health Protection and Medical Care for Seafarers, 1987; C165, Social Security for Seafarers (Revised), 1987; C166, Repatriation of Seafarers (Revised), 1987; P147 Protocol to the Merchant Shipping (Minimum Standards) Convention, 1976; C178, Labour Inspection (Seafarers), 1996; C179, Recruitment and Placement of Seafarers, 1996; C180, Seafarers Hours of Work and the Manning of Ships, 1996; Seafarers' Identity Documents, 2003.

[47] C160, Labour Statistics, 1985.

[48] P81 Protocol of 1995 to the Labour Inspection Convention, 1947.

[49] C168, Employment Promotion and Protection against Unemployment, 1988. See too, C169, Indigenous and Tribal People in Developing Countries, 1989.

[50] C181, Private Employment Agencies, 1997.

of whether international standards are hitting their mark. In his pathbreaking study, published in 1966, Landy observed that there are many pressures on countries to undertake premature ratification, before their national standards have been raised, and he noted the phenomena of 'empty' ratification and bogus ratification.[51] These pressures have increased over recent decades as governments have been required to adopt ILO-compliant labour codes in order to ensure assistance from the World Bank and IMF. It is therefore necessary to consider both the number of ratifications and the number of observations made by CEACR for non-compliance with ratified conventions. In the language of the ILO an 'observation' refers to a serious or long-standing violation of a ratified convention.[52] Countries with a high number of ratifications may not be complying with those conventions; countries with a high number of observations in respect of certain conventions may be adequately fulfilling their obligations under many other ratified instruments.

Table 2.A

CLASSIFICATIONS OF COUNTRIES ACCORDING TO THE NUMBER OF RATIFICATIONS OF ALL CONVENTIONS AND THE RECORD OF OBSERVATIONS OF NON-COMPLIANCE MADE BY THE COMMITTEE OF EXPERTS (1989–2003)[53]

Number of Countries	Record of Ratifications	Record of Observations
Category 1 (14)	80 or more ratifications	(A) *Low non-compliance* (4): Belgium, Bulgaria, Poland, Sweden (B) *High non-compliance* (10): Brazil, Cuba, Finland, France, Italy, Netherlands, Norway, Spain, Uruguay, United Kingdom
Category 2 (60)	More than 40 and fewer than 80 ratifications	(A) *Low non-compliance* (18): Azerbaijan, Belarus, Belize, Bosnia, Czech Republic, FYR Macedonia, Hungary, Israel, Kyrgyzstan, Latvia, Lebanon, Luxembourg, Malta, Serbia and Montenegro, Slovakia, Slovenia, Tajikistan, Ukraine (B) *High non-compliance* (42): Algeria, Argentina, Australia, Austria, Bolivia, Cameroon, Chile, Columbia, Costa Rica, Croatia, Cyprus, Denmark, Djibouti, Ecuador, Egypt, Germany, Ghana, Greece,

[51] Landy (1966).

[52] A 'direct request' usually relates to matters of secondary importance or may seek clarification on points on which there is insufficient information.

[53] As of December 2003.

		Guatemala, Guinea, Guyana, Iraq, Ireland, Japan, Kenya, Mauritania, Mexico, Morocco, New Zealand, Nicaragua, Panama, Peru, Portugal, Romania, Russian Federation, Switzerland, Syria, Tanzania, Tunisia, Turkey, Venezuela, Zambia
Category 3 (64)	More than 20 and fewer than 40 ratifications	(A) *Low non-compliance* (11): Albania, China, El Salvador, Estonia, Fiji, Grenada, Lithuania, Moldova, St Vincent, San Marino, Zimbabwe
		(B) *High non-compliance* (53): Angola, Antigua, Bahamas, Bangladesh, Barbados, Benin, Burkina Faso, Burundi, Canada, Central Africa Republic, Chad, Comoros, Cote d'Ivoire, DR Congo (Zaire), Dominica, Dominican Republic, Ethiopia, Gabon, Guinea-Bissau, Haiti, Honduras, Iceland, India, Jamaica, Jordan, Lesotho, Liberia, Libya, Madagascar, Malawi, Malaysia, Mali, Mauritius, Myanmar, Niger, Nigeria, Pakistan, Papua New Guinea, Paraguay, Philippines, Rwanda, St Lucia, Senegal, Seychelles, Sierra Leone, Singapore, South Africa, Sri Lanka, Suriname, Swaziland, Togo, Uganda, Yemen
Category 4 (24)	More than 10 and fewer than 20	(A) *Low non-compliance* (12): Botswana, Cambodia, Georgia, Kazakhstan, Korea, Mongolia, Namibia, Solomon Islands, Somalia, United States, Uzbekistan, Vietnam
		(B) *High non-compliance* (12) Afghanistan, Cape Verde, Equatorial Guinea, Indonesia, Iran, Kuwait, Mozambique, Sao Tome, Saudi Arabia, Sudan, Thailand, Trinidad
Category 5 (12)	Fewer than 10 ratifications	Armenia, Bahrain, Eritrea, Gambia, Kiribati, Lao, Nepal, Oman, Qatar, St Kitts, Turkmenistan, United Arab Emirates

Sources: ILOLEX, List of Ratifications December 2003
Reports of Committee of Experts

"High non-compliance":	Category 1 = 50 or more observations;
	Category 2 = 25 or more observations;
	Category 3 = 13 or more observations;
	Category 4 = 7 or more observations.

Table 2.A employs a similar methodology to that used by Córdova in respect of the earlier period 1986–91. Countries are classified according to the number of ratifications as at December 2003, and the record of observations of

non-compliance made by the Committee of Experts 1989–2003. This has been done in respect of all ILO Member States. The categories are the same as those used by Córdova. Category 1 comprises those countries with 80 or more ratifications; Category 2 those with more than 40 and fewer than 80 ratifications; Category 3 those with more than 20 and fewer than 40; Category 4 those with more than 10 and fewer than 20; and Category 5 those with fewer than 10. The first four categories are divided between (A) low non-compliance, and (B) high non-compliance. Córdova used five observations per year as the figure to separate low and high compliance. In this Table, the borderline used in Category 1 is a total of 50 or more observations; in Category 2, 25 or more observations; in Category 3, 13 or more observations; and in Category 4, 7 or more observations.[54] This refinement takes into account that there are fewer opportunities for the CEACR to examine government reports where the number of ratifications is low.[55] It does not, however, follow that there is a higher number of observations from countries with a higher number of ratifications.[56]

These non-ratifying countries, the vast majority of which also record high non-compliance, are overwhelmingly developing countries. The main exception is the US, with only 14 ratifications (including 2 conventions no longer in force) but low non-compliance. At the other end of the scale in Category 1, with ratifications of 80 or more conventions, there are 11 European states and 3 Latin American states, half of them with high non-compliance. In Category 2(B), three quarters of the countries which have ratified more than 40 but less than 80 conventions but record high non-compliance are developing countries. These statistics are not dissimilar from those produced by Córdova in 1993 in respect of an earlier period.

Table 2.B compares the number of ratifications of ILO Conventions (up to December 2003) by countries according to their place on the UNDP's Human Development Index. This ranks the level of development of countries on the basis of life expectancy, educational attainment and real income, number 1 being the most developed and number 173 the least developed. This indicates that there is relatively little difference between high-, medium-, and low-development countries in their ability to ratify conventions relating to the 'core' conventions on freedom of association, forced labour, child labour, and equality of opportunity and treatment. For example, 86 per cent of high-

---

[54] In calculating the number of observations account has been taken both of general observations and individual observations by CEACR.

[55] CEACR also examines government reports in respect of selected unratified conventions.

[56] For example in Category 1, there were only 17 observations in respect of Bulgaria with 84 ratifications and 31 in respect of Belgium with 89 ratifications. On the other hand, in Category 2, there were 125 observations in respect of Bolivia with 46 ratifications; in Category 3, 106 observations in respect of Sierra Leone with 33 ratifications; in Category 4, 35 observations in respect of Sudan with 12 ratifications; and in Category 5, 13 observations in respect of Nepal with 9 ratifications.

development countries have ratified Conventions 87 and 98 on freedom of association, the right to organise and collective bargaining, compared with 75 per cent of medium- and low-development countries. A higher percentage of medium- (93 per cent) and low- (96 per cent) development countries than high-development ones (86 per cent) have ratified C.29 and C.105 on forced labour. Countries in the three categories are relatively equal in their ratification of C.100 on equal remuneration of men and women and C.111 on discrimination (88 per cent, 90 per cent and 89 per cent respectively). As one might expect, low-development countries have had more difficulty in ratifying C.138 on minimum age in employment (40 per cent) than medium- (43 per cent) or high-development countries (49 per cent), and also in ratifying C.182 on the worst forms of child labour (77 per cent, compared with 90 and 87 per cent).

The most significant differences occur in respect to occupational safety and health and social security. While 35 per cent of high-development, and 28 per cent of medium-development countries have ratified C.155 on occupational safety and health, only 11 per cent of low-development countries have done so. Forty-nine per cent of high development countries have ratified C.102 (minimum standards in social security), only 19 per cent of medium- and 7 per cent of low-development countries have done so. Not a single low-development country has ratified C.168 on employment promotion and protection against unemployment, or C.183 on maternity protection. Only two of these countries has ratified C.128 on old-age, invalidity and survivors' benefits and C.130 on medical care and sickness benefits.

Table 2.B				
ILO RATIFICATIONS COMPARED BY HUMAN DEVELOPMENT INDEX[57]				
Category of Instrument	Up-to-date instruments	HHD[58] (1–53)	MHD[59] (54–85)	LHD[60] (86–173)
Basic Human Rights Freedom of association	C.87 (Freedom of association)	44	23	69

---

[57] Source: Human Development Report 2002, United Nations Development Program. Under the HDI, countries are ranked according to their development. 1 being the most developed country, 173 being the least. Development is measured according to life expectancy, educational attainment and real income.

[58] High Human Development. Countries ranked 1–53.

[59] Medium Human Development. Countries ranked 54–85.

[60] Low Human Development. Countries ranked 86–173.

Table 2.B (*cont.*)

Category of Instrument	Up-to-date instruments	HHD (1–53)	MHD (54–85)	LHD (86–173)
	C.98 (Right to organise and collective bargaining)	44	27	76
Basic Human Rights (cont.)				
Freedom of association (*cont.*)	C.135 (Workers' representatives)	30	11	30
	C.141 (Rural workers)	20	6	11
	C.151 (Public service)	22	9	10
Forced labour	C.29 (Forced labour)	47	29	79
	C.105 (Abolition of forced labour)	47	28	75
Equality of opportunity and treatment	C.100 (Equal remuneration of men and women)	47	29	79
	C.111 (Discrimination in employment and occupation)	47	27	77
	C.156 (Workers with family responsibilities)	18	6	7
Child labour	C.138 (Minimum age)	26	14	36
	C.182 (Worst forms of child labour)	48	26	67
Employment				
Employment policy	C.122 (Employment policy)	36	19	36
Employment services and fee-charging agencies	C.181 (Private employment agencies)	8	2	4
Vocational guidance and training	C.142 (Human resources development)	30	11	16
Rehabilitation and employment of disabled persons	C.159 (Vocational rehabilitation and employment)	33	12	27
Labour administration				
General	C.150 (Labour administration)	24	7	22
Labour inspection	C.81 (Industry and commerce)	41	22	61
	C.129 (Agriculture)	20	4	15
Statistics	C.160 (Labour statistics)	26	8	10
Tripartite consultation	C.144 (Tripartite consultation)	40	18	48
Industrial relations				
Industrial relations	C.154 (Collective bargaining)	15	8	10

Conditions of work

Wages	C.131 (Minimum wage fixing)	15	7	20
	C.95 (Protection of wages)	21	22	47
	C.173 (Employers' insolvency)	9	1	5
	C.94 (Labour clauses, public contracts)	17	12	25
Night work	C.171 (Night work)	6	1	1
Weekly rest	C.14 (Industry)	34	23	54
	C.106 (Commerce and offices)	16	13	29
Paid leave	C.140 (Paid educational leave)	14	7	7
Part-time work	C.175 (Part-time work)	7	1	2
Home work	C.177 (Home work)	3	0	1

Occupational safety and health

General	C.155 (Occupational safety and health)	19	9	10
	C.161 (Occupational health services)	11	4	4
	C.174 (Major industrial accidents)	3	4	2
Toxic substances and agents	C.115 (Radiation)	24	8	14
	C.139 (Occupational cancer)	20	5	6
	C.162 (Asbestos)	15	4	6
	C.170 (Chemicals)	4	3	4
Air pollution, noise and vibration	C.148 (Air pollution, noise and vibration)	21	5	11
Building industry	C.167 (Construction)	9	3	4
Underground work	C.176 (Mines)	12	3	5
Commerce and offices	C.120 (Hygiene)	19	10	19
Agriculture	C.184 (Safety and health)	2	0	1

Social security

Comprehensive standards	C.102 (Minimum standards)	26	6	6
	C.118 (Equality of treatment)	12	7	18
	C.157 (Maintenance of rights)	2	1	0
Medical care and sickness benefits	C.130 (Medical care and sickness benefits)	10	2	2
Old-age, invalidity and survivors' benefits	C.128 (Invalidity old-age and survivors' benefits)	12	2	2
Employment injury benefit	C.121 (Employment injury benefits)	13	3	5

Table 2.B (*cont.*)

Category of Instrument	Up-to-date instruments	HHD (1–53)	MHD (54–85)	LHD (86–173)
Unemployment benefits	C.168 (Employment promotion and protection against unemployment)	4	2	0
Maternity benefit	C.183 (Maternity protection)	3	2	0
Employment of children and young persons				
Medical examination	C.77 (Industry)	15	10	17
	C.78 (Non-industrial occupations)	14	8	16
	C.124 (Underground work)	18	7	16
Indigenous and tribal peoples, indigenous workers in non-metropolitan territories				
Indigenous and tribal peoples	C.169 (Indigenous and tribal peoples)	5	7	5
Seafarers				
General	C.108 (Identity documents)	25	15	20
	C.145 (Continuity of employment)	12	2	2
	C.147 (Minimum standards)	30	6	6
Training and entry into employment	C.179 (Recruitment and procurement)	3	3	1
General conditions of employment	C.146 (Annual leave with pay)	7	2	4
	C.166 (Repatriation)	4	4	1
	C.180 (Hours of work and manning)	10	2	2
Safety, health and welfare	C.163 (Welfare)	9	3	0
	C.164 (Health protection and medical care)	9	2	0
Social security	C.165 (Social security—seafarers)	2	0	0
Labour inspection	C.178 (Inspection of working and living conditions)	6	0	2
Dockworkers				
General	C.152 (Occupational safety and health)	10	4	4
Plantations				
General	C.110 (Plantations)	1	4	5
Nursing personnel				
General	C.149 (Nursing personnel)	15	5	15
Hotels and restaurants				
General	C.172 (Working conditions)	8	2	2

Córdova suggested that the laxity of developing countries might be due to the volume of the obligations assumed. Against this view, one must point out that the ILO's reporting system is principally concerned with whether a country's national legislation complies with the international standard in question. It does not examine in depth whether the convention is being complied with in practice, and the CEACR generally lacks the sociological information to make such an examination possible. So it is relatively easy, even for a small developing country, with ILO technical assistance, to bring its formal legal system into compliance. Indeed, it is notorious that there are states with model labour codes reflecting international standards which fail to enforce them due to lack of resources, incompetence or corruption. My own experience when providing technical assistance in developing countries has been that it is not the magnitude of the International Labour Code that prevents compliance but rather a deeply-held view, shared by governments and influential national and trans-national employers, that the ILO's standards are too remote from the reality of their stage of economic and social development. In theory, use can be made of flexibility clauses in ILO conventions to adjust the scope and level of protection, but it seems that in practice such clauses are infrequently invoked.

The real obstacle is an ideological one, namely the fear that adoption of ILO standards will put poor countries at a competitive disadvantage in international trade. Empirical analysis by Chau and Kanbur of the ratification of four core conventions, suggests that the decision to ratify a convention depends crucially on whether or not peer countries have done so.[61] A virtuous circle of ratifying countries depends on the initiative being taken by a competitor, with similar factor advantages. The result is that vast disparities continue to exist between an elite of industrialised countries complying with a relatively high number of conventions, and the great mass of developing nations with few ratifications and high levels of non-compliance in respect of conventions that involve significant costs, in particular those on occupational health and safety and social security. This is a vicious circle which serves to reinforce the belief in the socially advanced countries that the developing countries are practising 'social dumping', and in the developing countries that there is 'social imperialism' on the part of the industrialised countries.

5. Does the supervisory machinery work?

Supervision through reporting procedures

The ILO has a unique supervisory system. This falls into two categories. First, there are reporting obligations on governments. These reports form the basis for

---

[61] Chau and Kanbur (2001), analysing ratifications of Conventions 98, 105, 111 and 158.

dialogue to improve compliance with ILS, combining an independent technical body (the Committee of Experts on the Application of Conventions and Recommendations, CEACR) with a political body (the Conference Committee on the Application of Standards, CCAS). Secondly, there are the adversarial 'special procedures'. Contrary to traditional international law, non-governmental organisations, in particular workers' or employers' organisations, as well as other Member States, are able to set these procedures in motion.

The first reporting requirement, under Article 19 of the ILO Constitution, sets a time limit for the submission of a convention or recommendation to the 'competent authority' (usually the legislature), and to report to the Office. Workers' and employers' organisations can provide their observations. This is aimed at publicising ILS, and, in practice can lead to immediate improvements in national law and practice. The CEACR examines the reports and, where appropriate, reminds Member States of the possibility of obtaining technical assistance from the ILO.

Secondly, also under Article 19, the GB may request a Member State to report on 'the position of its law and practice in regard to matters dealt with in the Convention [or Recommendation], showing the extent to which effect has been given, or is proposed to be given, to any provisions of the Convention [or Recommendation]' and explaining the 'difficulties which prevent or delay the ratification.' These reports are analysed by the CECA in a general survey.

Thirdly, ratification places a Member State under the obligation, by virtue of Article 22 of the ILO Constitution, to provide a periodical report on the application of the Convention. The government draws up the report, but it is obliged to show it to workers' and employers' organisations, which are free to forward comments on the government's report directly to the CEACR (Box 2.3). The reporting cycles have been modified at various times and reports are now due at 2 or 5-yearly intervals, but they can be requested more frequently. In 2002–03, 2,368 reports were requested and 1,529 (64.57 per cent) were received. Four hundred observations were received from workers' and employers' organisations. Thirteen countries had not complied with requests for two or more years.[62]

The CEACR's observations are sent to the governments concerned, and the reports are made to the CCAS (Box 2.3). From 1994–2003, the CCAS examined an average of 27 cases each session, over 70 per cent relating to the priority conventions. The countries which feature most frequently in the CCAS report are from Latin America and the Indian sub-continent. Among developed nations, the UK is most frequently referred to. In 2003, two countries were included in a 'special paragraph'. These were Belarus and Myanamar in respect of Convention 87, on freedom of association.

---

[62] ILO (2003) at 28, 36.

Box 2.3

THE CEACR AND CCAS

The *Committee of Experts on the Application of Conventions and Recommendations* (CEACR) is composed of independent jurists, specialists in labour law or international law drawn from the world's major legal systems and chosen on the basis of their personal qualities. There are currently 19 members who meet in private in November each year to examine the reports and do so purely on the basis of documentary information. The CEACR publishes its observations and also each year a general survey reviewing the law and practice in a specific field in respect of both ratified and unratified conventions. Where a Member State repeatedly fails to report or to reply to comments, the CEACR may require non-periodic detailed reports, and the ILC then automatically examines those cases.

The *Conference Committee on the Application of Standards* (CCAS) examines, in June each year, the most serious cases in the CEACR report from a more political angle. The CCAS is a permanent tripartite committee of the ILC, which meets in public. It invites the representatives of the governments concerned to submit written replies or to participate orally in the discussions. The CCAS adopts conclusions. Cases of continued failure or deficiency can be mentioned in a special paragraph of the report. The report, drawing attention to particular cases, is discussed in a plenary session of the ILC.

Adversarial procedures

There are several special, more adversarial, procedures. First, representations may be made, under Article 24 of the ILO Constitution, to the GB by workers' or employers' organisations, complaining that a Member State has failed to secure effective observance of a convention which that State has ratified. If the representation is deemed receivable, the GB sets up a tripartite committee to examine the allegations and to make recommendations, which are then a matter for decision by the GB. The GB invites the government concerned to be represented at its meeting when it considers the matter. In 85 years, this procedure has been used on only 70 occasions, 58 of these in the decade 1994–2003.

Secondly, Article 26 of the ILO Constitution provides for a complaints procedure, reserved for the most serious cases of failure to observe ratified conventions. Complaints may be initiated by a State that has ratified the convention against another Member State that has ratified the convention, or by the Governing Body either of its own motion or on receipt of a complaint by any delegate to the ILC. This may result in the establishment of a Commission of Inquiry, which elaborates it own procedure. The Commissions were originally intended to be tripartite, but in practice experts of high legal standing are appointed. The procedure was used in the 1970s in the case of Chile, in the 1980s against Nicaragua, and in the 1990s against Nigeria, in respect of alleged violations of the freedom of association. In 1996, 25 workers' delegates set the procedure in motion against Myanmar for violation of Convention 29 on forced labour. This led to the application in June 2000, for the first time in the ILO's history, of measures under Article 33 of the ILO constitution to secure compliance (Box 2.4).

Article 33 provides that

> in the event of any Member failing to carry out within the time specified the recommendations, if any, contained in the report of the Commission of Inquiry, or in the decision of the International Court of Justice, as the case may be, the Governing Body may recommend such action as it may deem wise and expedient to secure compliance therewith.

Unlike the observations of the CEACR, the complaint procedure under Article 26 and the report of a Commission of Inquiry is the only way in which a legally-binding determination can be made that a Member has breached its obligations under a convention. The findings of the Commission become binding when the Member State agrees explicitly to accept them, or abstains from referring the matter to the ICJ, under Article 29 of the ILO Constitution. In none of the cases in which a Commission has reported has the government exercised this right of appeal. Failure to appeal means that the findings cannot be re-opened: the only issue is how to implement them.

Finally, and most importantly, there are the special procedures for freedom of association, the Committee on Freedom of Association (CFA) and the Fact-Finding and Conciliation Commission (FFCC) (see Box 2.5). In the period 1951–2003, the CFA examined over 2,300 cases.

Evaluation

The two most distinctive features of the ILO's supervisory system, like the rest of its Constitution, are tripartism and reliance upon voluntary action by Member States. Both are under increasing strain.

Historically, tripartism was an attempt to reconcile the interests of workers and employers. The presence of these groups provides a dynamic element. This is illustrated by the Myanmar case in which, according to Maupain,[63] the feeling of moral outrage on the part of the worker and employer delegates overcame any reluctance on the part of governments to act, and ensured a

---

[63] Maupain (forthcoming a), to whom I am much indebted for his analysis of this case.

Box 2.4

THE CASE OF MYANMAR (BURMA)

Until 1948, Burma was part of the British Empire. It was granted independence in 1948, but the military assumed power in 1962. British legislation, including the Penal Code and the Town and Village Acts (TVA) remained in force. Although the Penal Code makes forced labour unlawful, the TVA allow Village Heads to requisition forced labour for a variety of purposes. Britain never ratified ILO Convention 29 on Forced Labour in respect of Burma, but during a short period of civilian rule independent Myanmar did so. From 1964 onwards, the CEACR consistently pointed out that the TVA were inconsistent with the Convention. The military junta that took over in 1988 used forced labour on an unprecedented scale, not limited to the TVA. This led to the complaint by workers' delegates to the ILC in 1996, and the establishment of a Commission of Inquiry.

The Government refused to accept a visit from the Commission, which revealed, on the basis of evidence from victims, 'a saga of untold misery and suffering, oppression and exploitation of large sections of the population.'[64] The Government did not appeal to the ICJ against the Recommendations of the Commission of Inquiry. A resolution adopted by the ILC in 1999 imposed a ban on technical co-operation with Myanmar, and in 2000 the GB placed on the agenda of the ILC the question of implementing Article 33 of the ILO Constitution. This prompted the Government to accept a Technical Co-operation Mission (TCM) in May 2000. In June 2000, the ILC adopted a Resolution calling on ILO Members and international organisations to review their relations with Myanmar to avoid abetting the practice of forced labour and contributing to the implementation of the Commission's Recommendations. In 1999 and 2000 the Government adopted two orders making the requisition of forced labour illegal and subject to penal sanctions. The GB decided that this was not 'sufficiently concrete and detailed' as a response the Commission's Recommendations and activated the ILC Resolution. After lengthy negotiations, the Government accepted a far-reaching Understanding under which an international High level Team (HLT) would carry out an independent evaluation of implementation. The HLT found that the orders were not being adequately enforced, not least because of the absence of an independent judiciary and the disproportionate size of the military. In March 2002, as recommended by the HLT the Government agreed to the establishment of an ILO Liaison Officer in Myanmar to assist on the elimination of forced labour. In May 2003 agreement was reached on a Joint Action Plan for the Elimination of

[64] ILO, GB 273/5.

Box 2.4 (*cont.*)

THE CASE OF MYANMAR (BURMA) (*cont.*)

Forced Labour Practices. This includes provision for a 'Facilitator', an independent person who is a Swiss national, who will receive complaints and determine whether they represent a *prima facie* case of forced labour. If these complaints are not settled, they will be referred to the judiciary for prosecution. The process was, however, interrupted as a result of the suppression of the democratic movement following the 'massacre' of 30 May 2003.

Box 2.5

THE CFA AND FFCC

The *Committee on Freedom of Association* (CFA), established in 1951, is a tripartite body of 9 members with an independent chairman, appointed by the GB. It examines allegations of violation of the principles of freedom of association, on the basis of complaints brought by a State or by a workers' or employers' organisation. The CFA is not limited to complaints against a State which has ratified the relevant conventions. This distinguishes it from other international procedures which require the express consent of States to accept the supervisory body's jurisdiction. This is justified on the basis that when a State joins the ILO it accepts the fundamental principles embodied in the Constitution and the Declaration of Philadelphia, including the principle of freedom of association.[65] The CFA considers complaints primarily on the basis of documentary evidence. Its decisions are normally adopted by consensus. The CFA invites the government, after a reasonable period of time, to indicate the effect it has given to the Committee's recommendations. In cases where the issues relate to legislation and the State has ratified the conventions, the CFA refers these issues to the CEACR.

The GB may refer allegations of the infringement of trade union rights, by Member or non-Member States, to a *Fact Finding and Conciliation Commission* (FFCC). This is composed of 9 independent members, working in panels of 3. The consent of the government concerned is required. Cases may also be referred to a FFCC by the Economic and Social Council of the UN (ECOSOC). The FFCC normally holds hearings in the county concerned (as in the case of South Africa in the early 1990s), reports to the GB or (concerning States that are not Members of the ILO) to ECOSOC. These reports are also drawn to the attention of CCAS.

---

[65] This obligation is also assumed under the Declaration of Fundamental Principles and Rights at Work (1998), below.

majority for the Resolution and its subsequent implementation. In modern terms, tripartism is is usually described as a 'social dialogue', involving governments, employers' and workers' organisations. The unequal tripartism (2/1/1) of the ILC and GB[66] is tempered on the technical and supervisory committees, such as the CCAS and CFA, on which each group is equally represented (1/1/1). The principle of tripartism rests on the assumption that workers' and employers' delegates are able to make decisions without government instructions or interference. In practice workers' delegates and employers' delegates tend to vote together based on group interests rather than allegiance to their governments, although in some cases (such as the adoption of social clauses, chapter 6, below), nationalism rather than internationalism has prevailed. The end of the Cold War removed one problem, that of the representativeness and independence of delegations from the communist countries (above). Indeed, the ILO's dialogue with the communist governments, for example concerning Polish *Solidarity* (above), was a significant factor in the democratisation of those countries.

The real problem with the social dialogue model is that it becomes a fiction if independent trade unions or employers' organisations, at national level, are weak or non-existent. This is the case in many, perhaps most, of the States which have joined the ILO in the post-colonial period. In the informal sector of the developing countries, the tripartite model simply does not exist. In the formal sector, the standard-setting activities of the ILO, as well as its supervisory machinery, are contaminated by the weakness and lack of genuine independence of national organisations. This is exacerbated by the decline in trade union strength in the older developed countries. The main spokespersons for the workers in developing countries come from the international NGOs. However, these are not 'representative' organisations and most are dominated by activists from the developed countries. The ILO's Director-General has spelt out the advantages of an alliance between certain NGOs and the traditional workers' and employers' representatives.[67] The ILO itself invites some NGOs to participate (but not to vote) in meetings of various bodies, a practice permitted by Article 12 of the ILO Constitution, and draws some of its technical experts from these organisations.[68]

Resistance to more active involvement of NGOs in the ILO's standard-setting and supervisory mechanisms comes from the employers' and workers' groups who are anxious to protect their vested interests. Both groups have

---

[66] Unlike the ILC, for which the Member State appoints the worker and employer representatives, the representatives of employers and workers on the GB are elected respectively by the Employer and Worker groups of the ILC.

[67] ILO (1999) at 39–40.

[68] Art 12 refers to 'public international organisations'. Art 18 permits technical experts to be appointed to committees. These may be drawn from NGOs.

been totally opposed to any modification of the ILO's structure to include NGOs. As the ILO attempts to campaign for 'decent work' and to spread its activities into the informal sector (below), the contradiction between the principles of universality and tripartism is likely to be become acute. Even the greater involvement of NGOs would not, however, ensure that all the interests involved are fairly represented.

The challenges to voluntarism are well-illustrated by the British (Box 2.2) and Myanmar (Box 2.5) cases. These cases involved legislation for which the governments were directly responsible. Even more problematic are situations where the violations of conventions are committed by private corporations or individuals. The CFA goes further than other supervisory bodies, when it finds violation of the principles of freedom of association by a private employer, by advising the State to take measures to ensure compliance (eg the reinstatement of a worker dismissed for anti-union reasons). But this practice has not been generally followed by other ILO bodies.

The most frequent criticism of the supervisory mechanisms is that they depend on goodwill that is not present on the part of the worst offenders. There can be no doubt that in many cases that goodwill is present. The CEACR lists cases of progress. In 2003, the Committee expressed satisfaction with progress in 30 cases from 24 countries, bringing to 2,342 to number of cases in which such progress has been recorded since 1964.[69] The follow-up procedure of the CFA has, since 2002, made it possible to assess the impact of its procedure. There has been no systematic study of the impact of supervisory measures, and it would be difficult to determine precise criteria for measurement. But this does not mean that the supervisory machinery is not working, simply that diplomatic measures require patience and persistence. The ILO provides a great deal of technical assistance, either in response to requests or in the course of its regular work. 'Direct contacts' may be requested to follow-up matters raised by the supervisory bodies, and the Director-General may appoint an official or an independent expert to examine the situation and propose solutions acceptable to all parties. Although the Director-General proposed, as long ago as 1994, that a procedure of voluntary mediation and arbitration should be established, this has not yet happened.

In the case of Myanmar it took 30 years of persistent CEACR observations before a Commission of Inquiry was established. It was the threat that sanctions would be activated, coupled with sensitive and difficult negotiations, that ultimately caused a dictatorial government to respond. The agreement to an ILO Liaison Officer and a Facilitator in the country were important steps, but their success cannot be guaranteed until democracy is restored in Myanmar.

[69] CEACR Report III, Part IA (2003), paras 107–10.

The crucial reason why Article 33 has been invoked on only one occasion, and then only over the objections of several countries, especially from Asia, is the general hostility to trade sanctions as a means of enforcing ILS. It is sometimes argued that imposing sanctions in respect of ratified conventions would act as a disincentive to ratification. However, it can be justified on the grounds of reciprocity: one country cannot be expected to ratify if other ratifying countries are flouting the provisions of conventions they have purported to ratify. The argument is strongest when there is a flagrant breach of a fundamental right

There is some legal ambiguity as to the scope of the 'action' that can be authorised under Article 33. Before 1946, Article 28 of the ILO Constitution allowed the GB, in response to the findings of a Commission of Inquiry, to recommend 'the measures, if any of an *economic character*' that should be taken against a defaulting government. Either party could then approach the Permanent Court of International Justice (now the ICJ) which was to make the final decision on the merits and on 'any measures of an *economic character*'. This was dropped in 1946, no such measures ever having been recommended, and replaced by the current Article 33 which, as we have seen, refers only to 'such action' as may be deemed 'wise and expedient to secure compliance'. Maupain[70] believes that the change of wording does not rule out economic sanctions. The wording of the Myanmar Resolution in 2000 deliberately left Member States and international organisations with a wide discretion in this respect. They were asked to 'review' their relations with Myanmar and to take 'appropriate measures'. Without this ambiguity, leaving responsibility with the Member States, it is unlikely that the Resolution would have been adopted.[71] The key issue, Maupain points out, is the compatibility of trade sanctions imposed by Member States with their commitments as WTO members. This will be discussed in chapter 6, below.

Finally, it is obvious that the supervisory procedures could be streamlined and made more transparent. There is a considerable degree of overlap between the procedures under Articles 22 (CEACR) and Articles 24 (representations) and Article 26 (complaints). In practice, the CEACR does not examine aspects of the application of a convention that are the subject of a representation before the representation procedure is completed. Similarly, the CFA will submit the legislative aspects of a case it has examined to the CEACR. Although there is no overlap between the CEACR and CCAS, the selection of cases which reach the ILC tends to be haphazard. The procedures could be streamlined and made more transparent, with agreed criteria for the selection of cases. Consideration of cases could be more effectively distributed between the different committees.

---

[70] Maupain (forthcoming a).
[71] Maupain (forthcoming a).

There is a question whether a special international labour tribunal should be established to provide authoritative interpretations of conventions. This has become an increasingly pressing issue because of the adoption of regional instruments and bilateral treaties, which adopt sometimes subtle differences in wording from ILO conventions and recommendations. O'Higgins argues that the primacy of ILO standards could be ensured, and confusion overcome, by some overall supervisory authority, preferably a court, where authoritative interpretations could be given.[72]

Neither the CEACR nor the CFA adopt adversarial procedures, and their conclusions do not have legally-binding force. Nevertheless, the CEACR believes that its interpretations should be regarded as 'valid and generally recognised' unless contradicted by the ICJ.[73] The jurisdiction of the ICJ has not been invoked since the 1930s, and this forum lacks specialist knowledge and experience of labour matters. However, there is provision, in Article 37(2) of the ILO Constitution, for the appointment of a tribunal for the 'expeditious determination of any dispute or question relating to the interpretation of a convention.' Although there are some legal doubts as to the exact scope of this provision, the establishment of a specialist labour tribunal could help to resolve disputes between states and the supervisory bodies, and clarify the meaning of ILO instruments. Perhaps even more urgent than this is the creation of an international conciliation and arbitration service to resolve disputes between governments, TNCs and workers involving the alleged violation of rights under ILO conventions, bilateral treaties, corporate codes and international collective agreements (chapter 3, below).

6. New directions: fundamental rights and decent work

The ILO's response to the challenges discussed above has been threefold. First, promoting a Declaration on Fundamental Principles and Rights at Work, adopted at the International Labour Conference in June 1998; secondly, revitalising international labour standards by making them more coherent and integrated; and thirdly by a campaign for 'decent work'.

---

[72] O'Higgins (2002) at 68.
[73] CEACR Report, 1990, paras 7, 8.

Fundamental principles and rights at work

The then Director-General's reports to the 81st session (1994) of the International Labour Conference,[74] and to the 85th session (1997),[75] outlined the ILO's new vision for reconciling the liberalisation of trade with adherence to labour standards. This was to be achieved by universal respect for fundamental human rights in the workplace as defined in seven 'core' or fundamental conventions. These are: freedom of association and collective bargaining (C.87 and C.98), forced labour (C.29 and C.105), non-discrimination (C.100 and C.111) and the minimum age in employment (C.138). In 1999, an eighth core convention, adopted that year, was added, on the prohibition and immediate action for the elimination of the worst forms of child labour (C.182). This concentration on fundamental human rights followed a study by the OECD, begun in 1994 and completed in 1996, from which the Employment, Labour and Social Affairs Committee and the Trade Committee of the OECD drew a number of conclusions later endorsed by OECD Ministers.[76] The Report suggested that improved enforcement of non-discrimination standards, and the elimination of forced and child labour might raise economic efficiency, and concluded that concerns of developing countries that core standards, such as freedom of association and the right to collective bargaining, would negatively affect their economic performance or international competitive position are unfounded. This concentration on core rights was endorsed in Copenhagen in 1995, when the Heads of State and Government attended the World Summit for Social Development.[77] The US Government was influential in pressing for a promotional approach, in part because it was sensitive to criticisms that it had failed to ratify conventions.[78] The WTO Ministerial Conference held in Singapore in 1996 also expressed a commitment to core labour standards, but resolved that the ILO—and not the WTO—was the competent body to deal with these standards. This culminated in June 1998 with the adoption by the ILC of the ILO Declaration on Fundamental Principles and Rights at Work (Box 2.6).

---

[74] ILO (1994); cf Myrdal (1994) at 342–49, who disputes the notion of an internationally agreed 'core'.

[75] ILO (1997d).

[76] OECD, (1996); see too, ILO Governing Body, 267th session, Working Party on the Social Dimensions of the Liberalisation of International Trade, GB267/WP/SDL/2, November 1996; ILO Governing Body, 268th session, Statement by the Chairperson of the Working Party on the Social Dimensions of the Liberalisation of International Trade, GB 268/WP/SDL/D1, March 1997.

[77] Art 54(b) of the Programme of Action adopted by the Copenhagen Summit.

[78] Alston (2004) at 564–67.

Box 2.6

THE ILO DECLARATION OF FUNDAMENTAL PRINCIPLES AND RIGHTS AT WORK (1998)

[Preamble omitted]
The International Labour Organisation –

1. Recalls that in joining the ILO, all Members have endorsed the principles and rights set out in its Constitution and in the Declaration of Philadelphia, and have undertaken to work towards attaining the overall objectives of the Organisation to the best of their resources and fully in line with their specific circumstances; that these principles and rights have been expressed and developed in the form of specific rights and obligations in conventions recognised as fundamental both inside and outside the Organisation.

2. Declares that all Members, even if they have not ratified the Conventions in question, have an obligation, arising from the very fact of membership of the Organisation, to respect, to promote and to realise, in good faith and in accordance with the Constitution, the principles concerning the fundamental rights which are the subject of those conventions namely: freedom of association and the effective recognition of the right to collective bargaining; the elimination of all forms of forced or compulsory labour; the effective abolition of child labour; the elimination of discrimination in respect of employment and occupation.

3. Recognises the obligation of the Organisation to assist its Members, in response to their established and express needs, in order to obtain those objectives by making full use of its constitutional, operational and budgetary resources, including by the mobilisation of external resources and support, as well as by encouraging other international organisations with which the ILO has established relations, pursuant to Article 12 of the Constitution to support these efforts: by offering technical co-operation and advisory services to promote the ratification and implementation of the fundamental conventions; by assisting those Members not yet in a position to ratify some to all those conventions to respect, to promote and to realise the principles concerning fundamental rights which are the subject of those conventions; and by helping the Members in their efforts to create a climate for economic and social development.

4. Decides that, to give full effect to this Declaration, a promotional follow-up, which is meaningful and effective, shall be implemented in
   accordance with the measures specified in the annex hereto, which
   shall be considered as an integral part of this Declaration.
5. Stresses that labour standards should not be used for protectionist
   trade purposes, and that nothing in this Declaration and its follow-up
   shall be invoked or otherwise used for such purposes; in addition, the
   comparative advantage of any country shall in no way be called into
   question by this Declaration and its follow-up.

The choice of these 8 core conventions, and not others, rests on the view that
they are, in the words of the Preamble, of 'particular significance' in maintaining 'the link between social progress and economic growth'. This linkage exists
because the conventions enable 'the persons concerned to claim freely and on
the basis of equality of opportunity their fair share of the wealth which they
have helped to generate, and to achieve fully their human potential.'[79] This
justification, which treats economic and social policies as mutually reinforc-
ing, marks a significant shift from the priority given in earlier ILO conventions
to matters which were believed to have a direct effect on economic competitiveness, such as hours of work, night work, unemployment and minimum
age. It also differentiates the ILO core from the concept of 'internationally
recognised worker rights' enshrined in US trade legislation which includes
'acceptable conditions of work with respect to minimum wages, hours of work,
occupational safety and health' but makes no mention of discrimination in
employment and occupation. (chapter 4, Box 4.1). It has been argued that the
8 conventions are 'process-oriented', rather than 'results-oriented', and are
thus consistent with freedom of choice and free trade ideology.[80]

The unique legal character of the Declaration is that obligations are placed
on all Member States not by reason of ratification of the named conventions,
but 'from the very fact of membership'. This is, therefore, a constitutional
obligation not one which rests upon voluntary acceptance. So it has been
argued that the US is bound by the principles of non-discrimination and freedom of association purely as a result of its ILO membership, despite its failure
to ratify the relevant conventions. Such an argument is unlikely to make any
practical difference because the Declaration is regarded as purely promotional.[81] The more interesting question, from a legal viewpoint, is whether

---

[79] Preamble, 5th recital. Other recitals emphasise that the ILO should continue to deal with
other matters.

[80] McCrudden and Davies (2000) at 51–52.

[81] Alston (2004) at 469.

any of the fundamental principles and rights embodied in the Declaration have become part of customary international law. It would have to be established that they form part of 'habitual state practice', and that States appreciate that the practice is *required* by international law. Since 1986 the ICJ has stated that the practice of states must be 'broadly consistent'.[82] While the prohibition of slavery[83] and forced labour[84] may be said to be matters on which state practice is broadly consistent, it is much more difficult to show this in respect of the prohibition on child labour and the elimination of discrimination. Widespread abuses of the freedom of association and the denial of the right to collective bargaining in many countries make it virtually impossible to regard these human rights as part of consistent state practice, but the growing observance of the relevant conventions may in time change this.

The follow-up procedure (set out in the Annex to the Declaration) relies entirely on a reporting mechanism, not on sanctions. The validity of this mechanism rests on Article 19(5)(e) of the ILO Constitution which allows the Organisation to request reports on unratified conventions. The follow-up combines annual reviews of the situation in countries that have not ratified some or all the 8 conventions, with 4-yearly 'global reports' reviewing trends in each category of fundamental rights. The report is submitted to the annual ILC for tripartite discussion, and the GB may then draw on the conclusions from this discussion to determine priorities and plans for technical co-operation for the following 4-year period.

The main result of the Declaration has been a significant increase the number of ratifications of the 8 core conventions. The ILO aims to reach its goal of universal ratification of these conventions by 2015. By 2004, a total of 100 Member States had ratified all 8 core conventions, and 144 had ratified at least one convention in each of the four groups. Over 90 per cent of ILO Member States have ratified the 4 conventions on forced labour and non-discrimination. Developing countries, particularly in Africa, account for a growing percentage of ratifying States. The first full 4-year cycle of global reporting in respect of freedom of association ended in 2004. In that period a further 15 countries ratified C.87 and 9 ratified C.98. This left 18 countries that had ratified neither of these two conventions, 16 that had ratified C.98, but not C.87 and four that had ratified C.87 but not C.98. These numbers do not reflect one stark fact. This is

[82] *Nicaragua v United States* [1986] ICJ 14 at 98; 76 ILR 349 at 432; See generally Shaw (2003) at 68ff, and Rubin (1998) at 28–29.

[83] The Supplementary Convention on the Abolition of Slavery, the Slave Trade, and Institutions and Practice similar to Slavery, 7 September 1956, UN Treaty Series 3, Art 1, obliges all UN Member States to 'take all practicable and necessary legislative and other measures to bring about . . . the complete abolition of forced labour and other slave-like practices.'

[84] C29 requires states to 'suppress the use of forced or compulsory labour'. This has been interpreted by the ILO as not confined to these practices only within the territory of a Member State. See Mynamar case (Box 2.4 above).

that about half the world's workers still do not enjoy protection under C 87 and C.98, given that some of the largest countries in population size have not ratified the two conventions. These include Brazil, China, India, Mexico and the US.[85] Even in those countries which have ratified these conventions, national laws and practices frequently do not actually implement the international obligations. The ILO's resources for offering technical assistance to promote the core conventions are stretched by increasing demands. The 'quick-fix' of an ILO-assisted Labour Code provides no guarantee that the legal reforms will be sustainable or responsive to national conditions. This can occur only through the training of domestic experts and by the political will to make labour legislation work.

The ILO has recognised, in addition to conventions on fundamental rights at work, four other 'priority' conventions. These relate to effective labour inspection (C.81 and C.129), tripartite consultation (C.144) and employment policy (C.122). The four 'priority' conventions have far fewer ratifications than the 8 fundamental human rights conventions. Only 23 states have ratified all 4 (most EU Member States and Australia), 40 have ratified three (including the UK), 53 have ratified 2 (including China and the Russian Federation), and 59 have ratified less than 2.

The Declaration has been subject to a number of criticisms. The first of these is the absence of any express linkage with trade. Paragraph 5 of the Declaration specifically rules out any use of the Declaration for 'protectionist trade purposes'. This was demanded by a group of 113 non-aligned member states, plus five observers including China. They issued a statement at the ILC Conference rejecting proposals by the Director-General for a voluntary system of global 'social labelling'. Such a label would be awarded to countries that had shown comprehensive respect for core labour rights and had agreed to submit to reliable and legally autonomous international inspections. These inspections would not lead to judicially-imposed sanctions for violations but would simply have verified whether a country 'respects the spirit and principles.'[86] The group of 113 described the Director-General's argumentation as 'inherently flawed and it introduces an untenable link between labour standards and trade which we do not accept.' They claimed that the principle of equal remuneration for equal work (C.100) would 'question the comparative advantage of developing countries', that a binding Declaration would contravene the principle of voluntary adherence by states, that ILO reports on social progress would allow the ILO to determine what is an 'acceptable' level of comparative

---

[85] ILO (2004b) at 23.

[86] Response to the Director-General's Report, 30 May 1997. (I am grateful to Peter Brannen for providing me with a copy). It is understood that several non-aligned states (including South Africa) dissented from the statement whose primary advocates were Columbia and Egypt. Some countries, such as Belgium, have introduced national legislation to create a social label based on the Declaration.

advantage, and that social labelling would legitimise the use of labour standards for protectionism. ILO inspections would be 'beyond the legal and financial capabilities of the ILO.' Essentially, the statement is a plea to rely on free trade to produce social progress, with labour standards being seen as no more than 'the benchmarks in this process.'

Despite these objections to a trade-labour linkage, one of the consequences of the Declaration is that it has provided a ready-made set of core rights for those countries, and international organisations that wish to provide incentives for the observance of fair labour standards. These include the EU, in its Generalised System of Preferences, and recent US trade agreements, as well as the World Bank and some other financial institutions, but not yet the WTO. These linkages are discussed in chapters 4, 5 and 6 below. It is also increasingly common to find reference to the core standards in corporate codes and collective agreements (chapter 3, below). These linkages reflect recognition that the ILO is the primary international organisation for defining labour standards, and achieves one of the main aims of the Declaration, to make it easier for TNCs and national and international bodies to promote these standards. However, critics fear that this 'will narrow their gaze and focus on four core rights' taking 'the pressure off them in relation to non-core rights.'[87] This criticism would be well-founded if the 8 core conventions became the endpoint of the ILO's campaign. However, there are other 'priority' conventions and the ILO has understandably chosen to concentrate initially on those principles which enjoy the widest consensus. A wider consensus will be possible only if there is a fundamental reassessment of the scope and nature of conventions, particularly those relating to the informal economy (below).

A second, well-founded, criticism is the weakness of the follow-up mechanism and the soft 'promotional' emphasis of the Declaration. In part, this stems from the confusion in the Declaration itself between 'principles' and 'rights.'[88] The four core principles are selective, and they suggest that countries can adhere to these vague principles without observing the more numerous specific rights conferred by the 8 conventions. The Declaration is a useful means of promoting ratification; but it is only ratification that can confer rights and obligations in international law. Moreover, there is no express linkage between the follow-up mechanism and the regular supervisory machinery of the ILO (above). That machinery itself is in need of modernisation. A more satisfactory follow-up would have been to create a GB committee, similar to the CFA, to consider complaints of breach of the core standards by any ILO member. The GB or ILC could then consider action under Article 33 against serious defaulters.

---

[87] Alston (2004) at 484.
[88] Alston (2004) at 476–83.

Revision and integration of standards

The second ILO initiative has been the revision of conventions and a more coherent and integrated approach to their adoption. As a result of the recommendations of a Working Party on Policy Regarding the Revision of Standards,[89] the GB has decided that of the 185 conventions and 194 recommendations, only 71 conventions and 73 recommendations are up to date, 24 conventions and 15 recommendations have to be revised, 54 conventions and 67 recommendations are outdated. Five conventions have been withdrawn (they never entered into force) and 17 recommendations have been replaced by later instruments. Nearly 80 per cent of up to date conventions were adopted after 1960. In addition to this revision process, the ILO's Joint Maritime Commission has agreed that the ILO's maritime instruments should be consolidated by means of a new Framework Convention on labour standards applicable to the maritime sector. The ILO is also working towards better integration of standards among themselves and with other means of action available to the Organisation. This has led to in-depth reviews of existing standards and other means for achieving the goals in question. One area being examined in this way is occupational safety and health. The intention is to focus on general principles and to produce a framework instrument which is more promotional than prescriptive in content.

Decent Work Agenda

The third, and most important, refocusing of ILO activities, is the Decent Work Agenda launched by Juan Somavia, the Director-General, in 1999. He proposed that the ILO should set as its primary goal 'to promote opportunities for women and men to obtain decent and productive work, in conditions of freedom, equity, security and human dignity.'[90] This goal is based on the idea that social justice is 'about a set of regulations, institutions and policies that ensures a fair treatment to all members of society, and a relatively equal distribution of opportunities and income.'[91] The four strategic objectives are to: (1) promote and realise standards and fundamental principles and rights at work; (2) create greater opportunities for women and men to secure decent employment and income; (3) enhance the coverage and effectiveness of social protection for all; and (4) strengthen tripartism and social dialogue. These strategic objectives have been subdivided into operational objectives with indicators and targets that make it possible to measure the progress achieved.

[89] ILO, GB283/LILS/WP/PRS/1/1 (March 2002).
[90] ILO (1999) at 3.
[91] ILO (2002), point 3.

The most innovative feature of the ILO's definition of Decent Work, as Amaryta Sen pointed out in his address to the 1999 ILC,[92] is that it encompasses all kinds of productive work. Unlike classical labour law, it does not presuppose the existence of a contract of employment or employment relationship. It is not limited to 'dependent' or 'subordinated' labour on which ILS and domestic labour laws have traditionally been based. Labour law has tended to legitimise the inequalities between different categories of employed workers, between the employed and the self-employed, and between those who work and those who are unemployed or are cut off from work on grounds of age. The new objective of Decent Work proclaims the basic equality of all those who work and who seek work. It focuses policy on the needs of the unemployed as well as the employed and self-employed, the elderly as well as the young, and those in the informal as well as the formal sectors.[93]

Secondly, the Decent Work Agenda has given renewed emphasis to the ILO's action for poverty reduction. Economic growth is the starting point. The Director-General declared in 2004:[94] 'the principal route out of poverty is work, and to this end the economy must generate opportunities for investment, entrepreneurship, job creation and sustainable livelihoods.' This has to be accompanied by rights—'good laws that are enforced and work for, not against, their interests.' 'Without rights and empowerment,the poor will not escape poverty.' New ways have to be found to provide social protection for vulnerable groups, including the strengthening of women's capacity to renegotiate the distribution of unpaid work caring for family needs. Dialogue is 'the way to solve problems peacefully' and those living in poverty 'can gain from the ILO's experiences in negotiation, dialogue and conflict resolution.'

Thirdly, the Decent Work Agenda has enabled the ILO to reassert it position as the primary international agency for defining universal social rules. This role was recognised at the 1995 World Summit in Copenhagen, and in the WTO Ministers' statement in Singapore in 1996. The ILO has tried to persuade the Bretton Woods Institutions (the World Bank and the IMF) to pay more attention to the social repercussions of 'structural adjustments'—the draconian economic reforms and stabilisation programmes which these Institutions force developing countries to adopt.

Following the 1999 financial crisis the Bretton Woods Institutions refocused their policy on combating poverty and began to take a greater interest in social protection, albeit mainly short-term safety nets.Their approach to labour standards has been neither consistent nor uniform. While the IMF has supported fundamental labour rights and has promoted them in countries such as

---

[92] Sen (2000).
[93] Hepple (2001) at 9.
[94] ILO (2004b) at 16.

the Republic of Korea and Indonesia, the World Bank has, until recently, insisted that only those standards which it regards as economically justified should be applied. The Bank accepts the need for standards on child labour and forced labour and gender discrimination,[95] but it has been reluctant to promote freedom of association and the right to collective bargaining. Until 2003, the International Finance Corporation (IFC), the Bank's lending arm, required its borrowers to abide only by the principles of prohibiting child labour and forced labour. However, in 2003, the IFC announced that it intended to include the two remaining principles of freedom of association and collective bargaining and non-discrimination as standard conditions for its loans. Nineteen global financial groups have adopted the 'Equator principles', based on the policies and principles of the World Bank relating to the environmental and social impact of infrastructure projects funded by private banks. The Asian Development Bank (but not yet the African Development Bank) has agreed to co-operate with the ILO in promoting fundamental principles and rights at work. The European Bank for Reconstruction and Development (EBRD) approved core labour standards for guiding its work in 2003, but still refuses to include the principles of freedom of association and the right to collective bargaining.[96] The growing technical and policy co-operation between the ILO and the international financial institutions may, in the long term, break down this resistance and promote social responsibility in investment policies.

Finally, the Decent Work Agenda has given a new coherence to international social policy based on the idea of a 'socio-economic floor.' The World Commission on the Social Dimension of Globalisation,[97] set up by the ILO, endorsed the ILO's actions on fundamental rights at work, basic income and social protection. Disappointingly, the Commission failed to develop the idea of a socio-economic floor in any detail, beyond trite generalisations on fundamental rights at work, the combating of social exclusion and social protection. The Commission said that a socio-economic floor would have to reflect national circumstances and would need international support. Such platitudes do little to explain the ways in which relatively high standards in the formal sector in developing countries are to be reconciled with the abysmal poverty and absence of regulation in the informal sector.[98] The starting point has to be economic growth. The Director-General said in 2004 that the task of the ILO will be to help find mechanisms 'for spreading the benefits to the least advantaged and ensuring that the costs of change do not fall disproportion-

---

[95] In 2000 the Bank adopted a toolkit on core labour standards to guide the work of its operational staff.

[96] ILO (2004b) at 17.

[97] World Commission on the Social Dimension of Globalisation (2004), paras 287–89, 491.

[98] Review by Martin Wolf, *Financial Times*, 3 March 2004, at 19.

ately on any one group.'[99] The enormity of this task is illustrated by the ILO's estimate that about 2.0 per cent of the global Gross National Income would be needed to furnish all the world's poor with a minimum of income security, access to basic educational services and access to basic health care. The ILO has limited resources and a tripartite structure which represents predominantly those with vested interests in the formal economy of developing countries. The idea of social solidarity across national borders faces enormous obstacles. This long-term ideal might best be served by the ILO giving technical assistance to countries to enhance their own comparative advantages while progressing towards a realistic socio-economic floor.

Conclusion

The ILO's founding principles remain enormously relevant in the new global economy, but its methods of action have become out-dated. It is no longer possible for a small number of relatively wealthy developed countries to dictate labour standards for the whole world, reflecting the models adopted in the North. The 1998 Declaration was a worthy attempt by the ILO to re-establish the universal legitimacy of the fundamental principles on which the Organisation is based. Difficulties remain in translating these principles into national law and practice. They have to be interpreted sensitively, so as to take account of the level of socio-economic development in each country. For example, a simple ban on child labour without corresponding steps to provide education and family support, would be counter-productive. The concept of Decent Work makes us think more broadly about the *quality* of life of all those engaged in productive labour.

Beyond the core and priority conventions, the present subjects of international regulation do not serve the real needs of developing countries. The concept of Decent Work provides an opportunity to move away from the model of paid employment in the formal sector, towards international regulation of productive work, whatever its legal form, on the basis of minimum socio-economic rights. There also needs to be a change in the traditional division between conventions and recommendations,[100] replacing these with promotional or framework conventions which set principles and codes of practice directed at specific groups of countries at similar stages of development. The understandable reluctance of countries to adopt standards which their competitors ignore, could be overcome by regional dialogue based on the

---

[99] ILO (2004a) at 38.

[100] Maupain (2000) at 383, suggests that some new terminology is needed 'to describe what the limited evidence suggests, that in many cases there is a selective impact of some of the normative provisions of the instrument, but not necessarily of the instrument as an integrated whole'.

implementation of principles which are supplemented by flexible guidelines.

The implementation of such promotional standards requires different methods from the traditional juristic technique of judging whether laws and practice conform to an abstract standard. That technique will continue to be of great relevance in respect of the core conventions which lay down fundamental human rights at work. A rights-based approach is necessary and appropriate to the implementation of the 'core' standards, and that core should be regarded as progressive not static, taking in a wider range of fundamental human rights. Adversarial procedures should be improved for this purpose, including a complaints-mechanism for a wider range of human rights issues than freedom of association.

Outside this expanding core other framework conventions would set only general principles or common goals, which are to be progressively achieved. There has to be periodic evaluation of the outcomes, based on agreed indicators or criteria (benchmarking). The evaluation is not simply a technical process, but also a political one that requires active social dialogue. The operational strategy for implementing the Decent Work Agenda, to some extent adopts this methodology. This has similarities with new methods of integrating economic and social policy in the EU (chapter 9, below). There is room for cross-fertilisation and exchange of experience between the ILO and EU in developing these new 'soft law' methods within a framework of fundamental rights.

We must now turn to the principal actors in the new global economy: the TNCs that can play a crucial role in either thwarting or promoting international labour standards.

3

Privatising Regulation: Codes, Agreements, and Guidelines

1. The shift from public to private regulation
2. Corporate codes and labels
3. Trade unions, NGOs and collective agreements
4. The OECD Guidelines and the ILO Tripartite Declaration
5. Who wins in the 'race to the top'?

1. The shift from public to private regulation[1]

The most striking feature of current attempts to build on the best practices of TNCs is fragmentation. There are public codes from international sources, notably the OECD Guidelines for Multinational Enterprises (1976, revised 2000), and the ILO Tripartite Declaration of Principles Concerning Multinational Enterprises and Social Policy (1977), codes produced at regional level such as the EU standards for European enterprises operating in developing countries (1999),[2] and codes promulgated by national governments, such as the Canadian Code (1985) for companies with subsidiaries operating in South Africa during the apartheid era. There have also been many private initiatives notably, in the USA, the Sullivan principles to promote racial equality practices in American TNCs operating in South Africa (1977), the MacBride Principles relating to fair employment practices in Northern Ireland (1984),[3] and the Guidance Document for Social Accountability promoted by the US Council on Economic Priorities Accreditation Agency (SA 8000). In the UK, the Ethical Trading Initiative (ETI), an alliance of companies, NGOs and trade unions working to promote good employment practices, has developed a code of labour practice—the 'Base Code'—to which ETI member companies are

---

[1] This chapter is a revised and expanded version of Hepple (1999b).
[2] European Parliament (1999).
[3] McCrudden (1999a).

expected to conform. However, far more significant than these external codes has been the rapid growth in the number of internal self-regulatory corporate codes adopted in the 1990s.

What accounts for the shift from public to private regulation, and from external private initiatives to internal self-regulation? The story may be described as one of retreat from public international labour law, embodied above all in the conventions and recommendations of the ILO, to privatised 'soft' regulation. One may identify three periods in the post-Second World War period of international labour law. The first, from the Declaration of Philadelphia in 1944 until the 1960s, was dominated by the ILO's ambitious programme of conventions and recommendations which emphasised the centrality of collective labour law, especially freedom of association and collective bargaining (C.87 and C.98), and the principle of equality and non-discrimination (C.100 and C.111). These instruments, the outcome of a remarkable tripartite consensus between governments, employers and unions at international level, were addressed to Member States as the principal actors in a public international law regime. Although many of the texts concern action to be taken by private entities, they bind only States who are obliged to ensure that private action is taken by the employers and workers concerned. Tripartism in the ILO's unique supervisory system was the principal method for ensuring the participation of all parties not only at international level but also in the process of securing national compliance with international standards (chapter 2, above).

The second period from the late 1960s until the early 1980s, was one in which the focus shifted from governments to TNCs. Organised labour in the developed world and the governments of newly independent developing nations were increasingly alarmed by the domination of the TNCs—the ITT scandal in Chile and the campaign for sanctions against apartheid in South Africa were defining moments. The ICFTU made its first call for international regulation of TNCs in the late 1960s. The 1974 UN resolution advocating a new international economic order, the Report of the Group of Eminent Persons set up by the UN's Economic and Social Council, and the draft UN Code on TNCs were unsuccessful attempts to impose binding rules on TNCs. The non-binding OECD Guidelines of 1976 were a pre-emptive strike by the industrialised states to avoid more stringent controls. The ILO's disappointing reaction in 1977 was to adopt a Tripartite Declaration of Principles concerning Multinational Enterprises and Social Policy, which bears a close resemblance to the employment and industrial relations chapter of the 1976 OECD Guidelines, and like those Guidelines is voluntary. But while the OECD Guidelines are recommendations jointly addressed by OECD Member States to the TNCs operating in their countries, the ILO Tripartite Declaration is addressed to governments, workers' and employers' organisations, as well as

TNCs. At regional level, various codes—such as the Andean Investment Code, the US and Canadian Chambers of Commerce Precepts for Successful Business Operations, and the EC Code relating to South Africa—were also being developed. At national level, some 22 developing countries passed legislation controlling the activities of TNCs in the period 1967–80. The stream of national legislation and international public codes dried up in the 1980s, as the shift occurred to deregulatory market-oriented policies.

The third period, from the late 1980s, saw a phenomenal upsurge in the adoption and use of private corporate codes. There are several reasons for this. First, the corporate codes are a response to public pressure from consumers, investors, trade unions and NGOs. TNCs wish to avoid negative publicity—or worse still, organised boycotts. The definition of countries in which a TNC will not invest (eg Levi-Strauss and Timberland in relation to China, and one of the parts Heineken does not reach is Myanmar) and the transparency of practices in countries where it does operate enhance the corporate reputation.[4] Secondly, many managers believe that the benefits of good employment (and environmental) practices outweigh the costs. Those costs include monitoring and corrective action. The benefits may be improved employee morale, lower labour turnover, fewer accidents, enhanced product quality, and greater consumer and investor confidence. Thirdly, the codes can be used to strengthen the power of senior central management. This is particularly the case with outsourcing guidelines which enable central management to dictate the labour practices of sub-contractors and suppliers as part of a monitoring process which leads to better product quality. Contractors, too, may welcome a level playing field in the otherwise cut-throat competition for supply contracts. By complying with code standards they may be assured of long-term contractual relationships and protect themselves from 'free-riders'.[5] Corporate social responsibility, says the US Council for International Business (USCIB), is 'good business' helping to maintain 'the competitiveness of companies over time and in highly diverse parts of the world.'[6] In this new model of corporate social responsibility, social and environmental objectives are seen as an integral part of the corporation's core business strategy.[7] Linked to this has been the move towards 'socially responsible investment' (SRI). Groups of shareholders may use their voting rights to influence corporate social behaviour. 'Ethical investment' involves the screening of investment funds based on the social performance of companies.

---

[4] Eg: 'We are the acknowledged corporate leaders in human rights' (Reebok); 'we seek to do not only what is required, but whenever possible, what is expected of a leader' (NIKE code of conduct).

[5] van Liemt (2000) at 178–79.

[6] United States Council for International Business, *Position Paper on Codes of Conduct*, 1998.

[7] Parkinson (1993) at 269.

Since the late 1990s we have entered a fourth period of post-War history in which attempts are being made to reassert an element of public control over private regulation by TNCs. The first, and most important, political development was the adoption in June 1998 of the ILO's Declaration on Fundamental Principles and Rights at Work, and, in 1999, its Decent Work Agenda which now provide a socio-economic floor which TNCs are expected to observe (chapter 2, above). Secondly, in 1999 Kofi Annan launched the UN Global Compact which is designed to provide labour, human rights and environmental standards for TNCs.[8] These include the ILO's four core principles and rights. Thirdly, in 2000, the OECD made substantial changes to its Guidelines. Although these are still not legally binding, the links with public international law have been strengthened, for the first time substantive standards to be followed by TNCs in relation to their employees have been specified, and the international obligations of States have been spelt out.

The next section of this chapter examines the content and enforcement of private corporate codes and labels, section 3 looks at the attempts of unions and NGOs to influence them and to negotiate collective agreements, before turning, in section 4, to the scope and prospects of the OECD Guidelines and ILO Tripartite Declaration. In the final section, there is an evaluation of whether the codes, agreements and guidelines do, in fact, contribute towards a 'race to the top.'

2. Corporate codes and labels

Private corporate codes exist because of the absence of an enforceable internationally agreed labour regime. One must distinguish here between a statement of personnel policy adopted by a company in a local or national context, and the setting of standards applying to international business activity. Codes of the latter kind reflect the weakness of the ILO, the OECD and other public regimes. Research into the rapidly proliferating number of private corporate codes is in its infancy. The most significant reviews are those by the ILO into 215 available codes and 12 social labelling programmes,[9] by the OECD into 182 codes,[10] by the UK Department for International Development into 18 UK Company Codes,[11] and the general survey by the Overseas Development Group at the University of East Anglia (UEA).[12]

[8] For details see the website www.globalcompact.org.
[9] ILO (1998e).
[10] OECD (1999).
[11] Ferguson (1998).
[12] Seyfang (1999).

These studies indicate that most private codes are issued by individual companies, but some emanate from private business organisations, and others involve trade unions, NGOS, consumer campaign groups, charities, churches, and other bodies. What they share in common is that they are *voluntary* written commitments to observe certain standards in the conduct of business. They may cover a number of broad areas of ethical conduct, namely fair business practices, observance of the rule of law, environmental stewardship, corporate citizenship and fair employment and labour rights. Fair business practices and fair employment and labour rights are the most frequently mentioned subjects. But the choice of particular labour issues is highly selective, and seems to depend on the size of the company, the industry sector and the importance of the issue to the company's operations. So of the codes surveyed by the ILO, those in the textile, clothing and footwear sector, where abuses of child and forced labour have been well-publicised, tended to concentrate on these issues, while health and safety got special attention in the chemical and transport sectors All the surveys find that the most frequently cited labour standard is the minimum age of workers, and many make a commitment not to utilise child labour, reflecting the concerns among consumers in Northern countries.[13] In the UK survey, not all supplier codes included a provision on non-discrimination. While some UK codes included a reference to freedom of association, none of the UK company codes made explicit reference to collective bargaining. Even internationally, only 15 per cent of codes in the ILO survey addressed freedom of association, and only some of these referred to collective bargaining. The same survey found examples of codes aimed at the elimination of trade unions, or expressing a preference for individualised non-union representation.

Self-definition is the most common source of standards in company codes, the ILO noting that code provisions 'which only used portions of ILO instruments in many cases changed the meaning or intended protection of the instrument and qualified as self-definitions'.[14] The need to observe national law was frequently referred to, although only a few codes treated national law as a *minimum* standard. International standards (ILO conventions, ILO Tripartite Declaration and OECD Guidelines) were expressly referred to in only 20 per cent of the codes surveyed by the OECD, and in no more than one-third of those reviewed in the ILO. study. None of the codes surveyed in the UK study included a statement of commitment to all core ILO standards, and the wording in those which referred to specific international obligations were not as unambiguous as those in the model codes advocated in SA 8000 and by the ICFTU.

[13] Seyfang (1999) at 14.
[14] ILO (1998e) at para 50.

Most codes are limited in coverage. The UEA survey shows that only 50 per cent of codes apply to subcontractors (but 70 per cent of those instigated by NGOs).[15] A study, sponsored by the Swedish Ministry of Foreign Affairs,[16] of supply chain management by 147 global companies, found that only 20 per cent of them had formulated any policy for suppliers. In the particular sectors in which these companies were involved (retailing, clothes, sporting goods manufacture, and tobacco) UK-based companies (61 of which were in the sample) were much more likely to have active supply chain policies than companies based in other countries. For example none of the 32 Japanese companies in the study had developed any practices for working conditions in supply chains. This is a crucial gap, given the extensive use of outsourcing. The ICFTU developed a model code[17] which would make companies responsible for the violations of their subcontractors, but this is rejected by most TNCs on the ground that it would be unrealistic and costly given the extent of supply chains. The UEA survey also found that only 30 per cent of codes apply to homeworkers (but 42 per cent of those instigated by NGOs). This leaves unprotected the most vulnerable, largely female, section of workers in export industries.

The credibility of a private company code depends first of all on how it is made and interpreted, and secondly on how it is monitored and implemented. Is the code a genuine attempt to change corporate behaviour or is it simply a public relations exercise? One indicator of this is whether the code was unilaterally adopted by the company or was negotiated with trade unions or NGOs. The UEA survey shows that issues such as non-wage benefits, health and safety issues, reproductive rights, the provision of information on standards, and banning physical abuse, are more likely to have been included in codes with their origins in workers' organisations, than any other type of organisation. Those most likely to be included in codes instigated by NGOs are payment of minimum or living wages and independent verification.[18] The role of unions and NGOs is further considered in the next section of this chapter.

The main criticism of corporate codes is that of ineffective implementation. Codes launched in the glare of publicity in the TNC's host country, are not infrequently unknown, unavailable or unimplemented in the producing country, and workers in that country have no means of reporting non-compliance.[19] There is an absence of monitoring (ie checking that the code is followed), a lack of training and incentives encouraging managers to comply (eg performance bonuses), and of sanctions on those who do not comply. So

---

[15] Seyfang (1999) at 18.
[16] OECD (2002). The study is available on www.eiris.org.
[17] ICFTU (1997).
[18] Seyfang (1999) at 13–14.
[19] Van Liemt (2000).

far as monitoring is concerned, the USCIB SA 8000 standard draws a distinction between (1) internal or first-party assessment within the company itself; (2) second-party assessment by a purchaser of company products against a standard selected by the purchaser (eg a brand name retailer assesses its manufacturing supplier); and (3) third-party assessment, in which an external audit body, neither a purchaser nor consultant employed by the company, imposes a uniform standard (eg an industry association, NGO or certification agency), leading to certification of the company as meeting the required standard. The OECD survey found that a significant number of companies did not deal with the issue of monitoring at all, and of those that did so, almost all stated that in-house staff would monitor compliance. The UEA survey found that it is codes instigated by NGOs and firms that are the most likely to provide for independent monitoring (85 per cent and 60 per cent respectively).[20] But requirements for inspection and publication are rare. Although several of the codes in the UK survey referred to the use of their regular monitoring systems, none of them made reference to the use of unions or other civil society organisations as intermediaries in consultations with the workers involved. The ICFTU Working Party argued that without effective trade union and worker participation there could be no effective monitoring. By 'effective monitoring' is meant (1) auditable standards, with fairly precise requirements as to performance, and (2) verification, which may be limited to ensuring that there is an adequate system of internal monitoring, or may itself verify the achievement of the standards. A satisfactory outcome might lead to certification or accreditation indicating that the product was made under conditions required by the code. Such procedures are, however, still largely an aspiration and not a reality.

One form of communicating compliance is social labelling schemes, such as 'no sweat', 'union labour' and 'fair trade', or simply a symbol or logo like 'Rugmark' to indicate the absence of child labour. Licensing arrangements for the production of products such as footballs, sometimes make use of the label by licensees conditional upon code compliance. Some of these labels involve a high degree of trade union or NGO participation as part of public campaigns. Most of the instigators are in developed countries, but increasingly they involve coalitions in developing countries. Distinct from these independent labels that indicate compliance, there are unverified 'brand' labels developed by companies to signal code compliance as part of their marketing strategy.[21]

So far as sanctions are concerned, corporate codes are generally toothless. In the OECD survey, codes made little reference to the consequences of non-compliance. A few mentioned some form of corrective action, including

---

[20] Seyfang (1999) at 19.
[21] Diller (1999) at 103–4.

working with suppliers or business partners to make improvements. Even fewer stated that non-compliance could lead to termination of a contract or business relationship, and it is not clear whether this sanction has ever been invoked. None of the codes in the OECD survey provided for government involvement.

In summary, what is clear from all the reviews of corporate codes is that these private sector initiatives generally impose *lower* standards and are more *selective* in their choice of human and labour rights than the public regulatory frameworks, and that they are inadequately monitored and enforced.

3. Trade unions, NGOs and collective agreements

The ICFTU Working Party on Multinational Companies[22] alleged that some early codes were a form of avoidance of unions, and that very few codes respected trade union rights. Moreover, it was said that some companies sought to engage in a dialogue with NGOs as a substitute for dealing with trade unions. There were several high-profile public disagreements between NGOs and unions.[23] The picture seems to be changing as international unions adopt a more strategic role towards their involvement in the making and implementation of codes. They first became directly involved with codes of conduct in the 1990s as a result of campaigns relating to health and safety and child labour.

Distinct from codes of conduct, are framework collective agreements negotiated by trade unions. The fundamental problem is that international trade union structure cannot match the globalised activities of TNCs to negotiate framework agreements covering all the countries and sectors in which a TNC operates. The main international federation is the ICFTU, and there are 10 sectoral federations. Between 1994 and 2004, five of these sectoral federations negotiated a total of 31 agreements with TNCs. All but two of these TNCs are European-based and one of the critical factors in persuading these TNC to negotiate has been the European Works Councils Directive compelling the establishments of EWCs. The agreements are, in the ICFTU's words only 'the first building blocks in an international system of industrial relations'.[24]

An analysis of the content of the 31 framework agreements by Ewing[25] shows that their main point is to commit the TNCs in question to the core ILO

---

[22] ICFTU (1997).
[23] Diller (1999) at 110.
[24] ICFTU (1997).
[25] Ewing (2004).

international labour standards of eliminating child and forced labour, the principle of equality and non-discrimination, and rights to freedom of association and collective bargaining. In some cases the commitment goes further, for example to protect workers' representatives with an express reference to C.135. In some cases there is also a commitment to fair labour standards on matters such as minimum wages (C.94, C.95, C.111), employment promotion (C.168), and health and safety (C.155).[26] Not all the agreements go as far as the OECD Guidelines. Most of them are silent on whether they cover suppliers and licensees of the TNC or at best do no more than say that these third parties will be 'encouraged' to adhere to the standards in question. The most extensive agreement in this respect to date is that between Triumph International, its European Works Council (EWC) and the ITGLWF. This requires subcontractors, suppliers and licensees to provide Triumph with information, allow their work places and activities to be checked at any time, record details of all employees, make this data available, and inform employees about the Code. The agreement states that if the requested corrective measures are not carried out Triumph 'can stop the actual production, annul existing orders, suspend future orders or terminate the business relationship.' This is, however, worded as an aspiration rather than a legally binding obligation to place a contractual obligation on third parties.

One of the distinctive features of these agreements (like codes agreed with unions) is that unions or other workers' representatives are involved in monitoring. Many set up structures or procedures for this purpose. In some cases use is made of existing procedures, such as the agreement by Air France to use its EWC's employee-side select committee, and the agreement by Merloni to use a joint commission (already set up at national level in Italy). In others a new structure is created usually involving regular world-level joint meetings.[27] The number and scope of these agreements is likely to increase rapidly in those sectors where TNCs are vulnerable to consumer and shareholder pressures. For beleaguered international union federations, they present an opportunity to raise their profile. These unions have been able to take advantage of the EWCs to initiate such agreements. With few exceptions, it seems unlikely that US-based TNCs will be ready to bargain with unions on these issues. The existing public international legal framework, under C.87 and C.98, fails to impose obligations on TNCs to negotiate with international union organisations. In any event, as the analysis in chapter 2 showed, there is little likelihood that either the US or major developing countries would ratify and implement such obligations. In the absence of legal supports, international unions might wish

---

[26] ILO (2002a) at 25.
[27] *European Industrial Relations Review and Report* No 341, June 2002 at 29.

to rely on international solidarity action, but, as will be shown in chapter 7 below, this is neither practically nor legally feasible. In Ewing's words, 'it is difficult to avoid the conclusion that if trade unions are to have a role in transnational labour relations, they too will need the support of transnational government institutions.'[28]

4. The OECD Guidelines and the ILO Tripartite Declaration

The OECD Guidelines for Multinational Enterprises are addressed by the 30 OECD Member governments, and other adhering countries[29], to TNCs and all their entities operating in *or from* their territories.[30] The ILO's Tripartite Declaration of Principles Concerning Multinational Enterprises and Social Policy is addressed jointly to all governments, employers' organisations and workers' organisations and to TNCs in both home and host countries. Unlike the ILO, only governments are Members of the OECD, which adopted the Guidelines in 1976 and revised them in 2000, but Business and unions enjoy consultative status through the Business and Industry Advisory Committee (BIAC) and the Trade Union Advisory Committee (TUAC). These committees consist of the principal employers' and workers' organisations in the Member States. The ILO Tripartite Declaration was adopted by the ILO Governing Body (which includes government, employer and worker representatives) in 1977 and amended in 2000.

Both the Guidelines and the Declaration adopt a functional definition of the types of enterprise to which they are addressed.[31] Thus, in paragraph 6 of the ILO Declaration TNCs engaged in all types of activity are considered as falling under its provisions, irrespective of whether they are of public, mixed or private ownership or as to their type of activity, so long as there is cross-border economic management of entitites established in various countries. Like the ILO Declaration, the OECD Guidelines Employment and Industrial Relations Chapter applies to TNCs engaged in all types of activity regardless of their pattern of ownership or control. Moreover the OECD Guidelines are

---

[28] Ewing (2004).

[29] At present Argentina, Brazil and Chile.

[30] The 1976 version covered only TNCs operating in their territories. Although the Members account for only 16% of the world's population, they produce about two-thirds of its goods and services, and 60% of its exports.

[31] Both instruments use the term 'multinational enterprise' rather than the UN terminology 'transnational enterprise' [TNC]. References to TNCs in this book are equivalent to 'multinational enterprise' in the OECD and ILO terminology.

addressed both to the parent companies and local entities 'according to the actual distribution of responsibilities among them on the understanding that they will co-operate and provide assistance to one another as necessary to facilitate observance of the Guidelines.'[32] TNCs are told to 'encourage, where practicable, business partners, including suppliers and subcontractors, to apply principles of corporate conduct compatible with the Guidelines.'[33] Both instruments provide that, where their recommendations are relevant to domestic enterprises, they should be considered as applying to them as well. Neither the OECD Guidelines nor the ILO Tripartite Declaration are legally enforceable. They are voluntary and promotional, but their follow-up is monitored by institutional machinery of each organisation (below).

The OECD Guidelines are wider than the Tripartite Declaration. They cover general policies, disclosure of information, competition, financing, taxation and environmental issues and science and technology as well as employment and industrial relations (Box 3.1). The Guidelines are part of a package that together seek to provide a balanced framework for international investment issues.[34] The ILO Tripartite Declaration is restricted to employment and training issues, conditions of work and life and industrial relations (Box 3.2).

Box 3.1

OECD GUIDELINES: EMPLOYMENT AND INDUSTRIAL RELATIONS[35]

Enterprises should, within the framework of applicable law, regulations, and prevailing labour relations and employment practices:

1. (a) Respect the right of their employees to be represented by trade unions and other bona fide representatives of employees, and engage in constructive negotiations, either individually or through employers' associations, with such representatives with a view to reaching agreement on employment conditions;
   (b) Contribute to the effective abolition of child labour;
   (c) Contribute to the elimination of all forms of forced or compulsory labour;

---

[32] OECD Guidelines (2000) I Concepts and Principles, para 3.

[33] OECD Guidelines (2000) II General Principles, para 10.

[34] The Guidelines are one of four instruments making up the OECD's Declaration on International Investment and Multinational Enterprises. The others are instruments on National Treatment, committing countries to treat foreign-controlled enterprises no less favourably than they treat domestic enterprises, an instrument that calls on countries to minimise or avoid imposing conflicting requirements on TNCs, and an instrument on International Investment Incentives and Disincentives.

[35] Adopted 27 June 2000.

Box 3.1 (*cont.*)

    (d) Not discriminate against their employees, with respect to employment or occupation on such grounds as race, colour, sex, religion, political opinion, national extraction or social origin, unless selectivity concerning employee characteristics furthers established governmental policies which specifically promote greater equality of employment opportunity or relates to the inherent requirements of the job.

2. (a) Provide facilities to employee representatives as may be necessary to assist in the development of effective collective agreements;
    (b) Provide information to employee representatives which is needed for meaningful negotiations on conditions of employment;
    (c) Promote consultation and co-operation between employers and employees and their representatives on matters of mutual concern.

3. Provide information to employees and their representatives which enables them to obtain a true and fair view of the performance of the entity or, where appropriate, the enterprise as a whole.

4. (a) Observe standards of employment and industrial relations not less favourable than those observed by comparable employers in the host country;
    (b) Take adequate steps to ensure occupational health and safety in their operations.

5. In their operations, to the greatest extent practicable, employ local personnel and provide training with a view to improving skill levels, in co-operation with employee representatives and, where appropriate, relevant governmental authorities.

6. In considering changes in their operations which would have major effects on the livelihood of their employees, in particular in the case of the closure of an entity involving collective lay-offs or dismissals, provide reasonable notice of such changes to representatives of their employees, and, where appropriate, to the relevant governmental authorities so as to mitigate to the maximum extent practicable adverse effects. In the light of the specifiic circumstances of each case, it would be appropriate if management were able to give such notice prior to the final decision being taken. Other means may also be employed to provide meaningful co-operation to mitigate the effects of such decisions.

7. In the context of bona fide negotiations with representatives of employees on conditions of employment, or while employees are exercising a right to organise, not threaten to transfer the whole or part of an operating unit from the country concerned nor transfer employees from the

enterprises' component entitities in other countries in order to influence unfairly those negotiations or to hinder the exercise of a right to organise.

8. Enable authorised representatives of their employees to negotiate on collective bargaining or labour-management relations issues and allow the parties to consult on matters of mutual concern with representatives of management who are authorised to take decisions on these matters.

Box 3.2

THE ILO TRIPARTITE DECLARATION: SUMMARY[36]

1. *General Policies* (paras 8–12). All the parties concerned 'should respect the sovereign rights of states, obey the national laws and regulations, give due consideration to local practices and respect relevant international standards.' This includes the ILO Declaration on Fundamental Principles and Rights at Work. TNCs should 'take fully into account established general policy objectives of the countries in which they operate.'

2. *Employment* (paras 13–32). Governments are asked to pursue an active policy for promoting full, productive, and freely chosen employment, and policies to promote equality of opportunity. TNCs should endeavour to provide stable employment. In considering changes in operations, the TNCs should provide reasonable notice of such changes to the appropriate government authorities and workers' representatives. Governments should provide some form of income protection for those whose employment is terminated. Governments and TNCs should provide relevant training.

3. *Conditions of work and life* (paras 33–37). Wages, benefits and conditions of work offered by TNCs should 'be not less favourable to the workers than those offered by comparable employers in the country concerned.' Where there are no comparable employers they should provide 'the best possible' wages, benefits and conditions of work, within the framework of government policies. The minimum age for admission to employment should be respected by TNCs, and adequate safety and health standards must be provided.

4. *Industrial relations* (paras 42–59). The standards should be not less favourable than those observed by comparable employers in the country concerned. Freedom of association and the right to organise (as

---

[36] Adopted by the GB of the ILO at its 204th session (1977), as amended at its 279th session (2000).

Box 3.2 (*cont.*)

specified in ILO conventions) should be granted. Workers employed by TNCs should have the right, in accordance with national law and practice, to have representative organisations recognised for the purposes of collective bargaining. TNCs should enable workers' representatives to bargain with representatives of management authorised to take decisions on the matters under negotiation. They should not threaten to relocate or to bring in workers from other affiliates as a means of influencing negotiations. Information required for meaningful negotiations should be provided. There should be provision for regular consultations. Workers should be allowed to submit grievances without suffering adverse consequences; and voluntary conciliation and arbitration machinery should be established with workers' representatives.

The Guidelines have two major strands, sometimes inimical to each other: to protect states from interference by TNCs in their domestic policies, and to protect TNCs from less favourable treatment by national governments than domestic enterprises.[37] The first of these is reflected in provisions that encourage TNCs to comply with national law, policies and practice. A feature of the original Guidelines was that TNCs were judged almost entirely by their adherence to national standards, however much these offended international norms.[38] The ILO Tripartite Declaration, on the other hand, is firmly based in the framework of ILO conventions and recommendations, and was amended to make specific reference to the ILO Declaration of Fundamental Principles and Rights at Work. Under the revised OECD Guidelines, obeying domestic law is still the first obligation of TNCs, and the Guidelines do not override local law: 'they represent supplementary principles and standards of behaviour of a non-legal character.'[39] However, the revised Employment and Industrial Relations chapter now opens with a *chapeau* which urges TNCs to observe the principles 'within the framework of *applicable* law, regulations, and labour relations and employment practices.' This is meant to acknowledge the fact that TNCs, while operating within the jurisdiction of particular countries, may be subject to national, sub-national, as well as supra-national levels of regulations.[40] The terms 'prevailing labour relations and employment practices' are

---

[37] Murray (2001b) at 256–58.
[38] Murray (2001b) at 258–61.
[39] OECD, *Commentary on General Policies*, 27 June 2000.
[40] OECD, *Commentary on Employment and Industrioal Relations*, 27 June 2000.

sufficiently broad to permit a variety of interpretations, such as different options under national practice for collective bargaining arrangements. The revised Guidelines place emphasis on compliance with the ILO's 'core' principles and rights at work, which are specifically mentioned (para. 1), and reference is also made to other human rights instruments including the UN Declaration of Human Rights (Preface, para. 8).

The OECD has recognised that the ILO is the competent body to set and deal with international labour standards, and to promote fundamental rights at work, and has said that the Guidelines and the ILO Tripartite Declaration 'are intended to be parallel and not conflict with each other. The ILO Tripartite Declaration can therefore be of use in understanding the Guidelines to the extent that it us if a greater degree of elaboration.'[41] As well as the core ILO rights, some of the other provisions, such as those on consultation, are also taken from ILO instruments. There is thus a considerable overlap between the Guidelines and the Declaration, with the latter acknowledged as a significant aid to the interpretation of the Guidelines. Both instruments contain a good deal of useful guidance elaborating general ILO principles, such as freedom of association and the right to collective bargaining. For example, they state that TNCs should not use a threat to transfer operations to influence negotiations or to hinder the exercise of the right to organise, and should provide the information needed for 'meaningful negotiations'.

Although these instruments are rich in principle, they are weak in enforcement. Neither can be invoked before national courts or tribunals, and they both fall outside the ILO's normal supervisory regime. The ILO Tripartite Declaration has been ineffective because of the absence of sanctions to secure compliance with its standards, even by countries which adopt them. Although about two-thirds of countries submit triennial reports on their observance of the Declaration, less than half of these consult the social partners in preparing their replies. The disputes procedure is aimed purely at interpretation, has no means of enforcement and is rarely used. Requests for interpretation are examined by the GB's Subcommittee on Multinational Enterprises, which refers a draft reply to the GB for decision. The procedure can be used only where this would not duplicate or conflict with existing national or ILO procedures. Between 1977–2002, only five cases were the subject of decisions by the GB. One of these was held to be non-receivable, and the other four resulted in interpretations. Two were submitted by governments, and three by international workers' organisations on behalf of national affiliates.[42]

---

[41] OECD, *Commentary on Employment and Industrial Relations,* 27 June 2000.
[42] ILO (2002a) at 29; for details of the cases see Tergeist (2000) at paras 86–98.

The OECD Guidelines provide for National Contact Points (NCPs) which are responsible for encouraging observation of the Guidelines, handling enquiries about them, assisting in solving problems, gathering information on national experiences, and reporting annually to the OECD Committee on Multinational Enterprises (CIME). There are four types of NCP structure currently in use: a single government office, a multi-department government office, a tripartite body and quadripartite body including NGOs. The Guidelines provide for 'specific instances', a procedure that allows interested parties to draw the attention of an NCP to the alleged non-observance of the Guidelines by a TNC. The CIME can issue 'clarifications' on the application of the Guidelines in specific circumstances. It consults with BIAC and TUAC (above) on matters relating to the Guidelines and their effectiveness. About 30 'cases' (the employers object to this term because the findings are not seen as precedents) have been brought to CIME's attention. The procedures have been criticised on the grounds that NCPs have almost ceased to exist in some countries, and that CIME 'clarifications' show an extremely cautious, even opaque attitude to interpreting the Declaration so as rarely to favour the trade union position, an unswerving adherence to the national treatment principle, and give priority to national systems of industrial relations and labour law.[43] Despite attempts by the OECD to revitalise the NCPs,[44] there is little reason to expect that the Guidelines will have a significant impact until they are integrated into a new regulatory framework of the kind proposed in the next section.

The OECD Guidelines are of considerable relevance to foreign direct investment (FDI), and could become increasingly important should a multilateral investment framework be adopted.[45] In the course of negotiations in the late 1990s, for the OECD's proposed Multilateral Agreement on Investment (MAI), a majority of governments accepted the following approach. First there would be an affirmation in the preamble of their support for internationally recognised core labour standards, and that the ILO is the competent body to deal with these standards. Secondly, the OECD Guidelines would be annexed to the MAI text, without changing their non-binding character. Thirdly, there would be a binding obligation on Member States not to waive or derogate from their domestic health, safety, environmental or labour measures in relation to an individual investment or investor. This would not prevent governments from adjusting these measures for public policy reasons other than attracting a particular foreign investment.

---

[43] Murray (1998).

[44] Murray (2001b) at 268.

[45] At the WTO's Fourth Ministerial Meeting at Doha, 20 November 2001, it was agreed that negotiations for a multilateral framework for investment would be undertaken following the 5th Ministerial meeting in 2004.

No agreement could be reached on the MAI and it is, for the time being, in limbo. Few tears will be shed about this outcome. First, the OECD was an unsuitable forum for negotiating such an agreement. Although there are 30 Members of the OECD, these do not include the poor and developing countries that are seeking to attract FDI. These countries had to stand by and watch the Club of the rich countries determine the rules with which the poor and developing countries would have to comply to catch the crumbs of FDI that fell outside the OECD area. Secondly, and even more important, the MAI initiative was based in the neo-liberal dogmas of the 1980s. These are that economic development can best be secured by removing barriers to the free flow of market forces, coupled with the strong protection of property rights and the deregulation of labour standards. The draft negotiating text of the MAI sought, above all else, to protect investments and to liberalise investment regulation. There were many critics of the draft text, in particular trade unions, environmental groups and international social campaigners.[46] Their argument, broadly speaking, was that the MAI failed to provide a fair balance between liberalisation and adequate international regulatory standards.[47]

In the absence of multilateral agreement on how to achieve this balance, individual countries negotiating investment agreements could seek to negotiate 'social clauses'. The options range from general hortatory provisions encouraging TNCs to observe the OECD Guidelines and ILO Tripartite Declaration, to national legislation imposing legal duties to observe specified employment standards.[48] This issue is closely related to that of social clauses in trade agreements, which will be discussed in chapters 4, 5 and 6.

5. Who wins in the 'race to the top'?

This brief assessment of the public regulatory framework and of private initiatives indicates that the so-called 'race to the top' at present has more to do with legitimating 'sustainable capitalism' than with promoting sustainable social development in the world's poorest and most disadvantaged countries, with the active participation of the people of those countries. Arthurs argues that the most obvious explanation for the recent popularity of voluntary codes, is the interest of TNCs in avoiding disruption of their global activities. The codes help them to 'pacify workers, neutralise unions and reassure NGOs, governments and consumers.'[49]

[46] Compa (1998).
[47] Picciotto (1999) at 82–105.
[48] UNCTAD (2000) gives guidance on these options.
[49] Arthurs (2002) at 479.

The corporate codes, rather than reflecting international legal norms, tend to export American conceptions of corporate social responsibility.[50] From the universal framework of mid-20th century public international labour law, centred on the core rights of freedom of association, effective collective bargaining and equality, we have retreated to the 'soft' Guidelines addressed by governments to TNCs, and then witnessed the galloping privatisation, and lowering of public labour standards. This is a different kind of 'race to the bottom', not a genuine 'race to the top'. The ILO has sought to recover some of the lost ground by moving to its own soft law Declaration of Fundamental Principles and Rights at Work, and Decent Work Agenda.[51]

There are two major weaknesses in current international regulation of the employment relationship. The first is the absence of positive obligations on states to require TNCs to observe both core and core-plus standards. A strong example of such obligations at regional level is to be found in the EU, where treaty provisions, regulations and directives are binding on Member States. The European Works Councils Directive[52] provides legally enforceable duties aimed at improving information and consultation in TNCs. It requires 'Community-scale' undertakings and groups of undertakings to establish a European Works Council (EWC) or an alternative procedure for informing and consulting employees, which satisfies certain minimum requirements.[53] This has not been replicated in other regional trading and investment systems, and certainly does not exist at international level. The OECD Guidelines and ILO Tripartite Declaration are remarkably weak when compared with OECD financial instruments such as the Code of Liberalisation of Capital Movements, which imposes 'strict substantive commitments'.[54]

The second main weakness is the reliance that the international system places on national labour laws, at a time when there is widespread deregulation. This proved to be a fatal weakness of the Sullivan Principles, which if followed would in effect have required American TNCs operating in South Africa to breach apartheid laws. Since those TNCs were not willing or able to do so, the Principles lost credibility and a policy of divestment rather than engagement was pursued after the mid-1980s.[55]

The TNCs benefit from the National Treatment principle, embodied in the OECD Guidelines, and in the ILO Tripartite Declaration, that there must be no less favourable treatment of TNCs than that accorded in like situations to domestic enterprises. Before 2000, there was only one significant instance in

---

[50] McCrudden(1999a) at 175.
[51] Alston (2004).
[52] Council Directive 94/54, [1994] OJ L254/64.
[53] See Carley and Hall (2000) for a discussion of the implementation of the Directive.
[54] Murray (1998).
[55] McCrudden (1999a) at 178.

which the OECD Guidelines and ILO Tripartite Declaration placed an additional obligation on TNCs which are not applicable to purely domestic ones. This is the obligation to give reasonable notice of changes in their operations that would have major effects on the livelihood of their employees, even when such notice would not be obligatory under national law. The 2000 revision of the OECD Guidelines has placed specific obligations to observe international 'core' standards on TNCs, but these are not as extensive as the ILO conventions which the Tripartite Declaration mentions.

A major problem is that national labour laws are often not effectively enforced, especially in developing countries. This leaves TNCs which observe those laws at a competitive disadvantage in comparison with other foreign or domestic companies which flout the legal requirements. One approach which has emerged to counteract this is cross-border monitoring of domestic labour laws and employment practices, as in the North American Agreement on Labor Co-operation (NAALC), and other US trade agreements, discussed in chapter 5, below.

The greatest task of contemporary labour law on a transnational scale is to provide a framework within which the potential of TNCs to raise the labour standards of economically and socially disadvantaged groups of workers and producers can be encouraged and developed (chapter 1, above). The reality is that there is a transnational regulatory void,[56] evidenced by the fragmentation of corporate codes, the absence of legal supports for the participation of unions and NGOs, and the soft law of investment codes and the ILO's Declaration of Principles and Rights at Work. The 'race to the top' is won hands-down by the TNCs. What is lacking is a public international regulatory mechanism which can ensure that TNCs observe international norms, their best practices are disseminated, and, at the same time, countries are enabled to build on their comparative institutional advantages without interference by TNCs. This requires the re-invention of transnational labour regulation along lines proposed in chapter 10, below.

---

[56] Cf Murray (2001c) at 322–26.

4

Unilateral Social Clauses

1. Introduction

This and the next two chapters examine a controversial market-based approach that seeks to relocate globalised labour law into the field of international economic law. The aim of this approach is to secure compliance with specified labour standards by imposing trade and financial sanctions against countries that do not observe them, or by granting them trade or other preferences for doing so.[1] These are referred to generically as social clauses, although, as we shall see, they come in many forms.

There have been attempts to link trade and labour standards since the late 19th century—in Charnovitz's words, a 'long story of false starts, hollow promises and forgotten laws'.[2] Three broad objectives have been pursued. The first is to encourage labour standards in the exporting country that are comparable with those in the importing country, that is harmonisation or a

---

[1] The *Dictionnaire de Droit International Public* (2001) at 41–68, defines the social clause as: 'Provision included in regional trade agreements or the agreement establishing the WTO providing for the use of restrictive measures such as trade restrictions or the withdrawal of trade preferences, where fundamental rights at work are not respected' (ILO translation). For the purposes of this book, the social clause also embraces the unilateral application of trade measures, and clauses in bilateral and regional agreements.

[2] Charnovitz (1987) at 565, 580.

level playing-field, to prevent 'unfair' competition. The means used are characteristically the imposition of anti-dumping or countervailing duties.[3] The best-known example is the US Tariff Acts of 1922 and 1930 under which the President was empowered to adjust tariffs to equalise the differences in the cost of production between a domestic article and a similar foreign article. This applied to all factors of production, but was aimed particularly at products of cheap labour in foreign countries. Similar measures were adopted before the Second World War by several countries including Argentina, Austria, Czechoslovakia, Cuba, Spain and the United Kingdom. These provisions were popular in the 1930s, but have generally fallen into disuse as 'cost equalisation' arguments have been discredited (chapter 1, above).

A second objective has been to ensure compliance with common international labour standards, to which exporting nations must adhere. The means have included the 'stick' of quantitative restrictions on imports (negative conditionality), as well as the 'carrot' of preferential trade benefits (positive conditionality). The international standards to which such measures apply have developed over time starting with the trade in slaves, followed by bans on the importation of the products of prison labour, forced labour and child labour. Other standards sometimes enforced in this way include occupational safety and health (starting with the famous Berne Treaty of 1906 between 14 nations to prohibit the importation of matches containing white phosphorous), minimum wages and maximum hours of work. These subjects are today included in the concept of 'internationally recognised worker rights' utilised in US trade legislation (chapter 5, Table 5.A, below). A more widely utilised definition is that of 'core labour standards' corresponding to the four heads of the ILO 1998 Declaration of Fundamental Principles and Rights at Work (Table 4.A, below). These are regarded as essential human rights that should be protected through trade sanctions.

A third objective is to ensure the enforcement of domestic labour laws on defined subjects by the exporting country. Unlike the second objective, this recognises the sovereignty of each country to set its own labour laws, but holds them accountable to ensure compliance with certain basic principles. The most important example is the North American Agreement on Labor Co-operation (NAALC) which contains 11 labour principles including but going beyond the ILO's 'core' (chapter 5, Table 5.A, below). Under NAALC, fines can be levied on countries that persistently fail to enforce domestic laws relating to child labour, minimum wages and occupational health and safety. There are variations on this in other US trade agreements.

---

[3] A countervailing duty is one placed on certain imports to offset production or commercial advantages granted by the government of the exporting country.

Some of these objectives may be pursued *unilaterally,* that is by the action of a state or trading block without the agreement of the targeted state. The US is the major practitioner of unilateralism, particularly through its Generalised System of Preferences (GSP). This and other legislatively-mandated measures by the US to obtain the observance by other countries of internationally recognised worker rights will be assessed in this chapter. They will compared with the social clause in the EU's GSP. In chapter 5, the use of social clauses in *bilateral* and *regional* trading agreements will be discussed. Chapter 6 will consider the compliance of unilateral, bilateral and regional social clauses with the WTO trade liberalisation principles, and the limits of the WTO institutions as a means of protecting labour rights.

2. 'Aggressive unilateralism': US trade policy

Since the 1980s the promotion of labour rights in developing countries has become an increasingly important part of US trade policy. This is the result of pressure from labour and human rights activists in the US and marks a shift from the older purely protectionist campaigns of US unions to 'stop imports' or 'buy American.' The spate of legislation designed to protect the labour rights of workers in foreign countries has been characterised by some critics as 'aggressive unilateralism',[4] 'global bullying', and disguised protectionism.

The first major legislative achievement of the pressure groups was a labour rights amendment to the US Generalised System of Preferences (GSP) adopted by Congress and signed by President Reagan in 1984.[5] The GSP, as originally enacted by Title V of the Trade Act 1974, aims to provide developing countries 'fair and reasonable access' into the US for specified products. Under it, over 3000 products from more than 145 developing countries have duty-free access to US markets. The GSP has been renewed on several occasions most recently until 31 December 2006.[6] The labour rights provision prohibits access to US markets to any country 'that is not taking steps to afford internationally recognised worker rights to its workers (including those in export processing zones).'

The labour rights clause in the GSP was followed by a series of other measures which make trade and investment conditional upon observance of labour rights. In 1985, Congress amended the legislation governing the Overseas Private Investment Corporation (OPIC) requiring OPIC to withhold investment insurance from projects in countries that fail to adopt and

---

[4] Alston (1993), and Alston (2004) at 495–97.
[5] GSP Renewal Act 1984, Pub L No 98–577, 98 Stat 3019.
[6] Trade Promotion Act 2002.

implement 'laws that extend internationally recognised worker rights'.[7] In 1988, the Omnibus Trade and Competitiveness Act (OTCA)[8] amended section 301 of the Trade Act 1974 so as to make systematic violations of internationally recognised workers' rights (as defined in the GSP) an unfair trade practice against which the US could impose retaliatory sanctions. In 1990, the Caribbean Basin Economic Recovery Act (CBERA),[9] first enacted in 1984 as part of the Caribbean Basin Initiative (CBI) to grant duty-free entry for specified products from countries with designated beneficiary status (currently 27), was amended so to mandate the President not to designate any country as a beneficiary that does not conform to 'internationally recognised standards for worker rights' (as defined in the GSP).[10] A similar provision was enacted in the Andean Trade Preference Act 1991, which grants duty-free access to a range of products from Bolivia, Columbia, Ecuador and Peru. In 2000, the US–Caribbean Trade Partnership Act (CBTPA)[11] provided additional benefits for countries which satisfy certain eligibility criteria (currently 24).[12] The criteria include the extent to which the country provides 'internationally recognised worker rights'. In 2000, the African Growth and Recovery Act (revised in 2002) offered expanded GSP benefits to African countries (currently 37) provided they have established or are making progress towards establishing market-based economies and other specified objectives. These include 'internationally recognised worker rights' and commitments to eliminate the worst forms of child labour as defined in ILO C.182.[13] However, the President can override these requirements if he determines that it would be in the national economic interest of the US to do so. There are also several other Acts of Congress with worker rights provisions.[14]

[7] The Overseas Private Investment Corporation Amendment Act, Pub L No 99–204 (1985), codified at 22 USC §2191 (1988).

[8] Pub L No 100–418, 102 Stat 1107, codified at 19 USC §2411 (1988).

[9] 19 USC §§2701–4 (1984).

[10] Caribbean Basin Economic Recovery Extension Act 1990 (CBERA Extension).

[11] The CBERA, CBERA Extension, and CBTPA are collectively referred to as the Caribbean Basin Initiative (CBI). The CBTPA was labelled 'NAFTA-parity' because it aimed to give Central American and Caribbean countries the same duty treatment provided to Mexico under NAFTA.

[12] CBTPA continues in force until 30 September 2008 or the date, if sooner, on which a free trade agreement enters into force between the US and the CBTPA beneficiary concerned.

[13] S 502.

[14] These include Multilateral Investment Guarantee Agency Act (MIGA), Trade Act 1974, 19 USC §§2101–706 (975) (US representatives to MIGA must exert influence to ensure worker rights considered when making loans or insurance); International Financial Institutions Act, 22 USC §2600 (1994) (US directors in World Bank, IMF etc to use 'voice and vote' to screen loan proposals for effect on worker rights); Foreign Aid Appropriation law, Foreign Operations, Export Financing and Related Programs Act, Pub L No 102–391, 106 Stat 1633,1696 (1992) (bars US assistance to export processing zones or areas where labour etc laws do not apply); Foreign Aid Appropriations Law, Foreign Operations, Export Financing and Related Programs Appropriation Act, Pub L No103–87, S547,107 Stat 931, 959 (1993) (to prevent US aid to promote relocation of firms from US to developing countries using promise of union-free environment).

3. Effects on labour rights

The GSP and other measures have had both positive and negative effects.[15] On the positive side, labour rights violations have led to 13 countries[16] being suspended from GSP beneficiary status, and 17[17] being placed on temporary extension with continuing review. As a result several of the suspended countries have undertaken labour law reforms to regain GSP beneficiary status. A review by of the CBI apparel exporting countries in 1998 by the US General Accounting Office concluded that governments had reformed their labour laws to meet international standards and had been making efforts to improve and upgrade their labour departments. The reforms had included strengthening and streamlining procedures to form unions and negotiate collective agreements, establishing labour courts, enhancing labour inspection and enforcement capabilities.

However, despite the progress made, 'allegations of worker rights abuses persists, and enforcement of labour laws generally remains a problem in CBI countries.'[18] A 20-year review of labour rights in the GSP by Compa and Vogt provides detailed case studies of 6 countries (Chile, Guatemala, Malaysia, Indonesia, Pakistan and Belarus).[19] They conclude that 'the merits of a petition have little bearing on the outcome of a case. Geopolitics and foreign policy are the chief considerations for applying the GSP labour rights clause, not the merits of a country's compliance or non-compliance with the law.'[20] But in most cases the dynamics of petition and review led to alliances between unions and human rights groups in the US and those in the developing countries, and resulted in modest but significant changes in labour conditions. Compa and Vogt argue that the criticisms of the labour rights system in US trade law are arguments for improving the system and not renouncing it.

But critics have argued that unilateralism is a fundamentally flawed approach for three principal reasons: first, it undermines the rule of international law by the use or threat of sanctions against a country for failing to

---

[15] For a full review, see Compa and Vogt (2001).

[16] Romania (1987), Nicaragua (1987), Paraguay (1987), Chile (1987), Burma (1989), Central African Republic (1989), Liberia (1990), Sudan (1991), Syria (1992), Mauritania (1993), Maldives (1995), Pakistan (1996), and Belarus (2000).

[17] Benin (1990), Dominican Republic (1990), Haiti (1990), Nepal (1990), Syria (1990), Bangladesh (1991), El Salvador (1992), Mauritania (1992), Panama (1992), Thailand (1992, Bahrain (1993), Fiji (1993), Guatemala (1993), Indonesia (1993), Malawi (1993), Oman (1993), Pakistan (1994), Swaziland (1997).

[18] United States General Accounting Office, Caribbean Basin. Worker Rights, Progress Made, but Enforcement Issues Remain, GAO/NSIAD 98–205, July 1998 at 29.

[19] Compa and Vogt (2001) 199.

[20] Compa and Vogt (2001) 236.

adopt international standards which it has not accepted and do not form part
of customary international law; secondly, the processes are ineffective; thirdly
the motivation for the unilateral measures is primarily protectionist and
political; and finally, there exist suitable alternatives.[21]

4. Undermining the rule of international law?

The US GSP legislation[22] does not use the ILO concept of 'core labour standards. Instead, it applies to 'internationally recognised worker rights' (Table
4.A, below). This concept is used either expressly or by reference in virtually all
the US legislative measures. The first four of these rights correspond almost
exactly to those in the 1998 ILO Declaration, but the right against all forms of
discrimination, which features in the ILO Declaration, is excluded. This
important omission was the result of a political compromise on the labour
rights amendment in 1984.[23] The Reagan Administration successfully resisted
the proposal to include discrimination because of their fear of antagonising
oil-producing states which practise discrimination against women and non-
Muslims, and in order to protect Israel which was accused of discrimination
against Palestinian workers. The Administration also insisted on softening
language in the original draft which required the mandatory suspension of
those who violated rights, so as to make it sufficient for a country to be 'taking
steps' to achieve these rights. This was designed to give the Administration
maximum discretion in furthering the foreign policy interests of the US. The
definition does include 'acceptable conditions of work with respect to minimum wages, hours of work, and occupational safety and health', which are not
'core' ILO standards. But the language leaves a wide discretion for the
Administration to decide what is 'acceptable'.

   The critics point out that the US is demanding standards of others that it has
not accepted as part of its own international obligations. The US has ratified
only 14 ILO conventions (2 no longer in force). These includes those on forced
labour (C.105) and the worst forms of child labour (C.182), but not any of the
other 'core' ILO conventions, nor those relating to wages, hours of work or
occupational safety and health (with the exception of safety and health in
mines (C.176)). Moreover, many of the standards demanded have not yet been
accepted by the countries on which US practice imposes them (chapter 2,
above) Nor can the US claim to be enforcing customary international law, As

---

[21] Alston (1993).
[22] Trade Act 1974, 19 USCA, §2467.
[23] Compa and Vogt (2001) 203–4.

pointed out in chapter 2, it is unlikely that any of the ILO conventions apart from those relating to slave and forced labour can be said to be part of customary international law.

Moreover, the interpretations of 'internationally recognised worker rights' are not consistent with the interpretations made by the ILO supervisory bodies. For example, the murder of a trade union leader has been classified as a violation of 'human rights' not of a 'worker right' and so excluded from the GSP program.[24] A strict standard of proof appears to be required to show that the treatment of individuals was related to their union activities. When a petition was filed against Malaysia for suppressing unions in the electronic sector, Malaysia announced an end to the ban but later clarified this by indicating that only in-house unions would be allowed. Although this was a clear violation of ILO standards, the US Trade Representative accepted that Malaysia was 'taking steps' to improve its labour regime and simply issued an admonition while rejecting further petitions on the ground that they failed to provide new information.[25] The result of these idiosyncratic interpretations is that attempts to create a consistent set of international labour standards is frustrated.

Table 4.A	
ILO AND US STANDARDS	
ILO core labour standards	US 'internationally recognised worker rights'
1. Freedom of association and right to collective bargaining	1. Right of association and right to organise and bargain collectively
2. Elimination of all forms of forced or compulsory labour	2. Prohibition of any form of forced or compulsory labour
3. Effective abolition of child labour	3. Minimum age for employment of children and prohibition on worst forms of child labour
4. Elimination of discrimination in employment and occupation	4. *No corresponding provision*
5. *No corresponding provision*	5. Acceptable conditions of work with respect to minimum wages, hours of work, occupational safety and health

[24] US General Accounting Office, International Trade: Assessment of the Generalized System of Preferences, GAO/GGD-95–9, November 1994, 108–10.
[25] Above, 110.

5. Ineffective procedures?

Since adoption of the GSP labour rights amendment in 1984, the USTR has conducted approximately 100 reviews on whether countries were taking steps to afford worker rights. Allowing for repeated reviews of the same country, approximately 42 different countries have come under labour rights scrutiny in the GSP process. The first 15 reviews were part of a 'general review' mandated by the 1984 law.[26] Petitions filed by labour and human rights groups have prompted most of the subsequent country reviews.

The petition process allows organisations to request the US government to review a country's treatment of workers to determine whether or not GSP benefits should be suspended for lack of progress in respecting worker rights. Petitions are filed with the office of the US Trade Representative (USTR) which decides whether to dismiss them out of hand or accept them for review. Review essentially puts a country on probation. After a review period, USTR can end the country's review, suspend duty-free treatment on one or more products (eg sugar), or suspend the country from the program in its entirety. The most active petitioners have been the AFL-CIO, individual unions such as the United Electrical, Radio, and Machine Workers of America (UE), International Union of Electrical Workers (IUE), the United Food and Commercial Workers (UFCW), and several NGOs, such as the International Labor Rights Fund (ILRF), the US Labor Education in the Americas Project (US LEAP), and various divisions of Human Rights Watch—Asia Watch, Africa Watch, and Americas Watch.

The USTR has adopted regulations and procedural guidelines for filing petitions to challenge a country's GSP status due to worker rights violations[27]. The regulations establish a threshold to determine whether to accept or reject a petition for review[28] If accepted, the USTR proceeds to an investigation. Procedures include public hearings and other forums to present evidence and argue for the removal or suspension of trade benefits because of violations of workers' rights.[29]

The criterion used by the USTR is whether a country is 'taking steps', rather than being in full compliance with the standards. This allows a great discretion in the application of this criterion. In the case of Guatemala, the mere fact of presentation of legislation to bring the country into conformity with ILO

---

[26] Initiation of General Review under the US Generalized System of Preferences (GSP), 50 Fed Reg 6,294 (1985).

[27] Regulations of the US Trade Representative Pertaining to Eligibility of Articles and Countries for the Generalized System of Preference Program, 15 CFR §2007 *et seq* 2002.

[28] 15 CFR §2007.2 (a–b).

[29] 15 CFR §2007.2 (d).

conventions, even before any parliamentary approval, was taken by the USTR as proof that Guatemala was 'taking steps' to afford workers rights.[30] The GSP subcommittee has refused to review, without explanation, the majority of petitions filed by worker rights advocates.[31] A subsequent review of a petition previously denied, is not permitted unless the petitioners present 'substantial new information'.[32] The petition filed against Malaysia (above) is a good example of the way in which this has been used to deny review despite a clear violation of ILO standards after that country had been found to be 'taking steps'.

In 1990, a coalition of worker rights advocates brought a lawsuit charging the President, the USTR, and other government officials with failure to enforce the statutory worker rights provisions of GSP The District Court of Columbia dismissed the complaint, holding that section 701(a)(2) of the Administrative Procedure Act[33] provided the agency with discretionary authority over worker rights provisions because they (1) were so vague that they gave the court 'no law to apply' and (2) implicated the President's inherent foreign affairs powers. The District of Columbia Circuit affirmed this in a sharply divided opinion; one member of the panel relied on a jurisdictional argument rejected by the lower court although conceded by the government on appeal, another based his ruling on standing (an argument never raised on appeal by the government), and the third member dissented.[34]

The GSP review process differs in important respects from that under section 301 of the US Trade Act. Section 301 allows affected enterprises, domestic interest groups or individuals to petition the USTR to investigate a foreign government policy or practice and take action. The USTR may also initiate an investigation on its own initiative. In each investigation the USTR must consult with the foreign government whose practices are under investigation. If the consultations do not result in a settlement and the investigation involves a trade agreement, section 301 requires the USTR to use whatever dispute settlement procedures are available under the agreement.

The USTR, under the direction of the President, can withdraw previous GATT tariff concessions or impose new tariffs if the foreign country is judged to be in violation of the law, and if consultations between the USTR and the foreign government do not lead to a negotiated settlement. Most section 301 cases have resulted in a negotiated settlement, sometimes on the day the deadline for retaliatory action is reached. At the conclusion of the investigation if the matter is not resolved, section 304 of the Trade Act requires the USTR to

---

[30] USTR, Fact Sheet: Caribbean Trade Partnership Act, 3 October 2000.

[31] See GSP Assessment at 108 (demonstrating that of 80 worker rights petitions filed with USTR from 1985 to 1993, only 46 were accepted for review).

[32] 15 CFR ss 2007.0(b)(5), 2007.1(a)(4) (1993).

[33] 5 USC 701 (a)(2) (1988).

[34] *International Labor Rights Educ And Research Fund v Bush* 752 F Supp 295 (DDC, 1990), aff'd by a divided opinion, 954 F 2d 745 (DC Cir, 1992).

determine whether the practices in question deny the US rights under a trade agreement or whether they are unjustifiable, unreasonable or discriminatory and burden or restrict US commerce. If the practices are determined to violate a trade agreement or to be unjustifiable, the USTR must determine whether action is appropriate and, if so, what action to take. The time period for making these determinations varies according to the type of practices alleged. Generally, investigations of alleged violations of trade agreements must be concluded within 18 months, whereas investigations of alleged unreasonable, discriminatory or unjustifiable practices must be decided within 12 months.

The range of actions that may be taken under section 301 are broad and include: (1) suspension of trade agreement concessions, (2) imposition of duties or other import restrictions, (3) imposition of fees or restrictions concerning services, (4) entry into agreements with the subject country to eliminate the offending practice or to provide compensatory benefits for the United States, and (5) restriction of service sector authorisations. Since 1974 well over 100 investigations pursuant to section 301, have been launched, but none of these since 1993 has concerned worker rights. In March 2004, the AFL-CIO presented a petition claiming that China was in violation of worker rights, thus creating an unfair trade burden on the US.[35] This petition was rejected by the Bush Administration which, while acknowledging that China suppresses worker rights, said that 'accepting these petitions would take us down the path of economic isolationism' and would 'worsen the very problems they are trying to solve.'[36]

A comparison may also be made with the worker rights petition process of OPIC, which is required to conduct annual public hearings to afford any person the opportunity to present views as to whether OPIC is complying with the 1985 OPIC amendments (above). The annual public hearing is also a forum for persons to present evidence of 'whether any investment in a particular country should have been or should be extended insurance, reinsurance, guarantees, or financing.' This review process is open to any person and is not limited to parties that may be affected directly by OPIC's decisions. OPIC does require that participants in the public hearing express their views through a formal challenge procedure. To qualify as a formal challenge, OPIC requires complainants to support their accusations with factual information of the internationally recognised worker rights listed in the Trade Act 1974 (above). Several labour unions and human rights organisations have testified before OPIC's Board of Directors, alleging violations of worker rights and requesting that OPIC cease its activities in offending nations.

OPIC's practice has been to treat workers' rights cases as 'business confidential' avoiding all publicity and requiring its auditors to sign confidentiality

---

[35] *Financial Times,* 17 March 2004; Alston (2004) at 474–75.
[36] USTR, Statement of the USTR, Robert B Zoellick, on US–China Trade Relations, 28 April 2004.

agreements. It is therefore difficult to get records of employment standard reviews or petition information. This lack of transparency has been criticised. What is known is that OPIC has a two-track approach to facilitate the implementation of the worker rights provision. With respect to beneficiary countries under the GSP program, OPIC follows Executive Branch determinations of a host country's compliance. Any beneficiary country for which GSP eligibility is revoked on account of that country's failure to take steps to adopt and implement internationally recognised worker rights is subject concurrently to the suspension of OPIC programs. For non-GSP countries in which OPIC operates, OPIC conducts its independent analysis in consultation with the Departments of State and Labor as required by the statute.

In February 1987 OPIC's Board of Directors notified Congress of the results of its first annual review of employment standards in countries where OPIC-assisted projects are located. OPIC indefinitely suspended insurance, reinsurance, loan guarantee, and direct loan programs to investments in Nicaragua, Paraguay, Romania, and Ethiopia. OPIC's findings with respect to Nicaragua, Paraguay, and Romania were consistent with the President's decisions under the GSP program. With regard to Ethiopia, a non-GSP country, OPIC consulted with the Departments of State and Labor and other interested agencies prior to suspending its programs in that country. In 1991 OPIC determined that South Korea had failed to meet OPIC statutory worker rights criteria. In 1998, South Korea became eligible again for OPIC programs.

One may conclude that although the review procedures allow for petition by interest groups, and for hearings, they have been relatively ineffective because of the broad discretion allowed to the Executive Branch on matters such as whether there has been a violation of worker rights or a country is 'taking steps' to remedy this. Moreover, the procedures make it difficult to know the grounds on which decisions are taken. There is no requirement to have regard to the decisions of ILO supervisory bodies, there is no right to challenge the Executive's decisions, and subsequent petitions will often fail because of the stringent application of the requirement that there must be 'new information'. Not surprisingly relatively little use has been made of the procedures in worker rights cases over a 20-year period. Worker rights advocates have proposed—so far without success—that clear and specific criteria for the acceptance of petitions for review should be enunciated, ruling out only those that are frivolous, and revising the 'new information' standard discussed earlier. They also want the definition of worker rights to be based on ILO standards, including the right to non-discrimination.[37]

---

[37] GAO, Assessment of GSP Program (1994) at 119–22.

6. Protectionist and political motives?

In the first three decades after the Second World War the AFL-CIO was a keen supporter of free trade which it saw as a means to fight communism. Union leaders were converted to the 'fair trade' cause in the 1970s by the fear of low-wage foreign competition. The US apparel manufacturing industry went from a peak of 1.45 million workers in 1973 to 853,000 in 1996, a drop of 41 percent. One of the main reasons for this was intense price competition in the US market which manufacturers and retailers blamed for driving jobs to the Caribbean Basin.[38] Although the manufacturers claimed that US-owned plants had the best working conditions in the Caribbean countries, unions joined other interest groups who wanted to close US markets to those making use of 'unfair trade practices' in those countries. Lane Kirkland, President of AFL-CIO, put this firmly in the fair trade discourse by maintaining that 'competitive advantage in trade should not be derived from the denial of the right to freedom of association, the refusal to create a safe working environment, the exploitation of child labour and other such reprehensible practices.'[39]

It is debatable whether low wages in developing countries was the principal cause of the loss of jobs in the US. Technological innovation may have been even more significant—for example the increase in spinning speeds has decreased the need for labour by 40 percent—and much of the competition came from other developed countries.[40] However, the perceived link with off-shoring became the focus of demands for labour rights clauses in the CBI, GSP and other trade measures. It has been suggested that these are preferential programs which the US is free to establish under WTO rules subject to whatever conditions it chooses—benefits are conceded unilaterally, and conditions may be set unilaterally. This is said to justify labour rights conditions for preferential trade just as GSP benefits may be denied to countries that expropriate investments, or refuse to accept an international arbitration award, or fail to protect intellectual property rights.[41] In fact, as we shall see (chapter 6, below), WTO rules do not give carte blanche for preferential agreements with developing countries—there must be no discrimination between these countries.

In any event, this justification for labour rights conditionality, cannot be applied to section 301 of the US Trade Act (above), which, as amended in 1988,

---

[38] GAO, Worker Rights (1998) at 2–3.
[39] Van Roozendaal (2002) at 75, citing Lane Kirkland, Testimony before the Senate Finance Committee on the Goals of US Trade Policy, 20 January 1987.
[40] Dicken (1998) at 311.
[41] Compa and Vogt (2001) at 236.

allows mandatory retaliatory sanctions against unfair trade practices, including violations of the same 'internationally recognised worker rights' as specified in the GSP Renewal Act (above). This vague power is not limited to developing countries; sanctions may be applied to any country whose practices result in a burden to, or restriction upon, US commerce. The scale of sanctions is greater than under GSP, but these can only be used in the case of economic injury. It would be difficult to justify the use of section 301 in the case of labour rights violations under WTO rules (chapter 6, below).

The political nature of decisions made under the GSP program is illustrated by the case of Pakistan. In 1996, President Clinton suspended GSP benefits on selected goods, including sporting goods, surgical goods and hand woven rugs because of Pakistan's failure to take steps to remedy labour abuses, including child and bonded labour, the exemption of the Karachi Export Processing Zone from labour laws, and restrictions on the rights of state employees to strike or to resign. Despite the persistence of these violations, in 2002 the suspension of GSP benefits was lifted. Most observers believe that this decision, and other reductions of trade barriers, was a direct consequence of Pakistan's support for the US in the Afghanistan war.[42] The US has been willing to suspend benefits from countries whose trade has little impact on the US economy (eg Belarus), but not those (eg Thailand) where labour abuses are equally or more prevalent but the loss of trade would be detrimental to the US.

7. 'Soft unilateralism': the EU's generalised system of preferences

At the time the Treaty of Rome was negotiated Belgium, France, Italy and the Netherlands had colonial possessions in Africa, the Caribbean and Pacific (ACP). The Treaty of Rome dealt with the association of these territories, but did not cover the emerging independent countries. This gap and the accession in 1973 of another former imperial power, the United Kingdom, led to a series of association agreements providing for preferential trade access of products originating in ACP countries. According to Article 177(2) of the EC Treaty, EU development policy contributes to 'the general objective of developing and consolidating democracy and the rule of law, and to that of respecting human rights and fundamental freedoms.' But it was not until the revision of the fourth Lomé Convention (1989) by the Mauritius Agreement of 1995, that a specific commitment to 'human rights, democratic principles and the rule of

---

[42] Compa and Vogt (2001) at 231.

law' became an 'essential element' in the fourth Lomé Convention.[43] The development of this clause and of a clause on core labour standards in the new ACP-EC Partnership Agreement, signed on 23 June 2000, at Cotonou, Benin, will be considered in chapter 5.

Alongside these agreements with social clauses, there is also a unilaterally imposed Generalised System of Preferences (GSP). Since 1995, the EU GSP schemes have replaced the traditional approach of granting duty-free market access for restricted quantities of goods, by the concept of modulation which provides for limited preferences for unlimited quantities. At the same time new rules on graduation were introduced, allowing for the exclusion of specific sectors of exports from individual beneficiary countries. Subsequently additional preferences were offered in the framework of special incentive arrangements, meant to promote the objectives of sustainable development, in particular the protection of labour rights and of the environment.

The current scheme, embodied in Council Regulation 250/2001 of 10 December 2001,[44] adopts a 'carrot and stick' approach to core labour standards (positive and negative conditionality). The carrot is the 'special incentive arrangements for the protection of labour rights' in Title III, section 1 of the Regulation. A beneficiary country[45] has to request these preferences and must show that its national legislation incorporates the substance of the standards laid down in ILO C.29 and C.105 on forced labour, C.87 and C.98 on the freedom of association and the right to collective bargaining, C.100 and C.111 on non-discrimination in respect of employment and occupation, and C.138 and C.182 on child labour (the core standards).[46] The requesting country must also show that it 'effectively applies that legislation.'[47] Where the legislation is not applied in certain sectors (eg export processing zones) the special incentive arrangements may be granted only for those sectors in which it is applied.[48] The requesting country must give an undertaking to monitor the application of the special incentive arrangements and to provide the necessary administrative co-operation.[49] The products concerned must be accompanied by a statement issued by the authorities certifying that those products have been manufactured in the country of origin in conditions complying with the legislation.[50]

---

[43] Art 5(1) sub-para 3, Lome IV(1995).

[44] [2001] OJ L346/1 extended by Council Regulation 2211/2003, [2003] OJ L332/1 until 31 December 2005.

[45] The beneficiary countries are listed, and may be removed where for 3 consecutive years the country is (a) classified by the World Bank as a high income country, and (b) has a development index higher than −1.

[46] Council Regulation (EC) 250/2001, Art 14(2).

[47] Art 14(2).

[48] Art 18(2).

[49] Art 15(1).

[50] Art 19(1).

The flexibility of these provisions, leaving the European Commission with a number of discretions, is apparent. This, as we shall see (chapter 7, below) is significant for purpose of compliance with WTO requirements.

The additional preferences for countries complying with these requirements, are substantial. Under earlier rules the margin of preferences was relatively small. This together with the extremely complicated calculation of the additional preferences that beneficiaries might get on top of the normal ones, deterred countries from requesting them. In order to improve the incentives, the current scheme simplifies the additional preferences. The 'general arrangements' for beneficiary countries allow suspension or reduction of the common customs tariff. There are special incentives for observance of core labour rights,[51] and there is provision for the monitoring and evaluation of compliance with the ILO core standards.[52]

The 'stick' is the temporary withdrawal of preferential arrangements in respect of all or of certain products originating in a country which is a beneficiary of the scheme.[53] This can occur in three relevant circumstances:

(a) [the] practice of any form of slavery or forced labour as defined in the Geneva Conventions of 25 September 1926 and 7 September 1956 and ILO C.29 and C.105;
(b) serious and systematic violation of the freedom of association, the right to collective bargaining or the principle of non-discrimination in respect of employment and occupation, or use of child labour, as defined in the relevant ILO conventions;
(c) export of goods made by prison labour.

This goes somewhat further than the ILO core standards, by adding slavery and the products of prison labour.[54] In addition the special incentive arrangements for the protection of labour rights (above) can be temporarily withdrawn in respect of all or certain products for either of the following reasons:

(a) if the national legislation no longer incorporates the [core labour] standards . . . or that legislation is not effectively applied;
(b) if the undertaking [to monitor the special incentive arrangements] . . . is not respected.

In implementing the Regulation, the Commission is assisted by a GSP Committee composed of representatives of the Member States and chaired by the representative of the Commission.[55] When the Commission or a Member State receives information (eg from a trade union or NGO) that may justify temporary withdrawal and where it considers that there are sufficient grounds

---

[51] Arts 8–14.
[52] Art 10.
[53] Council Regulation (EC) 250/2001, Art 26(1).
[54] See further, ch 6 below, on the case for including these additional provisions.
[55] Art 37.

for an investigation, it must inform the GSP Committee and request consultations which should take place within 15 days.[56] Following the consultations the Commission may decide to initiate an investigation, publishing a notice in the *Official Journal*, and giving the beneficiary country every opportunity to cooperate in the investigation.[57] A clear link is established with the ILO procedures, by a provision that the 'assessments, comments, decisions, recommendations and conclusions of the various supervisory bodies of the ILO, including in particular the Article 33 procedures, shall serve as the point of departure for the investigation . . .'[58] The Commission has to report its findings to the GSP Committee. Where the Commission considers temporary withdrawal to be necessary it must submit a proposal to the Council which has to decide by a qualified majority within 30 days.[59]

There is a special procedure in cases where the Commission considers that temporary withdrawal is justified because of serious and systematic violation of core labour standards.[60] This effectively grants the beneficiary country more than a year to put its house in order. The Commission must monitor and evaluate the situation in the beneficiary country concerned for a period of 6 months. Where, at the end of that period the Commission finds that the country has not made the required commitment, it must present a proposal to the Council which has to decide within 30 days, by qualified majority, whether to impose temporary withdrawal. This decision does not enter into force until 6 months after it was taken.[61] There are thus many opportunities for an offending country to delay compliance.

There has thus far been only one case in which temporary withdrawal of GSP has been applied. This was in March 1997, when the Commission found that Myanmar was involved in the 'routine and widespread' use of forced labour, and the Council temporarily withdrew access to the tariff preferences granted under an earlier GSP regulation.[62] (The ILO's action in respect of Myanmar, including the application of Article 33 of the ILO Constitution is discussed in chapter 2, Box 2.4, above.) On the other hand, around the same time, the Commission did not seek temporary withdrawal against Pakistan for use of child labour because Pakistan had introduced legislation to outlaw child labour and kept the Commission regularly informed about implementation.

---

[56] Art 27.

[57] Art 28(1).

[58] Art 28(3).

[59] Art 29(4).

[60] Art 26(2)(b) which does not, however, refer to forced labour, which falls under Art 26(1)(a) and so does not appear to require this special procedure.

[61] Art 29(3)(5).

[62] Council Regulation (EC) 552/1997, [1997] OJ L 085/8. In January 2004, acting in information from international and European trade union bodies, the EC launched an investigation against Belarus for allegations of violation of freedom of association.

At that time the GSP regulation did not refer specifically to child labour, and the Commission was concerned that withdrawal of preferences might increase family poverty unless accompanied by positive measures.[63]

8. US and EU compared

Both the US and EU GSPs may be described as unilateral because they do not rest on agreement with the targeted countries. However, the EU system may be described as 'soft' unilateralism because it avoids most of the criticisms which have been directed at 'aggressive' US unilateralism. First, the EU does not under-mine the rule of international law. It applies the ILO 8 core conventions, which all EU Member States have ratified, unlike the US which has ratified only two of these. Compliance with the core standards is a condition of membership of the ILO, even by those countries that have not ratified the core conventions. Unlike the US, the EU does not require compliance with any other unratified conven-tions. In the EU, unlike the US, a clear link has been established with the various supervisory bodies of the ILO. These are 'the point of departure' for EU action.

Secondly, unlike the US, the EU has to follow transparent and fair proce-dures before withdrawing or refusing preferences. The European Commission does not have the same ambiguous discretions as the USTR, for example there is no equivalent in the EU to the US criterion of whether a country is 'taking steps' to afford worker rights. In the absence of a full-scale study, it is still too early to say whether the EU procedures have been fully effective, but it is clear that the carrot of preferences has induced countries to ensure that they have, at least, ratified the core conventions.

Thirdly, it is far harder to sustain the charge of protectionism against the EU GSP than it is against US trade measures. These preferences are a legacy of the historical relationship with former European colonies and are now part of a larger framework for the integration of developing countries. They appear to fall within the WTO's 'enabling clause' which allows the grant of non-reciprocal trade benefits provided that these benefit all developing countries without discrimination (chapter 6, below). There is no equivalent in the EU to the labour rights amendment to section 301 of the US Trade Act that permits mandatory retaliatory sanctions, and there is no evidence of preferences being granted or denied by the EU for protectionist or political purposes. This indi-cates that it is possible to maintain a policy of linking trade preferences with core labour standards. The US is unlikely to modify its approach to one that is more development-friendly without a push from the WTO and also from the developing countries.

---

[63] Brandtner and Rosas (1999) at 716–17.

5

Social Clauses in Bilateral and Regional Agreements

1. Introduction

The North American Agreement on Labor Co-operation (NAALC), the companion 'side agreement' to the North American Free Trade Agreement (NAFTA), was the first-ever trade agreement to make a significant link between trade and labour rights. The parties to NAFTA and NAALC are the US, Mexico and Canada. The Agreements came into force on 1 January 1994. They have been the model, with some significant variations, for later Free Trade Agreements (FTA) negotiated by the US with Jordan (2000), Chile and Singapore (2003),[1] and Australia (2004), and the proposed Central America Free Trade Agreement (CAFTA) between the US, Costa Rica, El Salvador, Guatemala, Honduras and Nicaragua. These models also feature in negotiations for a Free Trade Agreement of the Americas (FTAA), expected to include 34 countries, and a proposed regional free trade agreement with the Southern African Customs Union (SACU).[2] A new uniquely American system of cross-border monitoring of the enforcement of domestic labour laws is emerging.

---

[1] A somewhat different approach will be found in the US–Cambodia Bilateral Textile Agreement (1999, extended to 31 December 2004), discussed below.

[2] Comprised of South Africa, Namibia, Lesotho, Swaziland and Botswana. In 1996, the SA National Economic Development and Labour Council (NEDLAC) adopted a framework agreement on the social clause in bilateral treaties.

This is likely to become much more important than the current unilateral US measures, discussed in chapter 4. This chapter provides an analysis of the NAALC and FTA models, then examines the place of labour rights provisions in EU external trade agreements, and in the final section evaluates who are the winners and loses under these agreements.

2. The North American Agreement on Labor Co-operation

The core feature of the NAALC is that it requires the enforcement of *domestic* labour law by each of the parties, and not the application of *international* labour standards. The definition of 'labour law' for this purpose consists of 11 principles, which fall into three categories (Table, 5.A, below).[3] These categories determine the extent to which enforcement can occur (see below).

Table 5.A	
NAALC 'LABOR PRINCIPLES' AND FTA 'INTERNATIONALLY RECOGNISED WORKER RIGHTS'	
NAALC 'Labor Principles'	Other FTA 'internationally recognised labor rights'
CATEGORY I	
1. Freedom of association and right to organise	1. The right of association; *commitment to ILO core standards*
2. Right to bargain collectively	2. Right to organise and bargain collectively; *commitment to ILO core standards*
3. Right to strike	3. *No corresponding provision*
CATEGORY 2	
4. Prohibition of forced labour	4. Prohibition on use of any form of forced or compulsory labour; *commitment to ILO core standards.*
5. Elimination of employment discrimination	5. *No corresponding provision, but commitment to ILO core standards*
6. Equal pay for women and men	6. *No corresponding provision, but commitment to ILO core standards*
7. Compensation in cases of occupational injuries and illnesses.	7. *No corresponding provision (but see 11)*

---

[3] Art 42 and Annex 1.

8. Protection of migrant workers	8. *No corresponding provision*
CATEGORY 3	
9. Labour protections for children and young persons	9. Minimum age for employment of children; and *commitment to ILO core standards.*
10. Minimum employment standards such as wages and overtime pay	10. Acceptable conditions of work with respect to minimum wages, hours of work
11. Prevention of occupational injuries and illnesses	11. Acceptable conditions with respect to occupational safety and health.

NAALC does not demand adherence to supranational standards (such as 'internationally recognised worker rights' which are the cornerstone of US unilateral trade measures), nor does it create a supranational enforcement system. Instead, there is a review and dispute resolution procedure aimed at holding countries accountable for enforcement of their own laws and collective agreements. The Preamble affirms the parties' 'continuing respect for each party's constitution and law.' A general commitment in Article 2 by each party to 'ensure that its labour laws and regulations provide for high labour standards, consistent with high quality and productivity workplaces' is preceded by an affirmation of 'respect for each party's constitution,' and a recognition of 'the right of each party to establish its own domestic labour standards.'

The striking supremacy of the principle of national sovereignty can be understood only in the specific social, economic and political context in which NAALC was negotiated. The recently elected President Clinton was caught between his support for free trade and the pressure from his political allies in the US labour, human rights and green movements who claimed that the NAFTA (negotiated by President George Bush in 1990–1992) would lead to a loss of US jobs and harm to the environment. He agreed to support NAFTA only if side agreements on labour and the environment were negotiated. The US proposed a strong independent commission and the availability of trade sanctions to enforce labour standards. Canada and Mexico, fearing the economic, military and cultural dominance of the US, resisted this approach and called instead for a small administrative secretariat, no economic sanctions, and full respect for national sovereignty over the substance of labour law. The NAALC reflected a compromise, with trade sanctions being available in very limited circumstances, and only the enforcement of national labour laws being opened for review and dispute resolution.[4] The emphasis on enforcement stemmed particularly from the belief of US and Canadian unions that the explicit commitments to extensive labour rights in the Mexican constitution

---

[4] Compa (2001) at paras 7–9; Weiss [Marley] (2003) at 701–3.

and labour laws are far removed from the reality of life in the *maquiladoras*. But all the parties agreed to oversight by a review body in the government of one of the *other* parties, and in the case of some labour principles to evaluation and arbitration by independent non-government committees or panels.

The NAALC set up a Commission for Labor Co-operation that includes a Ministerial Council and a permanent Secretariat. There are National Administrative Offices (NAOs) in the Ministry of Labour of each country. Any person or group (the 'submitter') in a NAFTA country may file a submission with a NAO, not in the country to which the dispute relates, alleging that one or other of the governments has failed effectively to enforce its labour laws relating to these principles. If the NAO decides to accept the submission it may hold public hearings and consult with other NAOs [5]. A party may also request consultations at ministerial level relating to any of the 11 labour principles (ie categories 1, 2 and 3). Although such consultations can take place without the filing of a submission, in practice Labour Ministers have acted only in cases involving submissions.[6]

If a matter has not been resolved at ministerial level, a party may ask request the establishment of an Evaluation Committee of Experts (ECE), whose members are chosen 'on the basis of objectivity, reliability and sound judgment' and must be independent.[7] An ECE may be appointed only in respect of the 8 labour principles in category 2 and category 3. This excludes some of the matters most frequently raised, namely non-enforcement of laws relating to freedom of association and the right to organise, the right to engage in collective bargaining and the right to strike. Moreover, the matter giving rise to the setting up of an ECE must be 'trade-related' and 'covered by mutually recognised labour laws.' To be 'trade-related' it has to be 'related to a situation involving workplaces, firms, companies or sectors that produce goods or provide services: (a) traded between the territories of the parties; or (b) that compete in the territory of the party, whose labour law was the subject of ministerial consultations . . ., with goods or services produced or provided by persons of another party.'[8] 'Mutually recognised labour laws' means 'laws of both a requesting party and the party whose laws were the subject of ministerial consultations . . . that address the same general subject matter in a manner that provides enforceable rights, protections or standards.'[9] For example, since the US does not have a law like that of Mexico on profit-sharing with employers of 10 per cent of the firm's profits, it could not request an ECE to evaluate the

---

[5] Art 21. The NAO requested to consult must provide available data or information. The NAO of the third country is entitled to participate.

[6] Compa (2001) at para 76.

[7] Arts 23, 24.

[8] Art 49.

[9] Art 49.

enforcement of Mexican laws on this subject.[10] It is an open question whether a country with a law on a particular subject can complain about another country's failure to enforce a stronger law on the subject: for example could the US seek enforcement of Ontario's law on equal pay for work of equal value in view of the fact that the US legislation is limited to equal pay for equal work ? This and similar questions remain theoretical since, as at May 2004, no ECE had ever been convened.

If the parties are unable to achieve a 'mutually satisfactory resolution of the matter' after the ECE has published its final report, then a country can require consultations with any other party. This is, however, limited to the 3 labour principles in category 3 (occupational safety and health, child labour and minimum wage 'technical labour standards'[11]), and there must be a 'persistent pattern of failure' by the other party to effectively enforce the standards covered by the ECE report.[12] If these consultations fail to resolve the matter, a party may request a special session of the Ministerial Council, which may call on technical advisers and have recourse to concilaition and mediation.[13] If the matter is not settled after this, two of the three members of the Council can convene an arbitral panel. At this stage too, only category 3 matters are relevant, they must be 'trade-related' and 'covered by mutually recognised labour laws', and there must be 'persistent pattern of failure.'[14] The 5-member panel is appointed *ad hoc* from a roster of 45 independent experts. As at May 2004, no Arbitral Panel had ever been convened.

If the Arbitral Panel finds that there has been a persistent pattern of failure, it must make recommendations for the resolution of the dispute. These take the form of an 'action plan' 'sufficient to remedy the pattern of non-enforcement'. If the parties cannot agree that the action plan is being implemented, then the Panel can be reconvened and the Panel can then impose an action plan. If a government fails or refuses to implement this, the Panel can impose a 'monetary enforcement assessment' in an amount up to 0.007 percent of the total value of trade in goods and services between the disputing countries. The fine is to be paid into a fund expended at the direction of the Ministerial Council on improvement of labour law enforcement in the offending country. Finally, there are trade sanctions. If the US or Mexico fails to pay

[10] I am grateful to Lance Compa for this example.

[11] 'Technical labor standards means laws and regulations, or specific provisions thereof, that are directly related to' minimum wages, thus excluding consideration of whether the level set is adequate: NAALC, Art 49.

[12] Art 27. 'Pattern of practice' 'means a course of action or inaction beginning after the date of entry into force of [NAALC], and does not include a single instance or case'. 'Persistent pattern' 'means a sustained or recurring pattern of practice': Art 49.

[13] Art 28.

[14] Art 29.

the fine the complaining party may suspend the application of NAFTA benefits in an amount sufficient to collect the fine.[15] In the case of Canada not paying a fine, instead of suspension of benefits, any fine imposed by the Panel is treated as a judicial order under Canadian law and is enforceable in proceedings in Canadian courts.[16]

The three NAALC parties undertake six obligations. The first of these is the general commitment in Article 2 (see above) to 'establish and maintain high labour standards.' This has provided the basis for several NAALC complaints in which it has been argued that some laws, even if 'effectively enforced', fail to provide 'high labour standards.' An example in the *Pesca Union* case[17] (Box 5.1).

Box 5.1

THE *PESCA UNION* CASE

The *Pesca* [fisheries] union lost its registration when the Ministry of Fisheries merged with a larger Ministry of Environment and Natural Resources. Recognition was granted instead to a pro-government union at the enlarged Ministry. A federal labour law prohibited more than one union in a government entity. It was argued that this was contrary to the Mexican Constitution and also contrary to the standards in ILO C.87 on freedom of association. Mexico had ratified the Convention and under Mexico's Constitution ratified treaties are part of domestic law. The US NAO accepted the petition for review in 1996 and recommended ministerial consultations on relevant doctrines of Mexican law including the effect of ILO conventions on national labour laws. Mexico agreed to engage in consultations. However, further consideration became unnecessary because the Mexican Supreme Court ruled that the trade union monopoly was unconstitutional. Registration was restored to the *Pesca* union, which then tried (albeit unsuccessfully) to compete with the larger union.[18]

---

[15] Art 41, subject to the criteria for determining the fine in Art 41 Annex. Annex 41B provides that the collecting country may impose on the targeted goods the lesser of (a) tariff rates in effect prior to the date of entry into force of NAFTA, or (b) most-favoured nation (MFN) tariff rates in effect on the date of suspension. The complaining country must first seek to apply the sanctions to the same sector(s) where the government failed effectively to enforce its laws; if it is practicable or effective to do so, the sanction may be applied to other sectors to collect an amount in higher tariffs equal to the amount of the unpaid fine.

[16] Annex 41A.

[17] US NAO 9601.

[18] Compa (2001) at paras 142–46.

The second obligation is to 'promote compliance with, and effectively enforce its labour law through appropriate government action.' This includes appointing and training inspectors, monitoring compliance and investigating suspected violations, including through on-site inspections, seeking assurances of voluntary compliance, requiring record keeping and reporting, encouraging the establishment of worker-management committees to address labour regulation of the workplace, providing or encouraging mediation, conciliation and arbitration services, and initiating, in a timely manner, proceedings to seek appropriate sanctions or remedies for violations of its labour law.[19] This is, however, subject to an important limitation in respect of the exercise of discretionary enforcement powers, discussed below.

The third obligation is to ensure access for private parties to procedures for the enforcement of domestic labour law and collective agreements.[20] Fourthly, each party has to ensure procedural due process. This is spelt out in a number of detailed guarantees, such as open hearings, the right to present information and evidence, written decisions based on evidence in respect of which the parties were offered the opportunity to be heard, impartial and independent tribunals or courts, and appropriate remedies for the enforcement of labour rights including compliance agreements, fines, penalties, imprisonment, injunctions or emergency workplace closures.[21] Fifthly, there is a transparency requirement. Each party must publish or otherwise make available to interested parties its laws, regulations, procedures and administrative rulings of general application.[22] Finally, there is an obligation on each party to promote public awareness of its domestic labour law. This includes making public information available on enforcement and compliance procedures, and promoting public education regarding labour law.[23]

These are relatively strong obligations: 'high labour standards' must be established and maintained; parties must 'promote compliance' and 'promote public awareness'; they must 'effectively enforce' domestic labour law; and they must 'ensure' or 'guarantee' access, due process, and transparency. However, there is an important gloss on 'effective enforcement'. Article 49(1) states that a party has not failed to 'effectively enforce its occupational safety and health, child labor or minimum wage technical labour standards' or comply with Article 3(1) [government enforcement action] in a particular case where the action or inaction by agencies or officials of that party, (a) reflects a reasonable exercise of the agency's or the official's discretion with respect to

---

[19] Art 3.
[20] Art 4. In this context 'labour law' includes 'occupational safety and health, employment standards, industrial relations and migrant workers.'
[21] Art 5.
[22] Art 6.
[23] Art 7.

investigatory, prosecutorial, regulatory or compliance matters; or (b) results from bona fide decisions to allocate resources to enforcement in respect of other labour matters determined to have higher priorities. This escape clause appears to mean that non-enforcement can be challenged only if action or inaction was legally-speaking perverse, in the sense that no reasonable agency or official could have acted or failed to act in this way. Moreover, a genuine decision to concentrate resources in a particular sector or on particular laws constitutes a defence to a complaint of non-enforcement.

We have seen that the obligations are also weakened in the higher stages of the enforcement process following unsuccessful ministerial consultations. By holding out against pressure by the other disputing party, the determined violator can reduce the range of labour principles which it must enforce from 11 to 8 and ultimately to 3; it can avoid compliance by insisting that the domestic laws in question are not 'trade-related' or not 'mutually recognised' or by denying that there is a 'persistent pattern of practice' of violation.

Perhaps the greatest weaknesses are the absence of an express provision to prevent waiver or derogation from labour laws in order to attract trade or investment,[24] and the absence of an express link to the international floor of labour rights contained in ILO conventions. The 11 labour principles in NAALC are similar to but not the same as those in ILO conventions. They are less specific and sometimes lower than ILO obligations. There is provision for NAALC parties to establish co-operative arrangements with the ILO,[25] and submitters draw on ILO experience. But the Ministers, the ECE and Arbitral Panel are not obliged to have regard to the conventions or to the findings of the ILO Committee of Experts on the Application of Conventions and Recommendations, and the ILO Committee on Freedom of Association.

3. Variations in later Free Trade Agreements

NAFTA and NAALC were negotiated by the Administration and approved by Congress under presidential 'fast-track' authority—without amendment and with limited debate—granted by OTCA in 1988. That Act included three worker rights provisions in the principal US trade negotiating objectives: (1) to promote respect for worker rights; (2) to secure a review of the relationship of worker rights to GATT articles; and (3) to adopt as a principle of the GATT that the denial of worker rights should not be a means for a country or its

[24] Arguably, the commitment in Art 2 to establish and maintain high labour standards operates as a brake on waiver or derogation but this is not explicit.
[25] Art 45.

industries to gain competitive advantage in international trade.[26] The OTCA fast-track authority expired in 1994, and for the next 8 years the Republican majority in Congress was not willing to renew the worker rights provisions, apart from preventing governments from derogating from existing domestic labour standards. As a result, Congress could not agree on fast-track reauthorisation. However on 6 August 2002, President George W. Bush signed the Bipartisan Trade Promotion Authority Act 2002, which sets out a series of trading objectives in relation to subjects such as labour and the environment for agreements under the fast-track or trade promotion authority. These include: (1) ensuring that a party does not fail effectively to enforce its labour laws through a sustained or recurring course of action or inaction in a manner affecting trade; (2) strengthening the capacity of US trading partners to promote respect for 'core labour standards'; and (3) ensuring that labour policies and practices of parties to trade agreements with the US 'do not arbitrarily or unjustifiably discriminate against US exports or serve as disguised barriers to trade.' Fast-track treatment is conditional upon the FTA 'making progress in meeting the applicable objectives.'[27] If Congress determines that the Administration failed to meet these objectives, it may adopt a procedural disapproval resolution which renders the fast-track procedure inapplicable to the particular FTA.

The absence of fast-track authority after 1994 meant that the Clinton Administration was unable to conclude FTA negotiations with Chile which it had been hoped would accede to NAFTA. As a result Canada negotiated its own FTA with Chile, and this was accompanied by the Canada–Chile Agreement on Labour Co-operation (CCALC) and also an environmental side agreement. Subsequently, the Canada–Costa Rica FTA and labour and environmental side agreements were concluded. Broadly speaking, these agreements follow the NAFTA/NAALC model, with effective enforcement of domestic labour laws being the core obligation. Significantly, the Canada–Costa Rica Agreement on Labour Co-operation prescribes a minimum standard based on ILO instruments against which domestic labour law is to be measured. On the other hand, the agreement simply authorises ministerial consultations and does not provide for fines as an ultimate sanction.

In January 1999, the US Administration was able to use the President's power to negotiate textile agreements[28] in order to sign a bilateral 3-year textile agreement with Cambodia that included a commitment to expand the quota on textile and apparel imports from Cambodia by 14 percent if 'working conditions in the Cambodian textile and apparel sector substantially

---

[26] The second and third of these objectives is considered in ch 6 below.
[27] 19 USC § 3803(b)(2).
[28] 7 USC § 1854.

comply' with Cambodian labour law and 'internationally recognised core labour standards.'[29] The agreement was amended and extended for a further 3-year period from December 2001. The amended agreement offers a possible 18 percent annual increase in Cambodia's export entitlements provided that Cambodia supports 'the implementation of a programme to improve working conditions' including 'internationally recognised core labour standards, through the application of Cambodian labour law.' The US and Cambodia requested ILO technical assistance, and this led to an ILO project, substantially funded by the US, to monitor factories in the textile and apparel sector in Cambodia and to improve the capacity of government, employers and workers to improve working conditions. The operation of this unique experiment is considered in section 4 of this chapter.

The US–Jordan FTA, signed on 24 October 2000 by the Clinton Administration, with Congressional approval, is the first to contain labour rights and environmental obligations in the text of the main agreement instead of a side agreement. The significance of this is that disputes over labour rights are subject to the same dispute settlement procedures and remedies as the rest of the agreement. A Joint Committee is established to supervise the proper implementation of the agreement.[30] If consultations about any dispute fail to reach a mutually agreeable resolution, either party may refer the matter to a dispute resolution panel that must report to the Joint Committee. If the Committee does not then resolve the dispute the affected party is entitled to take 'any appropriate and commensurable measure'.[31] It has been suggested that this 'broad discretion could be abused' for protectionist purposes,[32] but it should be remembered that it would be subject to the WTO disciplines discussed in chapter 6.

The central labour rights obligation in the US–Jordan agreement, like NAALC, is effective enforcement of domestic labour law, but a significant difference from NAALC is that there is an express linkage between ILO and domestic standards. In Article 6(1) the parties 'reaffirm their obligations as members of the ILO and their commitments under the ILO Declaration on Fundamental Principles and Rights at Work and its Follow-up.' The parties undertake to strive to ensure that such labour principles and the internationally recognised labour rights set out in Article 6(6) of the agreement are 'recognised and protected by domestic labour law.' The 'internationally protected labor rights' omit some of the NAALC 'labor principles' (see Table 5.A, above). The definiton seems have been drawn from GSP 'internationally recognised worker rights' (chapter 4, above) rather than from NAALC. It omits express

---

[29] Cambodia Bilateral Textile Agreement, Art 10(D).
[30] Art 15.
[31] Arts 16 and 17.
[32] Elliott and Freeman (2003) at 87.

reference to compensation for injury and illness at work, but arguably this is encompassed by 'acceptable conditions of work with respect to . . . occupational safety and health'. Although it refers to the minimum age of employment and not to the elimination of the worst forms of child labour, the parties are bound to 'strive to ensure' that the ILO core principles, including the elimination of the worst forms of child labour, and of discrimination in employment are incorporated into domestic law.

Another significant feature of the US–Jordan agreement, unlike NAALC, is that each party agrees to 'strive to ensure' that it does not waive or otherwise derogate from domestic labour laws as an encouragement to trade with the other party. The encouragement to incorporate ILO core standards, and not to relax domestic labour laws responds to some of the criticisms of the NAALC, but this is only an obligation to 'strive to ensure.' Marley Weiss suggests that the mortar 'may be too thin and watery to do the job' of closing the gaps in NAALC.[33] On 3 September 2003, President George W.Bush signed into law, FTAs with Chile and Singapore. Like the Jordan FTA these locate labour rights in the body of the agreement, and contain the same basic obligations.[34] However, unlike the Jordan FTA, the Chile and Singapore agreements authorise sanctions only for sustained failure to enforce domestic labour laws in a manner affecting trade. Moreover, in contrast to the open-ended 'appropriate and commensurate measures' in the Jordan FTA, the maximum penalties under the Chile and Singapore agreements are $15 million annually, with failure to pay, as under NAFTA, leading potentially to suspension of benefits to the equivalent dollar volume. The proposed CAFTA also contains a labour clause weaker than that in the US–Jordan Agreement. The US–Australia FTA, concluded in 2004 and awaiting ratification at the time of writing, adds to the commitment to the ILO core principles, that the parties will strive to improve standards 'consistent with high quality and high productivity workplaces.' This seems to allow flexibility to relax the core standards where they appear to have an adverse impact on productivity (cf chapter 1, above). Enforcement of domestic labour laws is restricted to federal laws, and then only 'in a manner affecting trade between the parties.' Since matters such as child labour and forced labour are dealt with at state and not federal level in Australia (which has not ratified C.138 and C.182), the application of the US–Australia FTA will be limited.

It can be seen that there are several differences between the NAALC model, and later FTAs, and even between these FTAs (Table 5.B). However, the emerging American labour rights clause has several distinctive features likely to appear in future agreements: (1) incorporation in the body of the FTA rather than in a side accord as in NAALC and the Canada–Chile, Canada–Costa Rica

---

[33] Weiss (2003) 718.

[34] The non-waiver, non-derogation clause in the Chile and Jordan agreements extends to investment as well as trade.

agreements; (2) a core obligation to effectively enforce domestic labour law; (3) a commitment to 'strive to ensure' that domestic law complies with ILO core standards and the list of 'internationally protected labour rights'; (4) agreement not to waive or derogate from domestic labour law in order to expand trade or investment; (5) parity in enforcement procedures and sanctions in respect of labour rights and other rights.

Table 5.B		
COMPARISON OF NAALC AND OTHER FTAS		
NAALC US–SINGAPORE/CHILE	US–JORDAN	
Side agreement	Main agreement	Main agreement
1. Establish and maintain high labour standards	1. *No corresponding provision but ILO core and int.recognised worker rights protected*	1. *No corresponding provision but ILO core and int.recognised worker rights protected*
2. Compliance and effective enforcement of domestic labour laws in manner affecting trade	2. Shall not fail to enforce domestic labour laws in manner affecting trade	2. Same as Jordan
3. Access to private action and due process	3. *No corresponding provision*	3. Similar to NAALC
4. Transparency and public awareness	4. *No corresponding provision*	4. Same as Jordan
5. Discretion in enforcement and allocation of resources	5. Discretion in enforcement and allocation of resources	5. Same as Jordan
6. *No corresponding provision*	6. No waiver or derogation to attract trade	6. Same as Jordan, *adds investment*
Sanctions only for persistent pattern of practice on trade-related category 3 labour principles	Sanctions for all labour provisions	Sanctions only for sustainedfailure to enforce trade-related domestic labour laws
Maximum fine of 0.007% of total value of trade	Any appropriate or commensurate measure	$15m annual fine; suspension of benefits to equivalent dollar value

4. The effectiveness of the emerging American model

In the first ten years of its operation, 25 submissions were filed under NAALC, 12 of these against Mexico, 11 against the US and 2 against Canada. Some submissions related to single issues, others raised several grounds. The majority of issues concerned category 1 rights (collective labour law), which cannot proceed beyond the ministerial consultations stage to higher levels of enforcement. Ten of these were against Mexico, 6 against the US and 2 against Canada. Category 2 issues were raised in 9 submissions. These related to employment discrimination, compensation for occupational injuries and protection of migrant workers, all but one of these being targeted against the US and Canada. Category 3 issues, mainly prevention of occupational injuries, were raised in 12 submissions, 5 of these against Mexico, 5 against the US and 2 against Canada. None of these category 2 and 3 submissions had been taken beyond the first stage of ministerial consultations. Neither ECEs (available in respect of categories 2 and 3) nor Arbitral Panels (category 3) had ever been convened.

The first official review of NAALC, covering the first four years, took place in 1997–99, and the second commenced in 2002, but had not been published at the time of writing. In the first review, unions and employers' organisations in the three countries heavily criticised NAALC from different perspectives. Unions thought it had been a failure because the enforcement processes are too weak; employers' groups were worried about the support it gives to labour and human rights activists. The Mexican Government and corporatist unions complained that it had been used for 'Mexico-bashing' and had been captured by protectionist groups in the US. Some academics and independent experts were more willing to see positive results.

The small number of submissions has been explained in terms of the nature of the NAALC process which involves a 'soft law' review of the enforcement of domestic labour laws rather than the 'hard law' of enforcing labour rights which is left to domestic law.[35] The NAALC provides a long-term mechanism for changing the culture of law enforcement and promoting adherence to internationally recognised labour rights. NAALC advocates point out that the process has led to some positive outcomes. There have been conferences, seminars and public reports dealing with issues raised. For example, in response to concerns about gender-based discrimination, the NAFTA governments convened a conference to discuss women's rights at work in all three countries; another conference (arising out of the *Pesca Union* case above) dealt with the relationship between national laws and ILO conventions; and another case was resolved by holding three conferences and preparing an experts' study on union representation rights.[36] There have been some cases where settlements

---

[35] Compa (2001) at para 119.
[36] *Sony Case*, US NAO Case No 940003; see to the *Sprint Case*, Mexican NAO Case No 9501 which led to a public forum and a Secretariat research study on the effect of sudden plant closures on freedom of association.

have resulted in withdrawal of the submission.[37] Seven ministerial implementation agreements, covering 12 cases, have been reached. In the view of many
labour activists, the most important achievement of NAALC has been its contribution to international labour solidarity.[38] The cross-border complaints
mechanism provides a platform for the promotion of labour rights, and for
labour advocates to seek partners in other countries.[39] Most of the submissions have involved cross-border coalitions of unions and human rights and
community groups, but these alliances are still at any early stage and their
achievements are modest.

On the other hand, the weaknesses of the NAALC's core obligation—the
effective enforcement of domestic labour law—have been revealed. Several
submissions have been rejected because the alleged infringement of one of the
11 listed labour principles was in conformity with domestic labour law.
Striking flight attendants who accused the Mexican Government of violating
the right to strike because they were forced back to work when the
Government intervened by executive order to take over the airline and end the
strike, were denied a hearing of their case by the US NAO on the ground that
the takeover was in accordance with Mexican law.[40] The US NAO also refused
to review a complaint by Canadian rural letter carriers that they were excluded
from Canadian labour legislation, including the rights to organise and bargain
collectively, protection against occupational injuries and employment discrimination.[41] In the *Duro Bag* case,[42] the US NAO refused to hear a case
in which it was alleged that the Mexican Government had failed to fulfil a
commitment to promote the use inter alia of secret ballots in union elections
on the ground that Mexican law did not confer a right to a secret ballot, and
more generally because a review would not further the objectives of NAALC.
What is particularly disturbing about this decision is that Mexico had entered
into the commitment in a Ministerial implementation agreement following
earlier complaints of violation of union electoral laws. This was not a straightforward case of the absence of an enforceable right in domestic labour law, but
raised an issue as to the effectiveness of a Ministerial agreement, which the US
NAO was not willing to consider.[43] All of these are cases where the application

---

[37] *Department of Labour Case*, Mexican NAO Case No 9804, filed simultaneously with
Canadian NAO Case No 98–2.

[38] Esp Compa (2001) at paras 262–99.

[39] Compa (2001) at paras 268–77 provides a detailed study of the *Washington State Apples
Case*, Mexican NAO Case No 9802, in which such a cross-country alliance had notable success in
improving the working conditions of the 50,000 plus Mexican workers in the largest apple-
growing region in the US.

[40] *Aero México Case*, US NAO Case No 9801.

[41] *Canada Post Case*, US NAO Case No 9804.

[42] US NAO Case No 2001–01.

[43] See Weiss [Marley] (2003) at 741; cf La Sala (2001) at 319.

of ILO core standards on collective labour law would probably have led to a different conclusion. The NAALC core obligation tends to reinforce the status quo in domestic labour law, it lacks mechanisms to raise standards to a 'high level' (ambiguously promised in Article 2), and it does not prevent the relaxation of domestic standards to attract trade or investment. It remains to be seen how far stronger texts of the newer FTAs can overcome these deficiencies.

There is also an institutional problem. Enforcement is dependent upon the action of private parties, and decision-making ultimately rests in the hands of politicians and diplomats.[44] It is not surprising that the majority of submissions have related to collective labour law, because the complainants are usually unions. Marley Weiss argues that issues such as child labour and compensation for injury have rarely been raised because the victims lack an organised constituency. This leads her to propose an independent tri-national entity with prosecutorial authority, and a permanent impartial tribunal to deal with NAALC complaints.[45] There is also a question whether financial sanctions, of the kind found in NAALC and in the US–Chile and US–Singapore agreements are preferable to the open-ended discretion conferred by the US–Jordan agreement to impose trade sanctions. Arguments against the latter are that they can more readily be used for protectionist purposes, and that the more draconian the sanctions the less likely they are to be used in practice. Moreover, trade sanctions may result in those workers who are the subject of abusive working conditions losing jobs—this is a dilemma to which we shall return in chapter 6.

A different model of 'soft' enforcement is the US–Cambodia textile agreement which offers quota increases to Cambodia for the implementation of a programme to improve working conditions including core labour rights, monitored through a project directed by a Chief Technical Adviser appointed by the ILO and guided by a tripartite Ptoject Advisory Committee. As at September 2003, 200 enterprises in Cambdia had registered with the project, the key inducement being that only registrered factories are eligible to use allocated export quotas. These factories have to provide access to the 12 ILO monitors and to allow them to interact freely with shop stewards and workers both inside and outside the factory premises. In the first three years of the project (2001–2003) seven synthesis reports were issued, covering all the registered factories at least once. The inspectors have uncovered evidence of frequent incorrect payment of wages, overtime that is not voluntary in a substantial number of factories, anti-union discrimination in some factories, and strikes that have been organised in breach of legal requirements. The ILO inspectors have no enforcement powers, but it is clear that their work has

---

[44] Weiss [Marley](2003) at 748.
[45] Weiss [Marley] (2003) at 750–54.

resulted in improvements in a number of factories. The inspectors have pointed out that 'monitoring alone is not enough.' What is required, they say, 'is a change in attitudes of those involved.'[46] It is doubtful whether a purely voluntary approach can work effectively, but the ILO project provides some interesting pointers for future agreements.

5. EU external trade agreements

Respect for human rights and democratic principles became firmly enmeshed in the external policy of the EU in the 1990s, in trade agreements with the emerging democratic 'transition' states in Central and Eastern Europe. From 1992 a standard human rights clause was along the following lines:

> Respect for human right and democratic principles as laid down in the Universal Declaration on Human Rights[47] underpins the domestic and international policies of the Parties, and constitutes an essential element of this agreement.

The reference to these rights and principles as an 'essential element' means that a grave breach of human rights or democratic principles by one party would entitle the other to terminate the treaty or to suspend its operation in whole or in part.[48] This has been strengthened in some agreements by a non-compliance clause. One type of clause ('the Baltic clause') reserves the right of a party to suspend the agreement in whole or in part with immediate effect if a serious breach of the essential provisions arises, thus bypassing the lengthy procedures laid down in the Vienna Convention on the Law of Treaties.[49] Another type of clause ('the Bulgarian clause'), increasingly used since 1993, allows a broader range of options for enforcement:

> If either Party considers that the other Party has failed to fulfil an obligation under this agreement, it may take appropriate measures. Before so doing, except in cases of special urgency, it shall supply the Association Council with all relevant information required for a thorough examination of the situation with a view to seeking a solution acceptable to the Parties.
>
> In the selection of measures priority must be given to those which least disturb the functioning of this Agreement. These measures shall be notified immediately to the Association Council and shall be the subject of consultations within the Association Council if the other Party so requests.

---

[46] ILO, Seventh Synthesis Report on the Working Conditions Situation in Cambodia's Garment Sector, ILO, Geneva, October 2003 (availabe on http://www.ilo.org/public/english/dialogue/ifpdial/pub/cambodia7.htm).

[47] In treaties with Organisation for Cooperation and Security (OCSE) countries reference was also made to the Helsinki Final Act and the Charter of Paris for a New Europe.

[48] Vienna Convention on the Law of Treaties (VCLT), Art 60(3)(b).

[49] VCLT, Art 65.

This wording implies that a test of proportionality will be applied when deciding upon the 'appropriate measures'. 'Cases of special urgency', justifying unilateral action without examination by the Council, could include a grave breach of human rights justifying immediate counter-measures.[50]

In chapter 4, we saw that when the fourth Lomé Convention (1989) was revised by the Mauritius Agreement of 1995, a specific commitment to 'human rights, democratic principles and the rule of law' became an 'essential element' in the fourth Lomé Convention.[51] A non-compliance clause was added[52] containing a greater emphasis on consultation than the Bulgarian clause. These human rights and non-compliance provisions served as a model for other external EU agreements. They became standard clauses and thus part of the *acquis communitaire.*[53]

A new ACP-EC Partnership Agreement, signed on 23 June 2000, at Cotonou, Benin, continues (in Article 9) the commitment to 'respect for human rights, democratic principles and the rule of law' as 'essential elements' of the Agreement.[54] There is a non-compliance clause (Article 96), similar to that in Lomé IV. There must be a 60-day consultation period 'with a view to seeking a solution acceptable to the parties'. These consultations are excused in cases of 'special urgency', defined as 'exceptional cases of particularly serious and flagrant violation of one of the essential elements' that 'require an immediate action'.[55]

If consultations do not lead to an acceptable solution, or in cases of special urgency, 'appropriate measures' may be taken. These must be in accordance with international law, and proportional to the violation. In the selection of these measures, priority must be given to those which least disrupt the application of the agreement. Suspension is a measure of last resort,[56] but it was used against Zimbabwe, together with other restrictions, because of the continued serious violations of human rights and of the freedom of opinion, of association and of peaceful assembly, and the prevention of free and fair

---

[50] Joint interpretation declaration on the Partnership Agreement with the Russian Federation, 24 June 1994, later copied for treaties with other CIS states: Riedel and Will (1999) at 728.

[51] Art 5(1) sub-para 3, Lome IV(1995).

[52] Art 366a, Lomé IV (1995).

[53] Riedel and Will (1999) at 732. The *acquis* refers to the established body of EU law.

[54] ACP–EU Partnership Agreement, [2000] OJ L317/3, Art 9.2, sub-para 4. The agreement is for a period of 20 years from 1 March 2000. It is a 'mixed agreement' with both the EU and its Member States as contracting parties, since development co-operation is not an exclusive competence of the EC See generally, Martenczuk (2000) at 461. Agreements with other countries, such as Bangladesh, Cambodia and Mexico, contain a similar 'essential element' clause and refer specifically only to the UN Declaration of Human Rights.

[55] Art 96.2(b). This is similar to the definition adopted in a joint declaration on interpretation under Lome IV.

[56] Art 96(2)(c).

elections in that country. In other cases, such as that of the civil war in Liberia, the EU has tended to make the fulfilment of its treaty obligations, such as the continuation of aid, dependent upon the restoration of democratic structures and upon free and fair elections.[57]

An innovation in the Cotonou Agreement was the addition of a clause on Trade and Labour Standards (Article 50). This states:

1. The Parties reaffirm their commitment to internationally recognised core labour standards, as defined by the relevant International Labour Organisation (ILO) Conventions, and in particular the freedom of association and the right to collective bargaining, the abolition of forced labour, the elimination of the worst forms of child labour and non-discrimination in respect to employment.
2. They agree to enhance co-operation in this area, in particular in the following fields:
   • exchange of information on the respective legislation and work regulation;
   • the formulation of national labour legislation and strengthening of existing legislation;
   • educational and awareness-raising programmes;
   • enforcement of adherence to national legislation and work regulation.
3. The Parties agree that labour standards should not be used for protectionist trade purposes.

The reference to 'internationally recognised core labour standards' was clearly influenced by the 1998 ILO Declaration on Fundamental Principles and Rights at Work (chapter 2, above). There is room for argument as to whether the list of core standards is exhaustive, but the words 'in particular' suggest that a wider but unspecified list of conventions could be intended. A subsequent co-operation agreement between the EC and Bangladesh,[58] has widened the scope by a clause stating:

The Parties agree that human resources development constitutes an integral part of both economic and social development.

The Parties acknowledge the necessity of safeguarding the basic rights of workers by taking account of the principles in the relevant International Labour Organisation instruments, including those on the prohibition of forced and child labour, the freedom of association, the right to organise and bargain collectively, and the principle of non-discrimination.

The Parties recognise that both education and skills development as well as improving the living conditions of the disadvantaged sections of the population with special emphasis on women, will contribute to creating a favourable economic and social environment.

---

[57] [2003] OJ C 020 E. For other earlier examples, see Riedel and Will (1999) 740–41, and Brandtner and Rosas (1999) at 701–4, and (in relation to the former Yugoslavia) at 709–13. Consultations with Guinea under Art 96 in the light of a deterioration in the democratic environment took place in 2003: COM/2003/0517/final.

[58] [2001] OJ L118/48, Art 10.

This does not limit co-operation to 'core' rights, but widens it to an undefined category of 'basic' rights taking account of 'principles' established by the ILO instruments. Bangladesh has ratified 33 ILO conventions, including 7 of the 8 core conventions. The clause may therefore have been intended to focus on compliance with all those ratified conventions, and any others which Bangladesh may ratify in future. No such clause is to be found in the agreement with Cambodia,[59] which has ratified only 12 ILO conventions, 7 of them being core conventions. An extensive partnership agreement with Mexico,[60] which has ratified 67 ILO conventions, has clauses on human rights and democracy and on 'the need to respect the rights' of 'vulnerable groups, such as indigenous population, the rural poor, women on low incomes and other population groups living in poverty',[61] but makes no specific mention of core labour standards.

There is, however, a confusing overlap between the 'core labour standards' listed in Article 50 of the Cotonou Agreement, and the 'human rights' instruments which form the 'essential elements' of the Agreement under Article 9. Article 9 does not specifically define 'human rights' but the Preamble to the Agreement refers to a number of international and regional instruments: the UN Charter, the 1993 Declaration of Vienna and the Programme of Action of the World Conference on Human Rights, the UN Covenants on Civil and Political Rights and on Economic, Social and Cultural Rights, the Conventions on the Rights of the Child, on the Elimination of all forms of discrimination against women, on the elimination of all forms of racial discrimination, various instruments on refugees, the European Convention on Human Rights, the African Charter on Human and People's Rights, and the American Convention on Human Rights. All four of the 'core' labour standards will be found, in various forms of wording, in some of these international and regional instruments. It would, therefore, seem that Article 50 is merely declaratory, while Article 9 makes possible 'appropriate measures' against a Party which violates core labour standards, since these standards are already covered by that article as 'human rights'. There are also other labour standards which, although not described by the ILO as 'core' standards, embody human rights as listed in the instruments referred to in the Preamble to the Agreement (chapter 2, above). The overlap between social and civil rights is seen in a Council Regulation on the development and consolidation of democracy and the rule of law and respect for human rights and fundamental freedoms. This requires the Community to support operations 'aimed at promoting economic, social and

---

[59] [1999] OJ L 269/18. An objective of this agreement (Art 2(d)) is to 'contribute to Cambodia's efforts to improve the quality of life and the standards of living of the poorest sections of the population, together with measures for the country's reconstruction'.

[60] [2000] OJ L 276/45.

[61] Art 16.

cultural rights, including trade union rights, together with the civil and polit-ical rights proclaimed in the Universal Declaration of Human Rights.'[62] There is a strong case for an explicit social clause—at least covering core labour standards—so as to dispel the notion that human rights do not include these basic social rights.[63]

The European Parliament has, on a number of occasions, declared itself in favour of a specific social clause.[64] The European Commission, too, has pro-posed that trade and co-operation agreements should in future include specific provisions on core labour standards.[65] As we have seen, the current practice treats 'human rights'—which appear to include at least the 'core' ILO standards—as an 'essential element' with consequent sanctions for violation. However, other ILO standards are relegated as matters for co-operation, and are not sanction-based.[66] The reason for this is the developing countries' fear of disguised protectionism, a fear expressed in Article 50(3) of the Agreement. The European Council,[67] conscious of this, has decided to focus its strategy on capacity-building and co-operative programmes, rather than negative sanc-tions. A Council resolution of 21 July 2003 supported all forms of incentives to promote core labour standards, including corporate social responsibility, the generalised system of preferences, more effective dialogue between the ILO and WTO, strengthening the monitoring of the application of labour stand-ards by the ILO, technical assistance to developing countries, programmes with binding deadlines for abolishing all forms of child labour, and incentive measures such as social labelling.

6. Winners and losers

As a matter of theory, all the parties to a trade agreement benefit from the opening of their markets. This encourages each country to produce the goods and services which it can provide most efficiently and to import those which it

---

[62] Council Regulation 976/99/EC, [1999] OJ L120/8.

[63] Riedel and Will (1999) at 746.

[64] Eg, EP Resolution on the Introduction of a Social Clause in the Unilateral and Multilateral Trading System [1994] OJ C61/89; EP Resolution on the Commission communication entitled 'Promoting core labour standards and improving social governance in the context of globalisa-tion', 4 July 2003.

[65] Communication from the Commission, Promoting Core Labour Standards and Improving Social Governance in the Context of Globalisation, COM(2001) 416 final, 18 July 2001.

[66] Other issues on which co-operation for creating an 'appropriate framework' are stipulated, include gender (Art 31), environment and natural resources (Art 32).

[67] Council Conclusions on the Commission Communication adopted 21 July 2003, EC Bulletin 7/8–2003.

produces least efficiently, leading to increased profitability, lower consumer prices, and in the long-run more jobs and higher wages in both countries (see chapter 1). In developed countries the main gains are for high-skill, high technology exporters, for firms that use cheap imports from developing countries in their production processes, and for TNCs who are able to relocate in low-wage developing countries. The losers in developed countries are labour-intensive firms whose products and services compete with imports from developing countries, and the workers in those firms whose jobs and labour standards are placed at risk.

When a social clause is included in the trade agreement, this may change the equation. Potentially, firms and their workers in the developed country are in a win-win situation. Their products and services have access to the markets of the developing country, but the developing country is excluded from the developed country's market unless the prescribed social standards are met. In reality, however, this protection is likely to be illusory. First, it is only rarely that observance of human rights standards, ILO core labour standards or 'internationally protected worker rights' add significantly to labour costs (chapter 1, above). Secondly, NAALC and the free trade agreements surveyed in this chapter have had only relatively minor effects on labour standards in developing countries, and have not acted as an effective barrier against products and services produced by workers with low labour standards. US critics of NAFTA can point to the closure of US plants and the shifting of jobs to Mexico. The US–Cambodia textile agreement, while leading to some improvements in working conditions in Cambodia has not halted the continuing decline of the US textile industry. From the viewpoint of firms and workers in the developed countries, the march of trade liberalisation is relentless and social clauses of the kind found in NAALC and other American FTAs are powerless to stop it. Supporters of NAALC and other FTAs claim that against the loss of around 500,000 jobs under NAFTA some 14 million new jobs in the US since 1993 owe their existence to trade agreements like NAFTA.[68] It is virtually impossible to evaluate claims of this kind, given other major influences on trade and employment such as the devaluation of the Mexican peso in 1994 and the enormous turnover for many different reasons in the US jobs market.

The effect of social clauses on firms and workers in developing countries is equally problematic, but for slightly different reasons. The main winners from free trade agreements in these countries are TNCs and other exporting labour-intensive firms located in these countries. These firms are usually able to increase the number of jobs. Potentially, the pressure of social clauses for improved enforcement of domestic laws can also contribute to better working conditions. but under NAALC there is no incentive to improve the content of

---

[68] Compa (2001) para 243.

domestic laws. Only the newer FTAs provide a limited recognition of higher ILO core standards. Under NAALC there is not even a formal commitment, of the kind in newer FTAs, against lowering labour standards in order to attract trade and investment. To date, the improvements in domestic enforcement have been marginal, but the NAALC procedures have increased international labour solidarity and, in some cases, have enhanced the status and capacity of trade unions in the developing countries. Against this, the imposition of fines or withdrawal of benefits for non-compliance is feared as potentially counter-productive if it causes job losses in the very sectors in which workers are most abused.

The EU's partnership agreements provide a more balanced approach than NAALC and newer FTAs. The EU rewards countries for complying with ILO core standards, and places the emphasis not on possibly destructive sanctions but instead on capacity-building, education and training and other positive co-operative activities that will raise labour standards at the same time as expanding the economies and job markets in developing countries. Conversely, access to the markets of developing countries also benefits firms and workers in the EU.

6

The WTO and Social Clauses

1. Introduction
2. Reconciling social clauses with WTO Agreements
3. The principle of non-discrimination
4. An illustration: social labelling
5. Article XX exceptions
6. Other mechanisms for social clauses?
7. The integration of developing countries
8. Would WTO sanctions work?

1. Introduction

Attempts to integrate labour rights into the multilateral world trading and financial systems have so far failed.[1] A direct link between international trade and labour conditions was recognised in Article 7 of the draft Charter of the International Trade Organisation (ITO) signed in Havana in 1948 by 53 countries:

> [T]he members recognise that . . . unfair labour conditions, particularly in production for export, create difficulties in international trade, and accordingly, each member state shall take whatever action may be appropriate and feasible to eliminate such conditions within its territory.[2]

Although the Havana Charter was never ratified and the ITO was stillborn, Article 7 of the draft Charter proved to be influential in post-war trade agreements, such as the International Sugar Agreement of 1953 under which the parties agreed that:

---

[1] For a discussion of social clauses in international investment agreements and the failed MAI, see ch 2, above.

[2] This wording was influenced by recommendations of an ILO Technical Conference in 1937: Charnovitz (1987) at 567.

in order to avoid the depression of living standards and the introduction of unfair competitive conditions in world trade, they will seek the maintenance of fair labour standards in the sugar industry.

Similar multilateral agreements were concluded in the tin, cocoa and rubber industries.

No specific provision relating to labour standards was made in the General Agreement on Tariffs and Trade (GATT 1947), an inter-governmental treaty incorporating the commercial policy chapter of the Havana Charter. The only exception is Article XX(e) which allows prohibition on the import of products of prison labour. The GATT 1994, updating the 1947 treaty (Box 6.2) made no changes in this or other respects. We shall see that attempts to interpret the GATT so as to permit trade measures for non-observance of labour standards are likely to collide with the non-discrimination principles on which the GATT is based. Moreover, the general exceptions and safeguards provisions of the GATT do not appear to be apt to allow trade measures for breach of labour standards. An explicit amendment to the GATT would be required, but there is no political consensus to bring this about.

During the Tokyo Round of multilateral trade negotiations (1973–79) the United States raised the issue of labour standards, but failed to gain support.[3] The reciprocal allegations between developed and developing countries of social dumping and protectionism surfaced again during the Uruguay Round (1986–94). The United States requested that a working group be formed to study the issue. Although this had the support of the EU, the Nordic countries, Switzerland, Canada, New Zealand, some Eastern European countries and Japan, no agreement could be reached.[4] The issue was again put on the agenda at the WTO ministerial conference in Singapore in 1996 by the United States, France and Canada. The Ministerial Declaration at the end of that conference, while renewing the commitment 'to observance of internationally recognised core standards', said that the ILO 'is the competent body to set and deal with these standards'. The Ministers in effect accepted the position of the developing countries, and rejected 'the use of labour standards for protectionist purposes.' They stated that ' the comparative advantage of countries, particularly low-wage developing countries, must in no way be put into question.' The approach of the WTO ministers was echoed in paragraph 5 of the ILO Declaration of Fundamental Principles and Rights at Work (1998) (chapter 2, above). Attempts led by the United States to revive the issue at the Seattle (1999), Doha (2001) and Cancun (2003) Ministerial Conferences also failed.

---

[3] Cappuyns (1998) at 666.
[4] Van Roozendaal (2002) at 17.

As we have seen (chapter 2, above) Article 33 of the ILO Constitution authorises 'action', possibly including economic sanctions, against Member States that fail to observe their obligations. A controversial issue is whether such sanctions would be compatible with the obligations undertaken by WTO Member States. Similarly, WTO rules throw into doubt the legality of unilateral trade sanctions under the US GSP and EU GSP (chapter 4, above). This chapter examines these complex, and as yet unresolved issues, and discusses the limits of WTO institutions as potential protectors of labour rights.

Box 6.1

WORLD TRADE ORGANISATION (WTO)

- Came into being 1 January 1995 under Marrakesh Agreement (15 April 1994) concluding the Uruguay Round of Multilateral Trade Negotiations.
- Has 147 members accounting for 97 percent of world trade, compared to 15 members in 1947; any government acting on behalf of a separate customs territory possessing full autonomy in the conduct of its external commercial relations (eg EU, Hong Kong) may accede to the GATT.
- Functions include administering WTO agreements (Box 6.2), acting as forum for negotiations, reviewing national trade policies, assisting developing countries' trade policies through technical assistance, co-operating with other international organisations.
- Decisions are made by entire membership, usually by consensus.
- Top-level decision-making body is the Ministerial Conference, which meets every two years; between conferences the General Council with representatives of all members meets several times a year, acting as well as the Trade Policy Review Body (TRB) and Disputes Settlement Body (DSB).
- Secretariat based in Geneva.
- Dispute Settlement Understanding (DSU) sets out unified rules for disputes under all WTO agreements; a stage-by-stage procedure allows for rulings by panel of experts, with appeal on legal grounds to Appellate Body (AB); schemes for surveillance of implementation, and for payment of compensation and suspension of concessions as 'temporary measures'.

Website: *http://www.wto.org*

Box 6.2

GUIDE TO THE WTO AGREEMENTS

These are annexed to the Marrakesh Agreement establishing the WTO (Box 6.1).

General Agreement on Tariffs and Trade 1994 (GATT 1994)

This includes GATT 1947 as amended, with annexes (based on the commercial policy chapter of the draft Havana Charter establishing the International Trade Organisation 1947); provisions of legal instruments that entered into force under GATT 1947 before 1 January 1995; and understandings (Annex 1A).

Other sources of GATT law include side agreements/codes; decisions and waivers adopted by the CONTRACTING PARTIES [upper case characters are used when referring to decisions taken multilaterally]; and jurisprudence of GATT panels.

General Agreement on Trade in Services (GATS)

This includes general principles (eg most-favoured nation) affecting all trade in services, and specific commitments (eg national treatment) that apply only to service sectors listed in a member's schedule. There is an understanding that periodic negotiations will be undertaken progressively to liberalise trade in services. The attachments set out sector-specific disciplines and ministerial decisions (Annex 1B).

Agreement on Trade-Related Aspects of Intellectual Property Rights (TRIPS)

This includes basic principles (eg most-favoured nation and national treatment), sets out standards concerning the availability, scope and use of intellectual property rights, provisions relating to their enforcement, and on dispute prevention and settlement (Annex 1C).

Agreement on Technical Barriers to Trade (TBT)

This is designed to ensure that technical regulations are not used to create unnecessary obstacles to trade. Such regulations must not be more trade-restrictive than necessary to fulfil a legitimate objective (Annex 1A).

Understanding on Rules and Procedures Governing the Settlement of Disputes (DSU)

The common dispute settlement mechanism for all WTO agreements (Annex 2).

Trade Policy Review Mechanism (TPRM)

An instrument for the surveillance of members' trade policies (Annex 3).

Plurilateral Trade Agreements

Tokyo Round agreements (on civil aircraft, government procurement, dairy and bovine meat products) that were not multilateralised in the Uruguay Round. Unlike all the other agreements, which are binding on all WTO members, the plurilateral agreements are binding only on the signatories (Annex 4).

2. Reconciling social clauses with WTO Agreements

As noted earlier, the only explicit reference to labour standards in the WTO agreements is Article XX(e) of GATT 1947 allowing a prohibition on imports made with prison labour (below). However, it has been argued that various clauses in the GATT 1947 could be interpreted so as to permit the imposition of barriers on goods where labour standards have been violated. These are Article VI (anti-dumping), Article XIX (safeguards), Article XX (general exceptions), Article XXIII (nullification and impairment), Article XXIV (customs unions and free trade areas) of GATT, and Article XIII of the WTO (Marrakesh) Agreement (opt-out provision).

In approaching these arguments, one must remember the 'general rule of interpretation' under the Vienna Convention on the Law of Treaties (VCLT). The WTO agreements are treaties which are to be interpreted ' in good faith in accordance with the ordinary meaning to be given to the terms of the treaty in their context and in the light of its object and purposes.'[5] The main purposes are to be found in the first recital in the preamble to the Marrakesh Agreement which states that the parties recognise—

> ... that their relations in the field of trade and economic endeavour should be conducted with a view to raising standards of living, ensuring full employment and a large and steadily growing volume of real income and effective demand, and expanding the production of and trade in goods and services, while allowing for the optimal use of the world's resources, in accordance with the objective of sustainable development, seeking both to protect and preserve the environment and to enhance the means for doing so in a manner consistent with their respective needs and concerns at different levels of economic development ...

---

[5] VCLT, Art 31.1, codifying the customary rules of interpretation. The DSU provides that that the WTO agreements may be 'clarif[ied] ... in accordance with the customary rules of interpretation of public international law', DSU, Art 3.2.

It is striking that while environmental concerns are specifically mentioned in this preamble, those relating to human resources are not. There are similarities between environmental and labour issues. Both involve non-trade values, and both may be relevant to sustainable development. But there are also differences. Labour abuses do not give rise to pollution of the global commons nor to physical cross-border externalities. Charnovitz argues that there is a non-physical cross-border externality from low labour standards that may harm other countries.[6] This echoes the words of the Treaty of Versailles, that 'the failure of any nation to adopt humane conditions of labour is an obstacle in the way of other nations which desire to improve the conditions in their own countries,'[7] and can be supported by research which suggests that the level of ratification of ILO conventions depends critically on the level of ratifications by countries at comparable levels of development.[8] Countries see low labour standards in their peer countries as harmful to their own interests.

WTO Disputes Panels have not to date adopted interpretations which would allow non-physical externalities to justify trade conditionality, preferring to give a broad meaning to the 'physical' properties of a product and to recognise that the competitive price may depend on customer tastes and habits (below). Even if non-physical externalities were admitted, and the conditionality imposed could be shown to be necessary and proportionate, it would be extremely difficult in practice to quantify the 'harm' or injury sustained by country A as a result of low labour standards in country B. There is rarely a simple cause-and-effect relation between labour standards and costs (chapter 1, above).

Another relevant principle of interpretation is that account must be taken of 'any relevant rules of international law applicable in the relations between the parties.'[9] ILO conventions are treaties binding only on those states that have ratified them; a state must consent to being bound and where it does so it is agreeing to become subject to the ILO's supervisory mechanisms, not to those of the WTO. As we have seen (chapter 2, Box 2.4, above), in the case of Mynamar it was ILO, not the WTO, which recommended sanctions. For the WTO to give effect to ILO conventions, it would need to be shown that these have become part of customary international law, binding on all WTO Members. This, as we saw in chapter 2, is unlikely to be accepted, except arguably in respect of slavery and forced labour. Although the GATT is not to be read in isolation from the rules of international law, it seems that neither ILO conventions nor customary international law provide a sure basis for the interpretation of the WTO agreements.

---

[6] Charnovitz (1994) at 22.
[7] Treaty of Versailles, Part XIII, s 1 (the original ILO Constitution).
[8] Ch 2, above, citing Chau and Kanbur (2001).
[9] VCLT, Art 31.3(c).

A final relevant consideration when interpreting the WTO agreements is the preparatory work of the treaty and the circumstances of its conclusion. This is relevant only to confirm the meaning resulting from the general rules of interpretation (above), or where the meaning resulting from that interpretation is either ambiguous or obscure or leads to a manifestly absurd or unreasonable result.[10] Research by Alben[11] into the legislative history of the ITO and GATT shows quite clearly that the drafters did not approach labour standards from the contemporary human rights perspective. Although labour standards played a significant role in the negotiations for the ITO, the negotiators were primarily concerned with the effect of these standards on the costs of production. Article 7 of the draft Havana Charter (above) refers to 'unfair labour conditions' not to human rights. In the context of the aim of securing full employment, and with an express linkage between labour standards and productivity, Alben concludes that 'wage policy was at the heart of the ITO's conception of labour standards.'[12] GATT was the only part of the ITO agreement left standing but, Alben argues, this does not mean that there was a wholesale rejection of labour standards in a multilateral trade agreement. It was intended that various provisions of GATT 1947, such as Article XIX (safeguards) and XX (general exceptions) might be used where countries faced unfair competition because of lower labour standards. These countries could seek to justify safeguards when faced by a surge of imports resulting from the exploitation of cheap labour, and use the dispute settlement provisions to compel the offending party to halt the practices causing trade distortions. In subsequent negotiations,[13] in particular concerning the accession of Japan to the GATT in 1953, the focus was on safeguards and provisions to prevent the sudden influx of cheap goods produced with low labour standards.

This legislative history makes it difficult to accommodate labour rights that do not directly affect production costs, when interpreting the WTO agreements. Those who advocate a wider enforcement of labour rights as human rights, are likely to be frustrated by the terms of the WTO agreements.

3. The principle of non-discrimination

Any attempt to make trade conditional upon observance of labour standards risks falling foul of two important principles of international economic law: Most Favoured Nation (MFN) and National Treatment (NT). The MFN

[10] VCLT Art 32.
[11] Alben (2001).
[12] Alben (2001) at 1431.
[13] Alben (2001) at 1432–40.

principle has been a cornerstone of trade law for many centuries. In essence it is an obligation of non-discrimination between 'like' products. Country A must treat country B or its citizens at least as favourably as country A's most-favoured trading partner. If country A imposes a condition that goods produced in country B may be imported only if B observes certain labour standards, while granting unconditional access to like goods from country C, the principle is breached. The rationale of MFN is both economic and political—non-discrimination allows the market to work freely without regard to the origin of goods, it minimises the costs of making special rules for certain countries and the costs of enforcing those rules. The principle is a safeguard against politically-motivated, short-term policies that exclude certain nations from the benefits of the world trading system. The more trade liberalisation occurs, the greater the multiplier effect of MFN in bringing about economic growth which in turn should lead to the raising of living standards.

Most scholars agree that the principle does not form a part of customary international law.[14] The obligation applies only where a treaty obligation requires it. In the absence of a treaty obligation, a sovereign state is free to treat nations differently depending upon their observance of labour rights. The most significant treaty obligation is that imposed by membership of the WTO. The MFN principle is enshrined in Article I.1 of the GATT in relation to imports and exports of goods:

> . . . any advantage, favour, privilege or immunity granted by any contracting party to any product originating in or destined for any other country shall be accorded immediately and unconditionally to the *like product* originating in or destined for the territories of all other contracting parties (emphasis added).

A similar provision in relation to services is to be found in GATS, Article II. Other bilateral and multilateral treaties apply it to trade in services by foreign citizens and to freedom of establishment, allowing foreign businesses to set up offices in the country.

National Treatment is the second relevant principle, and is enshrined in Article III of GATT. Article III.2 prevents fiscal measures against imported products in excess of those applied to domestic producers. Article III.4 provides that

> The products of the territory of any contracting party imported into the territory of any other contracting party shall be accorded treatment *no less favourable* than that accorded to *like products* of national origin in respect of all laws, regulations and requirements affecting their internal sale, offering for sale, purchase, transportation, distribution or use . . . (emphasis added).

---

[14] Jackson (2000) at 158.

In the GATS,[15] NT is a specific commitment, applying to services listed in each Member's schedule. It is defined as treatment no less favourable than that applied to like domestic services and service providers. Country A could not require a firm based in country B to observe higher labour standards for workers posted from A to B than those provided for by the domestic law of A for its own workers. In addition to NT, the GATS has a market access obligation.[16] Six types of market access restrictions are prohibited, including the number of natural persons who may be employed and the type of legal entity (eg a branch or subsidiary) through which a service supplier is permitted to provide a service.[17]

4. An illustration: social labelling

The application of the MFN and NT principles may be illustrated by the controversial issue as to whether they preclude government-sponsored social labelling initiatives. We saw in chapter 3 that social labels and codes of conduct have become increasingly popular as voluntary means of improving labour standards. Most of the sponsors of social labels are NGOs. Their schemes are not directly subject to WTO rules, but Members must not require or encourage NGOs or local government bodies within their territories to act in a manner inconsistent with Article 2 of the Agreement on Technical Barriers to Trade (TBT) (discussed below). But some governments, such as that of Belgium,[18] have responded to pressures to promote 'socially responsible production' by awarding labels to products which satisfy certain criteria of social responsibility (eg compliance with ILO core conventions). In France and several other countries, local governments allocate public resources to social labelling and fair trade initiatives. The European Parliament has strongly supported such government-sponsored schemes.[19] What is their legality under WTO rules? And even if they are lawful (which is arguable), could a compulsory social labelling scheme ever survive WTO scrutiny?

Government-sponsored or mandatory schemes would generally raise the question of the scope of Article III of GATT (above). The purpose of this provision is to provide equality of competitive conditions for imported products

---

[15] GATS, Art XVII.

[16] GATS, Art XVI.

[17] The other restrictions are the number of service providers allowed, the value of transactions or assets, the total quantity of services or output and the participation of foreign capital in terms of limits on foreign equity or the absolute value of foreign investment. There are complex provisions for the application of these special commitments: see Jackson (2000) at 306–10; Hoekman and Kostecki (2001) at 250–65.

[18] Lopez-Hurtado (2002) at 723.

[19] EP Resolution, 13 January 1999.

in relation to domestic products. But not all measures that differentiate between like products will violate the Article, only those that are designed to afford protection to domestic products. Most social labelling schemes do not openly differentiate between products on grounds of national origin (*de jure* discrimination), but on criteria related to the *process* of production (eg use of child or forced labour). The latter could amount to *de facto* discrimination.

The key issues are first whether the imported and domestic goods are 'like products', and secondly whether the imported product has been accorded 'no less favourable treatment' than the domestic one. Could one argue that a football produced by child labour in country A is not 'like' a football produced in country B by adult labour? In the *EC-Asbestos* case,[20] the first in which the WTO Appellate Body examined the meaning of the term 'like' in the context of Article III.4, it concluded that the determination of the 'likeness' of two products involves an examination of the nature and extent of the competitive relationship between and among producers. The Appellate Body said that the general criteria to be applied include the properties, nature and quality of the products; the end-uses of the product; consumers' tastes and habits in respect of the products; and the tariff classification of the products. This list is not exhaustive. In the *EC-Asbestos* case, the Appellate Body decided that products containing chrystolite asbestos fibres were not 'like' products containing PVA, cellulose and glass fibres because chrystolite asbestos is a known carcinogen. Consequently the EC restrictions on asbestos products did not violate Article III.4. The significance of this decision for labour rights conditionality is that evidence relating to health risks was considered relevant. Moreover consumer tastes and habits—presumably including sensitivity towards the social conditions under which products are produced—was also recognised as a valid criterion.[21] But the Appellate Body did not go so far as to consider evidence of non-physical properties as a separate criterion. The question remains an open one. One straw in the wind is the view of a GATT panel in the *Tuna I* and *Tuna II*[22] cases that measures which refer to the processes and methods of production cannot fall under Article III, but only under Article XI (discussed below). Against this, in the *Korea-Beef* case[23] the WTO Appellate Body said that Article

---

[20] *European Communities–Measures Affecting Asbestos and Asbestos-containing products,* Report of the Appellate Body, WT/DS135/AB/R, 12 March 2001.

[21] Lopez-Hurtado (2003) at 729; Blackett (2002) at 384–87 argues that a relevant factor is that the measures were loosely based on ILO C162 concerning the use of asbestos; but it is to be noted that France, the country imposing the ban, had not ratified this convention.

[22] *United State–Restrictions in Imports of Tuna,* Report of the GATT Panel (unadopted), 35 ILM, 1993, 1598–623 (*Tuna I*) para 5.11; *United States–Restrictions on Imports of Tuna,* Report of the GATT Panel (unadopted) 33 ILM, 1994, 839–99 (*Tuna II*) para 5.8.

[23] *Korea–Measures Affecting Imports of Fresh, Chilled and Frozen Beef,* Report of the Appellate Body WT/DS161/AB/R,WT/DS169/AB/R, 10 January 2001.

III.4 applies to all governmental requirements and does not refer only to the physical characteristics of a product.

The second requirement of Article III.4 is that the treatment of the imported product must be 'no less favourable' than that accorded to the domestic product. In the *Korea-Beef* case the Appellate Body said that this occurs if a government intervention modifies the conditions of competition in the relevant market to the detriment of the imported product. But in the *EC-Asbestos* case[24] the Appellate body made it clear that a government may draw distinctions between 'like' products without for this reason alone according imported products less favourable treatment than like domestic products. This means that if a social labelling measure were challenged, a disputes panel would have to evaluate whether the 'design, the architecture, and the revealing structures' of the measure affects the equality of competitive opportunities between imported and domestic products.[25]

Even if a government-backed social label survives examination under Article III.4 of GATT, it faces the further obstacle of the Agreement on Technical Barriers to Trade (TBT).[26] This is aimed at protectionist measures which are disguised as 'technical standards'. No less favourable treatment must be accorded to imported goods than domestic goods in respect of such standards, and technical regulations must not be adopted or applied 'with a view to or with the effect of creating unnecessary obstacles to international trade.'[27] The regulations must be no more trade-restrictive 'than necessary to fulfil a legitimate objective taking account of the risks non-fulfilment would create.'[28] A non-exhaustive list of 'legitimate objectives' is provided: national security, prevention of deceptive practices, protection of human health or safety, animal or plant life or health, or the environment. There is no mention of labour rights, but arguably regulations that establish a mandatory social labelling scheme in order to promote the protection of core labour standards would be treated as a 'legitimate objective.'[29] The key question then would be whether the regulation was 'necessary' to achieve that objective. This may be difficult to

---

[24] *EC–Asbestos*, para 100.

[25] Lopez-Hurtado (2003) at 728–29.

[26] TBT, Art 3 requires WTO Members to take reasonable measures to ensure compliance by their local government or non-governmental organisations with the provisions of Art 2, and they must not require or encourage such bodies to act in a manner inconsistent with those provisions. Art 4 requires Members to ensure compliance with a Code of Good Practice for the Preparation, Adoption and Application of Standards (annex 3). This is concerned with procedures under which standards are developed and their transparency, and not with the substantive standards.

[27] TBT, Art 2.2.

[28] TBT, Art 2.2.

[29] Social labels to promote ILO standards do not benefit from the presumption in TBT, Art 2.5 that technical regulations in accordance with relevant international standards do not create unnecessary obstacles to trade, because this objective is not explicitly stated in Art 2.2.

prove, as we shall see later in relation to Article XX of GATT (general exceptions) which also requires necessity.[30]

A further obstacle to is to be found in Article XI GATT which bars Members from imposing non-tariff barriers to trade such as export or import quotas, licensing restrictions and embargoes, which are used to inhibit the importation of competing products. An example of an unlawful labelling requirement would be the case where a country required canned foods to have labels in the language of that country and no other, so that the producer loses economies of scale because different labels are needed for different markets.[31] In the *Tuna I* case, Mexico challenged US legislation that created a voluntary labelling standard for any tuna products exported from, or offered for sale in the US. The aim of the legislation was to restrict the importation of tuna caught in a part of the Pacific Ocean where techniques known to harm or kill dolphins were used. A GATT Disputes Panel—which looked at the question solely under Article XI and not Article III—found that the 'Dolphin Safe' label did not make the right to sell tuna or tuna products conditional upon the use of certain harvesting methods. It simply gave consumers a free choice. It did not discriminate on grounds of national origin because the regulations applied to all countries whose boats fished in that part of the Ocean. This favourable conclusion under Article XI does not, however, rule out the possibility that a voluntary government-sponsored social label would fail to meet the somewhat different requirements of Article III.4 (above), or those of the TBT Agreement (above).[32]

Whilst it may be argued that a voluntary label resulting from a government regulation does not necessarily lead to inequality of competition between imported and domestic products (but simply recognises consumer tastes), this cannot be said of compulsory labelling schemes which are, therefore, more likely to fall foul of Articles I, III and XI of GATT and also the TBT.

In summary, it can be seen that there is much scope for argument whether social considerations, in particular the observance of labour standards, will in future influence the interpretation of matters such as the likeness of two products, the less favourable treatment of imported products compared to domestic ones, and whether government-sponsored social labels are legitimate.

---

[30] The TBT has no equivalent to Art XX GATT, but similar issues arise under TBT, Art 2.2.
[31] Jackson (2000) at 155.
[32] Lopez-Hurtado (2003) 740.

5. Article XX exceptions

Where a trade measure violates GATT obligations, it may be possible to rely on one of the 'general exceptions' set out in Article XX GATT. Three of these are relevant to labour rights: measures ' necessary to protect public morals' (Article XX(a)), 'necessary to protect human, animal or plant life or health' (Article XX(b)), and 'relating to the products of prison labour' (Article XX(e)). The latter is the least problematic, reflecting as it does national provisions since the 1890s which prohibited imports made by 'convict' labour.[33] At the Havana ITO Conference in 1947 the United States sought to have included other 'involuntary' forms of labour but this was unsuccessful, as was the United States' proposal to include in ILO C.105 a prohibition on international trade in goods produced by forced or compulsory labour. The US imposed a ban on imports of low-sulphur coal from apartheid South Africa in 1974 because this was produced by indentured (ie forced) labour; this induced the apartheid government to repeal the relevant penal sanctions so as to gain access to US markets. This legislative history might influence a WTO disputes panel to place a narrow interpretation on 'prison' labour, although there is no logical reason to exclude products of other forms of forced labour, as defined in ILO conventions.[34] In the *Hormones* case the Appellate Body made it clear that the mere fact that these are stated to be 'exceptions' does not create a presumption in favour of a narrow interpretation.[35]

The more likely heading under which to justify bans on products of slave, forced or compulsory labour is Article XX(a) (public morals). This exception is potentially broad, but the legislative history of the GATT discussed earlier, indicates that the drafters were primarily concerned with the costs of production rather than with core labour rights. Those who advocate a broad interpretation place heavy reliance on the Appellate Body's statement in the *Shrimp/Turtle I* case, when interpreting the exception in Article XX(g) relating to conservation of natural resources, that the exception must be read 'in the light of contemporary concerns of the community of nations about the protection and conservation of the environment'.[36] Similar concerns about

---

[33] Charnovitz (1987) 569–70.

[34] In 1997 the US legislation banning the importation of products made with convict or forced labour was extended to cover indentured child labour. Arguably this is outside the scope of Art XX(e) but could be justified under XX(a) (public morals): see Charnovitz (1998) at 705.

[35] *EC Measures Concerning Meat and Meat Products (Hormones)*, WTO Appellate Body Report, WT/DS26/AB/R, 16 January 1998 (*Hormones*).

[36] *United States–Import Prohibition of Certain Shrimp and Shrimp Products*, WTO Appellate Body Report, WT/DS58/AB/R, 12 October 1998 (*Shrimp/Turtle I*); *United States—Import Prohibitions on Certain Shrimp and Shrimp Products*, WTO Appellate Body, WT/DS58/AB/RW, 22 October 2001 (*Shrimp/Turtle II*).

human resources would certainly include the conventions on slavery, forced and compulsory labour, and the worst forms of child labour (chapter 2, above). Charnovitz argues that only trade sanctions based on international, as distinct from national, views of morality should be recognised.[37] Arguably, the other ILO 'core' conventions (on freedom of association and collective bargaining, and discrimination), should also qualify on this evolutionary approach to 'public morals'. The ILO conventions on health and safety at work would not fall under this rubric but must be regarded as highly relevant to the interpretation of Article XX(b) (life and health).[38] But it would be the WTO, not the ILO, which would be the ultimate arbiter of this issue.

There are, however, a number of obstacles to the application of Article XX to labour rights. One is the jurisdictional question whether these exceptions are limited to protecting domestic public morals and life, or can be interpreted to allow measures targeted at violations of labour rights in other countries. Does public morality stop at the border? This is still an open question. In the *Shrimp/Turtle I* case, the United States had placed an embargo on certain shrimp or shrimp products for the purpose of protecting endangered sea turtles. The Appellate Body left open the question whether there is an implied jurisdictional limitation in Article XX(g), but found that the migratory nature of sea turtles created a sufficient nexus between the turtles and the United States. The implications of this finding for Article XX(a) and (b) are uncertain. Would it need to be shown that the low labour standards in the targeted country have substantial effects in the importing state? The Appellate Body pointed out that extra-territorial measures were not in themselves ruled out, indeed that interpretation 'would render most, if not all, the specific exceptions inutile.'[39] This is certainly the case with prison labour.[40] The real issue is whether a state can show a legitimate interest in the observance of international labour standards. This comes back to the question whether these standards are common concerns of the community of nations, as reflected in ILO core conventions (above). It is also relevant to know whether there are domestic labour laws which parallel the standards being demanded of the target country.[41]

Another potential obstacle is that Article XX(a) and (b) both require the measures to be 'necessary' to promote public morals or human life. The exception does not apply if there is a reasonably available alternative to trade

---

[37] Charnovitz (1998) at 73–74; cf the *Asbestos* case where the Appellate Body (para 168) said that 'WTO members have the right to determine the level of protection of health that they consider appropriate in a given situation.'

[38] Blackett (2002) at 384–87 argues that health and safety laws are a concrete embodiment of the 'right to life' in various human rights conventions.

[39] *Shrimp/Turtle I*, para 131.

[40] *Tuna-Dolphin II*.

[41] *Tuna-Dolphin I*.

measures. This has limited the effectiveness of Article XX(b) in relation to environmental protection. For example, US efforts to control smog-causing contamination by gasoline products was held not to justify trade measures because less trade-restrictive alternatives were available and had not been pursued.[42] In relation to human rights Cleveland gives the telling example of a ban on products made with exploitative child labour. 'The targeted state could argue that an available, less trade restrictive measure, such as foreign assistance to improve educational opportunities, would be equally, if not more, effective.'[43]

The Article XX(e) prison labour exception is not limited by a necessity requirement. It simply requires the measure to be 'relating to' the products of prison labour. In the *Shrimp/Turtle I* case, the Appellate Body, construing the words 'relating to' in Article XX(g) (conservation), held that the import restriction could not be 'disproportionately wide in its scope in relation to the policy objectives' which in this case was the protection and conservation of sea turtle species. The means used must be reasonably related to the ends. Cleveland argues from this that a 'tailored' sanction, which directly relates the traded product to a human rights abuse (eg carpets made with exploitative child labour) would be permitted, but not a 'semi-tailored' sanction which imposes a general ban on goods which do not directly cause the human rights violation.[44]

Even if these obstacles can be surmounted, the trade measure must also satisfy the non-discrimination requirements of the opening paragraph of Article XX (called the *chapeau*). This tries to prevent the use of the exceptions to justify disguised trade protectionism by making them subject to the proviso that 'such measures are not applied in a manner which would constitute a means of arbitrary or unjustifiable discrimination between countries where the same conditions prevail, or a disguised restriction on international trade . . . .' The *chapeau* amounts to a 'soft' version of the MFN and NT obligations to the extent necessary to promote the stated legitimate aims.[45] GATT panels and the Appellate Body have applied the *chapeau* stringently, requiring the interference with free trade to be proportional to the legitimate interest being pursued and the benefit likely to result from the measure (eg all imports could not be banned to prevent some products of child labour).[46] The restrictions must not be imposed in a manner which would constitute arbitrary or unjustifiable discrimination between countries where the same conditions

---

[42] *United States–Standards for Reformulated and Conventional Gasoline*, WTO Disputes Panel Report, WT/DS2R, 29 January 1996, as modified by Appellate Body in *Reformulated Gasoline*, WT/DS2/9, adopted 20 May 1996.

[43] Cleveland (2002) at 162.

[44] Cleveland (2002) at 140–45.

[45] Jackson (2000) at 234.

[46] Cleveland (2002) at 155–79.

prevail (below). In principle, this might involve an evaluation of the labour standards record of all comparable WTO members (including the State imposing the restriction), and there would need to be agreement on the criteria for such an evaluation.[47]

6. Other mechanisms for social clauses?

A number of other provisions of the GATT have been suggested as means of justifying social clauses. These share in common the requirement that some 'injury' to the domestic industry from the product sold must be demonstrated. For example, it has been argued that the anti-dumping provisions of Article VI could be extended to 'social dumping' and its corrollary social subsidisation. 'Dumping' is the practice by which the products of one country are introduced into the commerce of another country at less than the 'normal value' of the products. It is barred under Article VI GATT 'if it causes or threatens material injury to an established industry in the territory of a contracting party or materially retards the establishment of a domestic industry.' In chapter 1 a number of general reasons, both empirical and theoretical, were put forward for rejecting the concept of 'social dumping'. As a matter of interpretation of GATT it would be difficult to sustain the argument that Article VI is apt to cover low labour standards. The legislative history shows that the drafters considered the phenomenon of 'social dumping' but decided to cover only price dumping.[48] The 1994 Agreement on Implementation of Article VI contains detailed provisions on the meaning of 'fair value' which simply do not fit when one is talking about labour rights abuses, many of which have a neutral impact on prices. Moreover the Agreement requires that 'special regard must be given by developed country Members to the special situation of developing country Members when considering the application of anti-dumping measures . . .'[49] The close connection between the level of development and the implementation of labour standards (chapter 2, above) makes this a further obstacle to applying the anti-dumping provisions. Similar considerations would apply to any attempt to invoke the 1994 Agreement on Subsidies and Countervailing Measures.[50]

Another suggested approach is under Article XIX GATT (safeguards), which allows for the temporary suspension of GATT obligations, where imports of a

---

[47] Quershi (1996) at 38. This principle is, however, open to interpretation: see the *India-GSP* case, discussed below.

[48] Blackett (1999) at 48.

[49] Marrakesh Agreement Establishing the WTO, Annex 1A, Agreement on implementation of Art VI GATT 1994, Art XV. These obligations are elucidated in the Anti-Dumping Agreement and the Agreement on Safeguards.

[50] Agreement on Subsidies and Countervailing Measures; see Blackett (1999) at 52–56.

product are increasing as a result both of 'unforeseen developments' *and* of GATT obligations. The domestic producers of competitive products must be seriously injured (or threatened with such injury), *and* this injury or threat must be caused by the increased imports. While the anti-dumping and subsidisation provisions are basically aimed at trade that is 'unfair', the safeguards provision allows a state to protect its industries against imports that are perfectly 'fair'—in the sense of being untainted by illegal dumping or subsidies—but which cause cause unreasonable burdens of adjustment.[51] Even if, say, there is an 'unforeseen' series of labour rights abuses in the exporting country, similar problems to those under Article VI would arise in relation to Article XIX. It would be difficult to establish that the combination of these developments and GATT obligations caused an increase in imports and that this surge caused serious injury to domestic producers.

Finally, mention must be made of the opt-out clause. Article XXXV of GATT allowed either a prior Member or new Member to opt out of a relationship with the other at one time only. This was introduced in 1947 when the voting requirement to admit a new Member was reduced from unanimity to two-thirds. This opt-out clause was sometimes used for political reasons related in part to labour conditions, such as India's refusal to trade with apartheid South Africa.[52] Article XIII of the Marrakesh Agreement continues the opt-out clause between WTO Members at the time one or the other first enters the agreement, and it applies to all of the multilateral agreements in Annex 1 and 2 of the WTO agreement.[53] In theory, this would allow a Member to opt-out because of objections to low labour standards in a prior or new Member. In practice this has not occurred.

7. The integration of developing countries

The non-discrimination principles in the WTO agreements are facially neutral, but their impact can be indirectly discriminatory on weak non-industrial economies. This concern was first expressed in a demand for better than MFN access to the markets of rich countries. Such preferences were recognised by the imperial powers in particular the United Kingdom and France in respect of their colonies and dependencies. As developing countries won independence they sought exemptions from GATT rules. They argued that they should be allowed to impose trade barriers in order to improve their terms of trade, and to protect their infant industries, so that they could develop rapidly.

---

[51] Jackson (2000) at 177–78.
[52] Jackson (2000) at 61.
[53] Art XIII allows for continuation of the opt-outs for the GATT.

Article XVIII of GATT 1947 recognised the need of developing countries for infant industry protection, and in 1954–55 it was modified to allow some restrictive measures to protect their balance of payments. However, it was not until 1964, following the formation of the UNCTAD, and a committee on Trade and Development in the GATT, that the demand backed by a bloc of developing countries in the UN for 'special and differential treatment' (S & D) for developing countries came to the fore. A new Part IV of the GATT on Trade and Development was adopted in 1965, recognising the notion of non-reciprocity for developing countries.[54] In 1971, GATT granted a ten-year waiver allowing industrial countries to establish their own discretionary Generalised Systems of Preferences (GSP) to grant trade preferences on a non-reciprocal basis, provided that these benefited all 'developing countries'. In 1979, the GATT Contracting Parties adopted a Decision, known as the Enabling Clause, which allowed the indefinite continuation of GSP.[55] This Decision has been carried over into the WTO as part of GATT 1994. Although the requirements to qualify as a 'developing country' were not defined, the Enabling Clause appears to sanction a 'graduation' principle. This in effect allows unilateral or bilateral measures to differentiate between countries based on their levels of development, as is the case in EC Council Regulation 2501/2001 (see chapter 4). The aim is that the more successful developing countries should lose their preferences and be integrated back into the WTO/GATT system with reciprocal obligations.

The extent to which the Enabling Clause permits preferences for observing core labour standards is an open question. In 2003, India complained under the disputes settlement procedures against the special incentive arrangements in EC Council Regulation 2501/2001 (chapter 4, above). The complaint was directed at the Regulation's special arrangements to combat drug production and drug trafficking. Initially, India also complained about the special incentive arrangements relating to protection of the environment and labour rights. The last two complaints were withdrawn, but India reserved its right to raise them in the future should the EU apply them in a manner detrimental to India's interests. The decision of the Appellate Body (AB) in relation to the validity of the drugs arrangements, gives some pointers as to how a WTO disputes panel might approach the protection of core labour rights in future.

The drugs arrangements give preferences to products being developed in substitution for drugs by listed countries in the Andean region. The gist of

---

[54] GATT, Art XXXVI.8.

[55] Declaration on Differential and More Favourable Treatment. Reciprocity and Fuller Participation of Developing Countries. Decision of 28 November 1979, L4901 of 3 December 1979, GATT BISD Supp 203 (1980). The scope and nature of the Declaration is controversial: see Jackson (2000) at 323–24, Hoekman and Kostecki (2001) at 388.

India's complaint was that this preferential treatment violated the Most Favoured Nation principle contained in Article 1.1 of GATT 1994 (see above), and was not justified under the Enabling Clause, para.1 of which states:

> Notwithstanding the provisions of Art.1 of the General Agreement, contracting parties may accord differential treatment and more favourable treatment to developing countries, without according such treatment to other contracting parties.

The main issue was whether the drug arrangements are consistent with paragraph 2(a) of the Enabling Clause, which reads:

> The provisions of paragraph 1 apply to the following:
> (a) Preferential tariff treatment accorded by developed contracting parties to products originating in developing countries in accordance with the Generalised System of Preferences (3)

> 3. As described in the Decision of the CONTRACTING PARTIES of 25 June 1971, relating to the establishment of "generalised, non-reciprocal and non-discriminatory preferences beneficial to the developing countries . . .".

The AB upheld findings by the Disputes Panel, that the Enabling Clause is an exception to Article 1.1 GATT, and that it does not exclude the applicability of that Article. The AB held, further, that it is incumbent on the complainant to raise the Enabling Clause in making its claim of inconsistency with Article 1.1 GATT, but that the respondent (in this case the EU) then bears the burden of proving that the arrangements satisfy the requirements of the Enabling Clause.

However, the AB went on to decide, contrary to the Disputes Panel, that the term 'non-discriminatory' in footnote 3 of paragraph 2(a) of the Enabling Clause does not require identical tariff preferences under GSP schemes to be provided to all developing countries (apart from Least Developed Nations). The AB also reversed the Dispute Panel's ruling that 'developing countries' means *all* such countries. India's submission that there must be identical treatment for all developing countries was rejected, and the AB accepted the EU's argument that treating objectively different situations differently is not discriminatory. So long as the GSP is 'generalised' (ie generally applicable) it need not apply to all developing countries, but can refer to individual countries in response to their 'needs'. Responding to these 'needs' may entail treating different beneficiaries differently. Sub-categories of developing countries, according to need (eg Least Developed Nations) is permissible. It is only when similarly situated countries are treated differently that the non-discrimination principle is violated; where they are in the same situation then they must be afforded the same treatment. The AB held that the drug arrangements were inconsistent with the non-discrimination requirement, because there were no objective criteria and no procedures for adding countries to or removing them from the list of beneficiaries.

It is significant that the AB favourably contrasted the labour rights provisions (Article 8) of the EU Regulation with the drug arrangements. The labour rights clause has substantive criteria and a detailed procedure for dealing with applications for beneficiary status (chapter 4, above). The standards are applied to all developing countries, and they are objective. Their point of departure is the 8 core ILO conventions, and the available assessments, comments, decisions, recommendations and conclusions of the various supervisory bodies of the ILO.[56] This gives strong grounds for believing that the EU's labour rights clause would survive challenge in the WTO disputes procedures.

The position is far less certain in regard to the US GSP. As we have seen (chapter 4, above) the USTR has wide and subjective discretions in deciding whether a country is 'taking steps' to achieve internationally recognised worker rights, and whether conditions of work are 'acceptable.' Some of the interpretations adopted by the USTR (eg in regard to freedom of association) are inconsistent with the interpretations by ILO supervisory bodies, and there are examples of blatant political judgments (eg in relation to Pakistan). It would also be difficult to justify other unilateral US measures (eg under section 301 of the Trade Act) under the Enabling Clause. Although there are some useful pointers in the *India-GSP* decision, a number of key questions remain. How are the 'needs' of developing countries to be defined in labour matters? One approach would be to say that since the International Labour Conference unanimously declared in 1998 that all members of the ILO should comply with ILO core conventions, there is an existing standard of 'need' reflected in these conventions. But what of a Muslim country that does not ratify or comply with the ILO non-discrimination conventions for cultural or religious reasons? Is such a country 'similarly situated' to a secular developing country? All developing countries need to improve working conditions and to enforce their labour laws effectively. The objective criteria of ILO conventions provides an incentive for them to do so, but the requirement that countries must be 'similarly situated' is likely to be a source of continuing controversy.

8. Would WTO sanctions work?

Advocates of WTO sanctions for violation of labour standards have made several suggestions for amending the WTO Agreements.[57] One of these would be to alter Article XX GATT (exceptions) to include measures necessary to enforce core labour standards. Maupain points out that this would exacerbate

---

[56] Council Regulation 2501/2001, Arts 14.1,19 and 28.3.
[57] See generally, Vázquez (2003).

fears of protectionism because it would simply leave it to each Member State to decide whether to take action.[58] To overcome this objection, use could be made of Article XXIII GATT. This was the centrepoint of the GATT dispute settlement mechanism for obtaining compliance with GATT obligations and is still relevant under the WTO.[59] Article XXIII can be invoked on grounds of 'nullification or impairment' of benefits expected under the agreement. If a 'satisfactory adjustment' is not effected between the parties, then 'the CONTRACTING PARTIES may authorise a complaining country to suspend the application of such concessions or other obligations as the Contracting parties determine to be appropriate.' The Disputes Settlement Understanding (DSU), adopted as part of the WTO agreements, now provides a stronger framework for multilateral approval of sanctions. The DSU states that, after procedures have been exhausted, the Disputes Settlement Body (DSB) '*shall* grant authorisation to suspend concessions or other obligations.'[60] In contrast to discretionary GATT-authorised retaliation, the WTO-sanctions system for failure to observe recommendations and rulings is mandatory.

WTO-authorised sanctions for failure to observe labour standards would plainly be an improvement on unilateral sanctions. The former ensure that sanctions are rule-based and appropriate, and provide due process for the defendant state. The latter are 'power-based',[61] subvert the rule of international law, encourage protectionism and discrimination, and may lead to unregulated retaliation. The WTO system could also provide a route for consulting the ILO, because, under Article XXIII.2 'any appropriate intergovernmental organisation' (such as the ILO) may be consulted. Similarly, Article 13 of the DSU allows dispute panels to seek information and technical advice from 'any individual or body which it deems appropriate'. This has been utilised in intellectual property disputes, and would allow panels to seek advisory opinions in labour matters from the ILO.[62] However, this would leave the ILO in a subsidiary position. At present the ILO does not even have official observer status at the WTO, although it has a standing invitation to attend ministerial conferences which it did at Doha (2001) and Cancun (2003). (Conversely the WTO has observer status at the International Labour Conference and the ILO Governing Body.) Matters would be decided within the inter-governmental

---

[58] Maupain (1996) at 81–82.

[59] Jackson (2000) at 114.

[60] DSU, Art 22.6 (emphasis added).

[61] Jackson (2000) at 109. The UN has declared that '[n]o state may use or encourage the use of economic, political or any other type of measures to coerce another state in order to obtain from it the subordination of the exercise of sovereign rights': UN Declaration on the Inadmissibility of Intervention in the Domestic Affairs of States and the Protection of Independence and Sovereignty': GA Res. 2131(XX) para 2, UNGAOR 20th Sess, Supp No 14, Art 11. UN Doc A/1604 (1965).

[62] Cleveland (2002) 184–85.

structures of the WTO which, unlike the ILO, does not have the benefit of employers' and workers' delegates. It is trade ministers who are in the driving seat and their primary objective is free trade not labour rights. In practice, the WTO normally acts by consensus, effectively giving every Member a veto, unlike the ILO where conventions can be adopted by a two-thirds majority of delegates but require ratification before they are binding on a Member State. Decisions to impose sanctions for labour rights violations would be virtually impossible to achieve in the WTO. In contrast, the International Labour Conference may act by a majority under Article 33 to secure compliance with the recommendations of a Commission of Inquiry, as happened in the case of Myanmar (chapter 2, Box 2.4, above). ILO members are not bound to impose measures, but this is no different from the WTO where a consensus-based decision still leaves members free to decide whether or not take action once authorised by the WTO. Trade diversion to countries which choose not to impose sanctions remains a distinct risk.

The crucial question is whether WTO-authorised sanctions would be more effective than action under Article 33 of the ILO Constitution. Charnovitz has pointed out that the WTO has now achieved a sanctions-based dispute settlement system substantially similar to the one intended under Article 28 of the original ILO Constitution (chapter 2, above), 'but never embraced because of its poor fit to the ILO's mission'.[63] If the earlier ILO system failed to achieve its purpose, the institutional features of the WTO make it an even worse fit for the enforcement of international labour standards.

In chapter 10, we shall return to the appropriate place for sanctions in the transnational labour regime.

---

[63] Charnovitz (2002) 614.

7

Labour Laws Beyond Borders

1. Introduction

The methods of transnational labour regulation with which this chapter deals fall under the long-established legal rubric of the conflict of laws or private international law. The latter description is somewhat confusing because, unlike *public* international law, the subject does not deal with the relations between states, but rather with fact situations which arise for determination under national labour laws in disputes between employers and workers where there is a foreign element. It is a branch of national law.

As a result of modern globalisation, such situations are increasingly common. When workers from State A (the home state) are posted to work abroad in State B (the host state), State A may want to ensure that its laws and the collective or works agreements made by its firms are applied to those workers. On the other hand, State B will be anxious to avoid the import of lower labour standards from State A which have the effect of undermining established laws and agreements in State B. Workers in host states want to make foreign parent companies of local subsidiaries legally responsible for failing to observe the labour standards that they are obliged to follow in their home countries. Workers in both the home state and the host state are affected by cross-border transfers of undertakings and offshore outsourcing. There is a slow but steady growth in the number of transnational collective agreements and works council agreements. These raise difficult issues for the conflict of laws, and so too, do international strikes and other solidarity action by workers.

Each country has its own conflict of laws rules. Very few have specific legislation or case law dealing with employment relationships, and most simply apply the general conflict principles relating to contract and tort (delict) or ignore the problem by applying their domestic labour laws (the *lex fori*, ie the law of the country of the court or tribunal hearing the case) notwithstanding the foreign element. The assumption of extra-territorial jurisdiction has become an increasingly important feature of US labour law.[1] Some US statutes are expressly extra-territorial, for example the Civil Rights Act, the Age Discrimination in Employment Act and the Americans with Disabilities Act apply to US corporations employing US workers and operating overseas. The courts and the National Labor Relations Board (NLRB) have been willing in some cases to apply the National Labor Relations Act extra-territorially. There are also statutes which give the Executive Branch the power to apply US labour laws extra-territorially by importing their standards into trade agreements (chapter 4, above).

The EU provides as a useful model for resolving conflict of laws problems in employment on a regional scale, possibly as a forerunner to an international covenant, although the latter prospect still seems far-fetched. The EC Treaty facilitates the free movement of workers and this can give rise to trans-border contracts of employment. This is expressly recognised in Council Directive 91/533/EEC[2] which places special obligations on EC employers to provide information on contractual terms to expatriate employees required to work in a country other than the Member State whose law and/or practice governs the contract.[3] At the collective level, the implementation of Council Directive 94/45/EC[4] on European Works Councils, far from eliminating differences raises a host of conflicts problems. An attempt in the 1970s to enact a Community regulation on the conflict of laws in employment relationships failed, after severe criticism.[5] However, Article 6 of the Rome Convention on the Law Applicable to Contractual Obligations (1980)[6] together with the European Parliament and Council Directive 96/71/EC[7] on the posting of workers in the framework of the provision of services lay down rules which aim to ensure a measure of uniformity in the conflict rules of all 25 Member

---

[1] Stone (1995) at 1011–19.
[2] [1991] OJ L288/32.
[3] Art 4.
[4] [1994] OJ L254/64.
[5] [1972] OJ C/49/25 for critique see Hepple (1974).
[6] [1980] OJ L 266/1,applied in the UK by the Contracts (Applicable Law) Act 1990.
[7] [1997] OJ L18/1.

States.[8] There is also a Council Regulation on Jurisdiction and the Enforcement of Judgments in Civil Matters.[9]

This chapter will, therefore, focus on the European employment conflicts and jurisdiction model, and then consider the European rules relating to the protection of posted workers, and the legal issues to which cross-border transfers of undertakings and offshore outsourcing can give rise. Finally, there is a discussion of the support (or lack of it) for transnational labour-management relations, in particular collective bargaining and employee representation and international solidarity action. The law on these subjects is complex and, in many instances, uncertain. It is not possible in the scope of this book to do more than identify the problems and discuss some of the wider policy questions.

2. The applicable law

Let us take an example of the choice of law problem.[10] An English resident enters into a contract of employment with a Dutch company, in a standard form, described by Dutch law as an 'international contract' applicable to workers of all nationalities, to work on an oil derrick in the territorial waters of any country other than the UK. His salary is payable in sterling. The contract is signed and negotiated in England at a place of business of the Dutch company. The employee is injured while working on an oil rig in Nigerian territorial waters by the negligence of the company's other employees, and brings a claim for damages in an English court. The contract makes provision for compensation for the employee in the event of accident or illness. It also has an exempting clause under which the employee accepts this compensation as his 'exclusive remedy in lieu of any other claims, whether at common law or under the statutes of the United Kingdom or any other nation.' If there was a contract of employment governed by English law, this exempting clause would be void by virtue of a UK statute,[11] but it would be valid if the relationship was governed by Dutch law. Which law applies—Dutch, English or Nigerian?

---

[8] The Rome Convention applies to all contracts regardless of whether they are connected with a state which is a party to the Convention. The only qualifying requirement is that the dispute is being tried in a contracting state.

[9] Council Regulation No 44/2001 of 22 December 2000, [2001] OJ L12/1. This supersedes the earlier Brussels Convention except in Denmark to which the Brussels Convention still applies. Where the defendant is domiciled in Iceland, Norway, Switzerland (three EFTA countries) or Poland, then the Lugano Convention applies; this is broadly similar to the Jurisdiction Regulation.

[10] Adapted from Dicey and Morris (2000) §33–085, illustration 1.

[11] The Law Reform (Personal Injuries) Act 1948, s 1(3).

At least three approaches are possible. The first is that of the English common law. This applies the express choice of the parties or, in the absence of such a choice, the 'proper law of the contract', that is the legal system with which the contract is most closely connected. This might lead to the application of Dutch law on the grounds that an employer contracting with workers of many nationalities cannot be expected to apply different laws to each of them (the 'business necessity' argument), that the 'seat' of the employing enterprise is in The Netherlands, and that preference should be given to a rule which validates a contract rather than one which invalidates it.[12]

A second approach would be to classify the claim as being one in tort and not in contract. The English common law rule in claims characterised as arising in tort would be to determine liability by English law, subject to the condition that, if liability exists by English law, it must also be civilly actionable in damages by the law of the place where the conduct took place.[13] Since 1996, the common law rule has been replaced in England by a statutory provision which lays down the general rule that the applicable rule is the law of the country in which the events constituting the tort or delict in question occur.[14] This would not, however, resolve the question whether or not the exemption clause is valid. Collier points out[15] that it is necessary to distinguish three situations: (1) if the clause was invalid by the law of the place where the tort was committed, but valid by the contract's applicable law, the clause could not relied upon by the employer; (2) if the clause was valid by both the law of the place where the tort was committed and the contract's applicable law, it would provide a defence; and (3) if it was valid by the law of the place where the tort was committed but invalid by the applicable law of the contract, then the clause could not be used by the employer to defeat the worker's claim. In other words, it is only in the first of these situations that in English law it will make a difference whether the claimant sues in contract or tort: he or she will win if the claim is in tort, but lose if the claim is in contract. In the other two situations it makes no difference whether the claimant sues in contract or tort.

---

[12] This was the approach taken by the majority of the English Court of Appeal in *Sayers v International Drilling Co* [1971] 1 WLR 1176, CA, on facts similar to those on which this example is based. In addition to the reasons given in the text, the Court held that the effect of the contractual clause was to preclude English law from being applicable.

[13] *Chaplin v Boys* [1971] AC 356, HL, as explained in later cases such as *Coupland v Arabian Gulf Oil Co.* [1983] 1 WLR 1136, CA. In *Sayers* (above), Lord Denning misstated the rule, then perversely held that the proper law of the tort was Dutch law and the proper law of the contract English law, but applied Dutch law as the 'proper law of the issue': see Collier (2001) at 236–37; and see *Brodin v A/R Seljan* 1970 SC 213, where a Scottish Court (correctly) held that s 1(3) of the 1948 Act applied whenever the action was based on a delict committed in Scotland, whatever the law governing the contract.

[14] Private International Law (Miscellaneous Provisions) Act 1995, s 11(1).

[15] Collier (2001) at 237.

A third approach gives primacy to certain 'mandatory' rules of employment law, that is rules which cannot be derogated from by contract.[16] This is the approach taken by the Rome Convention. The Convention starts with the recognition in Article 3 of the freedom of the parties to a contract to choose the applicable law, either expressly or impliedly. In the absence of choice, the contract is governed by the law of the country with which it is most closely connected. But there are special rules for 'individual employment contracts'.[17] Article 6(2) provides that in the absence of choice such contracts shall be governed:

(a) by the law of the country in which the employee habitually carries out his work in performance of the contract, even if he is temporarily employed in another country [the place of work test]; or

(b) if the employee does not habitually carry out his work in any one country, by the law of the country in which the place of business through which he was engaged is situated [the place of business test],

unless it appears from the circumstances as a whole that the contract is more closely connected with another country, in which case the contract shall be governed by the law of that country.

Article 6(1) qualifies the free choice of the parties by providing that in the case of individual employment contracts a 'choice of law made by the parties shall not have the effect of depriving the employee of the protection afforded to him by the mandatory rules which would be applicable under [Article 6(2), above] in the absence of choice'. In the example given of an English resident employed by a Dutch company to work in outside the UK, English law would apply to the contract in the absence of a choice of law by the parties because the place of business through which the employee was engaged is situated in England, and the employee does not habitually work in any one country. The UK statute lays down a 'mandatory rule': it was passed in order abolish the doctrine of common employment which prevented an employee from suing his or her employer for damage arising out of the negligence of a fellow employee, and to prevent evasion, contracting-out was prohibited. Accordingly, even if the parties expressly or impliedly chose Dutch law and the tort was committed in Nigeria, the exempting clause would be void because this is the mandatory rule of English law, the law of the place of business through which he was engaged.

---

[16] Rome Convention, Art 3(3).

[17] There is no definition of 'individual contract of employment' in Art 6. The concept is obviously intended to exclude collective and works agreements. Different legal systems have different concepts of the 'contract of employment'. It is not clear whether the ECJ will develop an autonomous EU-wide definition of this concept so as to achieve uniform application of the Rome Convention, or will resort to the choice of law rules in Art 6 to decide under which legal system the relationship should be classified: see Dicey and Morris (2000) at §33–053–4.

The Rome Convention means that the courts of the Member States have to consider carefully whether a particular rule of employment legislation is mandatory. Article 7 of the Rome Convention provides that rules which cannot be derogated from by contract are mandatory 'whatever the law applicable to the contract'. The reason for the application of mandatory employment rules is the need to secure 'protection for the party who from the socio-economic point of view is regarded as the weaker in the contractual relationship.'[18] Allowing 'free' choice of law could deprive the employee of the protection guaranteed by the social policy of the state. For example, if a statute lays down criteria for selecting employees for redundancy the statute can only operate sensibly if those criteria are applied to all employment relationships with the employer, irrespective of the proper law.[19]

National mandatory rules are often subject to their own provisions on spatial limitation. There is an increasing tendency for legislation in the US, UK and Ireland to do this. For example, the British Race Relations Act 1976, as amended in 2003, applies to employment 'at an establishment in Great Britain.' This apparent territorial limitation is modified by specifying two situations in which the employment is to be regarded as being at an establishment in Great Britain. The first is 'if the employee does his work wholly or partly in Great Britain.' The second is where the employee does his or her work wholly outside Great Britain provided that three conditions are satisfied. These are that (1) the employer has a place of business at an establishment in Great Britain; (2) the work is for the purposes of the business carried on at that establishment; and (3) the employee is ordinarily resident in Great Britain either at the time when he or she applies for is offered the employment or at any time during the course of the employment.[20] Although, there is no express provision that this is the case irrespective of the proper law of the contract, it seems obvious that this is intended, so that the provisions of the Act are to be regarded as 'mandatory' for purposes of the Rome Convention.

The patchwork nature of British anti-discrimination legislation has the curious result that legislation on sex discrimination and equal pay for women and men does not yet apply as widely as the more recent legislation on race, religion and sexual orientation. The Sex Discrimination and Equal Pay Acts apply to employment at an establishment in Great Britain unless the employee does the work 'wholly outside Great Britain.'[21] So, if a flight attendant,

---

[18] Giuliano-Lagarde Report on the Convention Applicable to Contractual Obligations [1980] OJ C–282/1.

[19] Krebber (2000) at 534.

[20] Race Relations Act 1976, s 8(1)(1A) as amended by SI 2003/1626, Reg 11. A similar extra-territorial provision will be found in legislation relating to religious discrimination and sexual orientation discrimination.

[21] Sex Discrimination Act 1975, as amended by SI 1999/3163, Reg 2.

ordinarily resident in Great Britain, is employed to work for purposes of the airline's business carried on at London Heathrow but does all her work on flights to and from Saudi Arabia, she may not be able bring a claim for sex discrimination, but would be able to claim for racial, religious or sexual orientation discrimination irrespective of the proper law of the contract.[22] Some other statutes, such as the National Minimum Wage Act 1998 are applied if the worker 'ordinarily works' under his or her contract in the United Kingdom,[23] and this appears to apply irrespective of the proper law of the contract as a mandatory rule for purposes of the Rome Convention.

The Employment Rights Act 1996,[24] containing a number of individual employment rights, expressly applies irrespective of the proper law of the contract. However, the geographical scope of these rights is limited. Before 1999, those who 'ordinarily' worked outside Great Britain (the meaning of which subject to a considerable body of case law) were excluded from most of the individual employment rights, such as the right not to be unfairly dismissed.[25] This limitation was repealed apparently in order to implement the EC Posted Workers Directive (below). Does the repeal mean that the right not to be unfairly dismissed applies to an employee of a British-based company who works anywhere in the world?[26] Or does it apply wherever the employment has a 'substantial connection' with Great Britain?[27] Different divisions of the Employment Appeal Tribunal reached different conclusions. The Court of Appeal has now decided that the right not to be unfairly dismissed applies only to dismissal from employment *in* Great Britain, and that this has to be assessed in the light of all the circumstances of the case including the location of the employee's base and the residence of the parties.[28] This case-by-case assessment is likely to lead to uncertainty, and is curiously out of line with the approach taken in recent anti-discrimination legislation. It is unlikely to be the last word on the subject.

---

[22] Cf *Carver v Saudi Arabian Airlines* [1999] IRLR 370,CA, where the issue was whether the attendant was 'wholly or partly' employed outside Great Britain, prior to the deletion of the word 'partly' by SI 1999/3163. It is to be noted that the Race Relations Act 1976, s 6 allows racial discrimination where the purpose is provide training in skills which the trainee or employee appears to the employer to intend to exercise wholly outside Great Britain. There is also an exception for seamen recruited abroad for employment outside Great Britain: RRA, s 9 and see *Deria v General Council of British Shipping* [1986] IRLR 108, CA.

[23] National Minimum Wage Act 1998, s 1(2).

[24] ERA 1996, s 204(1).

[25] ERA 1996, ss 196,197 repealed by Employment Relations Act 1999, ss 32(3), 44.

[26] This was the view of the EAT in *Lawson v Serco Ltd,* [2004] IRLR 206, overruled by the CA.

[27] The view of the EAT in *Jackson v Ghost Ltd* [2003] IRLR 824, and *Financial Times Ltd v Bishop* EAT/0147/03.

[28] *Lawson v Serco Ltd* [2004] IRLR 206.

3. The appropriate forum

Mr Connelly, a Scotsman, was employed between 1977 and 1982 at the Rossing uranium mine in Namibia by Rossing Uranium Ltd (RUL), a local subsidiary of the 'parent' RTZ Corporation plc (RTZ), the latter being incorporated and doing business in England. When Mr Connelly returned to England it was discovered that he was suffering form cancer of the larynx. He claimed that this was the result of inhaling silica uranium and its radioactive decay products at the mine. He obtained a legal aid certificate to bring proceedings against the parent RTZ in England. His allegations were that RTZ had devised RUL's policy on health, safety and environment, or, alternatively, had advised RUL on the contents of that policy.

The issue was one of jurisdiction. It was common ground that Namibia was the forum with the most real and substantial connection with the dispute. But Mr Connelly could not afford to proceed without financial assistance, and no legal aid was available in Namibia. In England he could either obtain legal aid or enter into a conditional fee agreement with his lawyers and experts to fund the action. Much of the essential evidence was that of medical experts who were readily available in England but not in Namibia. The House of Lords (by a majority decision) allowed the action to proceed in England on the ground that substantial justice could not be done in Namibia but could be done in England.[29]

Ultimately Mr Connelly lost the case on the merits.[30] But the ruling on jurisdiction alarmed TNCs. In the words of Lord Hoffmann (who dissented): '. . . any multinational with its parent company in England will be liable to be sued here in respect of its activities anywhere in the world.'[31] The only real connection of Mr Connelly's claim with the English jurisdiction was that the parent company was registered and had its headquarters in England. Mr Connelly had abandoned his domicile of origin in Scotland and had emigrated to South Africa and then to Namibia. The House of Lords' decision seemed to put him in a better position than a native Namibian who had worked at Rossing and contracted an illness.

Some of the fears of the TNCs were confirmed in a later case when a group of South African workers, who did not live in England, were allowed to sue Cape plc in the English courts in respect of asbestos-related diseases which they had contracted while involved in mining blue and brown asbestos in South Africa (Box 7.1).[32]

---

[29] *Connelly v RTZ Corp plc* [1998] AC 854, HL.
[30] [1999] CLC 533.
[31] [1998] AC 854 at 876.
[32] *Lubbe v Cape plc* [2000] 1 WLR 1545, HL. The South African Government intervened on behalf of the claimants arguing that it saw no 'public interest in requiring its courts to adjudicate in a dispute which arises from alleged acts of an English company under the laws of the old South Africa'.

Box 7.1

THE CAPE ASBESTOS LITIGATION

From 1893 to 1948 Cape's operations in the North Western Cape Province were carried out directly by the parent company, incorporated in England, and after 1948 by a wholly-owned South African subsidiary. The operations in the Northern Transvaal after 1948 were also carried on by a wholly-owned South African subsidiary which later sold its shares to a third party buyer. Cape continued its interest in another wholly-owned South African subsidiary which manufactured asbestos products. In 1989 Cape pulled out of all its South African subsidiaries and by the time the writs were issued in these proceedings it had no assets in South Africa. The claimants argued that the South African operations were in fact controlled by Cape in London, that the parent company knew that its operations involved risks to the health of the workers, and had failed to ensure that proper working practices and safety precautions were taken, so breaching its duty of care to the workers and those living in the area of its operations. The evidence for the claimants indicated what were described as 'appalling and inhumane conditions'. The mill at Prieska in the Northern Cape was situated in the middle of the town and close to the school, with the consequence that the incidence of asbestos-related disease was extremely high and whole families were afflicted.

Cape argued that day-to-day control was entirely in the hands of local management, and that the action should be brought in South Africa. After a lengthy legal battle to get their cases heard, the claimants persuaded the House of Lords that although South Africa was the natural forum, this was outweighed by the interests of justice. Lord Bingham, who delivered the leading judgment, stressed that the onus was on the (defendant) parent company to show that there was another forum in which justice could be done in the interest of all the parties.[33] There was a strong probability that the claimants would be unable to obtain financial assistance and the expert evidence necessary to sustain their claims in South Africa. This conclusion was reinforced by the fact that by the time the case reached the House of Lords there were about 3,000 claimants and there was an absence of established procedures in South Africa to deal with multi-party claims. Before the matter came to trial the (by then) 7,500 claimants agreed terms of settlement with Cape. Cape agreed to pay £21 million into a trust fund which was to make payments to victims of Cape's operations in South Africa.

[33] [2000] 1 WLR 1545 at 1554.

These decisions show a willingness by English courts to overrule the claims of parent companies that it would be inconvenient for them to submit to a trial 'even where the corporation's world headquarters are located in the state where the suit is brought and three blocks away from the courthouse.'[34] The courts have also been prepared to investigate the restructuring of corporate groups motivated by the desire to put the group's assets beyond the reach of foreign claimants.[35] However, it must be remembered that the basis of the English court's common law jurisdiction is the inherently discretionary 'interests of justice', so that outcomes are not clearly predictable or consistent. The availability of higher damages, more complete disclosure of evidence, a longer limitation period or legal aid are to be taken into account but are not decisive factors, nor are the inadequate remedies, financial burdens and other difficulties faced by workers in developing countries who wish to hold parent companies accountable for the civil wrongs of their local subsidiaries. By way of contrast, the High Court of Australia has held that a stay of proceedings should be granted only where the chosen forum is clearly inappropriate and the continuance of the action would be vexatious and oppressive. The defendant parent company in Australia would have to show that there was an appropriate foreign forum which would exercise jurisdiction. This robust approach avoids the need to engage in a potentially embarrassing evaluation of the merits of a foreign jurisdiction. At the same time, if the chosen forum has no real connection with the dispute, it would be 'oppressive' to choose it simply because of the possibility of higher damages or more extensive discovery.[36]

The English and Australian approaches may be contrasted with that of US courts which add a 'public interest' element when deciding whether the US courts or those of the host country should hear the case. An example is the litigation in the US District Court against the Union Carbide Corporation arising out of over 2,000 deaths and 200,000 injuries sustained following a gas leak from a chemical plant operated by Union Carbide at Bhopal, India, in December 1984. The Court held that the better ability of the Indian legal system to determine the cause of the accident and fix liability, the presence in India of the overwhelming majority of witnesses and evidence, as well as the

---

[34] Reed (2001) 178.

[35] *Sithole v Thor Chemical Holdings Ltd* [2000] WL 1421183, CA, 28 September 2000. After two actions by South African workers against the English parent company of South African subsidiaries producing mercury-based chemicals had been settled, there was a corporate restructuring which left the parent 'deliberately isolated from the resources of the majority of companies within the group at the tune of a sum in excess of £20m.' In a third action by another group of workers, the parent company was ordered to disclose documents relating to the restructuring and to pay £400,000 into court. This third action was then settled out of court for £240,000.

[36] *Oceanic Sun Line Special Shipping Co Inc v Fay* (1988) 165 CLR 197, and *Voth v Manildra Flow Mills Pty Ltd* (1990) 171 CLR 538.

claimants, and the substantial public interest of India in both the accident and the outcome of the litigation required that the consolidated case be dismissed on the ground that the US Court was not the appropriate forum (*forum non conveniens*).[37] This decision was upheld on appeal.[38] It was not until 1991 that ensuing litigation in India produced a settlement of the claims, approved by the Supreme Court of India. But litigation in the US over the disaster lingers on. In 1999 further claims were brought under the Alien Tort Claims Act (ATCA)[39] for compensation in respect of alleged violations of international environmental and human rights law. These actions were dismissed primarily on the ground that the ATCA claims were barred by the settlement orders of the Supreme Court of India.[40] In 2003, nearly twenty years after the disaster, separate environmental claims were again dismissed.[41]

There has been much preoccupation in the US with the possibility of using the ATCA as a means of holding corporations responsible for violations of international human rights, which might include some labour rights. The ATCA is a statute of 1789 which gives US District Courts 'original jurisdiction' in any civil action by an alien for a tort committed in violation of a US treaty or the law of nations. Some scholars have argued that this might be used to sue TNCs, wherever based, for producing goods with forced or slave labour, or possibly even child labour, as part of a joint venture with a foreign government.[42] However, in June 2004, the US Supreme Court ruled that the ATCA is purely jurisdictional in scope and does not create any new private law rights of action. According to a majority of the Court the jurisdiction is limited to a small number of international norms that a federal court could recognise as enforceable within the common law without further statutory authority from Congress. To be actionable an international norm must be 'specific, universal and obligatory.' In the case in question, the unlawful detention of an alien in a foreign country, for less than a day, was unanimously held not to be actionable in a District Court.[43] The implications of this decision remain to be worked out, but it seems to be highly unlikely that all the ILO core labour standards can be said to fall within the narrow definition of the 'law of nations' adopted

---

[37] *Re Union Carbide Corporation Gas Plant Disaster at Bhopal India in December 1984*, 634 F Supp 842 (SDNY), 844, 12 May 1986, as amended 10 June 1986. There were numerous actions all assigned to the Southern District of New York.

[38] 809 F 2d 195 (2d Cir), 14 January 1987.

[39] 28 USC §1350.

[40] *Bano v Union Carbide Corp*, 273 F 3d 120, (2nd Cir), 15 November 2001.

[41] *Bano v United Carbide Corp* F Supp 2d, (SDNY), 18 March 2003.

[42] Eg, Cleveland (1997) at 1561–67.

[43] *Sosa v Alvarez-Machain*, US Supreme Court No 03–339, appeal argued 30 March 2004, decided 29 June 2004. Justice Scalia (joined by Rehnquist CJ and Thomas J), differed from the majority, holding that no international norms beyond those recognised in 1789 could be the subject of jurisdiction under the ATCA.

by the Court.[44] In principle, however, the majority of the Supreme Court does not entirely rule out the possibility of holding TNCs directly responsible in law for human rights abuses.

A simpler set of rules about jurisdiction and the enforcement of foreign judgments has been adopted in the EU. These rules provide a codified system for determining jurisdiction, and favour the employee as the weaker party. They give little discretion to national courts in accepting or rejecting jurisdiction. These rules were originally contained in the Brussels Convention of 1968, now superseded by Council Regulation 44/2001/EC of 22 December 2000 (the Jurisdiction Regulation).[45] The Regulation applies where the defendant is domiciled in an EU state and the matter falls within the scope of the Regulation (as almost all employment matters do). Where the defendant is domiciled in Iceland, Norway, or Switzerland (three EFTA countries), then the Lugano Convention 1988 applies.[46] This is similar (but not identical) to the Regulation.

The fundamental starting point of the Regulation is the 'home court' principle: if the defendant is domiciled in an EU state then he or she must be sued in that state. An exception to the principle is that where the claim is in contract the defendant may be sued in 'the courts for the place of performance of the obligation in question.'[47] Initially, the Brussels Convention had no special provision relating to individual employment contracts. The ECJ held that in employment cases the place of characteristic performance is the place where the work is carried out, even if some obligations (such as payment) are to be performed in another state.[48] This interpretation avoids a multiplicity of jurisdictions where different obligations are to be performed in different states, protects the weaker party by ensuring the application of the employment legislation of the place of work, and recognises that it is usually cheaper for the employee to sue in the place where he or she works.[49]

These special features of the employment relationship led to an amendment by the San Sebastian Convention. The Jurisdiction Regulation now makes it clear that, while an employer may bring proceedings only in the courts of the

---

[44] See eg the ongoing litigation which started in *Doe v Unocal Corp* 963 F Supp 880 (CD Cal 1997), a class action lawsuit alleging that Unocal (US) and Total (France) acting with Burma's ruling junta were aware of and supported slave labour and other human rights abuses in the construction of an oil pipeline.

[45] [2001] OJ L12/1, superseding EC Convention on Jurisdiction and Judgments in Civil and Commercial Matters, 1968, which entered into force in 1973.

[46] Poland also acceded to this Convention in 2000.

[47] Art 5(1).

[48] Case 133/81 *Ivenel v Schwab* [1982] ECR 1891.

[49] *Mulox IBC v Geels* [1993] ECR I–4075. In Case 226/85 *Shenavai v Kreischer* [1987] ECR 239, it was also recognised that the employee cannot be denied the protection of the mandatory rules of the place where he or she works (Art 6, Rome Convention), and this makes it preferable that the country whose mandatory rules apply should also have jurisdiction.

Member State in which the employee is domiciled,[50] the employee may also sue in a number of other jurisdictions in respect of individual contracts of employment.[51] An employer who is domiciled in a Member State may be sued in the courts of the Member State where it is domiciled.[52] The meaning of 'domicile' is all-important when workers want to bring claims against their corporate employer. This is the 'seat' of the enterprise, a concept whose interpretation varies from country to country. In the UK, a company has its seat in the UK if it has a registered office there or its central management or control is exercised there. The same test is applied by UK courts to determine the seat of a company which does not have its seat in the UK, except that it cannot be regarded by UK courts as domiciled in a foreign country if it would not be regarded by the courts of that state as domiciled there. A company may have two 'seats'. In one case, a company was incorporated in Panama but managemt control was in Germany. It was held that its seat in Germany was sufficient for jurisdiction, even though it also had a seat outside the EU.[53]

Alternatively, the employer may be sued in another Member State (1) in the courts for the place where the employee habitually carries out his or her work, or in the courts for the last place where he did so [place of work test], or (2) if the employee does not habitually carry out his or her work in any one country, in the courts of the place where the business which engaged the employee is or was situated [place of business test].[54] The place of work test has been interpreted in one case to mean the place where the employee had established the effective centre of his working activities,[55] and in another case as the place where, taking into account the whole term of employment, the employee spends most of his or her time engaged in the employer's business.[56] The purpose of the place of business test was to reverse an ECJ ruling in a case in which the employee was habitually working for a Belgian company in various countries outside the EU, so that he could only sue in the court of the place of the employer's domicile.[57] As a result of the amendment, the worker could now sue in the court of the place where the business is or was situated, which may be different from the court of the defendant's domicile, and could include a

---

[50] Art 20(1). This does not affect the right to bring a counter claim in the courts in which the original claim is pending.

[51] It is problematic whether this includes all employment relationships based on contract: see Kidner (1998) at 106–7.

[52] Jurisdiction Regulation Art 19 (1).

[53] *The Deichland* [1990] 1 QB 361. 'Control' implies that the business can be managed without any further control or recourse to higher authority (apart from shareholders): *The Rewia* [1991] 2 Lloyds Rep 325.

[54] Regulation, Art 19(2).

[55] Case C–383/95 *Rutten v Cross Medical Ltd* [1987] ECR I–57.

[56] Case C–37/00, *Weber v Universal Ogden Services Ltd* [2002] ECR I–2013.

[57] Case 32/88, *Six Construction v Humbert* [1989] ECR 341.

branch or agency of the employer.[58] Where an employee enters into an individual contract of employment with an employer who is not domiciled in a Member State (eg the US), but has a branch, agency or other establishment in one of the Member States, the employer is deemed to be domiciled in that Member State in any dispute arising out of the operations of the branch, agency or establishment.[59]

The freedom of parties to an employment contract to choose their own jurisdiction is restricted. They can do so only by an agreement which is entered into after the dispute has arisen, or which allows the employee to bring proceedings in courts other than those designated by the Jurisdiction Regulation. This again recognises that the employee is in a weaker situation than the employer and needs to be protected against inducements to limit the choice of courts.

In summary, we have seen that the common law *forum non conveniens* approach, which allows the court a wide discretion whether to stay proceedings in favour of a foreign court, has been subject to different interpretations in England, Australia and the US. The English approach has been replaced in respect of employment contracts cases in the EU by sensible non-discretionary rules which recognise the desirability of protecting the worker. But the EU rules raise several unresolved puzzles. Does the concept of an 'individual employment contract' subject to these rules include the whole range of employment relationships, such as agency, temporary and sub-contracted work? Does the Regulation apply in all cases coming before the courts of EU states, even those where the competing foreign court is not an EU state (eg courts of a state in the US)?[60] If this is so, then cases like those of Mr Connelly and of the workers at Cape would no longer be decided on *forum non conveniens* principles, but in accordance with the Regulation which would clearly confer jurisdiction on the facts of those cases against a defendant who is domiciled in England.

---

[58] Jennard-Möller Report, OJ 1990 C–189/7. The reference to 'was situated' has the curious result that if the place of business moves from country A to B, and then to C, where the employee is dismissed, the employee could sue in B where he has never worked. Kidner (1998) at 112 argues that this should not be allowed.

[59] Art 18(2).

[60] References have been made to the ECJ on this issue: *Owusu v Jackson* [2002] EWCA Civ 877, and *American Motorists Insurance Co v Cellstar Cor* [2003] EWCA Civ 206. There is an issue whether Art 2 of the Regulation is mandatory, meaning that the defendant may only be sued in the state of domicile or whether a stay may be granted in some circumstances, such as where the *forum conveniens*, which is the *Owusu* question. Although individual employment contracts are not strictly covered by Art 2 the *Owusu* decision may be important in determining whether the Regulation applies at all where the competing state is a non-member state: see generally Fentiman (2000). The ECJ has held that anti-suit injunctions cannot be granted against proceedings taking place in an EU state, as this would be antithetical to the fundamental principles underlying the Regulation: Case C–159/02, *Turner v Grovit* [2004] All ER (EC) 485.

4. Posted workers and social dumping

Rules on choice of law and jurisdiction may serve a variety of purposes where workers are posted by their employer to work in another country. If the terms of employment of posted workers are more favourable than those of workers in the host state, the home state workers will normally seek the protection of home state rules and access to home state courts. Where their terms of employment are less favourable than those of workers in the host state, the home state workers' interests are less clear. They will want to benefit from the host state's higher standards, but this might raise employment costs and so imperil their jobs. Pressure for the application of the law of the place of work is more likely to come from employers and workers of the host state to protect them from 'social dumping' alleged to result from the employment of workers with lower labour standards from another country.

As we have seen (chapter 1, above) arguments based on 'social dumping' are highly suspect. Lower wages do not necessarily mean cheaper goods or services because highly-paid workers may be more productive. Moreover, if the rules of international trade do not permit a country to exclude imports of goods or services produced by workers on lower wages than those of workers in the importing state (chapter 6, above), why should it make a difference if, instead of sending the goods or services the exporter sends its own workers into the importing state to manufacture the goods or provide the services? Where cheaper services can be provided electronically or by satellite across borders (eg call centres), it becomes even harder to maintain that there is any substantial difference between these situations.[61]

These issues have arisen in relation to posted workers in the EU. As we shall see in chapters 8 and 9, the integration of the European market is built on a variety of principles which seek to ensure the free movement of capital, goods, persons and services. Of particular relevance in the context of posted workers are Articles 49 and 50 of the EC Treaty. These Articles cover the situation where a service provider established in State A, holding the nationality of one of the Member States (not necessarily State A), provides services in State B and then returns to State A once the services have been provided. Their effect is to prohibit rules laid down in State A or in State B which obstruct the provision of services.[62] Service providers have rights of entry to a Member State to provide

---

[61] Davies (1997) at 598–99.

[62] See Barnard (2004) at 331. Usually the rules challenged are those in the host state, State B, but difficult questions would arise if, for example, an employer in State A challenged employment laws in State A which were alleged to obstruct the provision of services in State B, the host state.

services, and this applies not only to an individual or company, but also to its workforce. In the *Rush Portuguesa* case[63] a Portuguese company used its own workforce of Portuguese nationals to carry out a contract to build a railway line in France. At the time the transitional arrangements for Portuguese accession to the EC meant that the workers were classed as non-EC (third country) nationals. French law provided that only the French Immigration Office could recruit non-EC workers. The ECJ held that the Portuguese company could not be prevented by French law from moving freely with all its workers, even where that workforce consisted of third country nationals. The Court found that France could not make the movement of staff by a guest service provider subject to conditions, such as recruitment in France or an obligation to obtain work permits.[64]

This ruling caused alarm, particularly in France and Germany, that out-of-state service providers would take advantage of their cheaper workforce in order to win contracts in the host State. They were not entirely reassured by a dictum of the Court that: 'Community law does not preclude Member States from extending their legislation, or collective labour agreements, entered into by both sides of industry, to any person who is employed even temporarily, within their territory, no matter in which country the employer is established.'[65] This did not amount to a right for posted workers to equal treatment with host state workers. It simply enabled importers of posted workers to extend their domestic laws and agreements to them. Several states took the opportunity to do this.[66] The European Commission became concerned about the effect of these protective national laws on the cross-border movement of services, and sought to clarify and moderate the situation by proposing a directive based on Articles 47(2) (ex 57(2)) and 55 (ex 66) of the EC Treaty. Article 47(2) allows harmonising directives 'in order to make it easier for persons to take up and pursue activities as self-employed persons', and Article 55 is aimed at removing restrictions on the provision of cross-border services.

The resulting Posted Workers Directive 96/71/EC of 16 December 1996[67] *requires* all the Member States to apply to workers posted to their territory certain core terms and conditions of employment of their own labour laws (see Table 7.A). These terms and conditions may be laid down by law, regulation or administrative provisions.[68] In the building industry, they may be laid down as

---

[63] Case C–113/89, *Rush Portuguesa v Office National d'immigration* [1990] ECR I–1321.

[64] Such third country nationals must, however, return to their country of origin or residence at the end of the service contract, and must not seek to enter the labour market: Case C–43/93, *Van der Elst v Office des migrations* [1994] ECR I–3803.

[65] *Rush Portuguesa*, para 18.

[66] Eg, In France Loi no 93–131 of 20 December 1993; in Germany Arbeitsnehmer-Entsendegesetz- AentG of 19 February 1996, BGB I, p 227.

[67] [1997] OJ L18/1.

[68] Art 3(1).

well by collective agreements or arbitration awards that have been declared 'universally applicable'. This means agreements or awards which must be observed by all undertakings in the geographical area and in the profession or industry concerned.

The problems associated with posted workers were felt most acutely in the building industry in France and Germany where many of the core terms are prescribed by universally applicable collective agreements. For this reason, the Directive designates the terms of such agreements as part of the compulsory 'core' in that industry. However, Member States are also *permitted* to apply terms and conditions laid down in universally applicable collective agreements and arbitration awards concerning activities outside the building industry.[69] This would be of little value in countries, like the UK, where no such system of declaring agreements universally applicable exists. So the Directive also allows the Member States to base themselves on agreements or awards that are generally applicable to all similar undertakings in the geographical area and in the profession or industry concerned, and/or agreements which have been concluded by the most representative employers' and labour organisations at national level and which are applied throughout the national territory. In order to ensure equality between potential competitors, there is a proviso: the application of the collective agreement must ensure equality of treatment on the core terms and conditions between undertakings in a similar position.[70] This equal treatment proviso is designed to prevent the application of collective agreements to foreign undertakings in a situation where those agreements are not legally enforceable against all domestic undertakings. It is not clear whether only 'core' terms prescribed in such agreements and awards may be applied. The great diversity in the Member States as to the matters that are regulated by law and those by collective agreement, suggests that this provision may be applied to posted workers in all industries in respect of non-core standards.[71]

In addition, Member States may apply 'public policy'(*ordre public*) provisions, other than compulsory core terms and conditions, to national undertakings and the undertakings of other States.[72] 'Public policy' is not defined, but will presumably be interpreted in line with the general conditions which have to be satisfied in order not to breach the free movement provisions of the

---

[69] Art 3(10) second indent.

[70] Art 3(1) and 3(8), with Annex.

[71] Davies (2002) at 299; for arguments against this interpretation see Davies (1997) at 582 n 30.

[72] Art 3(10) first indent. The Directive has been of little importance in the UK for three reasons: (1) UK statutes usually apply to workers posted to work in the UK, and the exclusion of those posted to work wholly or mainly outside the UK was removed in 1999 (see above); (2) the decline in multi-employer bargaining means that very few agreements meet the criteria of generally applicable or made with representative organisations and nationally applicable; and (3) posted workers are not as yet a significant feature of the UK labour market: see Davies (2002) at 299.

EC Treaty, as applied to services.[73] When using either of these permissive provisions, the Member State is obliged to ensure equality of treatment between domestic and foreign undertakings, and to act 'in accordance with the treaty' (on which see below). These permissive provisions are in some ways far more significant than the compulsory ones. The Directive goes beyond the Rome Convention by allowing Member States to apply the provisions of collective agreements to workers in all industries, even where those agreements are not legally enforceable. They also allow the application of 'public policy' provisions which go beyond the 'core.' This is likely to be rare in practice.

Three types of employment relationship involving posted workers[74] are covered by the Directive.[75] The first is the *Rush Portuguesa*—type situation where an undertaking in the course of carrying out a contract for work or services posts a worker to the territory of another Member State on behalf of and under the direction of that undertaking. The second covers intra-firm or intra-group mobility, where an undertaking posts a worker to an establishment or to an undertaking owned by the group carrying out work in a Member State, provided there is an employment relationship between the undertaking making the posting and the worker during the period of the posting. The third is where a temporary employment undertaking or placement agency hires out a worker to a user undertaking established or operating in a Member State, provided there is an employment relationship between the employment undertaking or agency and the worker during the period of posting.[76]

There is only one compulsory exemption, and this is in the case of initial assembly or first installation of goods (outside the building industry) where this is an integral part of a contract for the supply of goods and necessary for taking he goods supplied into use and carried out by skilled or specialist workers of the supplying undertaking. This exemption applies only if the period of posting does not exceed 8 days.[77] There are also permissive exemptions. First, after consulting employers and labour, the State can decide not to apply minimum pay provisions where the length of the posting does not exceed one month, other than agency-supplied workers.[78] Secondly, without the need for

---

[73] See for these conditions Barnard (2004) at 241. They might include, professional rules designed to protect recipients of a service, road safety, guaranteeing quality of work and generally the protection of workers as defined in case law under Arts 49 and 50.

[74] 'Posted worker' means one who, for a limited period, carries out his work in the territory of a Member State other than the State in which he or she normally works: Art 2(1). The definition of 'worker' is that which applies in the law of the Member State to whose territory the worker is posted: Art 2(2).

[75] Art 1(3).

[76] This was the situation in Cases 62 and 63/81, *Seco SA v EVI* [1982] ECR 223.

[77] Art 3(2).

[78] Art 3(3). Art 3(4) allows this to be done by collective agreement. In order to prevent repeated postings amounting to more than one month, the length of the posting has to be calculated on the basis of a reference period of one year from the beginning of the posting and

consultation, the State may exempt these workers from the minimum pay and paid holiday terms where the work to be done by them is 'not significant'.[79]

One of the puzzles about the Directive is the extent of the jurisdiction of the home and host states' courts. Article 6 of the Directive states that ' in order to enforce the right to the terms and conditions of employment guaranteed in Article 3 [the compulsory terms] judicial proceedings may be instituted in the Member State in whose territory the worker is or was posted, without prejudice, where applicable, to the right, under existing international conventions on jurisdiction, to institute proceedings in another state.' Is the jurisdiction of the home state limited to the enforcement of the compulsory terms, or does it confer jurisdiction in respect of all aspects of the individual employment relationship ? The literal meaning of Article 6 ('in order to enforce . . .') supports the first interpretation. However, the posted worker is more likely to sue in the home state, which will have jurisdiction under the EC Jursidiction Regulation, either as the court of the domicile of the employer, or the place where the worker habitually carries out his or her work or the place where the business which engaged the worker is or was situated (above). The home state courts will have to apply the mandatory rules of the applicable law, in accordance with Article 6 of the Rome Convention. These will usually be the rules of the home state. The home state court has a discretion, under Article 7 of the Rome Convention, when applying their own law, nevertheless to give effect to the mandatory rules of another country with which the contract is closely connected. The Posted Workers Directive identifies the relevant mandatory terms of the host state's law and requires the home state courts to apply them (Table 7.A).[80]

The legal basis of the Directive (above) indicates that it is intended to facilitate the provision of services by a home state employer to a customer in another Member State. As Davies points out in his seminal analysis of the Directive, it is difficult to see how the imposition on the relationship between the home-state employer and its workers of standards derived from the host state's labour laws and agreements can be said to further this objective. Davies suggests that 'the primary beneficiaries of the Directive are in fact the systems of labour regulation of the host state.'[81] If this is so, then the Directive risks challenge as being invalid because it goes beyond the powers conferred by the Treaty. More likely, is that the ECJ will interpret the Directive so as to maintain its compatibility with the Treaty.[82] This is indicated in a number of cases in

account must be taken of previous periods for which the post has been filled [in that year] by a posted worker: Art 3(6).

[79] Art 3(5).
[80] Davies (1997) at 579; cf Kidner (1998) at 114–17.
[81] Davies (1997) at 573.
[82] Expressly stated in Art 3(10), and also a general principle of EC law that a directive cannot go beyond Treaty powers.

Table 7.A

HOST COUNTRY STANDARDS APPLICABLE TO POSTED WORKERS

Required core terms and conditions	Permitted terms and conditions
Maximum work periods and minimum rest periods	Public policy provisions
Minimum paid annual holidays	Core terms in collective agreements and awards generally applicable or made with representative organisations in building industry
Minimum rates of pay including overtime rates[83]	Terms outside core terms in collective agreements and awards in all industries, subject to equal treatment of all undertakings
Conditions of hiring out workers, in particular supply of workers by temporary employment undertakings agency[84]	Rules applicable to temporary workers in place of work, if worker employed by temporary employment undertaking or
Health, safety and hygiene at work	
Protective measures with regard to the terms and conditions of employment of pregnant women or women who have recently given birth, of children and young people	
Equality of treatment between men and women and other provisions on non- discrimination	
Collectively agreed terms or awards declared universally applicable in building industry	

which the ECJ appears to have retreated from the broad dictum in *Rush Portuguesa* (above). These cases were decided before the period for transposition of the Directive into national law had expired, but they provide a new method of analysis for deciding whether home state labour laws undermine the cross-border provision of services.

First, it has to be asked whether the home state rules have a restrictive effect, even though they are facially neutral between home and domestic suppliers of

---

[83] This point does not apply to supplementary occupational pension schemes.

[84] Art 3(9).

services ? In *Mazzoleni*,[85] a French company employed 13 workers as security officers at a shopping mall in a Belgian frontier region. They were paid less than the minimum rate laid down by Belgian law. The ECJ accepted that the application of host state rules on pay may lead to an administrative burden (for example in having to determine how much time has been spent across the border), and to payment of different wages to workers attached to the same operational base, resulting in tension between workers and threatening the cohesion of labour agreements. Secondly, the court has to examine whether the restrictive effect on the freedom to provide services is justified on grounds of 'overriding requirements relating to the public interest.'[86] In principle, the protection of workers, including minimum rates of pay, is regarded as an overriding public interest. However, the recent decisions of the ECJ emphasise that it is the protection of the posted workers that must be the main purpose. Government assertions of the purpose are not conclusive. The national court has to be satisfied that the host state's law 'confers a genuine benefit on the [posted] workers concerned which significantly adds to their social protection.'[87] Moreover, measures which restrict the cross-border provision of services cannot be justified by economic aims or by the host state's interest in protecting domestic businesses.[88]

Thirdly, the national court has to assess 'genuine benefit' on an objective basis, and to decide whether this benefit has been conferred by 'appropriate means' which are no more restrictive on the ability to provide cross-border services than is necessary. For example, in *Commission v Germany*,[89] the ECJ held that the German temporary work law infringed Articles 43 (ex 52) and 49 (ex 59) of the EC Treaty by giving partial exemption from the prohibition on the provision of temporary labour-only work in the construction industry to undertakings covered by a certain type of collective agreement. Only undertakings established in Germany could in practice be members of the relevant employers' associations and thus be covered by the collective agreement. This went beyond anything that was necessary to ensure the social protection of posted workers.

These recent decisions show that the Directive is likely to have only a limited impact. The ECJ, modifying its earlier statement in *Rush Portuguesa*, now attaches more importance to the freedom to provide cross-border services than the power of host states to protect the economic interests of their own employers and workers. The Directive is likely in future to be interpreted so as

[85] Case C–165/98, *Criminal Proceedings against André Mazzoleni* [2002] ECR I–2189, paras 30–41.

[86] Joined Cases C–369 and 376/96, *Criminal Proceedings against Arblade and Leloup* [1999] ECR I–8453, paras 33 and 34.

[87] Joined Cases C–49, 50, 52, 54, 68 and 71/98, *Finalarte Sociedade de Construçao Civil Lda* [2001] ECR I–7831, para 42.

[88] *Finalarte*, para 49; Case C–164/99 *Portugaia Construçoes Lda* [2002] ECR I–787.

[89] Case C–493/99, *Commission v Germany (contracting-out of labour)* [2001] ECR I–8163.

to protect posted workers, not to protect national labour law regimes against allegations of social dumping.

5. Cross-border transfers of undertakings and offshore outsourcing

The limits of choice of law and jurisdiction rules to protect workers can be illustrated in the context of cross-border mergers and offshore outsourcing. The growing scale of these activities and their economic and social consequences were outlined in chapter 1. The employment effects may include transfer of production or provision of ancillary services from one country to another, rationalisation measures including the closure of plants or offices in one country, cross-border transfers of senior management and workers with particular skills on either a temporary or indefinite basis, and the integration of terms of employment of workers in the undertaking in one country with those in another. Transfers and offshore outsourcing may also reduce or remove the influence of trade unions and other workers' representatives (section 6, below).

Research studies on the human resource implications of mergers and acquisitions indicate that the impact on individual workers can include a sense of loss and uncertainty, psychological problems and difficulties with personal relationships. There may also be reduced commitment, loss of productivity and high staff turnover.[90] The more hostile a takeover, the greater will be the degree of employee resistance to integration. It is fair to assume that there will be even greater suspicion and negative attitudes in the case of a takeover by a foreign firm.

It is widely recognised that in order to minimise such adverse consequences it is important to ensure that individuals do not perceive their terms and conditions of employment as being under threat, and that workers as stakeholders in the target undertaking as well as the transferor undertaking are properly informed and consulted about plans for transfers of undertakings. This led to the adoption by the EC in 1977 of Council Directive 77/187/EEC on the approximation of the laws of the Member States relating to the safeguarding of employees' rights in the event of transfers of undertakings, businesses or parts of undertakings or businesses (the Acquired Rights Directive). This Directive was amended in 1998, and consolidated in the current Acquired Rights Directive 2001/23/EC of 12 March 2001.[91] The preamble recognises that 'differences still remain in the Member States as regards the extent of the protection of employees in [respect of transfers] and these differences should be reduced.'

---

[90] Enderwick (1994) at 271.
[91] [2001] OJ L82/16.

The Directive uses three methods to safeguard the acquired rights of workers in the event of transfers of undertakings: (1) the automatic transfer of the employment relationship from the transferor to the transferee, ie from the old to the new employer; (2) the protection of employees against dismissal due exclusively to the transfer of the undertaking (but dismissals for an economic, technical or organisational reason entailing changes in the workforce are permitted); and (3) requirements for information and consultation with the representatives of employees in the transferor and transferee undertaking.[92] The basic aim is to ensure that whatever the level of employment protection employees enjoyed before the transfer of an undertaking (the 'acquired rights'), these rights continue to be enjoyed after the transfer. There is, therefore, a distinction between (1) the level and content of rights which existed before the transfer (the substantive rights), this being solely a matter for determination at national level by Member States, and (2) the circumstances in which those pre-existing rights are transferred and the transfer is made subject to participation by employee representatives (the 'transfer rights'), this being a matter for determination by the Directive. All that is safeguarded on transfer are the rights which existed in national law before the transfer.

The Directive applies to the 'transfer of an economic entity which retains its identity, meaning an organised grouping of resources which has the objective of pursuing an economic activity, whether or not that activity is central or ancillary.'[93] There must be a change of employer. The Directive does not apply to a transfer by the sale of shares in the acquired company, the most frequent form of takeover in the UK. The effect of this limitation was vividly illustrated in the celebrated Westland affair (Box 7.2).

The most controversial aspect of the Directive has been its application to outsourcing. This first came to the fore in the process of competitive tendering in the 1980s, when public authorities put out the supply of services to bids from in-house and outside service providers. Commercial enterprises have also increasingly resorted to the contracting-out of ancillary services. The ECJ has been ambivalent about the meaning of 'an economic entity that retains its identity'. On the one hand, the Directive was held to cover a situation in which a Bank contracted-out cleaning operations which it had previously performed itself, even though, prior to the contracting-out the work was carried out by a single cleaner.[94] On the other hand, when a school terminated its contract for the cleaning of the school with one contractor and awarded the contract to another, leading to the dismissal of 8 employees of the first contractor, the ECJ

---

[92] Only a person who is protected by national law as an 'employee' is protected: Case 105/84 *Mikkelsen* [1985] ECR 2639. This has led to a wide variation in the coverage of national implementing legislation: see Hepple (1990b).

[93] Art 1(1)(b) which attempts to codify the confusing earlier case law.

[94] Case C–392/92, *Schmidt v Spar-und Leihkasse* [1994] ECR I–1311.

Box 7.2

THE WESTLAND AFFAIR

In 1985, Westland was the only British firm engaged in the manufacture of helicopters for military purposes. The company was in financial difficulties. One option was a rescue by Sikorsky, an American company, taking a minority stake in the company. Another option was the acquisition of a stake by a European-based consortium, in order to avoid dependence on the USA. The rival bids led to a Cabinet crisis, with resignations of Ministers, and ultimately to a decision by shareholders to accept a Sikorsky/Fiat offer. Workers were left out in the cold, as voteless spectators in decisions which vitally affected their future. The rival offers put to the Westland shareholders involved the subscription of new ordinary and preference share capital by existing shareholders and the potential partners. There was no change in the identity of the employer (Westland), but the changes in control involved were no less serious for the workforce than had there been an actual transfer of the undertaking. The form of the transaction deprived the recognised trade unions of any legal right under the Directive and the implementing UK legislation to information or consultation.[95]

---

held that there was no 'transfer of an undertaking' because there was no concomitant transfer of significant tangible or intangible assets.[96] Amendments to the Directive in 1998 (consolidated in the 2001 version), and subsequent case law, have thrown little light on the outsourcing problem. A rule of thumb, used in practice, is that where there are significant assets upon which the undertaking depends, there is unlikely to be a relevant transfer unless those assets are transferred. Where few or no significant assets are transferred, the voluntary taking over of a majority of the workforce would be a strong indication that there has been a relevant transfer.[97]

A question of particular relevance in the case of offshore outsourcing is whether the geographical relocation of an undertaking is sufficient to prevent

---

[95] Hepple (1986b). The situation may change when the UK implements the Directive of the European Parliament and Council 2002/12/EC establishing a general framework for informing and consulting employees.

[96] Case C–13/95, *Süzen v Zehnacker Gebäudereinigung GmbH* [1997] ECR I–1259.

[97] Case C–172/99, *Oy Likenne Ab v Liskojarvi and Juntunen* [2001] ECR I–745; in Case C–340/01, *Abler v Sodexho MM Catering GmbH* [2004] IRLR 168, it was held that the assets were 'taken over' where a hospital catering contractor was obliged to prepare the meals in the hospital kitchen, even though these assets continued to be owned by the contracting authority.

it from retaining its identity. In the *Merckx and Neuhuys* case,[98] the Ford Motor Company transferred an exclusive dealership from Anfo to Novarobel, dealers who were situated in different municipalities in the Brussels conurbation. The ECJ held that it was irrelevant that the principal place of business was situated in a different area of the same conurbation provided that the contract territory [ie the dealership] remained the same. Would the economic entity still retain its identity if the geographical location were shifted to another country? An example would be the transfer of the services provided for the whole of England and Wales by a call centre in England, to a call centre in India, offering the same services for the same area. This point has not yet come before the ECJ. It could be argued that so long as the nature of the activity pursued remains the same and significant assets (eg the IT used by the centre) are transferred, there is a relevant transfer. However, in a labour-intensive undertaking (such as a call centre) the fact that there is no significant transfer of assets and a new workforce is employed in another country would be decisive pointers that there was no relevant transfer.

If there has been a relevant transfer, the crucial question is the territorial scope of the Directive. Article 1(2) states that the Directive applies 'where and in so far as the undertaking, business, or part of a business to be transferred is situated within the territorial scope of the Treaty.' The first preliminary draft of the Directive, published in 1974,[99] was much wider in scope than the final version. It applied to mergers and takeovers 'irrespective of whether such a merger or takeover is effected between undertakings in the territory of one or more Member States or is effected between undertakings in the territory of Member States and undertakings in third countries.' A revised 1975 draft proposed an even wider territorial scope by applying the Directive 'where and insofar as the transferring or dependent undertaking is situated in the territory of the Member States of the EEC or the transfer or concentration *affects* an undertaking within that territory involved in such a transaction' (emphasis added).[100] It was the *effects* of the transfer within the EC which was to be the decisive criterion. The final version of the Directive, however, limits its application solely on the geographical situation of the undertaking *to be* transferred, and this must be within a Member State. In the example given of a transfer of a call centre from England to India, assuming that there is a sufficient transfer of assets and/ or workers to make this a relevant transfer, this would trigger the information and consultation requirements of the Directive. But so far as the individual employees in England are concerned, the employer is likely to be

---

[98] Joined Cases C–171 and 172/94, *Merckx and Neuhuys v Ford Motor Co Belgium SA* [1996] ECR I–1253, para 21.

[99] COM(74) 351 final/2, 21 June 1974; OJ C/104/1, 13 September 1974, Art 1(2).

[100] COM (75) 429 final, 25 July 1975, Art 1(3).

able to justify their dismissal under Article 4(2) of the Directive as being for an economic, technical or organisational reason entailing changes in the workforce.

When implementing the Directive, most Member States have usually limited the application of their law to situations where the undertaking to be transferred is situated within their own territory. This means that the Directive is applied only where the undertaking to be transferred is within the territory of the Member State. The transferor may have no place of business in that state, and may be subject to the law of another state. For example, if a Texas corporation transfers the undertaking of its Belgian subsidiary situated in Belgium to an undertaking situated in France, the transfer will be subject in Belgian courts to the Belgian Decree and collective agreements implementing the Directive. Although the transfer may affect the interests of employees of the French undertaking (the transferee) they will not be able to challenge the breach of the information and consultation requirements because the undertaking is situated in Belgium. If the transferee undertaking was situated not in France but in Spain or Portugal, the Spanish court would have jurisdiction over the transfer in Belgium, but only if the Texas corporation or the Belgian undertaking was under the control of a Spanish/Portuguese undertaking at the time of transfer.

The Directive contains no conflict of laws provisions. The 1974 draft provided that the 'labour laws of a Member State which are applicable to employment relationships prior to the merger or takeover shall continue to apply after the merger or takeover has taken place.'[101] This was not to apply where the place of work of an employee was transferred to another Member State or the application of another body of labour law was validly agreed. This proposal was, however, dropped from later drafts, apparently because it was believed that the issue would be dealt with in the draft Regulation on conflict of laws in employment matters.[102] The draft Regulation was later withdrawn, so the Acquired Rights Directive unexpectedly had to operate without complementary provisions on the conflict of laws.

The Rome Convention (above) is therefore the source of conflict rules in relation to acquired rights. As we have seen, Article 6(1) provides that a choice of law made by the parties shall not deprive an employee of the protection of the mandatory rules of the law of the place of work, or if the employee does not habitually work in any one country, the law of the place of business. If it appears that the contract is more closely connected with another country, the mandatory rules of that country apply. There can be no doubt that the rules on

---

[101] COM (74) 351, final/2, 21 June 1974, Art 10.

[102] PJ 1972, C 49/26; OJ 1972 C142/5 (Economic and Social Committee); OJ 1973 C 4/14 (Parliament). After consultation this was amended: COM (75) 653 final.

acquired rights are mandatory[103] and so the implementing legislation of the law of place of work will normally be applicable. Where the Rome Convention does not apply, must the rules of the forum be applied as public policy irrespective of the choice of law by the parties? In some Member States the implementing legislation makes it clear that the rules on transfer of under-takings must be not less favourable than they would be if governed by the law of the place where the employee habitually carries out his or her work.

The purposes of the Directive would be undermined if the law applicable to the contract changed as a result of a cross-border transfer to one which is less favourable to the worker. Although the EC's Economic and Social Committee expressed fears that this could occur, it can be argued that Article 3(1) of the Directive[104] has the effect of crystallising the law applicable to the employment relationship at the time of transfer, and so no further choice of law under the Rome Convention is possible. Put another way, the mandatory rules of the host state which applied immediately before the transfer will continue to apply after the transfer by virtue of Article 3(1) of the Directive, unless the employer validly dismisses the employee for an economic, technical or organisational reason entailing changes in the workforce under Article 4(2) of the Directive. Where a transfer results in the posting of an employee, say a highly skilled per-son with a mobile contract, to an undertaking in another country, then the Posted Workers Directive will apply.

The Acquired Rights Directive does not include any provision relating to jurisdiction. The Jurisdiction Regulation means that the appropriate forum will normally be the courts of the place of work. If, let us say, a German com-pany transfers its undertaking in England to an English firm, the employee in England who claims that his or her rights have been infringed will normally sue the transferor or transferee in England, but could also proceed against the transferor in the German court as the court of the transferor's domicile.

In summary, it has been shown that EC law offers only limited protection to workers in the case of cross-border mergers and offshore outsourcing. First, the Acquired Rights Directive does not apply to share transfers and other con-centrations, but only to the transfer of a stable economic entity to a new employer. Secondly, most cases of offshore outsourcing will not be covered as relevant transfers, either because there is no transfer of significant assets or, where there are few assets to transfer, because the transferee does not voluntarily take over a significant number of the old workforce. Thirdly,

---

[103] Case 324/86, *Foreningen af Arbejdsledere I Danmark v Daddy's Dance Hall* [1988] ECR 17. This was applied in the UK to a contracting-out due to the transfer and for no other reason in *Wilson v St Helens BC, sub nom. British Fuels Ltd v Baxendale, Meade v British Fuels Ltd* [1998] IRLR 706, HL.

[104] Art 3(1) provides: 'The transferor's rights and obligations arising form a contract or employment or an employment relationship existing at the date of the transfer shall, by reason of such transfer, be transferred to the transferee.'

although geographical location as such as irrelevant, there are spatial limits to the territorial application of the Directive, that is the location of the undertaking to be transferred in the territory of a Member State. Member States themselves generally limit the scope of implementing legislation to their own territory. Finally, although the employees will enjoy the acquired rights rules as mandatory rules of the law of the place where they habitually work, they will usually not get the benefit of the more favourable rules of the law of the transferee company's domicile. The effects of transfers and outsourcing on collective agreements and works agreements are considered in the next section.

6. Collective bargaining and employee representation

The foundation of collective labour relations is the freedom of association and the right to organise, which along with the right to engage in collective bargaining, are 'core' ILO principles (chapter 2, above). Problems arise when workers have contracts of employment governed by foreign law that does not properly recognise these rights. In some cases the law of the home state guaranteeing freedom of association may have extra-territorial effect; in others it may not. In the UK the statutory rights to union membership and to participate in union activities apply irrespective of the proper law of the contract,[105] but there is a territorial limit excluding from some of these rights those who ordinarily work, or in the case of a prospective employee would ordinarily work, outside Great Britain.[106] If the right can be classified as arising out of an individual employment contract (as it could in Britain but not in many other systems which see this as a 'collective' right) then the Rome Convention will normally result in the application of the 'mandatory rules' of the law of the place of work. These rules may include a non-derogable right to join a trade union and participate in its activities. But this right does not feature among the core terms guaranteed to posted workers.

In countries which prescribe a duty on employers to recognise trade unions for collective bargaining, questions may arise such as whether workers who are foreign nationals or workers who have been posted abroad should be included when determining the representativity of the union or the definition of the 'bargaining unit'. This will turn on the wording of the national legislation. For example, in the US there have been rulings that persons working outside the country, even though they are US nationals and employed by a US under-

---

[105] TULRCA 1992, s 289.

[106] TULRCA 1992, s 285(1), relating to refusal of employment, action short of dismissal, and time off for union activities. Protection against unfair dismissal is governed by ERA 1996, which was amended in 1999 so as to remove the territorial restriction, but has been (controversially) interpreted so as to apply only to dismissal from employment in Great Britain: see above.

taking, may not participate in a bargaining unit, and that vessels flying a foreign flag and manned by foreign crews were not within the scope of he National Labor Relations Act.[107] In Britain, a union cannot request recognition unless the employer together with any associated employer employs at least 21 workers on the day the employer received the request, or employs an average of at least 21 employees in the 13 weeks ending with that day.[108] The union is not allowed to count any worker employed by an associated company incorporated outside Great Britain unless on the day the request, or in the relevant week, the worker ordinarily worked in Great Britain.[109]

The law relating to collective agreements is predominantly national, with great differences between countries, even within the EU. International (sectoral) collective agreements, outside the shipping industry, are few and relatively recent, and are generally worded in a way that is too vague to allow them to be legally enforceable. They contain broad declarations of human rights, and are subject to monitoring by the parties but contain no enforcement provisions or guidance as to which country's law is to apply. A sensible way of resolving disputes which the parties cannot settle would be by international arbitration. But it is extremely rare to find agreements with provisions for arbitration in accordance with UNCITRAL Arbitration Rules, an exception being agreements to eliminate child labour in the soccer ball and carpet industries in Pakistan.

The enforcement of trans-national agreements will grow in importance as the European social dialogue develops (chapter 9, below). Article 138 EC requires the European Commission to facilitate the social dialogue at European level, and Article 139 EC provides that 'should management and labour so decide, the dialogue between them at Community level may lead to contractual relations, including agreements.' It seems to be envisaged that these agreements will be governed by national laws. Article 139(2) provides that 'Agreements concluded at Community level shall be implemented either in accordance with the procedures and practices specific to management and labour and the Member States' or in respect of certain matters, at the joint request of the parties, by Council decision. Although it has been suggested that these social dialogue agreements are entirely a matter for substantive EC law,[110] national courts may find it necessary to apply choice of law rules. For example, there may be an agreement covering different cross-border regions of the EU, or the agreement may cover the same industry in several states, or it may be a multi-industry agreement. A European company operating in a number of states may conclude an agreement with one or more unions. In all these cases, there will be representatives of management and labour from more

---

[107] Morgenstern (1984) at 97.
[108] TULRCA 1992, Sched A1, para 7(1).
[109] Paras 7(3)(4).
[110] Krebber (2000) 505.

than one country, and this may include countries outside the EU. There is at present an absence of European-wide rules to govern these situations, particularly since the Rome Convention on contractual obligations does not apply. National conflict rules will apply.

In most national systems, collective agreements are governed by the 'proper law of the contract.' In England, in the absence of an express choice, the law with which the collective agreement has the 'closest and most real connection' will be applied (Box 7.3).

Box 7.3

MONTEROSSO SHIPPING CO LTD v ITF[111]

Maltese shipowners claimed damages from the International Transport Workers Federation (ITF), then based in London, on grounds, among others, of their failure to issue a certificate that the crew of a ship flying the Maltese flag and manned by a Spanish crew were engaged on terms acceptable to the ITF. The undertaking to issue the certificate was contained in a 'special agreement' on a printed form issued by the ITF in London, but executed in Bilbao, Spain. Under UK law, a collective agreement is conclusively presumed not to have been intended by the parties to be a legally enforceable contract, unless the parties expressly agree that it shall be enforceable.[112] The 'special agreement' contained no statement of enforceability. The Court of Appeal held that the 'proper law' of the special agreement was Spanish law and not English law. This was because the agreement, intended to be used worldwide, had been entered into in Spain and affected the recruitment of Spanish crews. Accordingly, its 'closest and most real connection' was with Spanish law. The Court regarded the non-enforceability provision of the UK statute as not being a material consideration, a surprising conclusion in view of the express provision of the statute that 'it is immaterial whether the law which (apart from this Act) governs any person's employment is the law of the United Kingdom, or of a part of the United Kingdom, or not.'[113] By treating the UK provision as substantive and not procedural the Court was able to apply the foreign law. On the other hand, in an earlier case, the English High Court treated an agreement concluded in a British port between a Liberian company and the ITF as governed by UK law, and hence unenforceable because of the absence of a statement of enforceability.[114]

---

[111] *Monterosso Shipping Co Ltd v ITF* [1982] ICR 675, CA.

[112] TULCRA 1992, s 179(1).

[113] TULRCA 1992, s 289.

[114] *Universe Tankships Inc of Monrovia v ITF* [1980] IRLR 239; this point did not arise in the subsequent appeals: [1980] IRLR 363, CA, and [1982] ICR 262, HL.

One problem with applying the proper law of the contract is that collective agreements are not like other contracts. They may both be a contract between the employer or employers' association and trade union, and also have a normative effect laying down terms, such as wages and hours of work, which will be incorporated in individual contracts of employment. It is the proper law of the individual contract, rather than that of the collective contract which should apply. This means that the wage rates and other terms incorporated into individual contracts will be subject in the EU to the special rules relating to such contracts in the Rome Convention and, where relevant, the Posted Workers Directive. Where there is a national system for the 'extension' of collective agreements so as to make them 'universally applicable' then these are generally regarded as akin to mandatory rules. Under the Rome Convention such agreements are among the rules of the law of the place of work and cannot be avoided by choice of a different law to govern the contract.[115] These agreements and generally applicable agreements or agreements made by representative organisations may also be regarded as core terms which must be guaranteed to posted workers (above).

Another problem is what happens to collective agreements in the case of cross-border transfers and offshore outsourcing? Article 3(3) of the Acquired Rights Directive obliges the transferee to continue to observe the terms of collective agreements on the same terms applicable to the transferor, until the date of termination or expiry of that agreement or the entry into force or application of another collective agreement. Member States may limit the period for observing such terms, with the proviso that it shall be not less than one year. In principle this provision applies to cross-border mergers, and the general provisions of Articles 3 and 4 of the Rome Convention will determine the choice of law. There may be an express choice of law in the collective agreement, if this has a transnational dimension. In the absence of choice, the collective contract will be governed by the law of the country with which it is most closely connected.[116] In practice, however, agreements are geared to a single country, region or plant. The expectation is that within a year an acquiring undertaking will join the appropriate employers' organisation (where that organisation is a party to the agreement) in the country in which the undertaking is situated, or will negotiate a new agreement with the trade union or workers' representatives in the undertaking. This expectation will be frustrated where the acquirer fails to join the employer's organisation or is able to de-recognise the trade union.

---

[115] Giuliano-Lagarde Report, [1980] OJ C 282.

[116] This assumes that the collective agreement is a contract. In the UK a collective agreement is conclusively presumed not to be intended to be a legally enforceable contract, unless the parties agree that it shall be legally binding: TULRCA 1992, s 179.

Moreover, the TNC may decide to relocate the activities of the acquired undertaking to another country because it regards the collective agreement negotiated with unions in that country as more favourable to its interests than the agreement applicable in the country where the undertaking is siuated. Although the Hoover affair (chapter 1, Box 1.3, above), concerned the relocation of a TNC's activities from a plant in France to one in Scotland, and not a transfer of undertaking to a new employer within the scope of the Directive, it illustrates the possibility of what in the US is called 'whip-sawing', in which large employers can play off their plants in different states against one another to secure the lowest labour costs.[117] Trade unions that seek to oppose such transfers by international solidarity action face considerable practical and legal obstacles (see below). Problems such as these cannot be resolved within the framework of the Acquired Rights Directive, because they raise far wider questions about the enforceability of collective agreements and the scope of permitted industrial action

German unions have complained about the *Flucht aus der Mitbestimmung* when undertakings in countries with strong participation rights are transferred to jurisdictions which have such rights at a lower level. Workers' representatives in different countries may receive different, even contradictory information from companies within a group. When the parent company has its seat in a different country the workers may be unable to negotiate with the real decision-makers, and they may not have facilities for cross-border communications and co-operation with workers' representatives in the same group of companies in other countries.

Improvements were made to the Acquired Rights Directive in 1998, to strengthen the legal duty to preserve the status and functions of employee representatives, and also to apply the obligations relating to information and consultation irrespective of whether the decision resulting in the transfer is taken by the employer (eg a local subsidiary) or by an undertaking controlling the employer (which may be a parent company in another country). Moreover, in considering alleged breaches of the information and consultation requirements, the argument that such a breach occurred because the information was not provided by an undertaking controlling the employer cannot be accepted as an excuse.[118] This is similar to provisions in the Collective Redundancies Directive 98/59/EEC, amending an earlier Directive of 1977,[119] and avoids the problem of extraterritoriality because no direct obligation is imposed on the controlling undertaking in another country. It simply deprives the local subsidiary which took the decision of the excuse that its parent had not revealed

---

[117] For details see (1993) 230 *European Industrial Relations Review* 14–20.
[118] Art 7(4).
[119] [1998] OJ L225/16.

the information. There are major legal obstacles to extending Community jurisdiction to an agreement entirely external to the EU.[120] Moreover, the Directive avoids using 'by-pass' mechanisms of the kind envisaged in the draft 'Vredeling' directive in 1983,[121] which proposed that in exceptional cases where local management failed to provide information, the employee representatives should be entitled to approach the parent management, who then had to provide the information to local management for communication to the employee representatives. Where the parent company is situated outside the EU or EFTA states there would be obvious practical difficulties for employee representatives in seeking to enforce their rights against a natural or legal person operating under a different system of law. As a matter of international law, it is generally accepted that laws may not be enforced outside their territorial jurisdiction without the consent of the state in whose territory the enforcement takes place.

The adoption of the European Works Councils Directive 94/95/EEC[122] has, in any event, put the problem of information and consultation in transnational undertakings in a completely new light. The aim of the Directive is not the harmonisation of national information and consultation requirements (that is the subject of another framework Directive adopted in 2002)[123] but the creation of an EU-wide framework for information and consultation within 'Community-scale' undertakings or groups. These are undertakings with at least 1000 employees within the territorial scope of the Directive including at least 150 employees in each of two or more Member States. The Directive has resulted for the first time in a transnational level of collective labour relations in TNCs operating in Europe.[124] The Directive encouraged the negotiation of voluntary arrangements. Article 13 exempts undertakings which had by 22 September 1996 (the implementation date) already negotiated agreements for transnational information and consultation. Since that date a European Works Council (EWC) or alternatively, an information and consultation procedure, has to be negotiated through a 'special negotiating body' (SNB) composed of employee representatives from each Member State in which the undertaking operates. The agreement has to cover certain matters specified in Article 6. The Directive has 'subsidiary requirements'—a strong incentive to reach agreement—set out in the Annex to provide a basic constitution for an EWC which will apply when management refuses to open negotiations, or SNB negotiations do not produce an agreement within three years.

[120] See eg Cases 89, 104, 116–117, 125–0/85 *Ahlstrom v Commission (Woodpulp)* [1988] ECR 5193.

[121] [1983] OJ C 297/80.

[122] [1994] OJ L254/64.

[123] European Parliament and Council Directive establishing a general framework for informing and consulting employees in the European Community, 2002/14/EC, [2002] OJ L80/29.

[124] See generally, Weiss [Manfred] (2004).

While the Directive deals with transnational information and consultation, it devolves to national-level regulation many of the key rules concerning EWCs or alternative procedures. The national measures adopted differ in significant respects. For example, transposition in the UK has peculiar features because of the UK's largely 'voluntary' system of employee representation.[125] It is the law of the country where the 'central management' is situated which determines transnational issues, such as the definition of 'Community-scale undertakings', the details of the SNB procedure including the size of the SNB and the distribution of seats between countries in which the TNC operates, the confidentiality of information and the regulations through which effect is given to the Directive's 'subsidiary requirements'.[126] Where central management is not situated in a Member State, the law of the Member State in which its representative agent is located applies to these matters. If there is no representative agent, the applicable law is that of the establishment or group undertaking employing the greatest number of employees in any one Member State.[127] 'Central management' means the central management of the Community-scale undertaking, or in the case of a Community-scale group of undertakings, of the 'controlling undertaking'.[128] The law applicable in order to determine whether an undertaking is a 'controlling undertaking' is the law of the Member State which governs that undertaking. Where the law governing the undertaking is not that of a Member State, the law applicable is the law of the Member State within whose territory the representative of the undertaking, or in the absence of such a representative, the central management of the group undertaking which employs the greatest number of employees is situated.[129]

Certain other aspects of the EWCs or alternative procedures are, however, governed by the law of each Member State in which the undertaking or group of undertakings is situated. In particular, the method of electing or appointing national representatives to an SNB or EWC is determined by the national provisions in each country.[130] The question as to who is an 'employee' will also be determined by those provisions. As is usual with EU measures, the enforcement mechanisms are also a matter for the national laws of the country in which the workers are employed. The 'Europeanisation' of employee participation has obviously left considerable scope for national diversity.

It seems that the validity and binding effects of an agreement to set up a EWC or alternative procedure should be determined by the 'proper law of the

---

[125] Carley and Hall (2000) at 104.
[126] Art 4(1).
[127] Art 4(2).
[128] Art 2(e).
[129] Art 3(6).
[130] Arts 5(2)(a), Annex para 1(b).

contract', like any other collective agreement (above). For example, if the agreement was signed in Brussels where the central management is situated, and the parties did not choose another law, the agreement should be interpreted and enforced in accordance with the general principles of Belgian contractual law.[131] However, the normal conflicts rule would give rise to difficulties where the proper law is that of a part of the UK, because of the presumption that collective agreements are not legally enforceable as contracts unless the parties expressly choose otherwise. For this reason, the implementing UK regulations provide special enforcement mechanisms for agreements between central management and the SNB under Article 6 of the Directive. However, Article 13 agreements (made before 22 September 1996), governed by UK law, are subject to the ordinary presumption of non-enforceability.

Brief mention must also be made of the Directive on employee involvement in the European Company.[132] This supplements the 'statute' for the European Company (*Societas Europaea*) (SE) which provides an optional new corporate form for businesses in the EU. As originally proposed the SE was intended to provide a uniform set of rules which companies merging across borders could adopt. However, the Council Regulation embodying the 'statute' of the SE has many gaps which have to be filled by the national company law of the state in which the SE is registered.

The Directive is based on two sometimes inconsistent principles encapsulated in the European Parliament's slogans: 'no escape route from employee participation' and 'no export of employee participation.'[133] On the one hand, where employee participation was a substantial feature of the national laws applying to the companies which formed the SE, then in default of an agreement between management and labour, board-level participation must form part of the constitution of the SE as well. For example, where a German company with mandatory participation under German rules, and a British one with no such participation, form an SE, employee representation on the board of directors is required, unless management and labour decide otherwise. This representation must be at the 'highest level' if there was more than one preexisting system. The 'highest level' is determined on a purely quantitative basis.[134] On the other hand, the Directive qualifies this 'no escape' policy with

---

[131] Blanpain and Engels (2003) at 619 point out that the Belgian Act of 5 December 1968 on joint committees and collective labour agreements could not apply because the parties on the employees' side are not all representative Belgian trade unions; cf Carley and Hall (2000) 106, who state that the law of the country in which central management is situated will determine the validity of Art 13 agreements.

[132] Council Directive 2001/14/EC supplementing the statute for a European Company with regard to the involvement of employees, [2001] OJ L294/22. The Statute of the European Company is in Council Regulation (EC) No 2157/2001, [2001] OJ L294/1.

[133] Cited by Davies (2003) at 87.

[134] Davies (2003) at 84–86.

a 'no export' one where a substantial proportion of the workforce was not subject to mandatory participation before the formation of an SE. In these cases board-level participation is not required. The detailed rules are complex and differ according to whether the SE was formed by merger or by transformation, and there is considerable scope for management and labour to negotiate 'up' or 'down' in the arrangements for participation in the SE. For the present, all these possibilities remain largely theoretical because of the absence of positive attractions for the creation of SEs.

Companies are likely to continue to prefer straight cross-border mergers, rather than the complex rules for adopting the status of an SE. At present the differences in national laws make transnational mergers extremely difficult; acquiring firms have to create local subsidiaries or invent complex holding structures. Proposals from 1984 onwards by the Commission to simplify procedures ran into the rock of German fears that the process might be hijacked by companies trying to escape the mandatory employee participation provisions of German law, by registering the new company in a country without such a system. Following the adoption of the SE Directive, the Commission launched a fresh proposal in November 2003.[135] This applies a similar system of protection of employee participation to that under the SE Directive, where, following a cross-border merger, the registered office of the new company created by the merger is situated in a Member State that does not have compulsory participation rules, while one or more of the companies being merged were operating under a participation system. In all other cases, the national law applicable to the company created by the merger determines the rules on employee participation. At the time of writing, these proposals are still under consideration.

7. International solidarity action[136]

The right to strike is generally seen as the necessary complement to the right to collective bargaining. Threats of 'strikes' by capital are greatly facilitated by the mobility of international capital, and by the legal guarantees of free movement of capital, goods and services. The freedom of movement of individual workers is no counterpart to these freedoms. Wedderburn argued in 1972 that 'the international function of the trade union movement as a countervailing power to management in the multi-national enterprise demands recognition

---

[135] Proposal for a Directive of the European Parliament and of the Council on Cross-Border Mergers of companies with share capital.COM(2003) 703 final, Brussels, 18 November 2003.
[136] This section draws upon Hepple (2002a) at 252–55.

by *national* systems of labour law of a right to take collective action in support of industrial action in other countries against companies which are, in an economic sense, part of the same unit of internationalised capital.'[137] Yet, transnational industrial action is subject to severe legal restrictions, sometimes outright prohibition, in almost every country, and these restrictions have increased over the past few decades. A recent survey[138] indicates that among OECD Member States only Belgium appears to leave national and international solidarity action unregulated.

International solidarity usually takes one of three forms. The first, is the secondary boycott which involves direct pressure on a secondary (sometimes called 'neutral') employer, to induce it to cease doing business with another (primary) employer which has a dispute with its own workers. Secondly, indirect pressure may be put on the secondary employer by inducing that employer's workers not to perform work which would aid the primary employer's business (secondary strike). Thirdly, there may be pressure on the secondary employer through a consumer boycott by that employer's customers. Outright prohibition of all these forms of secondary or sympathy action is a feature of UK law, a legacy of the Thatcher Government which was left undisturbed by the New Labour Government after 1997. In most other OECD countries solidarity action is permissible only if at least two conditions are satisfied. The first is that the action taken by workers in the primary dispute must itself be lawful. The second is that the secondary boycott or strike must have a direct connection with the primary dispute. This connection is sometimes made to depend on the secondary employer not being a 'neutral' in the primary dispute (Sweden), or on there being a 'common interest' between the sympathy strikers and the workers in the primary dispute (Italy), or on the secondary strikers having a 'personal' interest in the primary dispute or being in a position to affect its outcome (France and Germany).[139]

These restrictions of national law on secondary or sympathy action have an added bite when applied to international labour disputes. The first question which arises is whether national legislation has extra-territorial effect. In the UK section 244(3) of the Trade Union and Labour Relations (Consolidation) Act 1992, allows a dispute relating to matters occurring outside the UK to constitute a protected 'trade dispute' only if the persons whose actions in the UK are said to be in contemplation or furherance of a trade dispute relating to matters occurring outside the UK 'are likely to be affected' by the outcome of the dispute in respect of one or more of prescribed matters. This prevents solidarity action being taken in the UK (even if all the other restrictions on

---

[137] Wedderburn (1972) at 19.
[138] Germanotta (2002).
[139] Pankert (1977) at 71.

industrial action are surmounted) where there is no immediate connection between the outcome of that dispute and UK workers. This is unduly restrictive, as the ILO supervisory bodies have recognised. The criterion should be whether the sympathy action relates directly or indirectly to the social or economic interests of the workers involved, and the test of this should essentially be a subjective one, that is a genuinely held belief of the workers taking the secondary action. Sympathy action of this kind will rarely be taken if the workers do not feel that they have something to gain, either immediately or through the implicit promise of future support from those with whom they are expressing solidarity.

The second question in international disputes is which country's law should be applied? If the law applied is that of the country in which the primary dispute occurs, this may make it impossible to take solidarity action with workers in a country where strikes are prohibited or severely restricted. Testing the legality of the primary dispute by the law of the country in which the sympathy action occurs—the usual rule[140]—is also beset with difficulties because of the different institutional arrangements and collective bargaining procedures in each country. The perceived impossibility of applying the law of the country in which the sympathy action occurs to determining the lawfulness of primary industrial action in another country, led a German court in 1959[141] to decide that sympathy action should not be allowed at all!

The subject is one that is ripe for regulation at the level of the EU. It has been strongly argued that the right to strike, including the right to take secondary action, should be protected by EU law.[142] One of the paradoxes of the new European social model, discussed in chapter 9, is that it relies on the social dialogue, which depends on strong representation of management and labour at European, national and sectoral level, but at the same time provides no mechanisms for strengthening and protecting collective organisations. Indeed, the procedures under Article 137 (ex 118) EC do not apply to the right of association, the right to strike or the right to lock-out.[143] The main emphasis of EU collective labour law has been on the subjects of information and consultation, but the sanctions for non-compliance are essentially a matter for national law and practice subject to the overriding requirements of 'adequacy' and 'proportionality'. Article 28 of the EU Charter of Fundamental Rights, based on the revised European Social Charter (Article 21), recognises the 'right to negotiate and conclude collective agreements at the appropriate level and, in cases of

---

[140] Morgenstern (1984) 114.

[141] Cited by Moregnstern (1984) 115.

[142] Germanotta and Novitz (2002) 67.

[143] Art 137(6) EC Treaty. Arguably, even though the Art 137 procedures do not apply to the right to strike, the EU could still adopt legislation concerning strikes under Arts 94 or 308 EC. This seems unlikely to happen in practice.

conflicts of interest, to take collective action to defend their interests, including strike action.' However, there is no EU law to protect strike action or other international solidarity between workers.

At international level, the ILO's stance has been equivocal and contested.[144] Although the Director-General has spoken strongly about the need for the ILO to contribute to the empowerment of workers, the ILO's Governing Body has not moved beyond inconclusive discussions. The 1998 ILO Declaration, with its reassertion of freedom of association and collective bargaining as fundamental principles and rights, does provide a framework for new ILO initiatives. The crucial issue is the extent to which the ILO's supervisory bodies, in particular the CEACR and the CFA, are willing to recognise that solidarity action, particularly across national boundaries, is encompassed by the freedom of association. The right to strike, including the right to solidarity action, is not expressly recognised in C.87, but the CEACR has derived the right to strike from Articles 3 and 10 of the Convention. In relation to solidarity action, the CEACR and CFA have generally taken the position that 'a general prohibition on sympathy strikes could lead to abuse, and workers should be able to take such action, providing the initial strike they are supporting is itself lawful'.[145] The applications of these standards have been ambiguous. In relation to the UK, the CEACR has recently repeated that 'workers should be able to participate in sympathy strikes provided the initial strike they are supporting is itself lawful'.[146] In 1989, the CEACR said that 'where a boycott relates directly to the social and economic interests of the workers involved in either or both the original dispute and the secondary action, and where the original dispute and the secondary action are not unlawful in themselves, then that boycott should be regarded as a legitimate exercise of the right to strike.'[147] It would, therefore, make sense for the ILO's supervisory committees to apply simply a test of 'common interest' between the workers involved in the primary and secondary actions.

8. Conclusion: the limits of extra-territoriality

The basic objection to extra-territoriality is that, in the absence of unilateral or multilateral agreement, it involves an infringement of the principle of national

---

[144] Novitz (2003).

[145] Freedom of Association and Collective Bargaining, *General Survey* (Geneva, 1994) para 168; and Novitz (2003) at 290–302.

[146] ILO, *Report of the Committee of Experts*, Report III (Part IA), International Labour Conference, 87th session, (Geneva,1999); and ILO, *Report of the Committee of Experts*, Report III (Part IA), International Labour Conference, 77th session (Geneva,1989).

[147] CEACR, 1989 Report.

sovereignty. Morgenstern points out that 'no country has a monopoly of excellence in labour law: all that can be said is that in some countries certain aspects of such law are more favourable to the worker than they are in others.'[148] A worker may want to enjoy the high salary and fringe benefits of a US contract of employment, but would prefer the protection of European dismissal laws in place of US termination-at-will. Any ideas of unification or even full harmonisation of labour laws on a global or regional scale in order to avoid extra-territoriality or to minimise conflicts are pure fantasy. Even in the EU the Treaties do not give competence to achieve the unification of labour laws. There is only provision for partial harmonisation (chapter 8, below). The wide variations in the domestic labour laws of the Member States, and the limited subject matter of Regulations and Directives applying throughout the EU, means that conflict of laws rules continue to be crucial.[149]

In this chapter we have seen that common law rules on choice of law give primacy to freedom of contract. In unequal employment relationships this could result in widespread avoidance of the mandatory provisions of national labour laws. This danger is recognised in the Rome Convention which precludes a choice which has the effect of depriving the employee of the protection of the mandatory rules of the place of work or, where the worker is mobile, the place of the employer's business. National legislation is generally limited in its spatial effect to the national territory. In the UK the statutory provisions on extra-territoriality are fragmented and inconsistent. As a matter of principle, compatible with national sovereignty, labour legislation should be applied to all those who work within the national territory (including the Continental Shelf). The legislation should also apply to mobile workers who are ordinarily resident within the national territory, where their employer has a place of business within that territory.

The courts have traditionally aimed to prevent forum-shopping by litigants who are seeking the court in which they are most likely to succeed in obtaining the highest award although that court has no real connection with either party. However, 'having rules which allow a claimant to choose a forum which suits the claimant best is not necessarily prejudicial to justice.'[150] Workers in developing countries who have suffered injury through the mismanaged operations of a TNC should be seen as having justice on their side when they seek to make the parent company accept responsibility in the courts of its home state. The *forum non conveniens* principle has been subject to varying interpretations in common law countries, and can lead to inconsistent results. 'If all other things are equal, it is to both parties' advantage to have a speedy final

---

[148] Morgenstern (1984) at 2.
[149] Krebber (2000) at 504.
[150] Collier (2001) at 85.

judgment from a single forum',[151] avoiding litigation tactics which seek either to drive the defendant into an inflated settlement, or to make the claimant run out of funds or lose the will to continue before trial. This consideration makes the 'home state' principle embodied in the EU Jurisdiction Regulation attractive. In employment cases this allows the worker to sue in the EU or EFTA state where the defendant employer is domiciled, or in the state of the place of work, or in the case of a mobile worker in the state of the place of the employer's business. The employee may be sued only in the country in which he or she is domiciled.

The case of workers temporarily posted to work in another state raises fundamental issues about the purposes of applying the law and using the courts of the host state. The history of the EU Posted Workers Directive suggests that the primary motivation was a fear of 'social dumping' and undermining the higher labour standards of the host state. This runs against the grain of the EU Treaty which aims to facilitate the competitive cross-border provision of services. Recent ECJ decisions have stressed the overriding importance of removing barriers to free movement, and that the Directive can be invoked only to protect the posted workers not the businesses of the host state. The posted workers, however, are most unlikely to invoke the Directive, if the only effect of this will be to lose the service contracts on which they are engaged in the host state. The Directive symbolises fears about globalisation, but offers no panacea.

While the EU has acted on this symbolic issue, it has done relatively little about the threats to jobs posed by cross-border transfers of undertakings and offshore outsourcing. Even if, as some economists argue, these transactions lead in the longer-term to increased growth and employment, they have an immediate and often adverse impact on workers (chapter 1, above). We have seen that the Acquired Rights Directive offers only limited protection. It turns a blind eye to changes in control of the employing undertaking through share transfers and concentrations, excludes most cases of offshore outsourcing because these do not constitute 'transfers of an economic entity which retains its identity', its application is limited to the territory of the Member States, and workers are not entitled to the more favourable employment rules of the transferee undertaking's home state.

One strategy for fostering 'countervailing workers' power'[152] to the forces of globalisation is to provide effective transnational rules for freedom of association, the right to collective bargaining, and the right to take transnational industrial action. However, such rules are virtually non-existent. Rights to union membership are usually strictly territorial in scope, and the representativity of

---

[151] Collier (2001) at 85.
[152] This concept is derived from Klare (2000) at 63.

unions is limited by excluding from bargaining units those working outside the national territory. International collective agreements are underdeveloped as legal instruments and there is an absence of effective mechanisms for concilia- tion, arbitration or legal enforcement. Agreements made under the European social dialogue at multi-industry, industry or company level lack effective European-wide legal underpinning. National conflicts rules apply the 'proper law of the contract', an inappropriate concept for collective agreements which have both contractual and normative effects. It is relatively easy in some coun- tries for a foreign employer acquiring an undertaking to derecognise a union or to avoid the continuation of a collective agreement (in the EU after one year). TNCs can play off establishments in one country against those in another in order to negotiate the lowest labour costs, with little regard for the acquired rights of employees. International solidarity action is usually unlawful at national level, there is no right to strike at EU-level, and there is only limited recognition of such a right in ILO instruments.

These weaknesses of countervailing workers' power on a transnational scale, lead some to put their faith in 'institutional redesign'[153] that is altering the institutional structure of enterprises so as to take account of the transnational dimension. The European Works Councils Directive is undoubtedly a significant development. Although limited to certain large 'Community-scale' undertakings or groups of undertakings, it provides the first steps towards a genuinely transnational level of labour relations. With the decline of collective bargaining and trade union strength in most countries, and the absence of effective international collective bargaining, the 'information and consulta- tion' model may be the only realistic way of securing workers' participation. However, the influence of the new structures on managerial prerogative is lim- ited because 'management decisions are . . . increasingly dictated by market conditions and are often made at headquarters, situated in other countries, even in other continents, outside the EU. Experience also with the European Works Councils, shows that strategic economic management decisions are, as a general rule, not fundamentally changed by the involvement of employees [through information and consultation].'[154] So far as the statute for the SE, and the accompanying Directive on employee involvement, is concerned, it is an open question as to what extent it will be translated into practice. The underlying question, to which we shall turn in chapter 10, is whether any of these patterns of labour relations can prevail in the face of global competition.

[153] Klare (2000) at 67.
[154] Blanpain and Engels (2003) at 643.

8

Negative and Positive Harmonisation in the EU

1. Introduction
2. The making of EU social and employment policy
3. Negative harmonisation
4. Positive harmonisation

1. Introduction

How can the aims of economic integration in a globalised economy be reconciled with the ideals of social and labour rights under the rule of law? The development of the social dimension of the EU provides many lessons for other regions as they move from bilateral agreements and free trade areas to regional markets which guarantee free movement of goods, services, capital and labour. This and the next chapter critically examine the main methods which have been used in the EU to link economic and employment growth with rising social and labour standards. (The EU and EU Institutions are described in Boxes 8.1 and 8.2.)

The conventional wisdom of liberal economists is that labour laws cause 'rigidities' in the market. For the market to function efficiently there must be 'flexibility' in the sense of a relative absence of regulation. The price mechanism should be left to operate without impediment. On this view, national labour laws of the EU states should be subject to the same disciplines as apply to other apparent barriers to free trade in goods and services and the free movement of capital. This approach subordinates labour laws to competition law and other laws which aim to guarantee the market freedoms. As a method of market integration it has been called *negative harmonisation*.

A second method is *positive harmonisation*. This aims at achieving compatability between the legal systems of the Member States. One method is by EU Regulations which automatically become part of the national legal systems and give rise to rights enforceable in national courts not only against the State but also against private individuals. Such Regulations are few and far between in labour law, the main example being the Regulations on migrant workers.[1] EU Regulations are also relevant to the conflicts of law and the enforcement of foreign judgments (chap. 7, above). The labour laws and social protection systems of the Member States are far too diverse to permit the use of regulations of this inflexible kind. Harmonisation has generally been pursued by means of Directives, which are binding on Member States as to the results to be achieved, but leave the choice of form and methods to national authorities (Box 8.3).The European Commission has sought to encourage harmonisation in a variety of other ways such as through Decisions, Recommendations and Opinions, and reports and studies on social and labour legislation.

These two traditional methods will be examined in this chapter. In the next chapter our attention will be turned to the 'new' social model that has been emerging since the Treaties of Maastricht, Amsterdam and Nice. This model is characterised by the use of the 'open method of co-ordination' (OMC), and 'social dialogue'. There is also emerging a framework of fundamental social rights within which these methods should operate.

These methods are not neutral techniques. They derive their construction and effects from the changing economic, political, social and ideological contexts of the EU. The first section of this chapter therefore provides a brief historical analysis of the ways in which these contexts have shaped the legal developments.[2]

2. The making of EU social and employment policy

Differentiated integration

The story of European economic and political integration has been one of growth from a relatively small and homogeneous community of six states, predominantly concerned with the four economic freedoms of movement of goods, services, capital and workers, to an increasingly large and diverse European Union (EU) of 25 States (Box 8.1), with co-ordinated and converging social and employment policies which remain rooted in the market freedoms.

---

[1] Notably Council Regulation No 1612/68, as amended, on the freedom of movement for workers within the Community [1968] OJ Sp ed L257/475.

[2] For excellent detailed accounts of EC employment and labour law, see Barnard (2000b) and Kenner (2003), and for a shorter version Syzszczak (2000a).

Box 8.1

THE EUROPEAN UNION

The European Coal and Steel Community (ECSC) was founded by the Treaty of Paris in 1951, to put coal and steel production under a common authority. The European Economic Community (EEC) was established by the Treaty of Rome in 1957, to create a common market in all sectors other than coal and steel. The European Atomic Energy Community (EURATOM) was also founded in 1957. The founding members of each Community were the same six Continental European states (France, Germany, Italy, Belgium, Luxembourg and the Netherlands). The EEC, renamed the European Community (EC) in 1992,[3] was enlarged by the accession of the United Kingdom, Ireland and Denmark in 1973, Greece in 1981, Spain and Portugal in 1986, Austria, Sweden and Finland in 1995, and Poland, Hungary, the Czech Republic, Slovakia, Slovenia, Estonia, Lithuania, Latvia, Cyprus and Malta in 2004. There are four candidate members: Bulgaria, Croatia, Romania and Turkey. Together, the Member States constitute the European Union (EU), established in 1992 by the Maastricht Treaty on European Union (TEU) (in force 1 November 1993) which was amended by the Treaty of Amsterdam (in force 1 May 1999) and by the Treaty of Nice (in force 1 February 2003). The EU and EC Treaties have been merged into a consolidated version. The EU has three 'pillars':

(1) *The Community Pillar* (incorporating the EC Treaty)
(2) *Common Foreign and Security Policy*
(3) *Police and Judicial Co-operation in Criminal Matters*

It is the first pillar (the EC) which is directly relevant to labour law and social policy, The common provisions (Title I) set out the fundamental principles of liberty, democracy and respect for human rights on which the EU is founded.

The Treaty establishing Constitution for the European Union, signed on 24 October 2004, and awaiting ratification by the end of 2006 by all 25 Member States, will replace these three pillars with a single Treaty. The Constitution refers throughout to the EU, and not the EC. *The term EU is used throughout this book to refer to the EC pillar. References to articles in the EC pillar are cited thus: Article 137 EC. The new Constitution adopts a different scheme of numbering.*

---

[3] The name EC now refers to all three communities. The ECSC Treaty expired and its assets and liabilities were transferred to the EC in 2002.

Box 8.2

EU INSTITUTIONS

(1) *The Council.* This consists of a ministerial representative of each Member State authorised to commit the government of that State. In practice, there is a series of Councils each dealing with separate topics (e.g, the Labour Ministers deal with employment and social policy). The Council's role is to co-ordinate the general policies of the Member States and to pass or approve all legislation. Qualified majority voting (QMV), which gives more votes to larger than to smaller states was introduced in 1986 and extended by later Treaties. It is now allowed in respect of most areas of social policy. Under the EU Constitution, instead of the present rotating Presidency, there will be a President elected for 2.5 years.

(2) *The European Commission.* This consists of 25 members, including one from each Member State. Their 'independence shall be beyond doubt' (Article 231 EC). They are led by a President appointed by the Council and approved by the Parliament Under the EU Constitution, the number of voting Commissioners will be reduced from 2014. The Commission has the monopoly of legislative initiatives, and has the duty to ensure that the provisions of the Treaty and measures taken by the institutions are applied.

(3) *European Parliament.* This consists of a maximum of 732 representatives of the people of the EU elected by direct suffrage every five years. The Parliament shares legislative power with the Council (co-decision) in most areas, further extended by the EU Constitution, giving it the right to veto proposed legislation; it scrutinises the work of the Commission and other EU institutions; and it approves the Community budget. The Parliamentary Committee on Employment and Social Affairs has an important influence on labour law and employment.

(4) *Economic and Social Committee* (ECOSOC). This advisory body consists of 222 members drawn from NGOs, employers' bodies, trade unions, and other organisations of civil society (Articles 257–262 EC). It must be consulted on social and employment matters (Article 137 EC), and can issue opinions on its own initiative.

(5) *European Court of Justice* (ECJ), based in Luxembourg. This has one judge from each Member State supported by Advocates General. The Court considers preliminary references made by national courts seeking guidance on points of EU law (Article 234 EC), hears appeals from the Court of First Instance (renamed the High Court in the EU Constitution) which deals mainly with actions by private persons against Community Institutions; and hears actions between Community Institutions and between Community Institutions and Member States.

Box 8.3

EU LEGISLATION

(1) *Regulations.* These are binding on all Member States, and are directly applicable, ie they are taken to be part of national legal systems automatically, and they give rise to individual rights which can be enforced in national courts, if their wording is clear, precise and unconditional. Under the EU Constitution, these are called European laws.

(2) *Directives.* These are addressed to Member States, and are binding as to the result to be achieved, but leave to national authorities the choice of form and methods. Directives can have direct effect enabling individuals to rely on them against the state (but generally not against other persons), and a Member State may be liable to individuals in damages for non-implementation or incorrect implementation of a Directive. Under the EU Constitution these are called European framework laws.

(3) *Decisions.* These are binding in their entirety on those to whom they are addressed.

(4) *Recommendations and Opinions.* These are intended for guidance only, and have no binding force.

The EU Constitution provides for a European Regulation, a non-legislative act of general application for the implementation of legislative acts and other provisions of the Constitution. This will be particularly important in the context of the social dialogue (chap. 9, below). A European Regulation may be (a) binding in its entirety and directly applicable in all Member States, or (b) binding as regards the result to be achieved on all Member States to which it is addressed, but leaving the national authority free to choose the form and means of achieving that result.

It is common to describe the development of the social dimension in the integration process in a linear way, culminating in a new 'European social model' based upon consensus. In reality, there is no 'end of history' in the EU, and the 'model' is a changing one. There are continuing conflicts between liberal and social democratic values, at both national and EU levels. Political struggles are unabated between those groups—particularly strong in the UK—who wish to restrict the EU to functionalist economic aims based on intergovernmental treaties, and those—led by France and Germany—who seek 'ever closer' political and social integration based on European supra-nationalism.

There are conflicting pressures for integration and fragmentation of labour laws and social policy. These conflicts are masked by idealised notions of a European social model.

From a legal perspective, the process has been described as one of 'differentiated integration'[4] or 'flexibility'.[5] The EU is based on treaties which define the competence of the European institutions and the Member States. In order to act in a given area the EU requires a legal base in the treaties giving it exclusive or concurrent competence. The EU has never had exclusive competence in the area of labour law and social policy; such integration as has occurred has not been aimed at total harmonisation or unification. Barnard points out that there has been flexibility in two senses.[6] First, there has been 'strong' flexibility in the form of opt-outs for particular States—'variable geometry' in social matters—with the consent of others who wish to integrate their social policies more deeply. The prime example is the UK's opt-out from the Social Chapter of the Maastricht Treaty (1991) which ended with the Amsterdam Inter-Governmental Conference (1997). Secondly, there have been 'softer' forms of flexibility. One set of examples relate to so-called 'internal flexibility':[7] provisions in Community secondary legislation allowing all or specific Member States to opt-out of particular EU norms. Another example is the increasing use of 'soft' measures, or 'informal law-making by exhortation':[8] Employment Guidelines, Codes of Practice and Recommendations which set goals but do not create legal obligations. A final example is the use of the 'social dialogue' between management and labour at Community-level in creating framework agreements which can be translated into secondary legislation, and also in the use of local collective and workforce agreements in the implementation of EU norms (chapter 9, below).

These new forms of governance are developing in a 'Fortress Europe' based on the four market freedoms *within* EU borders. The EU promotes 'fair' external trade particularly with developing countries (see chapter 5), but seals its labour markets from external economic migrants and many claiming asylum.[9] Although the aim of the founders was, in the words of the Treaty of Rome of 1957, by 'pooling their resources to preserve and strengthen peace and liberty', there is a dark side: an inward-looking Union with restrictive immigration and asylum policies, rifts between ethnic communities and continuing or worsen-

---

[4] Tuytschaever (1999) at 1–3, and de Búrca (2000) at 133.

[5] Barnard (2000c) at 198, who distinguishes constitutional flexibility from the connotation it has in labour law of adapting to competitive labour markets.

[6] Barnard (2000c) at 198.

[7] Barnard (2000c) at 204 *et seq.*

[8] Barnard (2000c) at 206.

[9] The European Employment Strategy (EES) does, however, recognise managed migration of skilled labour (ch 9, below).

ing racial disadvantage;[10] a democratic deficit in decision-making processes, a lack of transparency and accountability, and an absence of clear constitutional rights.[11] It is an interesting question how far, if at all, this will be changed by the new EU Constitution.

The economic constitution: 1957–72

From the Treaty of Rome in 1957 until 1972, labour law and social protection were seen as almost exclusively national functions. The Community institutions were solely concerned with building the common market. At the national level there was a new managed capitalism, with workers throughout Western Europe gaining significant legal rights and welfare benefits, a growth of institutionalised 'industrial democracy' as well as collective bargaining. Within these general trends there was considerable diversity as a result of the different economic, political and legal evolution of the Member States. Despite—perhaps because of—the growing importance of labour law at national level, there was little pressure for harmonisation at Community level.

Ideologically, the founders of the Community were undoubtedly economic determinists. Although Article 2 of the 1957 Treaty proclaimed the task of promoting 'an accelerated raising of the standard of living' this was firmly based on the ideas of economic liberalism. The task, said Article 2, was to be performed 'by establishing a common market and progressively approximating the economic policies of the Member States.' Similarly Article 117 of the Treaty declared the faith of the founders in the economic functioning of the common market as the automatic guarantee of improvements in living and working conditions. Approximation of municipal laws was described as an objective but 'only to the extent necessary to the functioning of the activities of the common market.' Article 118 contained a non-exhaustive list of areas, including labour law and working conditions, in which the Member States were expected to co-operate, but the role of the supranational Commission was entirely procedural.

In the negotiations for the 1957 Treaty, Germany and the Benelux countries argued that the harmonisation of social costs would be the inevitable outcome of the common market. Their view was supported by the majority of a group of experts (the Ohlin committee), set up by the six founding States in collaboration with the ILO. They expressed the opinion that special social provisions should not be included in the Treaty. They believed that all these countries were already striving to achieve, or adhering to, ILO standards at the national level and did not need supranational EEC rules. The proper supra-national

[10] Hepple (2004a).
[11] Szyszczak (2001) at 1170.

basis for workers' rights was to be found in ILO Conventions, and in the Council of Europe's Convention for the Protection of Human Rights and Fundamental Freedoms of 1950 (ECHR), and European Social Charter (ESC). (The latter then in draft form was adopted in 1961 and revised in 1996.) The Ohlin Report concluded that—

> International competition in a common market would not prevent particular countries from raising workers' living standards and there is no sound reason to think that freer international markets would hamper in any way the further improvement of workers' living standards, as productivity rises, through higher wages or improved social benefits and working conditions . . . [12]

The experts plainly regarded differences in social costs as fair comparative advantages, so long as these differences reflected improvements in productivity. The only exceptions were unequal pay between women and men, and paid holidays. In this respect, the Ohlin Report supported the French position. Although all six States had constitutional provisions declaring equality between women and men, and four of them had ratified the ILO Equal Remuneration Convention 1951 (No 100), only France was then in the process of enacting specific legislation requiring equal pay. The French argued that they would be at a competitive disadvantage if they alone had to bear the costs of equal pay. The Ohlin Report distinguished between the *general level* of labour costs, which were said to reflect different levels of productivity, and *inter-industrial* patterns of costs, where it was said that intervention was justified in particular industries with exceptionally low wages or social costs, thus giving them a competitive advantage. The committee explained that—

> Countries in which there are large differentials in sex will pay relatively low wages in industries employing a large proportion of female labour and these industries will enjoy what might be considered as a special advantage over their competitors abroad where differentials according to sex are smaller or non-existent. [13]

The Spaak Report, by the foreign ministers of the Six in 1956,[14] accepted the same reasoning. This Report regarded a 'gradual coalesence of social policies' as one of the elements of a common market, but made it clear that this was related solely to two purposes. The first of these was the removal of obstacles to the free movement of labour. Accordingly Articles 48–51 of the EEC Treaty (now Articles 39–42 EC) created a new form of labour market administration in order to remove these obstacles. The second purpose was to remove 'distortions' of competition. The theory was that differential burdens on employers

---

[12] Ohlin (1956) at 115.
[13] Ohlin (1956) at 107.
[14] *Rapport des chefs de délégation aux ministres des affaires étrangéres* (Brussels, 21 April 1956), as translated by Kahn-Freund (1960).

in the Member States would not themselves falsify the conditions for competition, so long as there was free movement of labour. It was argued that as demand for labour increased where labour was cheapest, wage rates would tend to rise and free circulation of labour would facilitate an equalisation of conditions of employment. 'Equalisation, so far from being a condition precedent to the operation of the common market is, on the contrary, its result' declared the Report. This was not a plea for unbridled *laissez-faire*, but supranational labour legislation was only to be resorted to when there were 'specific distortions'. Equal pay and paid holidays fell into this exceptional category.

The Title on Social Policy (Title III) of the 1957 Treaty was, therefore, a compromise between the German and French positions. On the one hand there was the exhortatory Article 117, circumscribed by Article 118 (above) promising improved working conditions as a result of the functioning of the common market. On the other hand, there was Article 119 (now as amended 141 EC) which embodied the principle of equal pay for equal work, albeit in a weaker form than the ILO standard of equal pay for work of equal value, and Article 120 (now 142 EC) which protected paid holiday schemes. The declared objective of achieving equal pay by the end of the first period of the EEC (1962), and when this failed, by the extended date of 1964, was in Warner's words 'either made without conviction or was remarkably naïve'.[15]

Social market vs deregulation: 1973 to 1985

After the expansion of the Community from 1 January 1973, to include the United Kingdom, Ireland, Denmark and, from 1981, Greece, 'social market' and 'deregulatory' ideas came into sharp conflict. The first initiatives for a more active social policy were taken during the period of mini-boom in 1972–73. On the eve of expansion of the EEC in October 1972, the Heads of Government declared 'that they attribute the same importance to energetic proceedings in the field of social policy as to the realisation of the economic and financial union.'[16] This prompted the first Social Action Programme in 1974. By then the EEC was in the midst of the crash which followed the oil crisis in the winter of 1973–74. The economic boom began to fall apart, with rising inflation. Unemployment, grew from 3 percent in 1973 to 6 percent in 1980. Economic integration within a common market was visibly failing to protect working and living standards, and a wave of strikes and wage explosions swept across Europe. Not surprisingly, the central measures adopted under the Social Action Programme were designed to harmonise the raft of national laws which sought to use state intervention and workers' participation as ways of mitigating the

[15] Warner (1984) at 143.
[16] This section draws on Hepple (1987) at 79–85.

impact of mass redundancies, the growing concentration of enterprises and the insolvency of employers. Community labour law came to life between 1975 and 1980 in the shape of three employment protection Directives—on collective redundancies,[17] acquired rights of workers on the transfer of undertakings,[18] and insolvency.[19] These were not, however, a full-scale 'harmonisation upwards'. For instance they did not require prior authorisation by public authorities of economic dismissals as under the law of January 3, 1973 of the Giscard Administration in France.

From 1980 onwards a crisis developed in European labour law. European employers' organisations and several American-based TNCs campaigned vigorously against the Commission's more ambitious proposals for the harmonisation of employment rights, and for industrial democracy. The requirement of unanimity on the Council enabled the UK's Thatcher Administration (with the active or tacit support of some other governments) to block these proposals, because of the need under Article 100 (now 94 EC) of the Treaty for unanimity in respect of approximation measures. The impetus for workers' participation on the German or Dutch models, proposed in the draft Fifth Directive on company structure and administration in 1972,[20] was already meeting powerful opposition by the end of the 1970s. The draft Vredeling Directive[21] on procedures for informing and consulting employees in large national and multinational enterprises had the misfortune to be presented to the Council on 24 October 1980, just as the steam had run out of the moves for greater worker involvement. The only new Directives adopted in the 1980s were in the fields of sex discrimination[22] and health and safety.[23]

The fierce economic logic of the crisis demanded the speedy completion of the common market. Free movement of labour, guaranteed by the Treaty, had not, as the founders believed, resulted in large-scale movements of labour to countries with higher social standards; it had, instead, created a secondary labour market within several Member States, populated by a sub-class of 'guest workers' (or 'third country nationals') from outside the Community. While the free movement of capital encouraged relocation in areas of low

---

[17] Council Directive 75/129/EEC, [1976] OJ L48/29, now replaced by Council Directive 98/59/EC, [1998] OJ L225/16.

[18] Council Directive 77/187/EEC, [1977] OJ L61/26, now replaced by Council Directive 2001/23/EC, [2001] OJ L82/16.

[19] Council Directive 80/987/EEC, [1980] OJ L283/23, amended by European Parliament and Council Directive 2002/74/EC, [2002] OJ L270/10.

[20] [1972] OJ C131/49.

[21] [1980] OJ C297/80; See generally Docksey (1985).

[22] Council Directive 79/7/EEC, [1979] OJ L 6/24 (equal treatment in social security); Council Directive 86/378/EEC [1986] OJ L225/40 (equal treatment in occupational social security); Council Directive 86/613/EEC, [1986] OJ L359/56 (equal treatment for self-employed).

[23] In particular the framework health and safety Council Directive 89/391/EEC, [1989] OJ L183/19.

social and wage costs, this had met the obstacles of low productivity, lack of skills, energy and resources, and weak infrastructure in those areas. The removal of the remaining technical, fiscal and physical barriers to free movement of capital, goods and services was therefore seen as essential to the lowering of real labour costs.

Just as important was increased labour 'flexibility' in all its forms, including the easing of legal and collective bargaining restrictions on working time and on working practices such as part-time work, temporary work and subcontracting. The debate about 'flexibility' became the central issue after 1980 in response to three powerful pressures: unemployment which had grown to an average 11.8 percent in the Community by 1987, the need to adapt to new technologies, and the competitive models of labour 'flexibility' in the US and Japan. These pressures were reflected in a raft of proposals by the Commission and by the European Parliament.[24] It was at this point that the crisis in Community labour law was revealed. The Commission's proposals were based on two premises which were unacceptable to the Thatcher Administration. The first was that workers' participation (albeit in the attenuated form of 'information and consultation' rather than negotiation and consent) had an essential role in the management of change. The second premise was that 'flexibility' and 'deregulation' are not synonymous. In the words of a senior Commission official at the time: 'the objective of more labour flexibility is not to go back on social achievements and social rights, but rather to seek an improvement in the functioning of the common market: consequently it will be necessary to encourage economic efficiency and the ability of enterprises to increase employment, and at the same time to safeguard the social values of justice and security.'[25] These notions came into conflict with the Thatcher Administration's position that flexibility 'involves not just working patterns and hours' but a 'better balance of bargaining power in industry', and that there needed to be a great reduction at Community level, as well as national level, of the 'burdens on the regulation of business.'[26] A stalemate had been reached between the conflicting pressures for harmonisation and deregulation. The difference between the Thatcher Administration and its Continental partners was not in the direction of change—reducing the real costs of labour and enhancing employers' ability to respond effectively to new markets and processes—but in the methods necessary to achieve this.

---

[24] For details see Hepple (1987) at 81.

[25] Gaetano Zingone, speaking at an International Colloquium on 'Flexibility and Labour Law—a European Challenge', Institute of Labour law and Industrial Relations in the EC, Trier, 20–21 February 1987.

[26] Department of Employment (1983) paras 7.5 and 7.16. For a comparison with the attitude of other EC states to deregulation see Vranken (1986).

A fragmented Social Europe: 1986–97

Social policy received an unexpected impetus following the adoption of the Single European Act of 1987 (SEA), coinciding with the accession of Spain and Portugal. However, the continuing dominance of a market-oriented approach meant that the steps which were taken lacked any clear organising principle.[27] The Commission's White Paper on *Completing the Internal Market* (1985)[28] had a 'distinctly deregulatory bias'[29] and concluded that in the process of completing the single market by 1992, Community social policy should be limited to health and safety and the objectives of free movement. Similarly the Cecchini Report on European integration[30] claimed that removing the physical, technical and fiscal barriers to a single market would generate 2 to 5 million new jobs. While recognising that widespread industrial restructuring and the need for flexibility would lead to short-term unemployment the Cecchini report did not propose any complementary social policies. The lead in developing a social dimension came from Jacques Delors. Ironically, he had been supported by Thatcher for the Presidency of the Commission because of his strong commitment to market integration. But, unlike the Thatcher Administration which treated market integration as an end in itself, Delors saw market integration as only the first step to the goal of political integration. He antagonised Thatcher and won the support of the labour movement by declaring that

> the creation of a vast economic area, based on the market and business co-operation is inconceivable—I would say unattainable—without some harmonisation of social legislation. Our ultimate aim must be the creation of a European social area (*l'espace sociale Européenne*).[31]

What, then, was to be the justification for social policy? An inter-departmental Commission working party on *The Social Dimension of the Internal Market* (1988) acknowledged the risks of 'social dumping' in specific sectors which 'are at all events very much in the minority', but concluded that this would be offset by other comparative advantages in terms of productivity, technical innovation and location.[32] The Working Party contrasted two 'less than ideal' approaches to social policy: a normative approach which would create a single, binding framework on social matters, and a decentralised approach with only health and safety and sex discrimination being subject to

---

[27] Davies (1992) at 331–42.
[28] COM (85) 310.
[29] Kenner (2003) at 75.
[30] Cecchini (1988).
[31] Bull EC 2 (1986) at 12.
[32] *Social Europe* (1988), special edition, at 65–66.

Community-wide rules. They recommended a 'middle way' which might combine a 'social dialogue' with a range of other 'minimum social provisions.'

This inconclusive debate took place in the context of the SEA which had the support even of Margaret Thatcher as being preferable to an ambitious draft Treaty on European Union favoured by the European Parliament and the French and German governments. She could not have envisaged the impact this 'modest document' would have on social policy. The aim of the SEA was to create a new institutional dynamic for economic liberalisation. The main Treaty base for the implementation of internal market[33] proposals was a new Article 100a (now 95(1) EC) which allowed qualified majority voting (QMV) for approximation measures. However, this expressly excluded those relating to 'free movement of persons' and 'the rights and interests of employed persons' (section 4, below).

The significant boost for social policy came from two new Treaty provisions which supplemented the original Article 118 EEC (now as amended 137(1) EC), so as to give powers to adopt harmonisation measures by QMV in respect of the working environment, in particular health and safety. The second, even more important, innovation were new articles (now as amended 138 and 139 EC) which charged the Commission with the duty to develop the dialogue between management and labour at European level (see section 4 below). A social area was emerging based on 'minimum requirements', laid down by Community legislation, coupled with arrangements for reaching consensus through 'social dialogue.'

The missing dimension, as the Economic and Social Committee recognised in 1987, was Community legislation guaranteeing 'basic social rights immune to competitive pressures.'[34] This idea had been launched during the Belgian Presidency in the first half of 1987, and subsequently elaborated by a series of seminars organised under the auspices of the Commission in 1987 and 1988,[35] and by an Opinion of the ESC in February 1989.[36] One proposal was for the Community to monitor and enforce the 'social constitution' of Europe embodied in the Council of Europe's ECHR, and the ESC.[37] The obligations under these instruments had nearly all been accepted by the Member States, but attempts to incorporate them directly into Community law had been rejected.[38] The Commission decided, instead, to propose its own Social Charter. As amended, this Community Charter of Fundamental Rights of

[33] It is highly controversial whether the nomenclature of 'internal market' in place of 'common market' was significant: cf Kenner (2003) at 80.

[34] *Opinion of the Economic and Social Committee on the Social Aspects of the Internal Market (European Social Area)*, 19 November 1987, CES(87) 1069, para 1.5.

[35] *Social Europe*, Supp 7/88, esp at 55–65.

[36] CES 270/89, 22 February 1989.

[37] Hepple (1987) at 86–87; Hepple (1990) at 653.

[38] Kenner (2003) at 110–11.

Workers, was adopted in December 1989 by the Heads of Government of all the Member States, with the notable exception of the UK. The Charter was not an international treaty and had no binding force. The first Title restated 12 'fundamental' labour and social rights.[39] There were glaring omissions, such as racial discrimination, coverage was limited to 'workers' rather than citizens, and there was confusion between rights and the policies necessary to achieve them.[40] In the second Title the signatories committed themselves to take appropriate steps to guarantee these rights by legislative measures or collective agreements.

The main importance of the Community Charter was as an inspiration for an action programme containing 47 specific proposals including 18 Directives. In the end 13 Directives were adopted, including those on proof of the employment relationship,[41] health and safety of fixed-term and temporary workers,[42] safety and health of pregnant workers,[43] a revision of the collective redundancies directive,[44] as well as a series of directives on specific safety hazards. In addition there was 'soft' law such as the Recommendation and Code of Practice on the protection of the dignity of women and men at work (sexual harassment),[45] and a medium-term Community action programme on equal opportunities for women and men.[46] Proposals that were stalled included one on atypical employment relationships, which was sponsored by Germany but opposed by the UK on the ground that this would have negative effects on employment. The piecemeal approach of the Commission was criticised for failing to take proper account of the different functions which particular normative provisions of labour law serve in each Member State. 'For example to select the topic of hours of work for uniform regulation throughout the Community is to ignore the complexity of compensation packages and flexible working practices in different Member States and the varying roles of collective bargaining and legislation in establishing norms.'[47]

The time was plainly ripe for a framework of fundamental rights of the kind set out in the Community Charter, while creating conditions in each Member

---

[39] Freedom of movement, freedom to choose and engage in an occupation, fair remuneration, improvement of living and working conditions, the right to freedom of association and collective bargaining, the right to vocational training, the right of women and men to equal treatment, the right of workers to information, consultation and participation, the right to health protection and safety at work, the protection of children and young persons, the elderly and disabled persons.

[40] See Hepple (1990a) for a detailed critique.

[41] Council Directive 91/533/EEC, [1991] OJ L288/32.

[42] Council Directive 91/383/EEC, [1991] OJ L206/19.

[43] Council Directive 92/85/EEC, [1992] L348/1.

[44] Council Directive 92/56/EEC, [1992] OJ L245/3.

[45] [1992] OJ C27/1.

[46] [1991] OJ C142/1.

[47] Hepple (1990a) at 653.

State conducive to decentralised negotiation of ways and means to achieve these rights. A further step in this direction was taken in the Maastricht Treaty on European Union (TEU) agreed in December 1991. From 1988, the major States, apart from the UK and Denmark, had been set on the course of establishing a European Monetary Union (EMU). This would involve the co-ordination of economic policies, a central European bank, and a single currency. The EMU would require a tightening of public expenditure, the reform of welfare systems, wage flexibility and labour mobility. This was seen as necessitating two complementary social strategies: the adoption of a new 'Social Chapter' replacing the original Articles 117–122 of the Rome Treaty, and a Community-wide policy to combat unemployment and social exclusion through labour market and antipoverty programmes.[48] The rhetoric of the opening articles of the TEU recognised the promotion of *social* progress on equal terms with economic progress, but this was to be 'balanced and sustainable.'[49] In other words the social dimension would be dependent on the effects on national budgets of the EMU convergence criteria and the interest rate policy of the Central Bank.[50] These monetary policies would also affect the impact of the new commitments in the revised EC Treaty to a 'high level of employment and social protection'[51] and the strengthening of 'economic and social cohesion'.[52]

When it became clear at the Maastricht European Council in December 1991 that the opposition of the Major Government in the UK to the draft Social Chapter threatened to wreck the whole Treaty, Ruud Lubbers, the Dutch Prime Minister, brokered a deal by which the Social Chapter was taken out of the Treaty. Instead all 12 Member States agreed to a separate Protocol No 14 on Social Policy, to which the unaltered draft Social Chapter was annexed,[53] as an Agreement on Social Policy applicable only to 11 States (ie excluding the UK). The result was to create two parallel social policy regimes. The first, for the Community of 12 comprised the social policy provisions of the (renamed) EC Treaty in the form embodied in the SEA. The second for the Community of 11 consisted of the Agreement on Social Policy. The link between these regimes was provided by Protocol No 14 which allowed the 11 to have recourse to the procedures and mechanisms of the Treaty for 'applying as far as they are concerned' the acts and decisions required to give effect to the Agreement. The UK was excluded from the Council of 11. This messy compromise generated much academic debate as to the legality of the Protocol and Agreement.[54] Happily

---

[48] Kenner (2003) at 220–21.
[49] Art B (now 2) TEU.
[50] Kenner (2003) at 228.
[51] Art 2 EC.
[52] Art 3 EC.
[53] This came into force in November 1993.
[54] Kenner (2003) at 223–27.

these controversies disappeared after Blair's New Labour Government, elected in May 1997, resolved to 'sign up' to the Social Chapter. This led to the reintegration of the Social Chapter into the TEU by the Treaty of Amsterdam (1997) which came into force in May 1999. Interim measures allowed the four Directives which had been adopted under the Agreement to be applied to the UK. These related to parental leave,[55] part-time work,[56] European Works Councils[57] and the burden of proof in sex discrimination cases.[58] Overall, Kenner concludes that the Agreement was of little 'added value' so far as the 11 Member States were concerned. Social rights of citizenship of the Union were not emphasised. The principle of subsidiarity was used to create a presumption that national measures were to be preferred even where there was a case for Community action.[59] The fear of social dumping by the UK—highlighted by the Hoover case (chapter 1, Box 1.4, above)—inhibited the 11 from racing ahead on the social front. Above all, social provisions remained anchored in the economic imperatives of the internal market.

The emerging social constitution since 1997

The major change in thinking and action on labour market issues occurred in the period between the coming into force of the Maastricht Treaty and the Treaty of Amsterdam. In 1994, the Commission issued an important White Paper, *Growth, Competitiveness, Employment,*[60] which identified a deep structural crisis. Over a 20-year period, the EU's global competitiveness had worsened in comparison with the US and Japan. While the rate of employment of the population of working age was 60 percent in the EU it was 70–75 percent in the US and Japan. Similarly, the EU's share of export markets, research and development and investment ratio was significantly lower than in the US and Japan. The EU's rate of growth had shrunk over the 20-year period from around 4 percent to 2.5 per cent per year. Unemployment had risen from cycle to cycle and stood at around 12 percent of the EU working force.[61] The

---

[55] Council Directive 96/34/EC, [1996] OJ L145/4 as amended and extended to the UK by Directive 97/75/EC, [1998] OJ L10/24.

[56] Council Directive 97/81/EC, [1998] OJ L14/9, as amended and extended to the UK by Directive 98/23/EC, [1998] OJ L131/1.

[57] Council Directive 94/45/EC, [1994] OJ L254/64, as amended and applied to the UK by Directive 97/74/EC, [1998] OJ L10/22.

[58] Council Directive 97/80/EC,[1998] OJ L14/6, as amended and extended to the UK by Directive 98/52/EC, [1998] OJ L205/66.

[59] The principle of subsidiarity has been used in the social policy field in two ways: (1) to defend national sovereignty; and (2) as a justification for devolving decision-making to the social dialogue.

[60] European Commission (1994b).

[61] European Commission (1994b) at 9.

Commission rejected miracle cures such as protectionism, reduction in working hours or severe wage reductions. They favoured active labour market policies, including job creation on 'an unprecedented scale', the development of a Community labour market with a high level of skills, greater flexibility in the organisation of work and the distribution of working time, and reduced non-wage labour costs.

The Directorate-General on Employment, Industrial Relations and Social Affairs (DGV), for its part, initiated a major debate on the future of social policy in Green and White Papers.[62] At the same time an ad hoc *Comité des Sages*, proposed the integration of civic and social rights as a basis for social policy.[63] There was a growing consensus for a European 'third way' which would combine social and economic integration. There were four main features of this consensus. The first was employment growth. The Essen Council meeting in 1994 drew up priorities around which Member States were asked to organise their policies. These 'Essen priorities' involved promoting investment in vocational training, improving the employment intensiveness of growth, reducing non-wage labour costs, avoiding measures that negatively affect availability for work, and improving measures for groups most affected by unemployment (women, young people, older employees and long-term unemployed).

Secondly, the new European model was to be a 'social' rather than a narrowly 'labour' one. The emphasis was no longer primarily on labour laws but on social protection. The 'classic' model of labour and welfare legislation viewed working men as the breadwinners and women as the carers, with a sharp division between working time and other time. The reality of European societies was a massive entry of women into the labour market in many cases as main breadwinners who were segregated in low-paid jobs. At the same time, there were growing pressures to dismantle the welfare states so increasing inequalities between the shrinking elite protected by labour laws and the 52 milllion Europeans living below the poverty line—the 'socially excluded'. The alarming rise of racism and xenophobia against third country migrants and visible minorities had exacerbated this social divide. Not surprisingly, therefore, the social policy White Paper emphasised the need to combat social exclusion. The idea of the 'European citizen'—an individual whose social standards are guaranteed in and out of work by indivisible social and civic rights—became a central concept. Equality of opportunity for women and men required measures to desegregate the labour market, to reconcile employment and family life, and to accelerate the participation of women in decision-making. Social integration was to be promoted by fighting against poverty and

---

[62] European Commission [DGV Green Paper] (1993); European Commission (1994a). [DGV White Paper].

[63] European Commission (1996).

social exclusion, and taking action to help disabled people and older people. The Commission said that the Treaty should be revised to introduce specific powers to combat discrimination on grounds of race, religion, age and disability.

Thirdly, the White Paper on social policy emphatically rejected total harmonisation as an objective of social policy. It was the 'convergence of goals and policies over a period of time by fixing common objectives that is vital, since it will permit the coexistence of different national systems and enable them to progress in harmony towards the fundamental objectives of the Union.'[64] There was 'not a need for a wide-ranging programme of new legislative measures' for workers.[65] Instead the role of the EU would be mainly programmatic and goal-setting, within a framework of minimum standards.

Fourthly, the creation and implementation of this social model would, increasingly, be through the social dialogue. This would be a 'European model of social consensus reconciling economic efficiency and social solidarity'.[66]

The Treaty of Amsterdam created the institutional framework within which this new vision could be achieved.[67] At Maastricht, Article 2 EC had been revised to include the words 'and a high level of employment' among the aims of the Community. At Amsterdam 'employment and social protection' were moved up to second place in the list of objectives in Article 2 just behind 'a harmonious, balanced and sustainable development of economic activities.' The EU Constitution takes this even further by listing 'full employment and social progress' 'with a high level of protection' as objectives of the EU, along with combating social exclusion and discrimination, the promotion of equality between women and men, and solidarity between generations.[68] The most important change was that the European Employment Strategy (EES) (a development following the Essen process described above) was brought into the Treaty by inserting a new Title VIII EC on Employment as the legal basis for a 'co-ordinated strategy' by the Community and the Member States. This has now been incorporated as Articles III–97 to 102 in section 1 of Chapter III of Part III in the EU Constitution

The Social Chapter was reintegrated in amended form into the EC Treaty as Title XI EC. This was amended by the Treaty of Nice (2000) and is now incorporated without significant change as Articles III–103 to 112 in section 2 (Social Policy) of Chapter III of Part III of the EU Constitution. A new Article 13 EC, introduced by the Treaty of Amsterdam, conferred on the Council the

---

[64] European Commission (1994a) at 12.
[65] European Commission (1994a) at 13.
[66] European Commission (1994a).
[67] This was amended in various respects by the Treaty of Nice (2000).
[68] Art I–3.

express power to 'take action' against discrimination beyond the existing prohibitions on sex discrimination.

The final element in the new structure is a credible system of fundamental
rights. Following the *Comité des Sages* report (above), and a proposal for
fundamental rights in the EU supported by 109 experts in labour law,[69] a
second group of experts appointed by the Commission (the Simitis Report)
recommended that fundamental rights should be included in the Treaties.[70]
The drafting of a new Charter of Fundamental Rights of the European Union
was entrusted to a Convention with representatives from the Member States.
At the Nice Council meeting in December 2000, the European Parliament, the
Council and the Commission signed this Charter as a political declaration.
This has now been incorporated as Part II into the EU Constitution.

It can therefore be said that a genuine 'European social constitution' is
emerging, but, as we shall see, this is not without contradictions or problems.
The first of the problems is that of 'negative harmonisation', that is the potential of the market freedoms on which the Community is based to undermine
national labour laws and social protection.

3. Negative harmonisation

The EC is founded on the four freedoms of movement of goods, services,
capital and labour. To what extent do these fundamental freedoms—'the heart
of the Community undertaking'[71]—inhibit Member States from enacting
their own labour regulations, or invalidate collective agreements? Take some
examples. Member State A seeks to attract capital by repealing its minimum
wage laws and allowing employers to refuse to negotiate with trade unions.
Can Member State B, which has a minimum wage and strong unions, place
restrictions on goods or services produced by cheap or non-union labour in
State A? Must a Member State prevent demonstrations by workers in its state
which have the effect of blocking a highway which is vital to inter-State commerce? Can a Member State apply laws designed in part to protect workers,
which have the effect of restricting the sale of both domestic and imported
goods and services? Can Member States restrict the freedom of employers to
provide private pensions by requiring them to affiliate to a pension fund which
enjoys a monopoly? Can a State assist small or medium employers by excluding them from the coverage of labour laws, or help employers in financial
difficulties to retain workers threatened with redundancy?

---

[69] Blanpain, Hepple, Sciarra, Weiss (1996).
[70] European Commission (1999).
[71] Davies (1995) at 50.

The answers have to be sought in the Treaty provisions relating to the free movement of goods (Articles 28 and 29 EC) and services (Article 49), and also the rules which prohibit anti-competitive practices (Article 81), abuse of a dominant position within the common market (Article 82), the regulation of state monopolies (Article 86), and state aids which allow domestic providers to compete unfairly with imported goods and services (Articles 87–89).

It has fallen to the ECJ to balance these free movement and competition provisions with regulations on working conditions, collective agreements, and fundamental rights. Prior to the Treaty of Amsterdam, as Davies has pointed out,[72] the ECJ tended to refuse to recognise overtly that a conflict existed, and resolved the issue either by concluding that the national rule did not fall within the scope of the Community provision, or by declining to deal in any serious way with the possible justification of the national rule. However, in the *Albany* case[73] the ECJ recognised that, as a result of changes in the wording of Articles 2 and 3 EC (section 2, above), the Community has both social and economic objectives. When deciding that a collective agreement, which made affiliation to a pension fund compulsory, was compatible with Community competition law, the ECJ for the first time clearly 'opened the field of analysis to social law.'[74] 'A policy in the social field' (Article 2 EC) was seen as much a part of the activities of the Community as 'a system ensuring that competition in the internal market is not distorted' (Article 3(1)(g) EC). Similarly, the ECJ has recently been willing to recognise the observance of fundamental rights as a free-standing justification for restrictions on the freedom of movement of goods.[75] This was in a case where the Austrian Government was able to justify its failure to ban a demonstration blocking the Brenner motorway (a major route for trade between Northern Europe and Italy) on the ground that it was respecting the fundamental rights to free expression and assembly under Article 10 of the ECHR and the national constitution. Whether this could be extended to the protection of social and labour rights recognised in the EU Charter of Fundamental Rights and some national constitutions remains uncertain. But the importance of the case, as Barnard points out,[76] is that

[72]   Davies (1995) at 52.

[73]   Case C–67/96, *Albany International BV v Stichting Bedrijfspensioenfonds Textlelindustrie* [1999] ECR I–5751, para 54.

[74]   Sciarra (2002) at 109.

[75]   Case C–112/00 *Eugen Schmidberger Internationale Transporte und Planzüge v Republic of Austria* [2003] ECR I–5659. This can be distinguished from the earlier Case C–265/95, *Commission v France (Spanish strawberries)* [1997] ECR I–6959, where there were serious and repeated disruptions to public order. See generally, Barnard (2004) at 66–71, and Council Regulation 2679/98,[1998] OJ L337/8, setting up a special procedure for dealing with serious disruptions to free movement, which contains a special exemption for freedom of assembly and association.

[76]   Barnard (2004) at 70.

fundamental rights were treated not simply as constituting the express public policy derogation, but as a free-standing objective justification.

The judicial review of social and labour legislation to test its compatibility with market rules remains possible. The national court are bound to undertake a balancing exercise in order to decide whether the interference with the freedom of movement or competition rules is proportionate to the aims of social policy or the fundamental rights being pursued. The significance of the Court's recognition of the changed objectives of the Community is that in future, in cases which fall within the scope of the Treaty, there is likely to be greater emphasis on social objectives and fundamental rights.

There is still an objection to balancing on the ground that it undermines the autonomy of the Member States to set their own labour standards. This can be illustrated by the early Sunday trading cases which reached the ECJ. Could Member States restrict Sunday trading? This raised the compatibility of social legislation and the free movement of goods. Article 28 prohibits quantitative restrictions 'and all measures having equivalent effect' on imports. Article 29 contains a similar prohibition in respect of exports. In the *Dassonville* case[77] it was said that Article 28 applied to 'all trading rules enacted by Member States which are capable of hindering, directly or indirectly, actually or potentially intra-Community trade.' Potentially this could affect national labour regulations or agreements which affect production costs, such as those on working time. Article 30 provides an exhaustive list of derogations from the Articles 28 and 29 prohibitions. These allow restrictions to be justified on grounds such as public morality and protection of life. The list does not expressly include the protection of working conditions or other labour regulations.

Problems for labour law have arisen with so-called 'indistinctly applicable' measures, those which apply equally to domestic and imported products but put imported ones at a particular disadvantage.[78] Notwithstanding the broad scope of the *Dassonville* ruling, in *Cassis de Dijon*[79] the ECJ developed an open-ended list of 'mandatory requirements' applicable to indistinctly applicable measures, to supplement the Article 30 derogations. These include the protection of working conditions and the protection of fundamental rights. National restrictions on free movement justified by a mandatory requirement must be proportionate to the aim pursued.[80] This involves the court in balancing the

---

[77] Case 8/74, *Procureur du Roi v Dassonville* [1974] ECR 837.

[78] Barnard (2004) at 100. Broadly speaking, this corresponds to the discrimination law concept of 'indirect discrimination', but the impact is not on persons of a particular social group but on commercial providers of goods and services.

[79] Case 120/78, *Rewe Zentrale v Bundesmonopolverwaltung für Brantwein ('Cassis de Dijon')* [1979] ECR 649.

[80] *Case 261/81 Rau (Walter) v de Smedt* [1982] ECR 3961, para 12; Barnard (2004) at 112.

objectives of the measure against its adverse effects on free movement. The restrictions must be both necessary and suitable.

It can be argued (as the Ohlin report did) that labour standards, as distinct from product requirements, do not impede access to markets, so Article 28 should not be considered at all.[81] Yet, in *Torfaen*,[82] the first of the British Sunday trading cases to reach the ECJ, the Court disregarded the advice of the Advocate-General that Article 28 did not apply to legislation prohibiting retailers from opening their shops on Sundays because the national rules were not directed at imports and gave no protection to domestic products. Instead, the Court held that the trading hours rules fell under Article 28 but could be justified under the mandatory requirements doctrine. The rules were 'a legitimate part of economic and social policy, consistent with the objectives of public interest pursued by the Treaty', and the 'restrictive effects on Community trade which may result therefrom do not exceed the effects intrinsic to rules of that kind.' This ambiguous ruling gave rise to much confusion in the national courts—for example did it make a difference if the reason for the restriction was to protect workers rather than to 'keep Sundays special'?—until the ECJ held that French rules banning Sunday work were not disproportionate,[83] and that Article 28 did not apply to UK legislation prohibiting shops from opening on Sundays because the restrictions were proportionate to the social aims of the legislation.[84] The approach in all these cases was based on an analysis of Article 28 as being directed at any restriction on freedom to trade, rather than as applying only to direct or indirect discrimination against imports.

It was only in 1993, in the *Keck* case,[85] that the ECJ finally accepted the Advocate General's advice that Article 28 does not apply to non-discriminatory national provisions, if the requirements are not such by their nature to prevent access to the market any more by imported goods than by domestic ones. The Court did so by drawing a distinction between 'product requirements' (which fall under Article 28) and 'certain selling arrangements' which do not. Sunday trading rules were subsequently held to be 'certain

---

[81] Deakin (1996) at 73.

[82] Case C–145/88, *Torfaen Borough Council v B & Q plc*[1989] ECR 3851. The Court referred to its earlier decision in Case 155/80, *Summary proceedings against Sergius Oebel* [1981] ECR 1993 (German prohibition on night work in bakeries did not breach Treaty because restrictions applied to all producers and trade within Community remained possible at all times).

[83] Joined Cases C–312 and 332/89, *UDS CGT de l'Aisne v Sidef conforama; Criminal proceedings against Marchandise* [1991] ECR I–1027.

[84] Case C–169/91, *Stoke-on-Trent and Norwich City Council v B&Q plc* [1992] ECR I–6635. UK law was later changed to allow Sunday shopping with accompanying protections for shopworkers by the Sunday Trading Act 1994.

[85] Joined Cases C–267 and 268/91, *Keck and Mithouard (Criminal proceedings against)* [1993] ECR I–6097. The potential, rather than the actual impact of the national rule could be sufficient to trigger Art 28: See Case C–322/01, *Deutscher Apothekerverband eV v 0800 DocMorris*, [2003] ECR CELEX 611, 11 December 2003. Cf Joined Cases C–34–36/95, *De Agostini* [1997] ECR I–3843.

selling arrangements.'[86] The result is that the Court no longer has to evaluate non-discriminatory national labour law regulations and agreements in such cases. This is a result consistent with national autonomy in labour laws and also with the economic philosophy of the Treaty. This falls 'a long way short of identifying free competition with uniformity of national laws.'[87]

There is similarly a recent trend to exclude labour regulation from the scope of competition law. This is exemplified by the important decision in *Albany* (above). Albany, a company in the textile business, wanted to be exempted from making contributions to the Dutch supplementary pension scheme which was managed by funds created within the context of collective agreements. At the request of the social partners, a Minister had exercised his powers to make affiliation to the fund compulsory for every employer in the sector concerned. Albany thought the scheme was inadequate and had made its own arrangements with an insurance company so as to provide more generous pensions. The company's application for exemption was refused. So it challenged a demand for contributions in a Dutch subdistrict court, claiming that the system of compulsory affiliation was contrary to several Treaty articles, in particular Articles 81, 82, 86 and 87. Article 81 EC prohibits agreements between 'undertakings', decisions by associations of 'undertakings' and concerted practices 'which may affect trade between Member States and which have as their object or effect the prevention, restriction or distortion of competition within the common market.' Article 82 prohibits abuses by undertakings of a dominant market position. The requirements of these and other Treaty articles are also applied by Article 86, to state support for undertakings, subject to limited derogations. Article 87 severely restricts state aid 'in any form whatsoever' if this 'distorts or threatens to distort competition by favouring certain undertakings or the production of certain goods.'

The first question the Court had to decide was whether the pension fund was an 'undertaking' within the meaning of these articles. The Court held that it was since it was carrying out an economic activity. Its function was to make investments, the outcome of which determined the amount of benefits paid to members. This distinguished the Dutch fund from other pension funds whose function was 'solidarity', that is 'the inherently uncommercial act of involuntary subsidisation of one social group by another.'[88] The second question the

---

[86] Joined Cases C–401/92 and C–402/92, *Tankstation 't Heukske and JBEBoermans (Criminal proceedings against)* [1994] ECR I–2199; Joined Cases C–69/93 and C258/93, *Punto Casa SpA v Sindaco del Commune di Capena and others* [1994] ECR I–2355; Joined Cases C–418/93 et.al, *Semerero Casa Uno Srl and others* [1996] ECR I–2975.

[87] Deakin (1996) at 73.

[88] Case C–70/95, *Sodemare v Regione Lombardia* [1997] ECR I 3395, per AG Fennelly, para29. For an example see Cases C–159/91 and 160/91, *Poucet v Assurances Générales de France* [1993] ECR I–637, and compare Case C–244/94, *Fédération Française des Sociététes d'Assurance* [1995] ECR I–4013.

Court had to answer was whether making membership compulsory nullified the effectiveness of competition rules applicable to undertakings. The Court held that Article 81 had not been infringed because these collective agreements were excluded from its scope. Its starting point was that the amended Treaty aims both at ensuring competition and social protection It said that 'agreements concluded in the context of collective agreements between management and labour in the pursuit of such objectives must, by virtue of their nature and purpose, be regarded as falling outside the scope of Article [81(1)] of the Treaty.' The third question was whether conferring an exclusive right on the compulsory fund was incompatible with Article 87. The Court accepted that the fund enjoyed a dominant position. Earlier case law had decided that Article 87 was infringed only if the body was 'manifestly unable' to meet demand, and the Court doubted whether this was the case with the the pension fund. The Court then examined the justification under Article 87(2): was the measure necessary for the performance of a particular social task of general public interest? The Court examined this issue itself, rather than leaving it to the national court as the Advocate-General had advised, and held that the supplementary pension served an essential social function because of its role in the Dutch social security system of topping up a basic state pension based on the minimum wage. The exclusive rights of the fund were necessary to enable it to perform the taks of general economic interest assigned to it.

This case has been related at some length because of its significance in recognising the role of the Member States and the social partners in regulating labour and social protection. Some commentators go even further and suggest that *Albany* 're-establishes' the social rights recognised in national systems in a way which is compatible with market rules.[89] Yet many questions remain. First, the inclusion of some pension funds within the category of 'undertakings' leaves open the possibility that they may fall foul of competition rules. The test of 'solidarity' excludes only those labour market institutions which do not operate on commercial principles; such bodies are increasingly rare due to extensive privatisation and the demands for economic efficiency in the public sector. In the *Macrotron* case[90] (decided before *Albany*) the ECJ applied the competition provisions to the German Federal Employment Commission, which had a monopoly over executive recruitment. There is nothing in *Albany* or other cases to suggest that a non-profit recruitment agency is not an economic entity. However, the ECJ has not drawn a consistent line between commercial and non-commercial activity.

---

[89] Sciarra (2002) at 105.
[90] Case C–41/90, *Höfner and Elser v Macrotron* [1991] ECR I–1979; Case C–55/96 *Job Centre* [1997] ECR I–7119.

Secondly, what types of collective agreement are excluded from the scope of Article 81(1)? The Court referred to the 'nature and purpose' of the agreements, and identified two features of the Dutch agreements. Their 'nature' was that they were like the category of agreements that emerge from the 'social dialogue' now specifically encouraged by the Treaty (chapter 9, below); their 'purpose' was to guarantee a certain level of pensions. A narrow reading of the reasoning relating to purpose, would lead to the conclusion that while collective agreements on pay (broadly defined) are excluded from competition rules, agreements on non-pay issues such as parental leave and child-care are not.[91] The implication of this is that positive harmonisation measures are needed to protect collective and workforce agreements on family-friendly policies. Flexibility agreements resulting from the European employment strategy may also need to be given legal status.

Thirdly, while the collective agreements in *Albany* were considered to be necessary for the performance of tasks of 'general economic interest', it does not follow that this conclusion will be reached in all cases. For example, in the earlier *Merci Convenzionale* case,[92] the maintenance of a dock work monopoly at the port of Genoa was held not to be necessary for the performance of work of 'general economic interest'. All that can be said is that, in future, cases of this kind are likely to undergo a more rigorous analysis of their social objectives than in *Merci*, where the Court took no account of the purposes of the monopoly, namely to combat casualisation of dock labour.

Finally, it is in the area of state aids that 'social dumping' issues are most likely to continue to arise. The Court neatly avoided these issues in *Kirshammer-Hack*,[93] in which it held that provisions of German labour law excluding those working for employers who employed five or fewer employees did not amount to illegitimate state aid contrary to Article 87(2) even though the effect of this exclusion was to subsidise small employers in Germany. The reason given was a narrow one, namely that the exclusion of small employers did not involve a transfer of state resources. However, in more recent cases, the ECJ has taken an expansive view of state aid where state measures or collective agreements have sought to reduce unemployment. Thus, French measures to mitigate the effect of redundancies by joint financing of social plans have been held to be state aid,[94] as have measures to relieve employers from certain social security contributions in respect of employees earning more than the minimum wage in return for the social partners agreeing to reorganise working time and maintain

---

[91] Vousden (2000) at 189.

[92] Case C–179/90, *Merci Convenzionali Porto di Genova SpA v Siderurgica Gabrielli SpA* [1991] ECR I–5889.

[93] Case C–189/91, *Kirshammer-Hack v Sidal* [1993] ECR I–6185; See too, Joined Cases C–72/91 and C–73/91, *Sloman Neptun* [1993] ECR I–887.

[94] Case C–241/94, *France v Commission* [1996] ECR I–4551.

employment.[95] A Belgian scheme to increase reductions in social security contributions in some sectors in order to increase the employment of low-wage manual workers has been held to be illegal.[96] Although *Albany* has taken some collective agreements outside the scope of competition law, national labour and social law has still not achieved full autonomy from the market freedoms.

4. Positive harmonisation

Level playing field or floor of rights?

As distinct from negative harmonisation which subordinates national labour regulations and collective agreements to the market freedoms, positive harmonisation requires the active involvement and co-operation of the Community Institutions, the Member States and the social partners.

Two distinct justifications have been used to support harmonisation measures: removing distortions of competition by achieving 'parity of costs' or a 'level playing-field', on the one hand, and setting 'minimum requirements', or a floor of rights, on the other hand. As we have seen, the original Article 117 in the Treaty of Rome proclaimed the *objective* of 'approximation'. In this context, 'approximation' can be regarded as 'an indicator of the degree of harmonisation taking place rather than as a separate legal process clearly distinguishable from harmonisation.'[97] In the period before 1987, the means to achieve this objective had to be found in Article 100 of the Rome Treaty (now Article 94 EC) which permits directives for the approximation of such laws, regulations and administrative provisions of the Member States 'as directly affect the establishment or functioning of the common market' provisions. The employment protection Directives adopted from 1975 to 1980 were expressly based on these articles. When interpreting these Directives, the ECJ held that they were intended 'both to ensure comparable protection for workers' rights in the different Member States and to harmonise the costs which such protective measures entail for Community undertakings.'[98]

When QMV was introduced in 1987, by Article 100a (now Article 95(1) EC) to facilitate the adoption of measures relating to the 'internal market', this expressly excluded 'provisions relating to the free movement of persons' and those 'relating to the rights and interests of employed persons'.[99] The latter

---

[95] Case C–251/97, *France v Commission* [1999] ECR I–6639.
[96] Case C–75/97, *Belgium v Commission* [1999] ECR I–3671.
[97] Watson (1980) at 31.
[98] Cases C–382 and 383/92, *Commisson v United Kingdom* [1994] ECR I–2479, paras 15 and 16.
[99] Art 100a(2) (now Art 95(2) EC).

required unanimity. Although the precise meaning of 'the rights and interests of employed persons' is controversial,[100] recent case law has emphasised that, in any event, Community competence under Article 95(1) is limited to measures which contribute to removing obstacles to free movement of goods and services or the removal of distortions on competition.[101] After 1987, in the face of opposition from the Thatcher Administration (section 2, above), the Commission attempted to justify some proposed Directives regulating part-time and temporary work on the economic grounds of removing distortions on competition. They did so by drawing a fatuous distinction between the differences in wage levels between countries, which 'do not hamper the operation of healthy competition in the Community', and differences in non-wage costs resulting from social charges and employment regulations.[102] Deakin[103] persuasively argues that there is no economic logic in this distinction, not least since the distortions referred to are not attributable solely to different employment rules. If sound, the Commission's distinction would undermine Article 141 EC (ex 119), which requires equality between women and men in respect of both pay and non-pay terms of employment.

Since the Treaty of Amsterdam, the most important legal basis for harmonisation in the social field is to be found in Articles 136–137 EC, as amended by the Treaty of Nice (Box 8.4). These articles give power to impose harmonising Directives setting 'minimum requirements for gradual implementation'. Harmonisation is stated, in Article 136, as the objective. This is to be achieved while the improvement in living and working conditions 'is being maintained'—a clear signal against levelling down. The danger that 'minimum requirements' might be used to deregulate more favourable national conditions is illustrated by the successful action of the Conservative UK Government in 1995 in altering the threshold necessary to trigger the obligation to consult workers' representatives from the higher UK standard to the lower EU requirement.[104] Some recent Directives have sought to prevent this by including non-regression clauses expressly providing that implementation

---

[100] Kenner (2003) at 84–91.

[101] Case C–376/98, *Germany v European Parliament and Council (Tobacco Advertising)* [2000] ECR I–8419. In Case 491/01, *R v Secretary of State for Health, ex parte British American Tobacco (Investments) Ltd,[BAT]* [2002] ECR I–11453, the ECJ recognised that different national rules might themselves be obstacles to free movement.

[102] European Commission (1990) at paras 22 and 25.

[103] Deakin (1996) at 78.

[104] When the UK was required by the ECJ in Cases C–382 and 383/92, *Commission v UK* [1994] ECR I–2435 to change UK law so as to comply with the Collective Redundancies Directive 75/129/EEC [1975] OJ L48/29, the UK took the opportunity to withdraw information and consultation rights where only one worker is made redundant, and sought to use Art 1(1) of the Directive to justify raising the threshold to 20 redundancies over a period of 90 days to trigger the obligation to inform and consult. This was held to be lawful by the High Court in *R v Secretary of State for Trade and Industry, ex parte UNISON, GMB and NASUWT* [1996] IRLR 438.

of the Directive 'shall not constitute valid grounds for reducing the general level of protection provided to workers.' Despite such a clause in the Working Time Directive, in 2003 the Berlusconi Government in Italy reduced the higher Italian standards in respect of rest periods to the lower EU 'minimum requirement.' This seems to be a flagrant breach of the non-regression clause, and the general aim of maintaining a floor of rights.

The aim of providing a floor of rights is supported by the express provision that Member States can maintain or introduce more stringent measures for the protection of working conditions so long as these are compatible with the Treaty.[105] As a concession to the deregulators, however, it is provided that 'such Directives shall avoid imposing administrative, financial and legal constraints on the creation and development of small and medium undertakings.'[106] Despite this limitation and the subtlety of its wording, Article 137(1) has provided an important legal base for the Commission to propose measures not only in respect of health and safety (where there is a framework Directive and an extensive range of 'daughter' Directives) but also in areas such as working time, the protection of pregnant workers and young workers.[107] In the *Working Time* case,[108] the UK argued that the Working Time Directive could not be adopted by QMV under Article 137(2) because the Directive concerned the functioning of the internal market in relation to employment. Instead recourse should have been had to Articles 95(1) or 308 which requires unanimity. The ECJ held that Article 95 is a residual provision. Since the principal aim was protection of the working environment, Article 137(2) had to be used even though there might be ancillary effects on employment and the functioning of the market. Moreover, the notion of 'minimum requirements' did not mean, as the UK had argued, a minimalist approach to social matters. 'Minimum requirements' involves a 'high degree of convergence'; it is not the lowest level acceptable to Member States but a compulsory minimum beyond which Member States are free to adopt more protective rules.

The retreat from positive harmonisation

Paradoxically, at the very time when this clear justification and legal base had been provided for harmonisation by directive the Commission underwent a

---

[105] Art 118a(3), now 137(5) EC.

[106] Art 137(2) EC.

[107] See Barnard (2000b), ch 6.

[108] Case C–84/94, *United Kingdom v Council* [1996] ECR I–5755, paras 11–12. The ECJ gave a broad interpretation to 'working environment' and also rejected the claim that a scientific link needed to be shown between working hours and health and safety in order to justify Community action (para 39).

Box 8.4

ARTICLES 136 AND 137(1) EC (as amended)

Article 136

The Community and the Member States, having in mind fundamental social rights such as those set out in the European Social Charter signed at Turin on 18 October 1961 and in the 1989 Community Charter of Fundamental Social Rights of Workers, shall have as their objectives the promotion of employment, improved living and working conditions, so as to make possible their harmonisation while the improvement is being maintained, proper social protection, dialogue between management and labour, the development of human resources with a view to lasting high employment and the combating of exclusion.

To this end the Community and the Member States shall implement measures which take account of the diverse forms of national practices, in particular in the field of contractual relations, and the need to maintain the competitiveness of the Community economy.

They believe that such a development will ensue not only from the functioning of the common market, which will favour the harmonisation of social systems, but also from the procedures provided for in this Treaty and from the approximation of provisions laid down by law, regulation and administrative action.

Article 137(1)

With a view to achieving the objectives of Article 136, the Community shall support and complement the activities of the Member States in the following fields:
(a) Improvements in particular in the working environment to protect workers' health and safety;
(b) working conditions;
(c) social security and social protection of workers;
(d) protection of workers where their employment contract is terminated;
(e) the information and consultation of workers;
(f) representation and collective defence of the interests of workers and employers, including co-determination, subject to paragraph 5 [which excludes pay, the right of association, the right to strike and the right to impose lockouts];

Box 8.4 (*cont.*)

(g) conditions of employment for third-country nationals legally resid-
    ing in Community territory;
(h) the integration of persons excluded from the labour market, without
    prejudice to article 150 [vocational training policy];
(i) equality between men and women with regard to labour market
    opportunities and treatment at work;
(j) the combating of social exclusion;
(k) the modernisation of social protection systems without prejudice to
    point (c).

*Note to Box 8. 4: Directives may be adopted by QMV in respect of (a) to (i),
apart from (c), (d), (f) and (g), which require unanimity. A Decision may be
adopted by QMV in respect of (d), (f) and (g). QMV has been extended to
social security for migrant workers by the EU Constitution.*

---

crisis of confidence in this regulatory model.[109] In 1996, the Commission
informed the Parliament and Council that 'outright harmonisation of social
policies is not a Community objective'.[110] This was repeated in the
Commission's social policy agenda in 2000.[111]

What explains this retreat from harmonisation by directive? Several reasons
may be suggested. First, the diversity of labour law and social protection systems in an enlarging EU renders illusory any idea of a common code of labour
regulation. An analogy may be drawn with the free movement of goods. In the
celebrated *Cassis de Dijon* case[112] (above) the ECJ enunciated the presumption
of equivalence or mutual recognition: goods lawfully produced and marketed
in one Member State can in principle be sold in another Member State without further restriction. Each State must recognise the other's standards as
equivalent to its own, unless it can justify its own more stringent mandatory
requirements as being proportionate (see section 3 above). The Commission
realised that the significance of this decision was to obviate the need for much
harmonisation legislation.[113] In the field of labour law and social protection,
mutual recognition is also a plausible response to diversity in the interests of
the market. However, mutual recognition can be used in a deregulatory way:
since there is freedom of movement of capital there is a risk that businesses will

---

[109] Lo Faro (1999) at 10.
[110] European Commission (1996).
[111] European Commission (2000) at 7.
[112] Case *120/78, Cassis de Dijon* [1979] ECR 649, para 8.
[113] Barnard (2004) at 105–8.

move to countries with unacceptably low labour and social standards.[114] In the case of free movement of goods this problem has been met by the notion of 'minimum requirements' (section 3, above). The field of labour law is different from free movement of goods. French *cassis*, produced according to French standards, is placed in direct competition with German fruit liqueurs, produced according to German standards, on the German market. Labour law, by contrast is territorial, and those affected do not move in the same way. Mutual recognition—as an alternative to harmonising legislation—is workable in respect of labour laws only if accompanied by a core of fundamental rights which all States must respect.

A second reason for the disillusion with harmonising directives is the difficulty of reconciling flexibility with effective implementation. A Council Resolution of 6 December 1994 said that Community legislation in the social field must 'take account of the situation in all Member States' and 'neither overstretch any one Member State nor force it to dismantle social rights.' Directives must be 'flexible enough and confine themselves to provisions which can be incorporated into the various national systems.'[115] One method for achieving this has been partial rather than full harmonisation. For example, the Directive on transfers of undertakings[116] is limited to harmonising the circumstances in which 'acquired' rights of workers go over to the new employer when an undertaking is transferred (transfer rights); the Directive does not attempt to harmonise the substantive rights which existed before the transfer, this being solely a matter to be determined at national level. Moreover, there are several optional clauses in the Directive which leave it to Member States to decide on the extent of 'transfer rights'[117] Another example is the Working Time Directive[118] which allows an individual to opt-out of the requirement for a maximum 48-hour week. A study of the effect of this on the UK (which had insisted on the opt-out) indicates that it has diluted the impact of the Directive on the UK's long working hours culture. More generally, the study found that the UK's individualised workplace bargaining is ill-placed to adapt to a continental European model of working time regulation.[119] A final example is the European Works Councils Directive,[120] Article 13 of which exempted from the provisions of the Directive any undertaking covered by an

---

[114] Lo Faro (2000) at 39–41.

[115] [1994] OJ C368/6; see Barnard (2000b) at 204–6.

[116] Council Directive 2001/23/EC, [2001] OJ L82/16, replacing Council Directive 77/187/EEC, [1997] OJ L61/26.

[117] Eg, in respect of joint liability of transferor and transferee employer; the observance of collective agreements; the extent of unfair dismissal coverage.

[118] Council Directive 93/104/EC [1993] OJ L307/18.

[119] Barnard, Deakin and Hobbs (2003).

[120] Council Directive 94/45/EC, [1994] OJ L254/64 as amended and extended to the UK by Council Directive 97/74/EC, [1998] OJ L10/22.

agreement already in existence by 22 September 1996 which covered the entire workforce.[121]

Another method which recognises national autonomy, has been to rely on national legal orders for the enforcement by workers of Community rules. After a phase of active intervention by the ECJ before 1990 to allow individuals to rely on Directives in actions against organs of the state, and to make the State liable for serious failures to implement a directive, the mood of the 1990s and 2000s has been one of restraint by the ECJ allowing autonomy to national courts in providing remedies.[122] The result of ambiguous Directives, partial harmonisation, opt-outs, exceptions and the reliance on national procedures for enforcement has been to render Community legislation relatively ineffective.

A third, and decisive reason for the move away from harmonisation by directive is political. We have seen (section 2, above), that opposition from employers and some governments (notably the UK) has frequently stopped legislative action, or led to the dilution of proposals. The grounds of opposition have been both quantitative—the 'burdens on business'—and qualitative—'obstacles to growth and competitiveness'. The post-Amsterdam period has been marked by a new spirit of political co-operation, the main priority being job growth. The activities of the Commission and Council have been directed towards securing co-operation between States, using 'soft' measures rather than legislation, but within a framework of fundamental social rights. This is the subject of the next chapter.

---

[121] In the case of the UK, this date was 14 December 1999. 386 such agreements had been signed by the relevant date, 58 of these by UK companies.

[122] Malmberg (2003) at 296.

9

New Methods of Integration in the EU

1. The open method of co-ordination
2. Social dialogue
3. Fundamental rights
4. Conclusions

1. The open method of co-ordination

The Employment Title of the Treaty of Amsterdam was a legal and constitutional, as well as social and economic, turning point in the evolution of EU labour law. In place of centralised harmonisation, the new approach has been presented as being based on the principle of subsidiarity. This principle, according to Article 5 EC is that the Community should take action 'only if and so far as the objectives of the proposed action cannot sufficiently be achieved by the Member States and can therefore, by reason of the scale or effects of the proposed action, be better achieved by the Community.' It uses the Open Method of Co-Ordination (OMC), a 'decentralised but carefully co-ordinated process, involving the exchange of best practices, the use of benchmarking, national and regional target-setting, periodic reporting, and multi-lateral surveillance.'[1] Its methods are intergovernmental, rather than supra-national, being modelled to some extent on methods of fiscal and economic co-ordination among the EU Member States.[2]

The institutionalisation of the OMC in relation to employment strategy, marked the culmination of a process, initiated at the Essen Council in 1994, which linked the objective of a 'high level of employment' with 'flexibility' in the labour market (chapter 8, above). Article 125 EC requires both the Member States and the Community 'to work towards developing a co-ordinated strategy for employment and particularly for promoting a skilled,

---

[1] De la Porte (2002) at 38.
[2] De la Porte (2002) at 40–41.

trained and adaptable workforce and labour markets responsive to economic change'. Article 127(2) EC has the effect of mainstreaming the aim of a 'high level of employment' so that it must be taken into account in the formulation and implementation of all EU policies. This is known as the European Employment Strategy (EES) or 'Luxembourg process' following its launch at the Luxembourg Jobs Summit in November 1997.

At the Lisbon European Council in March 2000, a new strategic goal was formulated that the EU should become 'the most competitive and dynamic knowledge-based economy in the world capable of sustainable economic growth with more and better jobs and greater social cohesion'. This was aimed at regaining the conditions for *full* employment. The Lisbon strategy set targets of an overall EU employment rate of 70 percent and women's employment of more than 60 percent by 2010. The Stockholm Council (March 2001) added some intermediate targets, and a new target of 50 percent employment for older workers by 2010. A mid-term review in 2003 resulted in a number of changes. The revamped strategy aims at 'full employment, quality and productivity, and strengthened social inclusion and cohesion.' The EU Constitution now formally states 'full employment and social progress' with a 'high level of protection' as EU objectives, along with the combating of social exclusion and discrimination, the promotion of equality between women and men, and solidarity between generations.[3]

The EES is designed to guide the employment policies of the Member States and to co-ordinate them. The European Council adopts Employment Guidelines, on the basis of a Recommendation from the Commission, following consultation with the European Parliament, the Economic and Social Committee and the Committee of the Regions. These Guidelines, revised annually, set out common priorities for Member States' employment policies. Each Member State has to submit a National Action Plan reporting on the employment situation and the steps taken to implement the Guidelines. On the basis of these reports, and after receiving advice from an Employment Committee,[4] the Council examines the implementation of the Member States' policies in the light of the guidelines. The Council may, on the basis of a Commission proposal, make Recommendations directed at specific Member States as to how they should improve their employment performance.

The working method under the EES has been called the Open Method of Co-ordination (OMC). This has several significant features. First, the Member States remain responsible for their employment policies, and, the Treaty

---

[3] Art I–3.

[4] This Committee, established under Art 130 EC consists of experts from the Member States and the Commission. It is separate from the Standing Committee on Employment on which the social partners are represented.

declares, their 'competences shall be respected.'[5] Article 126(2) EC imposes on the Member States the crucial duty 'to regard promoting employment as a matter of common concern' and to 'co-ordinate their action in this respect with the Council.' This mirrors the wording of Article 99(1) EC which places similar obligations on Member States in respect of economic policy. The role of the EU is to encourage co-operation between Member States, supporting and, if necessary, complementing their action.

Secondly, the OMC relies on *soft law* rather than legal sanctions. The only legal base for Community action against Member States is Article 129 EC. The Council may adopt 'incentive measures', but must do so with the European Parliament under the co-decision procedure.[6] These measures are aimed at developing exchanges of information and best practices, providing comparative analysis and advice as well as promoting innovative approaches and evaluating experiences, in particular by recourse to pilot projects. They may not include 'harmonisation of the laws and practices of the Member States.'[7] Szyszczak describes the regulatory framework of the Employment Title as 'an attempt to give employment policy a legal framework whereby the soft law discourse may be translated into binding normative rules'[8] and Biagi regarded the Employment Guidelines as 'certainly normative in character'.[9] But, as Ball pointed out,[10] there are no formal legal sanctions for failure to take the Guidelines into account.

Thirdly, the OMC is concerned with a *convergence of objectives*. The aim is to achieve commonly agreed employment outcomes through concerted action. Each Member State is expected to make its contribution towards raising average EU performance. This is managed by quantified measurements and benchmarks are used to monitor and assess the success of the EES. The use of targets and indicators is said to make the process transparent and open to public scrutiny. The annual reports allow for best practices to be identified. Exchange of experiences and peer pressure give an incentive to improving performance.[11]

This process has been criticised for placing the emphasis on *more* jobs rather than *better* or *decent* jobs.[12] There are ten specific Guidelines. Some of these undoubtedly have a deregulatory edge. 'Addressing change and promoting adaptability' means changes in contractual arrangements, to increase

---

[5] Art 127(1) EC
[6] Art 251 EC.
[7] Art 129 EC.
[8] Szyszczak (2000b) at 206.
[9] Biagi (2000) at 160.
[10] Ball (2001) at 357.
[11] For details see de la Porte (2002) at 46–51.
[12] Ball (2001) at 366–74.

'flexibility'; 'entrepreneurship' entails reducing the 'administrative burdens' on businesses, which may in practice result in less protection for workers in small and medium enterprises; 'making work pay' means tightening the qualifying conditions for eligibility or duration of social benefits. On the other hand, the Guidelines encourage many positive measures such as individual job search and guidance at an early stage of unemployment; 'developing human capital' by improving participation in education and training; promoting 'active ageing' involves increasing the participation of older workers, discouraging early retirement, and reforming pensions; promoting gender equality through policies to reconcile work and life, such as improved childcare provision; and improving the labour market situation of people with disabilities, migrant workers and ethnic minorities. There is, however, no mention of rights at work. The balance between flexibility and security is weighted in the Guidelines against legal rights for workers.

The Joint Employment Report for 2003/4 noted that the EES had led to a range of labour market reforms in EU States, but said that there was a grave danger that the key employment targets would not be met by 2010. In December 2003, a European Employment Taskforce (chaired by Wim Kok) identified the need for increased 'adaptability' of workers and enterprises, attracting more people into the labour market; investing more effectively in human capital; and ensuring effective implementation of reforms through better governance. Once again, there was no mention of employment rights.

Finally, the OMC is an attempt to *integrate* employment, economic and social policy. The Guidelines are not restricted to active labour market policies but extend to social, educational, tax, enterprise and regional policies. Since 2003, the EES has been more closely aligned with the Broad Economic Policy Guidelines process. There is, however, an underlying tension between the economic and monetary policies of the EU and aim of high or full employment. Member States facing the national budgetary constraints required to meet the convergence criteria for entering the single currency may find it difficult to satisfy the Employment Guidelines. Articles 126 EC and 128(2) EC require the Member States' employment policies and the Council's Guidelines to be consistent with the fiscal and economic policies adopted by the Council. Despite statements at Council meetings that employment and economic policies are of equal importance, the wording of these Articles makes employment policy subservient to economic policy, a point underlined by the presence of sanctions for failure to comply with fiscal policy and their absence in respect of employment policy.[13] There is a 'hard' co-ordination of fiscal policy, under which Member States agree to pool their sovereignty and to comply with

---

[13] Ball (2001) at 360, who also discusses the potential constraints imposed by competition policy on state aids for training, at 363–67.

certain benchmarks. Deviation from the policy of the so-called Stability and Growth Pact can result in a Council Recommendation for corrective action, and in the case of infringement of the Pact, the Council can issue a formal sanction. In the case of the Broad Economic Policy Guidelines and the EES, the Council can issue a non-binding Recommendation against a deviating Member State, but no formal sanction.

What is the potential for extending the OMC beyond employment policy into other aspects of social policy? The Commission's Social Policy Agenda (SPA) for the period until the end of 2005, approved at the Nice Council in December 2000,[14] plainly envisages this development. A legal basis was provided by an amendment, agreed in the Treaty of Nice, to Article 137(2) EC. This allows the Council to 'adopt measures designed to encourage co-operation between Member States through initiatives aimed at improving knowledge, developing exchanges of information and best practices, promoting innovative approaches and evaluating experiences.' Harmonisation of laws and regulations is expressly excluded. This means that the areas of social policy traditionally the subject of Directives are increasingly likely to be dealt with under the OMC. This is reinforced in the EU Constitution which states that the EU may adopt initiatives to ensure 'co-ordination' of Member States' social policies.[15]

Two areas in which the OMC had been particularly important are social protection and social inclusion. 'Modernisation of social protection systems' was added by the Treaty of Nice to the areas of social policy in which the Community supports and complements the activities of Member States.[16] This is seen as a crucial response to the problems of an ageing population, as well as a means to reduce public expenditure and raise employment rates. In the rhetoric of the SPA this 'means adapting social protection systems to make work pay and provide secure income, make pensions safe and sustainable, promote social inclusion and ensure high quality and sustainability of health care.'[17] Although placed in the Social Chapter, the power to co-ordinate social protection is seen as a 'productive factor', and as essential to maintain the capacity and financial sustainability of these systems.[18]

There has been extensive action to co-ordinate policies for combating social exclusion. This was also added to the areas of social policy by the Treaty of Nice,[19] but harmonisation of laws and regulations on this topic is expressly

---

[14] European Commission (2000).

[15] Art I–14(4); cf Art I–14(3) which says that co-ordination must be used in respect of employment policies.

[16] Art 137(1)(k). For details of the application of OMC to poverty and social exclusion, see de la Porte (2002) at 51–56.

[17] European Commission (2000) at 19.

[18] European Commission (2000) at 19.

[19] Art 137(1)(j).

excluded. The effect of this is that although harmonising Directives are possible under the Social Chapter in respect of ' equality between men and women with regard to labour market opportunities and treatment at work',[20] such Directives cannot be used for other forms of social exclusion, for example in respect of disabled persons and ethnic minorities. There are Directives under Article 13 EC relating to discrimination against these and other groups (section 3, below), but social inclusion is a far wider concept involving positive integrative measures. A hierarchy of social inclusion has thus been created. Significantly, the Conclusions of the Nice Council described social inclusion as a 'precondition for better economic performance'.

The major question mark which hangs over the OMC is whether it will be able to deliver not only high levels of employment, but also a high quality of jobs, social protection and social inclusion. Beneath the wording of the Treaties of Amsterdam and Nice, and the 'third way' rhetoric of the Commission's communications, an important shift in the governance of the EU is taking place. The OMC 'respects' the Member States' competence, but the convergence of objectives and the Community's guidelines and monitoring in effect leave 'less room for manoeuvre and innovation at national level'.[21] The weakness of the OMC is that it applies only incentives and peer pressure. There are no sanctions for failure to follow Council Recommendations. The 'rights deficit' may be filled, to some extent, by the development of fundamental rights (section 3, below). There is also a democratic deficit, with only limited participation of the European Parliament and the social partners.[22] The usual response to this criticism is to point to the social dialogue. It is to this method that we must now turn.

2. Social dialogue

'Social dialogue' is Eurojargon for the participation of representatives of European-level employers' organisations and trade unions (the 'social partners') in the formulation of policy and legislation at EU-level. It is said, by the Commission, to be uniquely 'rooted in the history of the European continent' and to be 'at the centre' of the European social model.[23] This is misleading because it confuses the EU-social dialogue with the many systems of autonomous collective bargaining that have developed in European countries. Those systems rest on freedom of association including the right to strike, and

---

[20] Article 137(1)(i). Directives relating to gender equality are also made under Art 141(3) EC.
[21] Syzszczak (2001) at 1169.
[22] Syzszczak (2002).
[23] COM (2002) 341 final, at 6.

on the negotiation of agreements between representative organisations of workers and employers. The 'right of association, the right to strike or the right to lock-out' are expressly excluded from the EU's legislative competence,[24] and the European-level trade unions lack the membership of workers sufficient to mobilise the social power which is essential to effective collective bargaining. European social dialogue is not a replication of national level bargaining. It is, as Lo Faro observes, 'merely a regulatory technique potentially useful in overcoming the regulatory problems affecting the Community decision-making and implementation processes.'[25] As such, it purports to give democratic legitimacy to EU governance, and serves as a dynamic element in what the Commission calls 'the positive management of change',[26] and its critics label 'the transmission belt of transnational competition.'[27] Unlike collective bargaining, social dialogue is not supposed to be adversarial. The term 'social partners' implies an equality between management and labour which may be illusory in practice.[28]

The origins of the social dialogue lie in the SEA 1986 which introduced a new Article 118B in the Treaty requiring the Commission to 'endeavour to develop the dialogue between management and labour at European level which could, if the two sides consider it desirable, lead to relations based on agreement.' No procedures were prescribed, and the legal results of the dialogue were so ambiguous as to be meaningless. Indeed, it is difficult to characterise Article 118B as more than a political gesture legitimising the talks which had already begun in 1985. Following the failure of earlier informal consultations, the Commission's President, Jacques Delors, invited the employers' bodies, UNICE and CEEP, and the European Trade Union Congress (ETUC) to attend a meeting at Val Duchesse in January 1985. This revealed that both sides supported the objective of creating a single market. Further meetings were held in 1985 and 1986 and by 6 November 1986 a 'joint opinion' had been delivered on co-operative growth strategy, and on 6 March 1985, a 'joint opinion' on training, motivation, and information and consultation relating to new technologies. Gradually, further consultations took place and joint opinions emerged, but the Commission recognised that the dialogue 'remained in Brussels' without wider involvement. In addition to inter-sectoral dialogue, there was a revival of sectoral committees. By 1990, 8 such committees were functioning.

The constitutional turning point came in the Maastricht Treaty agreed in 1991, subject to the UK's opt-out from the Social Chapter (chapter 8, above).

---

[24] Art 137(6) EC.
[25] Lo Faro (2000) at 159.
[26] COM (2002) 341 final at 6.
[27] Mahnkopf and Altvater (1995).
[28] The EU Constitution now uses the term 'social partners' throughout in place of 'management and labour'.

The Social Dialogue Steering Group had set up an ad hoc group to consider the role of the social partners in the new Social Chapter. These discussions led to an agreement on 31 October 1991 which was incorporated almost in its entirety into the Maastricht Social Agreement, which came into force in 1993. This then became the Social Chapter of the TEU as a result of the Treaty of Amsterdam. Article 138 EC requires the Commission to promote the 'consultation' of management and labour at Community level. It must take 'any relevant measures to facilitate their dialogue by ensuring balanced support for the parties.' This form of consultation is distinct from that developed in a number of standing committees in which the social partners participate, whose task is to advise the Commission on specific issues such as employment, health and safety, vocational training, equal opportunities and social security for migrant workers. In the period 1993–2004, the Commission consulted the social partners at inter-sectoral level on 15 occasions (Table 9.A). In practice even more significant are the opinions and agreements produced by 28 sectoral social dialogue committees, covering most of the main branches of trade and industry.

There can be little doubt that the employers' enthusiasm for the new role given to the social dialogue in the Maastricht Agreement was that they preferred to keep social regulation in their own hands, and to reduce the role of the Council and Parliament. Zygmunt Tyskiewicz of UNICE declared: 'we are there to take the place of the legislator'.[29] On the other hand, Emilio Gabaglio of the ETUC believed that the legislative and dialogue approaches 'must be complementary rather than mutually exclusive. There are some minimum rights which must be guaranteed by law. Other aspects can be added through collective bargaining.'[30]

The Commission has an apparently neutral role, to ensure 'balanced support', but there is a two-stage consultation process which effectively leaves the Commission in the driving seat. In the first stage the Commission must consult management and labour on the possible direction of Community action *before* submitting proposals in the social policy field. On completion of that stage, if the Commission considers that Community action is 'advisable' it must consult management and labour again on the 'content of the envisaged proposal', but it is under no obligation to follow any Opinion or Recommendation. The crucial shift from consultation to negotiation occurs when, and if, 'on the occasion of *such* consultation' the social partners inform the Commission that they want to invoke the dialogue procedure under Article 139 EC.[31] The Commission then has to allow nine months for this procedure, a period which can be extended by agreement between management, labour

---

[29] Interview in *Social Europe* 2/92 at 20.
[30] Interview in *Social Europe* 2/92 at 14.
[31] Art 138(4) EC (emphasis added).

Table 9.A

CONSULTATIONS WITH SOCIAL PARTNERS 1993–2004

	Subject	Outcome
1993	European Works Councils	Opinion following attempted negotiations. Council Dir. 94/5/EC
1995	Work and family life	Agreement on parental leave implemented by Council Dir. 96/34/EC
1995	Burden of proof in sex discrim.	Separate opinions. Council Dir. 97/80/EC.
1995	Flexible working time	Agreement on part-time work implemented by Council Dir. 97/81/EC Agreement on fixed-term work implemented by Council Dir. 99/70/EC Failure of negotiations on temporary work. Proposed Council Dir.
1996	Prevention of sexual harassment	Separate opinions
1997	Worker information and consultation	Separate opinions. EP and Council Dir. 2002/14/EC
2000	Modernising employment relations	Agreement on telework, implemented by Member States' own procedures
2000	Protecting workers against employer's insolvency	Separate opinions. Council Dir. 2002/74/EC
2000	Protecting workers against exposure to asbestos	Separate opinions
2000	Safety and health for self-employed	Separate opinions
2001	Protecting employees' personal data	UNICE does not wish to negotiate
2002	Social aspects of corporate restructuring	Draft text agreed by UNICE, but not ETUC
2002	Portability of supplementary pensions	UNICE not willing to negotiate
2004	Revision of working-time directive	In progress
2004	Revision of European Works Councils Directive	In progress

and the Commission. It is ambiguous whether management and labour can initiate the Article 139 EC process at the time of the first stage consultation, or only at the second. This turns on the meaning of the words 'such consultation'. In practice, the negotiations have been shaped by the Commission's second-stage proposals. In Bercusson's phrase, the social partners have negotiated 'in the shadow of the law'.[32]

The Article 139 dialogue procedure 'may lead to *contractual relations*, including agreements.' The impression that this conveys of legally-binding collective contracts at European level is problematic. A preliminary point is that the emphasised words were the result of translation by civil servants, first in the Community Charter, and then in the Social Policy Agreement, of the French *relations conventionelles*, which means simply 'relations based on agreement.' For good measure, the words 'including agreements' were added. It is by no means clear that the Treaty now creates a new legal category of European collective contracts; indeed the addition of 'agreements' shows that at most such contracts were only one (unlikely) method of implementation. In practice, the social partners have made 'framework agreements', which lay down procedural rules and establish minimum standards. They include exhortatory language and general aspirations rather than unconditional and legally exact rights and obligations.

The agreements concluded at Community level may be implemented in one of two ways. The first is 'in accordance with the procedures and practices specific to management and labour and the Member States.'[33] To date, this procedure has been followed at inter-sectoral level on only one occasion, for an agreement in May 2002 on telework. The problem with this method is that a Declaration annexed to the Treaty of Amsterdam (originally annexed to the Maastricht Social Policy Agreement) provides that it 'implies no obligation on the Member States to apply the agreements directly or to work out rules for their transportation, nor any obligation to amend national legislation in force to facilitate their implementation.'[34] The Declaration envisaged that this method 'will consist in developing, by collective bargaining, according to the rules of each Member State, the content of the agreements.' The difficulty is that the labour law systems of the Member States generally do not impose legal obligations to bargain at national level, nor do national organisations usually have the mandate to reach agreements on behalf of their members. Collective agreements do not all have the same legal effects, and they can be limited in their coverage.[35] For these reasons, this method of implementation is feasible only where the agreement (such as that on telework) is not in a form suitable

---

[32] Bercusson (1992) at 185.
[33] Art 139(2) EC.
[34] Declaration No 27 annexed to the Treaty of Amsterdam.
[35] Hepple (1993) at 28–31.

for a binding Community Directive, or covers an area (such as pay) which falls outside the scope of Article 137 EC, and so cannot be made the subject of a Directive.

The second method of implementation is by a 'Council decision' on a proposal from the Commission.[36] There can be no doubt that the Council can reject a Commission proposal to implement an agreement.[37] The Council can act by QMV, but must act unanimously in relation to any of the areas of social policy covered by Article 137(3) (see chapter 8 above). It is debatable whether as a matter of law the Council could amend the agreement, rather than reject it outright. On one occasion when the Council expressed reservations about an agreement (on parental leave), the Commission threatened to withdraw the proposal because it regards the agreements as sacrosanct.[38] To date, three inter-sectoral framework agreements (on parental leave, part-time work and fixed-term work) and two sectoral agreements (on working time for seafarers and mobile workers in civil aviation) have been implemented by Directive (Table 9.A). The Council is not bound to use Directives because a 'Decision' is understood, in this context, to cover a variety of binding and non-binding instruments. The EU Constitution makes a subtle change in wording, replacing 'Decision' with the words 'European regulation or decision' (chapter 8, Box 8.3). It appears that a 'European framework law' (replacing Directives) will not be possible, but the change may not be significant because although a European regulation is a non-legislative act, it can be binding in its entirety.[39]

Where the social partners fail to agree, it remains open to the Commission to make its own proposal to the Council. This has occurred on several occasions, most notably in the case of the proposal for a draft Directive on European Works Councils. The Commission had proposed a text broadly based on a joint opinion of UNICE, CEEP and ETUC of 1987. This was accepted by the trade union side, but rejected by the employers' organisations. The Commission then launched its own fresh proposal which was then converted into a Directive.[40] When the social partners refused to negotiate on the subject of the burden of proof in sex discrimination cases, the Commission proceeded with its own proposal,[41] and it is has also done so in relation to the subject of temporary work basing its last draft on what was conceived to be the 'consensus' (but not agreement) of the social partners.

---

[36] Art 139(2) EC.

[37] The social partners had wanted the Treaty provision to oblige the Council to implement their agreement 'as concluded' but this was deleted: Hepple (1993) at 19.

[38] Kenner (2003) at 253.

[39] Art I–32(1).

[40] Council Directive 94/45/EC, [1994] OJ L254/64; see Kenner (2003) at 248.

[41] Council Directive 97/80/EC, [1998] OJ L14/6.

Much of the criticism of the social dialogue has been directed at its lack of democratic legitimacy. In particular, it provides an opportunity for sidelining the European Parliament, the only directly elected Community institution. Where the Commission makes a proposal for a Directive under Article 137(2) in the area of social policy, the Council and Parliament are put on an equal footing under the co-decision procedure. However, where negotiations between the social partners result in an agreement, there is no role for the involvement of the Parliament under the co-decision procedure. This led the CFI in the *UEAPME* case to conclude that in order to satisfy the democratic principle, the Commission and the Council are obliged to refuse to implement an agreement unless the parties are 'sufficiently representative.'[42] UEAPME, claiming to represent the largest number of small and medium-sized employers at European level, challenged the Parental Leave Directive before the CFI, on the ground that it had been excluded from the negotiations which led to the adoption of the framework agreement. In particular, UEAPME said that it should have been involved because of the requirement in Article 137(2) EC that Directives in respect of social policy 'shall avoid imposing administrative, financial and legal constraints in a way which would hold back the creation and development of small and medium-sized undertakings.' The CFI rejected this attempt to annul the Directive on the ground that the framework agreement set minimum requirements applicable to all employment relationships and therefore the signatories had to represent all categories of undertakings. UNICE included SMEs in its membership in the private sector, and CEEP had members across the public sector. Two-thirds of the workers affected worked for SMEs connected with UNICE. It was sufficient that UEAPME had been consulted prior to the dialogue stage, and the framework agreement made some provision for SMEs.[43]

There is an underlying confusion in this judgment, as several authors have pointed out, between representativeness and democratic legitimacy.[44] Trade unions can be sufficiently representative of workers as a whole to negotiate agreements on part-time, fixed-term and temporary work, even though relatively few of these categories of workers belong to unions; similarly UNICE and CEEP can be representative of all employers, even though UEAPME exists exclusively to represent SMEs. Democratic legitimacy, on the other hand, requires broader participation by the people and their representatives. The judgment does, however, underline the nature of the social dialogue as part of

---

[42] The Commission has published widely criticised criteria for determining 'representativeness', COM (93) 600, as updated COM (98) 322; see esp. Bercusson and van Dijk (1995).

[43] Case T–135/96, *UEAPME v Council* [1998] ECR II–2335.

[44] See Kenner (2000) at 262–63.

a regulatory technique which is subject to judicial review. In this it differs strikingly from autonomous collective bargaining.[45]

The use of the social dialogue as a regulatory technique is being extended beyond the traditional area of social policy into a macroeconomic dialogue on economic and monetary policy, a dialogue on all aspects of the EES, and a dialogue on social protection. The Standing Committee on Employment is being replaced by a new Tripartite Social Summit for Growth and Employment. The OMC may increasingly become the main method for implementing and monitoring the joint opinions of the social partners.[46] The Employment Guidelines specifically encourage the participation of the social partners, for example in concluding lifelong learning agreements and agreements for reducing the gender gap.[47] The Commission sees an important role for social dialogue at local level to produce 'innovative solutions to employment development, combating exclusion and improving the quality of life and work.'[48] It sees the European works councils in transnational undertakings, as a 'sound foundation' for extending worker information and consultation to matters such as equal opportunities, training, mobility and environmental policy and, in some cases providing negotiated commitments on restructuring.[49] The EU Constitution gives prominence to 'The Social Partners and the Autonomous Social Dialogue' by placing it under Title VI entitled 'The Democratic Life of the Union.'

There are currently more than 230 joint sectoral texts and 40 cross-industry texts. When these are examined, one is struck by the fact that they are geared to economic integration or to narrow issues such as aspects of atypical work. The poverty of subject-matter reflects the fact that despite the much proclaimed new social model, EU social policy has still not broken free from the straitjacket of market integration. The 'subservience to the process of market integration',[50] continues to hinder the development of a rationale for social and labour regulation. The exclusion of pay, the right of association and the right to strike, prevents the social dialogue from fulfilling the role of collective negotiation in a European industrial relations system. As Wedderburn has said, 'honeyed words about a "social dimension", "social dialogue" or consultation will mean little to workers if those who hold the initiative fail to

---

[45] Bercusson (1999) at 159–63, who argues that the constitutional law paradigm of democratic scrutiny and judicial review is inappropriate to collective bargaining.

[46] COM (2002) 341 final; Council Decision 2003/174/EC of 6 March 2003, establishing a Tripartite Social Summkit for Growth and Employment, [2003] OJ L70/31.

[47] Syzszczak (2001) at 1149–50.

[48] COM (2002) 341 final, para 1.3.3; Barnard and Deakin (2002) at 140–47.

[49] COM (2002) 341 final, para 1.3.4.

[50] Davies (1992) at 361.

defend [the core rights of labour]'.[51] The key question is whether the EU's emerging framework of fundamental rights can fill this gap.

3. Fundamental rights

The original EEC Treaty contained no express recognition of fundamental human rights, nor of social rights. This is not surprising given the historical origins of the Community as a common market and not a political union (chapter 8, above). However, many of the provisions of the Treaty were, and still are, concerned with rights of the individual, using 'rights' here in the sense of claims that are justiciable in national courts, or in the terminology of Community law, that have 'direct effects'. The main examples are the right of free movement of EU citizens, the right of the self-employed to establish businesses, and the right of EU citizens not to be discriminated against on grounds of nationality. By definition, these rights do not apply to third-country nationals, and so they cannot properly be described either as 'human' rights or even as rights which apply to all those lawfully working within the EU.[52]

The 'principle', under Article 119 (now 141 EC), that women and men should receive equal pay does apply to all workers. It was turned into an enforceable 'right' only after a series of actions brought in the early 1970s by Gabrielle Defrenne, a Belgian air hostess, and a report to the European Commission in 1972 by Evelyne Sullerot, a French sociologist, which concluded that there was still widespread sex discrimination in the Member States.[53] An Equal Pay Directive in 1975[54] widened the concept of equal pay by including a reference to the ILO's standard of work of equal value, and an Equal Treatment Directive in 1976[55] introduced the principle of equal treatment for women and men as regards access to employment, vocational training, promotion and working conditions. The reason for these extensions of the apparently limited provisions of Article 119, has to be found in the political rather than in the economic or legal sphere. Action against sex discrimination provided a vehicle for politicians to appease women voters. As Ellis points out, sex equality 'provides a relatively innocuous, even high-sounding, platform by means of which the Community can demonstrate its commitment to social

---

[51] Wedderburn (1997) at 33.
[52] Hepple (2004a) at 4–13.
[53] Hepple (1996) at 242.
[54] Council Directive 75/117/EEC, [1975] OJ L45/19.
[55] Council Directive 76/207/EEC, [1976] OJ L39/40 now amended by Directive of the European Parliament and Council 2002/73/EC, [2002] OJ L269/15.

progress.'[56] The result, according to Neilsen, was 'state feminism', that is, equality laws 'which are neither mobilised for, nor implemented by, women, and which create rights only on an individual basis.'[57] Significantly, however, the ECJ came to interpret Article 119 as being part of a fundamental principle of equality between women and men, based on the common constitutional traditions of the Member States.[58] But the ECJ was not willing to allow the fundamental right to equality to be used in order to extend the competences of the Community, for example to prohibit discrimination on grounds of sexual orientation.[59]

The Community legislature also did little to extend this fundamental right beyond the area of gender discrimination,[60] before the Treaty of Amsterdam introduced a new Article 13 EC empowering the Community to 'take appropriate action to combat discrimination based on sex, racial or ethnic origin, religion or belief, disability, age or sexual orientation.' This provision too, was largely a response to political pressures: the growing expressions of racism in certain countries, and also the increasing influence of NGOs representing the interests of other minorities. Article 13 has no 'direct effects' in the Member States, but it has given rise to two Directives requiring Member States to introduce enforceable rights against discrimination in all these new fields, in addition to sex discrimination.[61]

The major impetus for the development of fundamental rights and general principles as standards binding on Community institutions came, not from the Council, but from the ECJ. It did so in two main ways. The first was by asserting the supremacy of Community law and the principle of direct effects where this appeared to conflict with the fundamental rights guaranteed by national constitutions. In the early period the ECJ restricted individual rights to those made explicit in the Treaty. Then, starting in the late 1960s, after the courts in Germany and Italy had expressed concern that the fundamental rights in their national constitutions would be eroded as the competence of the Community increased, the ECJ decided that the protection of such rights was a general principle of Community law derived from the constitutional traditions of the Member States and from international standards. The ECJ said

---

[56] Ellis (1998) at 61–62.

[57] Cited by O'Donovan and Szyszcak (1988) at 195.

[58] The furthest the ECJ went in proclaiming a general principle of equality based on human dignity was in Case C–13/94, *P v S and Cornwall CC* [1996] ECR I–2143, discussed by Barnard (1997) at 59; see generally Szyszczak (1997) on equality as a constitutional principle in the EU, and Kilpatrick (2001) on the dialogue between national courts and the ECJ on gender equality.

[59] Case C–249/96,*Grant v South-West Trains* [1998] ECR I–621, para 45. The case law has since been overtaken by Council Directive 2000/78/EC [2000] OJ L303/16, which outlaws discrimination on this and other grounds.

[60] Hepple (1996) at 238–40.

[61] See generally Bell (2002), and for a critique Hepple (2004a).

that human rights protection must be ensured within the Community's institutions and objectives, but qualified this by saying that the Treaty would only
justify limiting fundamental rights where the substance of the rights was not
affected. In this way the ECJ was able to assert the supremacy of Community
law and the principle of direct effects, but at the same time it restricted the
potential use of Community law. This use of 'fundamental rights' has been
called 'defensive'.[62] The second use of 'fundamental rights' has been described
as 'offensive'.[63] This is the elevation of the four freedoms—of workers, services,
goods and capital—to the status of 'fundamental rights'which must be balanced against other rights enshrined in national constitutions. This offensive
usage is certainly controversial. It leaves it uncertain how far the Member
States may depart from the Community's economic freedoms in order to pursue a national constitutional right. There are many unresolved issues, as to
how classic first-generation civil and political rights are to be compared with
the economic freedoms, now classified as 'rights', and with the nascent social
rights which emerged in the Community Charter of 1989 and were developed
in the EU Charter of Fundamental Rights of 2000.

The ECJ has said that citizenship is the fundamental status of all Member
State nationals. The principle of non-discrimination combined with the right
to free movement illustrates the potential of fundamental rights to come into
conflict with the economic viability of national social protection systems. In a
series of recent cases, the ECJ has held that a national of a Member State lawfully residing in another Member State has the right not to be discriminated
against on grounds of nationality in respect of any social benefit available to
nationals of the State in which she resides.[64] This is the case even if she is not
economically active. In these cases, the right to move and to reside in another
Member State has been successfully combined with the right against discrimination on grounds of nationality. Szyszczak points out that this 'raises
fears that expansive rights to the non-discrimination principle could lead
individuals exploring the benefits of the free market: to actively search for the
most attractive form of social protection, be it social advantages, health care,
education.'[65] Fundamental rights of EU citizenship and nationally-based
social solidarity are uneasy bedfellows.

The ECJ's case law is in the process of being complemented by the Charter
of Fundamental Rights. The nature and future role of the Charter has been the

---

[62] Coppell and O'Neill (1992).

[63] Coppell and O'Neill (1992); but see the response by Weiler and Lockhart (1995).

[64] See eg Case C–85/96, *Martinez Sala v Freiestaat Bayern* [1998] ECR I–2691; Case C–184/99,
Grzelczyk v Centre public d'aide sociale d'Ottignies-Louvain-la-Neuve [2001] ECR I–6193; Case
C–413/99, *Baumbast and R v Secretary of State for the Home Department* [2002] ECR I–7091; and
generally Barnard (2004) at 403–21, and Szyszczak (2004).

[65] Szyszczak (2001) at 1158.

subject of widely divergent opinions. The UK Government's view is that its sole purpose is to raise the visibility of fundamental rights at EU level, to provide a 'showcase' of civil, social and other rights already achieved by the EU.[66] The Charter brings together these rights in a single document of 54 articles grouped in seven Chapters headed respectively 'Dignity', 'Freedoms', 'Equality', 'Solidarity', 'Citizens' Rights', 'Justice' and 'General Provisions'. According to this view, the Charter is purely an exercise in transparency and has no independent legal status or effect. An alternative perspective is that the Charter is intended to provide a bill of rights as part of the political constitution of a future federal Europe. The incorporation of the Charter into Part II of the EU Constitution can be seen as a step in that direction, but this is so carefully hedged with restrictions and safeguards that the Charter's main importance in the foreseeable future is likely to be as a benchmark of the common values which bind together the Member States, as an inspiration for action by the Commission, Council and Parliament, and as an aid to the ECJ and national courts when interpreting EU legislation. Amendments made to the Charter by the EU Constitution, requires the Charter to be interpreted in accordance with the explanations prepared and updated under the authority of the Praesidium of the Convention which drafted the Charter. The courts of the Union and the Member States must have 'due regard' to these explanations, which set out the sources from which the Charter is derived.[67]

The Charter provides an explicit link between EU law and existing human rights structures, such as the Council of Europe's European Convention on Human Rights and Fundamental Freedoms [ECHR] and European Social Charter [ESC]. Article II–52.3 establishes the important interpretative principle that 'insofar as this Charter contains rights which correspond to rights guaranteed by the [ECHR], the meaning and scope of those rights shall be the same as those laid down by the [ECHR]'. Moreover, according to Article II–53, the Charter may not be interpreted as restricting or adversely affecting human rights and fundamental freedoms as recognised by EU law, international law and international agreements to which the EU or all the Member States are party, including the ECHR, and by the Member States' constitutions.[68]

A particular concern of the UK Government was that the Charter might be used as a back-door means of enlarging the competence of the EU. This point is specifically met by Article II–51.2 which states that the 'Charter does not extend the field of application of Union law beyond the powers of the Union, or establish any new power or task for the Union, or modify powers and tasks

---

[66] Goldsmith (2001).

[67] EU Constitution, Annex 10, inserting fifth para, Preamble and Art II–52.7.

[68] Art I–7 of the EU Constitution provides that the EU (which is given legal personality) shall accede to the ECHR, but this shall not affect the EU's competences. Accession will make it possible for individuals to challenge an EU measure on the grounds that it contravenes the ECHR.

defined in the other Parts of the Constitution.' The Charter is addressed to 'institutions, bodies and agencies' of the Union 'with due regard to the principle of subsidiarity'.[69] It is, therefore, a means for ensuring that individuals are protected against infringement of their fundamental rights by EU institutions and bodies. In this sense, the Charter can be seen as an important limitation on the EU's powers. Although the Community legislature is allowed a wide margin of discretion, this will not be allowed to 'render meaningless the implementation of a fundamental principle of Community law such as the elimination of indirect discrimination on grounds of sex.'[70]

Another concern of the UK Government was that the Charter might disturb existing legal relations between citizens and domestic authorities in areas of national competence. This was thought to be particularly important in the UK, in view of the implementation of the Human Rights Act 1998 (in force since 2 October 2000) which has incorporated the ECHR into domestic UK law. This is a major shift in the legal and political culture of the UK which previously had no entrenched or fundamental rights. All new legislation is scrutinised to ensure compliance with ECHR rights. Remedies provided against public authorities which violate ECHR rights, and courts and tribunals are obliged to interpret both primary and secondary legislation as far as possible to be consistent with those rights. If there is incompatibility in the case of secondary legislation the legislation can be set aside. In the case of primary legislation, the principle of parliamentary sovereignty has been maintained, but the court can make a declaration of incompatibility so forcing the Government and Parliament to consider amendment in order to comply with the convention rights. The courts and tribunals themselves must observe convention rights. This means that the common law is likely to be developed in a way which is consistent with convention rights—this is already having a significant effect in areas such as privacy of employees and freedom of expression at work.[71] Any confusion between the domestic enforcement of ECHR rights, and the implementation of the EU Charter would create enormous difficulties. So, from the UK's perspective the limitation in Article II–51(1) of the scope of the EU Charter to EU institutions and to Member States only when they are implementing EU law was regarded as essential. This limitation may, however, prove to be illusory because the case law of the ECJ indicates that fundamental rights also apply when Member States are *derogating* from EU law.

---

[69] Art II–51.1. All references are to the Charter as incorporated in the EU Constitution.

[70] Case C–25/02, *Rinke v Arztekammer Hamburg,* [2003] ECR I–8349, at para 39. In this case, however, an indirectly discriminatory requirement in Community legislation on the training of part-time doctors (a considerable proportion of whom are women) was held to be objectively justified on grounds of providing a high level of health protection.

[71] See Hepple (1998a).

Perhaps the most important concern in the UK was that the Charter should not create any new rights. It was claimed, for example, that the right to strike, recognised in Article II–28 'could return Britain to the dark days of mass strikes and industrial conflict,' and 'this Charter would lock Britain into the steel hand-cuffs of an old-fashioned social model.'[72] The Engineering Employers' Federation argued that what is now Article II–38 on protection in the event of unjustified dismissal creates a new right not yet covered by EC directives. The Confederation of British Industry argued that some social rights, such as those to rest periods and annual leave, parental leave, and to information and con-sultation, although well-established in EC legislation, are of a different nature to fundamental rights. They were described as 'limited and qualified employ-ment rights' that are not universal or inalienable. It was contended that their inclusion in the Charter 'would devalue the notion of fundamental rights'. On the other hand, many trade unions and NGOs were disappointed that the Charter does not include all the rights set out in the revised European Social Charter 1996 or even those in the 1989 Community Charter such as the rights of migrant workers and the right to equitable remuneration.

The charge that the Charter creates 'new rights' can be readily rebutted. Its aim, as envisaged by the conclusions of the Cologne European Council meet-ing in June 1999, was to create legal certainty by defining the 'human rights and fundamental freedoms' upon which, according to Article 6(1) of the TEU the Union is founded, and to set out both the rights guaranteed by the ECHR, and the rights which result from the 'constitutional traditions common to the Member States.' The Union is pledged by Article 6(2) TEU to respect these rights. The Cologne conclusions expressly contemplated that in addition to civil and political rights, the Charter would include certain economic and social rights, as contained in the ESC and the 1989 Community Charter. This was plainly necessary because Article 136 EC regards the 'fundamental social rights' contained in those instruments as the basis of Community social pol-icy. The rights to collective bargaining and collective action in the case of conflicts of interest are recognised in the ESC 1961 which the UK has ratified, and also (in a somewhat more limited way) in the case law of the European Court of Human Rights under Article 11 of the ECHR. So there is no novelty in recognising these right in the Charter of Fundamental Rights. This does not add to the EU's competence (see Article II–51(2)) since Article 137(6) EC expressly excludes the right to strike and to lock-out. The right to protection against unjustified dismissal is contained in Article 24 of the revised ESC 1996. The UK has signed but not yet ratified the 1996 instrument but has no difficulty in accepting this right because it has been recognised in UK law since

---

[72] F Maude MP, Opposition spokesman, as quoted by the *Daily Mail*, 11 October 2000.

1972. The argument that incorporation of this right in the Charter may lead to unfair dismissal rights being extended to everyone with qualifying requirements (eg from day one of employment) overlooks the limitation clauses in the Charter,[73] and in the ESC, which permit necessary and proportional qualifications on any right. The real importance of the Charter, as Advocate General Tizzano has said, is that it provides 'the most reliable and definitive confirmation of the fact' that the right in question constitutes a 'fundamental right' which, in the absence of clear limitations, should be upheld by the Court when interpreting Community legislation.[74]

It is unfortunate that the Charter does not draw the clear line envisaged by the Cologne conclusions between those provisions of the ESC and 1989 Community Charter which contain 'fundamental social rights' and those which are merely 'objectives for action by the Union'. Indeed, the 'constitutional traditions' common to the Member States respect the division between justiciable rights and guiding principles of social policy. A clear example is provided by the separation in the Spanish Constitution between Chapter II on 'Rights and Freedoms' such as equality, freedom of expression, the rights to associate and the right to free selection of work or occupation, and Chapter III entitled 'On the Guiding Principles of Economic and Social Policy,' which places obligations on public authorities to pursue certain policies.

What criterion should be applied in order to distinguish 'fundamental social rights' from 'principles' or objectives? This question was much discussed in the UK and the House of Lords Select Committee on the European Communities[75] concluded that to use justiciability as the criterion for inclusion in the Charter would be both legally and politically controversial. Instead, the Select Committee proposed that the 'non-binding' nature of certain 'rights' should be made apparent on the face of the Charter. They suggested that social and economic rights that are not justiciable should be put in a different Chapter of the Charter, so that their status, as compared to core civil and political rights, would be clear. Instead of following this approach, the Charter uses three forms of wording (Box 9.1). The first is in those articles which set out clear individual rights. The second is in those articles which state that the 'Union recognises and respects' certain rights. Here no specific right is conferred, and the formulation is more akin to a guiding principle of social policy. The third category is those articles which state pure objectives. There are some articles whose exact status is difficult to determine. For example, Article II–27

---

[73] Art II–52(1).

[74] Case C–173/99, *R v Secretary of State for Trade and Industry, ex parte BECTU*, [2001] ECR I–4881, Adocate General Tizzano, para 28.

[75] 8th Report, Session 1999–2000, 16 May 2000 at paras 144–46.

says that 'workers or their representatives must, at the appropriate level, be guaranteed information and consultation in good time in the cases and under the conditions provided for by Community law and national laws and practices'. Is this simply an objective? Or is it intended to be a 'right', and, if so, what is the 'appropriate level' (a highly contentious issue), and under what conditions? This may be contrasted with Article II–28 which specifically states that workers and employers, or their respective organisations, have a 'right to negotiate and conclude collective agreements.' The authors of the Chapter of the Charter on 'Solidarity' can also be accused of a static approach to social rights.[76] For example, while Article II–27 limits the rights of workers or their representatives to 'information and consultation', the Commission's second group of experts (the Simitis report) went further by including 'participation in respect of decisions affecting the interests of workers'.[77] On the other hand, one may share Weiss' doubts whether some of the provisions—such as those on working time and paid leave—really state 'fundamental rights' or are simply the means by which the health, safety and dignity of the worker are to be achieved.[78]

Despite these limitations, the Charter gives the EU judges and Institutions a clear and systematic statement of social rights which have been endorsed at the highest political level, and are due to be entrenched in the EU Constitution. There is also no reason why courts and tribunals in the Member States should not have regard to the Charter when interpreting domestic legislation which implements EU obligations. The days of centralised positive harmonisation are over, for the time being at least. The EU is now seeking market integration through soft law techniques such as the OMC and social dialogue. This new decentralised and diverse approach makes fundamental social rights expressing common values indispensable. There is, however, an ever-present danger that by codifying the international sources of human rights, the case law of the ECJ, and the 'constitutional traditions of the Member States', the creative dialogue between national and European courts will be frozen in a time warp. Rights can never stand still. They have to be developed as society changes. Will lawyers and courts treat Charter rights as written on stone tablets, or will they develop them creatively? No one can predict the answer with any degree of certainty.

---

[76] Weiss (2002) at 86.
[77] European Commission (1999) at 24 (in the German version *Mitbestimmung*).
[78] Weiss (2002) at 86; cf the Opinion of Advocate General Tizzano in the *BECTU* case (above), stating that the right to paid annual leave is a fundamental right.

Box 9.1

THE CHARTER OF FUNDAMENTAL RIGHTS OF THE UNION
(References to Part II EU Constitution)

Rights of individuals
- Right to life (II–2)
- Right to integrity of the person (II–3)
- Prohibition of torture and inhuman or degrading treatment or punishment (II–4)
- Prohibition of slavery and forced labour (II–5)
- Right to liberty and security (II–6)
- Right to respect for private and family life (II–7)
- Right to protection of personal data (II–8)
- Right to marry and to found a family (II–9)
- Right to freedom of thought, conscience and religion (II–10)
- Right to freedom of expression and information (II–11)
- Right to freedom of assembly and association (incl. trade unions) (II–12)
- Right to education (II–14)
- Right to engage in work and pursue a freely chosen occupation (II–15)
- Right to property (II–17)
- Right to equality and non–discrimination (II–20,21,23)
- Rights of the child to care and protection (II–24)
- Rights of workers to information and consultation (II–27)
- Right of collective bargaining and action (II–28)
- Right of access to placement services (II–29)
- Right to protection against unjustified dismissal (II–30)
- Right to working conditions which respect health, safety and dignity (II–31)
- Prohibition of child labour and protection of young people at work (II–32)
- Right to protection from dismissal for reason connected with maternity (II–33.2)
- Citizens' rights and rights to justice (II–39 to II–50)

Guiding principles of social policy
- Human dignity is inviolable (II–1)
- Dignity and independence of elderly (II–25)
- Integration of persons with disabilities (II–26)
- Entitlement to social security and social assistance (II–34)
- Access to services of general economic interest (II–36)

Other objectives
- Respect for cultural, linguistic and religious diversity (II–22)
- High level of health protection (II–35)
- High level of environmental protection (II–37)
- High level of consumer protection (II–38)

3. Conclusions

The methods of integration that have developed over nearly half a century are in many respects uniquely European, and are not transplantable to other regions of the world. However, a number of general lessons emerge.

The first is that differentiated integration or flexibility is inevitable where states wish to develop social policy in different ways and at variable rates, and to preserve their national autonomy. In Europe, the shared goal of politicians has been to make another war impossible, and since 1989 to end the divisions of the cold war. For some this political ideal makes it essential to create a federal European 'social state', based on a principle akin to that of German public law of 'social government based on the rule of law'.[79] The underlying belief is the compatibility of a free market order with a socially responsible state. *Rechtstaat*, protecting the individual from the state, and *Sozialstaat*, requiring the state to create a just social order, are ideas which have come into the ascendant in the EU, particularly since the adoption of the Community Charter of 1989 and the Nice Charter of 2000, now incorporated in the EU Constitution. Not surprisingly, the greatest opposition has come from the UK whose constitutional and legal order, prior to the incorporation of the ECHR from October 2000, did not recognise any notion of 'fundamental human rights', and still does not acknowledge social rights. Many aspects of the British industrial relations system, including the absence of institutionalised workers' representation and of a national 'social dialogue', have also created obstacles to the acceptance of Continental-style forms of participation and regulation. The differences between Member States have been exacerbated by the enlargement of the EU to include countries that are moving at different speeds from the extremes of state-centred bureaucratic systems of labour law of the communist era to the extremes of managerial freedom in the market economy. In the foreseeable future there will be little pressure for harmonisation of labour laws from these new states whose competitive advantage in the EU depends to a

---

[79] Art 28(1) of the German Constitution which together with Art 20, defining Germany as a 'social federal State' forms the constitutional basis of the principle.

large extent on labour costs that are significantly lower than those in Germany and France.[80]

Secondly, differentiated integration cannot succeed without a credible, consistent and transparent social policy at regional level. 'Good markets need good governments.'[81] They also need good social policies. The initial belief of the founders of the common market that social progress would be an automatic consequence of market integration proved to be unfounded. The Community politicians and bureaucrats were then forced into a series of fragmented and spasmodic interventions in the social field lacking any underlying principle.

Thirdly, market and competition rules have to be harmonised with national labour laws in a way that respects the social objectives of the Union. Despite recent case law of the ECJ, there is still a lack of clear guiding principles. The substantive market and competition laws should exclude labour laws and collective agreements from their scope altogether, on the ground that human labour is not a commodity.[82] Short of providing a complete immunity from competition and state aids law, it would be useful to require the courts to apply a proportionality test, leaving Member States a wide margin of discretion in their collective bargaining arrangements and in providing state support for employment creation and legitimate social objectives.

Fourthly, the principle of mutual recognition of labour laws is as important for the functioning of a common market as is the mutual recognition of other regulations. However, to avoid the risk that businesses will move to countries with unacceptably low labour standards, positive harmonisation measures can be justified as a means of establishing 'minimum requirements' or a floor of rights. This would be the case where some countries are obtaining special cost advantages not linked to productivity (eg from cheap female labour), or there are unacceptable abuses of core labour standards. This floor needs to be adequately secured by effective non-regression clauses that prevent the use of harmonisation as an excuse for levelling-down standards.

Fifthly, the open method of co-ordination is an innovative approach that has the advantage of recognising national autonomy while seeking a conver-

---

[80] A study by the Institut der Deutschen Wirtschaft Köln [IW], indicated that labour costs in countries bordering Germany are, on average, $1/6$ of costs in western Germany, and $1/4$ of the costs in eastern Germany. The IW estimates that labour costs in the Czech Republic will reach $1/3$ of those in Germany by 2017 and $1/2$ by 2039: *European Industrial Relations Review* 366, July 2004, at 21.

[81] Wolf (2004) at 73.

[82] In the USA, the Clayton Act 1914, s 6, declared that labour is not an article of commerce. However, the anti-trust exception is not available to employers who adopt uniform employment standards as a means of thwarting labour unions. Nor can employers impose collectively bargained terms on other employers who have not agreed to this approach: cf the *Albany* case in the ECJ (ch 8 above).

gence of objectives. The use of 'soft' law to achieve this is not objectionable in itself. It may encourage governments and employers to adopt best practices beyond 'minimum requirements'. Soft law can play a significant part in system-based approaches, for example in respect of health and safety enforcement and equal opportunities. Here the aim is to achieve change by co-operation of management, workers and their representatives, and state regulators. To this extent the OMC using soft law allows a flexible approach. This requires long-term commitment, adequate resources and ultimate sanctions. However, when soft law is used as an excuse or justification for not providing binding sanctions in the case of violation of basic rights, 'it is at best naïve and at worst abject surrender to those whose only motive is profit.'[83] The EU Charter of Fundamental Rights now provides a systematic statement of rights but it lacks the direct enforceability necessary to provide an adequate legal framework for the OMC.

Finally, the social dialogue is no substitute for autonomous collective bargaining. It is a useful, but peculiarly European, regulatory technique. For it to work effectively there needs to be strong and representative independent trade unions and employers' associations, willing to work closely with the government in corporatist structures. Social dialogue simply masks inequalities of power where unions are weak or are political appendages of the ruling parties. The aim should be to create conditions in each Member State conducive to decentralised negotiation of the ways and means of achieving common objectives. The emphasis needs to be on effective procedures and remedies at local level when the fundamental rights to participate in decision-making, through collective bargaining are infringed.

---

[83] Hepple (2002) at 256.

10

The Comparative Advantages of Labour Laws

1. Introduction
2. Economic models
3. Political models
4. Seeking comparative institutional advantage
5. Re-inventing transnational labour regulation

1. Introduction

The orthodoxy of much of the literature on the 'new' labour law is that globalisation undermines the ability of nation states to regulate their own labour relations, enables TNCs to put pressure on governments to reduce labour costs, weakens the capacity of trade unions and civil society to resist, and so inevitably leads to a deregulatory convergence. Since labour is relatively immobile and international solidarity action is difficult to organise and frequently unlawful, while capital has many 'exit' routes, it is argued that the balance of power has shifted overwhelmingly in favour of transnational business interests (chapter 1, above).

This simplistic argument is increasingly challenged from a variety of perspectives. One view is that the internationalisation of trade and finance is not as extensive as believed.[1] Another is that governments are either corrupt or disingenuous when they use pressures from TNCs or the international financial institutions as an excuse to pursue policies they want. The problem is bad governments, and, according to Wolf, 'one of the strongest arguments for the open economy is that it puts a degree of competitive pressure on government.'[2]

---

[1] Hirst and Thompson (1999).
[2] Wolf (2004) at 75.

The most interesting and influential challenge to the orthodox view comes from new theories of comparative institutional advantage or 'varieties of capitalism'. The orthodox approach assumes that the strategies and structures of firms are similar across states, and links competitiveness to unit labour costs, which will lead firms to shift production abroad if they find cheaper labour there. Hall and Soskice[3] argue against this that firms are not essentially similar across nations and that they react differently to similar challenges. Their analysis indicates that firms will not automatically move their activities offshore when offered low-cost labour abroad. These scholars' conception of comparative institutional advantage is that firms may shift particular activities to other countries to secure the advantages of the institutional frameworks those countries offer.[4] They distinguish two core types of political economies: liberal market economies (LMEs) and co-ordinated market economies (CMEs). In LMEs, firms co-ordinate their activities through hierarchies and competitive market arrangements; in CMEs firms are more reliant on non-market relationships, including systems of workers' participation, social insurance and protection of employment and income.[5] Examples of LMEs in the OECD are the USA, Canada, Britain, Australia and New Zealand. Examples of CMEs are Germany, Japan, Switzerland, the Netherlands, Belgium, Sweden, Norway, Denmark, Finland and Austria. Mediterranean countries, such as France, Italy, Spain, Portugal, Greece and Turkey, are in a more ambiguous position tending to combine non-market co-ordination in some spheres with liberalising strategies in others, notably labour relations.

This differentiation enables Hall and Soskice to predict different responses in LMEs and CMEs to global competitive pressures. In LMEs firms co-ordinate their activities primarily through the market, so they will tend to put pressures on governments to sharpen market forces, unions will be unable to put up more than limited resistance, and there will be substantial deregulation just as the orthodox view predicts. In CMEs, on the other hand, governments should be less sympathetic to deregulation because this threatens their country's comparative institutional advantage from regulatory regimes that support non-market methods of co-ordination. While workers' representation tends to be voluntary in LMEs, it is an integral part of economic governance in CMEs. Similarly labour market regulation is partial in LMEs but universal in CMEs, for example through national or sectoral collective bargaining or mechanisms for the extension of collective agreements to unorganised sectors.

This analysis helps to explain why—contrary to many predictions—globalisation has not in fact led to across-the-board deregulation of labour laws or

---

[3] Hall and Soskice (2001).

[4] Hall and Soskice (2001) at 56–57.

[5] Hall and Soskice (2001) at 8, 17–21.

weakening of collective representation of workers. A universal cause-and-effect relationship between globalisation and deregulation has not been established. One of the paradoxes of globalisation is that 'nations often prosper not by becoming more similar, but by building on their institutional differences.'[6] In Hall and Soskice's analysis the institutional frameworks of LMEs offer companies the best opportunities for radical innovation. For example, firms wanting to develop a new product can hire and fire personnel with relative ease and do not have to engage in co-determination with workers' representatives. They place a premium on transferable industry skills. This has proved to be advantageous in areas such as biotechnology and telecommunications. By contrast, CMEs are better placed for incremental innovation, supported by consensus rather than adversarial decision-making, job security and firm-specific skills. This has been preferred in sectors such as mechanical engineering, product handling, consumer durables and machine tools.[7]

These are the bare bones of Hall and Soskice's theory which this chapter seeks to develop in respect of labour laws. It must be remembered that these laws are but one element of a wider political economy that includes industrial relations, corporate governance, vocational education and training, and inter-firm relations. The theory helps to explain the similarities and differences between the ways in which labour law systems are responding to globalisation. The next section presents some economic models of labour laws from the viewpoint of competitive advantage. Section 3 examines the main political models which have developed as regulatory responses. Section 4 considers which of these economic and political models offers nation states the maximum comparative advantage. The final section discusses how far transnational labour regulation needs to be modified in order to enable countries to enhance their institutional advantages.

2. Economic models

An institutional theory of labour law systems has to start with the employment relationship. Along with limited liability, the contractual relationship between employer and worker provides the essential foundation of the modern business enterprise.[8] This relationship enables firms and workers in a market economy to bargain for the exchange of work in return for wages. In reality, the idea of a 'bargain' is a fiction for unorganised workers, unless they have

---

[6] Hall and Soskice (2001) at 60.
[7] Hall and Soskice (2001) at 41 and fig 1.5.
[8] Marsden (1999) at 3.

highly-sought skills. They must usually take-or-leave work on the employer's terms. This is little different from standardised consumer contracts, but with the crucial distinction that human labour is not a commodity.

The essence of the employment relationship is that it enables management to decide on detailed work assignments after the workers have been engaged; it rests on the worker's agreement to be available to undertake certain types of work as and when their manager directs.[9] Only in the most exploitative regimes, however, does the employer have unlimited powers. A key economic function of labour laws is to determine how and when managerial authority is delimited.

These limitations on managerial power can be classified in different ways. Here a typology from the viewpoint of competitive advantage sketched in an important article by Charny will be developed.[10] The first model is that of 'static' or 'direct' benefits. This relates to matters such as working-time, health and safety, protection against unfair dismissal and harassment. As Charny points out, an economically 'efficient' benefit simply substitutes for a cash payment.[11] This confers no comparative advantage—either in terms of trade or attracting investment—since the employer's costs remain the same whether the benefit is in cash or is mandated as a non-wage benefit. If the net effect on costs is zero then a country would not gain any advantage by diluting these requirements. In reality, of course, some workers value the benefit at cost, some below cost and some above cost. For example, older highly-paid workers may value a pension or health benefit above cost, while younger, low-paid workers may value them at less than cost. A country with a large supply of young skilled but low-paid workers may be induced to maintain low standards so as to attract trade or investment; a country with an older skilled workforce may find that employers are tempted to outsource to such jurisdictions.[12] This appears to have occurred, for example, in the case of outsourcing of call centres from the USA and Europe to India (chapter 1, Box 1.2, above).

A second model describes labour laws that aim at 'dynamic' effects on the employment relationship. An example is a minimum wage law, which outlaws sweatshops thus giving employers an incentive to develop technology and invest in the skilled workforce that the technology requires.[13] Another example is the prohibition of child labour. There is historical evidence that employers in textile factories in Britain realised not only that the competitiveness of their factories was not jeopardised by statutory regulation of child employment, but also that children who went to school would become more

---

[9] Marsden (1999) at 3.
[10] Charny (2000). I have amplified this typology in various respects.
[11] Charny (2000) at 287.
[12] Charny (2000) at 288.
[13] Charny (2000) at 289.

skilled and therefore more productive workers.[14] A final pair of examples are 'family-friendly' laws, which provide for child care, parental leave, maternity pay, and the like, and anti-discrimination laws which mandate equal treatment and equal pay for women and men, and for other disadvantaged groups and ethnic minorities. These broaden the recruitment pool making it easier for women and other disadvantaged groups to enter and remain in the labour market, and give them an incentive to raise their skills. Although laws of these kinds raise the employer's costs, and are redistributive between groups of workers, the effects are dynamic, raising skills and productivity. From the viewpoint of comparative advantage dynamic standards should have a neutral or even positive impact on labour costs.

A third model is apt for labour laws aimed at spreading economic risks among workers as a group. These are a form of social insurance. They include pensions and laws relating to redundancies and the protection of acquired rights on the transfer of undertakings. Charny points out that risks arising from jurisdictional competition—where workers in one country are made redundant or are transferred to new employers as jobs shift across borders— could be eliminated by an insurance scheme that pooled workers across borders.[15] To a very limited extent this has been done in the EU by Directives on collective redundancies and transfers of undertakings (chapters 7 and 8, above). On a global scale, however, there is an incentive for capital to move to those jurisdictions where these 'social insurance' costs are low or non-existent.

The final model consists of laws that empower groups of workers, for example by protecting rights to organise and to bargain collectively, and by requiring information, consultation or co-determination with workers' representatives. These empowerment rules may serve some or all the different economic purposes described above: efficiency, redistribution, dynamic goals or social insurance. Giving workers a 'voice' generally improves efficiency. On the other hand, where collective bargaining power enables unions to raise wages above productivity levels, this imposes a cost on the employer, and may have effects on investment and terms of trade. This in turn can lead governments to impose restrictions on unions and collective bargaining, as occurred in Britain under the Thatcher Government. Diluting empowerment rules can, however, have adverse effects. The system for distributing rents between capital and labour could be disrupted, and employers could lose the advantages they gain from bargaining with representatives of workers. In both LMEs and CMEs employers need workers' representatives and find them useful for achieving peace, stability and continuous production.[16] Political and social conflicts are likely to be exacerbated without workers' participation.

---

[14] Hunt (1981) at 11.
[15] Charny (2000) at 291.
[16] Thelen (2001) at 76.

In summary, these models postulate that different national labour laws impose no competitive disadvantage where they enhance the efficiency of the employment relationship. On the contrary, competitive advantage is improved by laws that are dynamic and lead to an improvement in skills and productivity. However, where labour laws are primarily redistributive, jurisdictional competition will lead to pressures to deregulate or dilute these laws. Countries which face strong competition from others with weaker redistributive laws are at real risk of deregulation. Employers faced with redistributive labour regulation will be the ones most tempted to move.

3. Political models

Labour laws and power relations

While the economic models set the parameters of comparative institutional advantage, it is political choices that determine the outcomes. One of the best ways to understand the regulatory responses to economic globalisation at national level is in terms of four 'ideal types' or deductive models: (1) the liberal state; (2) the social democratic welfare state; (3) the neo-liberal state; and (4) the rights-based model. Models of this kind, freed from specific national features, help to illuminate the common tendencies and divergences in different countries, but they are not a substitute for close analysis of the actual circumstances in each country or locality at a particular time. Labour laws have not developed as a series of evolutionary stages, or as a 'necessary' or 'natural' response to globalisation. The laws in each country have been the outcome of complex, protracted and sometimes bitterly contested struggles.[17] The comparativist has to examine the specific features of historical change in each country in order to explain differences in the laws which have shaped labour markets. For example why was the work-book or 'pass' system a feature of labour markets in some countries but not others? Why was the 8-hour day achieved in some places by collective bargaining and in others by national legislation? Why is 'protection' treated as a gift from the state in some periods and as a 'right' in others?

In seeking answers to questions such as these one has to examine how particular rights came to be introduced into each country. Labour laws are the outcome of struggle between different social groups—monarchy, aristocracy, bureaucracy, middle class, workers and peasants—and of competing ideologies of conservatives, liberals, social democrats and socialists. The rights which

---

[17] Hepple (1986a) at 4.

any particular group gets 'is not just a matter of what they choose or want but what they can force or persuade other groups to let them have'.[18] The crucial element in the making of labour laws is *power*. Many of the demands by labour movements and reformers were unsuccessful because they were unacceptable to those with greater economic and political power. It is in power relationships, which are rooted in social structure, that we may find a key to the achievement and denial of rights at work.

The Liberal State: toleration and protection

In pre-industrial societies the worker is a member of a closed society and a closed economy with little freedom of movement. In Western Europe this covered broadly the period before the French Revolution of 1789. The employment relationship was within the family or guild controlled by the head of the household or the master. Master and servant or apprentice, employer and labourer, had mutual obligations. So a master had to provide professional training to an apprentice and to protect him, while the apprentice had to swear obedience and loyalty to the master. Public authorities regulated the rules of the guilds.

Under the early factory system in Europe, the factory owners enjoyed almost absolute rights or prerogatives within their own domain. They could also rely on penal master and servant laws to enforce their rights or prerogatives, for example by imprisoning workers who breached their contracts, or who combined into trade unions or went on strike. The work-book (*livret* or 'pass') system restricted the worker's freedom, especially on termination of employment. In colonial countries, master and servant laws and pass systems were maintained in order to enforce strict labour discipline and to prevent unionisation, long after these laws had disappeared in the metropolitan countries.[19]

The liberal constitutional states which emerged in Europe in the 19th century actively promoted liberal doctrines, purporting to leave the economy alone (*laissez-faire*). This was, of course, a form of intervention in the sense that it gave uncontrolled support to the power of property in the form of capital. Under the influence of liberal contractual ideas, the formal equality of employer and employee was proclaimed. The pre-industrial remnants of penal master and servant laws and laws against combinations were removed. Trade unions and collective bargaining were tolerated and sometimes gained legal recognition. The social problems resulting from industrialisation, including the degradation of children and women, urban poverty, unemployment and strikes, became political questions. The enfranchisement of (male) workers

[18] Abrams (1982) at 15.
[19] Braithwaite and Drahos (2000) at 225–27.

increased the pressure for state action to ameliorate these problems. Protective legislation was enacted for workers who were regarded as particularly vulnerable, starting with children and women, and later for other groups of workers. This was generally described as 'protection' rather than in the language of rights. The subjects included the length of the working day, the fencing of dangerous machinery, minimum wages and other basic working conditions

The Social Democratic Welfare State: equality, security, and other workers' rights

The challenges to the liberal model of toleration and protection came from two directions. One was from the Marxian socialists and communists whose primary aim was not to establish 'rights' under a capitalist order but was the assumption of political power by political parties claiming to represent the working class so as to end the system of wage labour itself. In the Soviet Union this took on the distinctive Leninist form of the 'dictatorship of the proletariat' (in reality the dictatorship of the Party). The centralised state took control of the economy and trade unions degenerated into the 'conveyor belts' between the 'vanguard' Party and the workers. The protection, welfare and job security of individual workers was seen as the reward for loyalty and strict observance of labour discipline. 'Evasion of socially useful work', declared Article 60 of the Soviet Constitution, 'is incompatible with the principles of socialist society.'

   The other challenge was from the social democrats whose aim was to redress the inequality of the supplier and purchaser of labour power. Labour 'rights' were demanded for subordinate or dependent labour. This is an idea that comes from Gierke, Weber and Durkheim and it stands in contrast to liberal and neo-liberal theories which ignore the inequitable distribution of wealth and power in society. The social democratic model of rights was tried in the German Weimar Republic (1919–33). It also appeared in some other countries such as the Mexican Constitution of 1917. The aim of the social democrats was—in Kahn-Freund's words[20]—'to legalise the class system in a class-divided society and to make it a component of the legal system.' They did this in Weimar Germany by giving constitutional protection to workers' rights and enabling the works councils to act as custodians of individual protection. It was in the quest for some kind of substantive and not merely formal equality between employer and worker in a pluralist society that they put their faith. The fragile collectivist system of the Weimar Republic came crashing down in the economic crisis of 1929–33. The huge rise in unemployment which virtually destroyed the new state system of unemployment insurance, and the

---

[20] Kahn-Freund (1981) at 190–91.

effective abolition of collective bargaining by presidential decrees, was followed by the victory of the National Socialists over a divided labour movement.

The theory of balanced industrial pluralism was still the dominant model of labour law in the 1970s when Kahn-Freund[21] wrote: 'the main object of labour law has always been, and we venture to say, will always be, to be a countervailing force to counteract the inequality of bargaining power which is inherent and must be inherent in the employment relationship.' Labour law was seen as providing institutions and processes, mainly collective, that created a fair balance between employers and workers. The focus was on subordinated workers within the employment relationship and not on wider aspects of the labour market. Labour law was regarded as serving primarily a social, and not an economic function. 'Rights' were a useful tool to end the distinction drawn in liberal societies between the 'private' sphere of economic life—what Adam Smith called civil society—and the 'public' sphere of what was directly controlled by the state. This was conceptualised in Continental European countries in the distinction between private law and public law. In the liberal state protective legislation for groups such as women and children could be justified on the ground that these groups lacked capacity to contract as equals. The idea of 'rights' changed the character of the legislation from being the gift of an enlightened ruling class into a right of the workers. These new rights—such as the right to work—were different from the rights of the individual proclaimed in the French Revolution and in most liberal constitutions. They were claims on the state to provide work and economic security and to recognise the collective interests of workers through the rights to organise, to bargain collectively and to strike.

However, not all democratic states answered the problem of inequality in the employment relationship by the creation of 'rights'. For example, in Britain 'Labourism' rather than any ideology of social rights was the dominant influence. The British approach was to defend social and organisational 'rights' won through industrial struggle, using the law on a pragmatic basis only when voluntary means were inadequate. Instead of social revolution or social democratic constitutionalism, the ideology shared by the majority of employers and trade unions was a 'very special, very British' variant of pluralism.[22] This, in its classic formulation by the 'Oxford School',[23] is in essence an ideology of 'enlightened management'. The focus was on equalising the position of employers and collective organisations of workers 'while leaving room for the continuing effects of market forces'. By the 1970s voluntary collective

---

[21] Kahn-Freund (1976) at 8; Kahn-Freund (1983) at 18.
[22] Streeck (1992) at 55.
[23] See esp. Clegg (1975); Fox (1966).

bargaining between employers and trade unions had come to cover about 85 percent of the workforce. Individual employment rights granted by legislation were mainly relevant in the absence of collective bargaining. However, from the 1960s onwards there was an increasing volume of legislation conferring rights on individual employees. Some of this fulfilled the function of what Wedderburn famously called a 'floor of rights',[24] that is a basis upon which collective bargaining could improve (eg unfair dismissal and redundancy compensation). Other legislation dealing with subjects outside the limited sphere of collective bargaining (eg race and sex discrimination) introduced the notion of fundamental human rights in the employment relationship. The decline of collective bargaining and trade union density since the 1980s in Britain has given greatly enhanced importance to individual rights.

In the United States, too, the approach was market-centred rather than rights-centred.[25] The ideal of free labour after the abolition of slavery became enmeshed with the idea of freedom of contract. Following the Supreme Court's decision in the *Lochner* case (1905),[26] almost every kind legislation establishing employment rights was struck down as an unconstitutional interference with the right of employers and of workers to buy and sell their labour on such terms as they saw fit. The only guaranteed right was the liberty to contract without state protective legislation. However, in 1937 a new majority of the Supreme Court largely repudiated the constitutional liberty to contract.[27] The Court upheld the National Labor Relations Act (NLRA) which prohibited discrimination against union activists and established a legal framework for union representation and collective bargaining. The Court also upheld the Fair Labor Standards Act which prescribed minimum wages and maximum working hours. What is striking is that these decisions were grounded in the federal government's power to regulate inter-state commerce, rather than on fundamental rights at work. The Supreme Court recognised that substandard labour conditions are an illegitimate subsidy to low wage employers, and the federal government was therefore justified in prohibiting inter-state traffic in goods produced under such conditions.[28] Two major shifts occurred after 1960. The first was civil rights legislation against discrimination on grounds of race, gender, age and disability. The second was the development, largely by courts on a state-by-state basis, of individual legal rights, derived from the common law, on matters such as discharge from employment and the right to privacy.

---

[24] Wedderburn (1971) at 8, 16; Wedderburn (1980) at 83.

[25] Estlund (2002) at 196–99.

[26] *Lochner v New York* 148 US 45 (1905), which struck down a state law limiting the hours of work of bakers.

[27] See esp *West Coast Hotel Co v Parrish* 300 US 379 (1937); *NLRB v Jones & McLaughlin Steel Corp* 301 US 1 (1937); *United States v Darby* 312 US 100 (1941).

[28] Barenberg (2000) at 303.

With the coming of welfare regimes after 1945 protective legislation changed its character. New social rights were supported by theories of 'social citizenship'. Citizenship was seen as a source of social cohesion. Citizens enjoyed political rights (to participate in the exercise of political power), and civil rights (to make contracts, to speak and to associate). These political and civil rights provided the means to secure social rights (to welfare and security on the basis of equality with others). Social rights were regarded as a component of the concept of citizenship. As we have seen in this book social and labour rights were internationalised through the UN and ILO (chapter 2, above), and also in regional treaties, most recently the Charter of Fundamental Rights of the EU (chapter 9, above).

Another feature of the welfare states was a change in the nature of the wage-work bargain. Under the model of the welfare state, there was a trade-off between economic dependence and social protection. While the worker continued to be subject to the commands and organisation of a hierarchy of management, it was understood that in return there would be a guarantee of a secure livelihood and job security.[29] Social legislation in the fields of workers' compensation for accidents, social insurance and employment protection was enacted.

The Neo-Liberal State: deregulation

The post-War consensus based on the notion of equality between employer and worker and support for collective representation within a welfare state has broken down since the 1970s. In place of the traditional ideologies, the focus has been on varieties of regulatory models. These all take the market system as their foundation. They assume that individuals are rational beings motivated solely by self-interest. Individuals are able to satisfy their preferences of which they are the best judges, through the mechanism of the market, in this way increasing their wealth. Values are measured by what people are willing to give up, their lost opportunities. So for example, a woman who seeks part-time work loses the opportunity to be paid at the same rate as a man doing full-time work because of her 'preference' for time to look after her children. The employer's 'taste' for discrimination is balanced against the cost to the woman. She is assumed to be a person of indeterminate gender or social background, but a calculating person able freely to choose her economic relations. Her preferences, such as caring for her children, are valued only in the process of exchange. Her right, as a human being to equal treatment and respect is not seen as a social value in itself: the only value recognised by this theory of markets is self-interest.

---

[29] Supiot (2001) at 151–55.

In regulatory theories, law is a means of intervening in the market order. Collins remarks that 'the regulatory agenda for the traditional field of labour law commences with a disarmingly naïve question: why regulate the employment relation?' Or, put another way, 'why should we exclude ordinary market principles such as the general law of contract and property from employment relations in favour of special rules?'[30] There is a 'heavy burden of proof' on advocates of employment rights 'to establish the superiority of regulation over ordinary market rules,' and 'the special regulation must be demonstrated to be efficient in the sense that its costs do not outweigh the potential benefits or improvements.' The question Collins poses and the burden of proof he stipulates to justify labour regulation, neglects the existing inequitable distribution of wealth and power. This is to treat the market and the private law of contract and property as a state of nature into which legal institutions intrude. It does not recognise that labour markets are themselves social institutions structured by law and that these laws can be made to reflect a different set of social values from those drawn solely from economic self-interest. Moreover, the cost-benefit calculations tend to ignore the costs of protecting the so-called negative rights of property and contract enjoyed by employers. 'The assignment, interpretation and protection of property rights of the owners of a business are not cost-free but are delivered as a cost to taxpayers, workers and consumers. Employment rights are part of an ancillary exchange by which government and employers recompense or give recognition to workers for the inequality of outcomes of the employment relationship.'[31]

Not surprisingly, in view of the presumption in favour of private law rules, regulatory theory has been used to justify deregulation of the employment relationship. By 'deregulation' in this context is meant leaving employment relations to ordinary market principles as underpinned by the private law of obligations. Hayek argued that trade unions used labour law to cartelise the market, so in the British context they had to be stripped of their 'special privileges' which protected them from the operation of the ordinary law of obligations.[32] In relation to individual rights—such as against unfair dismissal, and against discrimination—Epstein[33] claims that such special legislation interferes with efficient incentive structures provided by private law contracts. The arguments for de-collectivisation helped to shape the policies of many governments in the 1980s, but most of those governments never went as far as supporters of the Chicago School would have liked in deregulating individual employment rights. While legislation such as that on minimum pay and working time was repealed, and welfare rights were dismantled, the individual

---

[30] Collins (2000) at 4.
[31] Hepple and Morris (2002) at 249.
[32] Hayek (1980) at 89–90.
[33] Epstein (1984); Epstein (1995).

right not to be unfairly dismissed was generally not removed, and rights to equal pay and equal treatment between women and men were expanded. Even neo-liberal governments, intent on individualising the labour market, saw the need for laws which regulated termination of the contract, and guaranteed certain fundamental rights such as those against discrimination.

The main critique of the deregulatory model in the context of labour law, is that the economic model of freedom of individual choice and action is in practice illusory. Free markets are presumed to achieve allocative efficiency because the parties will trade with each other until they cannot further improve their position. This wrongly equates efficiency or cost-effectiveness with wealth-maximisation; and it makes claims about the links between labour regulation and job creation which are not evidence-based. Criticisms such as these led, in the 1990s, to alternative regulatory models being applied to labour law, with a view to improving economic performance. These are of particular importance to developing countries.

Rights-based regulation

The new model accepts that special regulation of the employment relation may be justified on two grounds. First, there may be market failure. This occurs when there is a significant deviation between the ideal outcomes which would result from perfect competition and the actual operation of the labour market. Secondly, regulation may be needed to correct unacceptable distributive outcomes. These justifications may sometimes conflict or they may overlap.

Rights-based regulation sees employment rights as beneficial and necessary to economic development. According to this version, workers come into the labour market with different levels of education and training, as well as differences in gender, class and race, and markets tend to generate differentials in wages and conditions which bear no relationship to the value added by individual workers. The labour of some is over-valued while that of others is under-valued. Under-valued labour leads to productive inefficiency, hampers innovation and leads to short-term strategies and destructive competition. Only regulation (eg a minimum wage, equal pay for women and men etc) can correct this market failure.

Secondly, rights-based regulation rests on the redistributive purposes of labour law. While the deregulators would say that competitive market outcomes are always the just distribution, because they are dictated by individual choice, rights-based regulation tends to favour a transfer of resources to enable those who wish to enter the labour market to do so, for example by providing better education, training and child care. Unlike the deregulators who see wealth maximisation (or allocative efficiency) as the primary goal, the rights-based model regards this as only a partial criterion of distributive justice.

Accordingly, in this model certain claims or entitlements, sometimes labelled 'fundamental rights', are treated as priorities among the distributive objectives of labour laws. However, there remains a presumption against regulation unless it can be shown that the regulation will not harm those whom it was designed to help. So if an increase in rights on termination of employment would lead employers to hire or retain fewer workers, this needs to be balanced against the benefits of being more careful about the selection and training of workers and the monitoring of their standards of performance. The question of redistribution is also linked to that of externalities: the self-interested market decisions of the parties to a contract may affect others adversely. For example, redundancies may cause costs to taxpayers who fund the social security system. The regulatory mechanism may therefore seek to transfer all or part of the social costs on to the parties to the employment relationship.

Thirdly, some advocates of the rights-based regulation argue that labour market institutions which encourage high trust or co-operative workplace 'partnership' lead to superior economic performance. This is the common argument for legal provision for better information, consultation and other forms of workers' participation in the enterprise, and for the improvement of corporate governance.[34]

Finally, the use of the language of rights to describe this model of regulation suggests that the claim of workers to distributive benefits is morally and legally superior to general claims to economic welfare which may result from free trade. Labour movements in the 19th and 20th centuries sought civil and political rights to enable them to use political power against the abuse of economic power in the labour market. They have also pressed for the recognition by the state of social rights such as the right to work, to education, to adequate food and housing, to healthcare and social security. Claims against employers have often been asserted as 'rights' to decent conditions of work, fair pay and job security, and the right to participate in trade unions and to engage in collective bargaining. Rights have been seen as a means of redressing the inequality in bargaining power between employer and worker. There was traditionally a strong emphasis on freedom of association and collective bargaining as core values.

The distinctive feature of rights discourse in the employment context in recent decades has been the individualisation of these claims. Whether one follows Rawls' 'first principle' that 'each person is to have an equal right to the most extensive total system of equal basic liberties compatible with a similar system for all',[35] or Dworkin's right of all to equal treatment and respect,[36] it is

---

[34] Deakin and Wilkinson (2000) at 56–61.
[35] Rawls (1973) at 11–15.
[36] Dworkin (1977) ch 6.

the *individual* and not the collective that is to be protected. So Article 11 of the ECHR protects the freedom of association and the right to join trade unions as an *individual* right, and is not directed at the inequality of the employment relationship.[37] Although social rights are nowadays not infrequently included in the constitutions of democratic societies, it is rare for them to be justiciable or legally enforceable.

The argument that social and labour rights are not human rights at all, is now widely discredited. But it has to be recognised that there are serious limitations on the use of such *individual* rights as a basis for the modernisation of labour law in the face of regulatory competition. First most social and labour rights—other than a few core values such as the freedom from slavery, forced and child labour, freedom of association and freedom from discrimination—are not universal or unqualified. Rights to decent working conditions and fair pay depend upon the level of socio-economic development in a particular country and they generally presuppose economic growth and expanding social welfare. Secondly, there is a contradiction between the inequality of class in the marketplace and the democratic element of citizenship and equal rights in the political sphere. British experience in the 1980s showed that social rights can be devalued by political action because industrial citizenship does not match political citizenship. Thirdly, there is a conflict between civil rights (such as the freedom to contract) which generally favour the operation of markets, and some social rights which may come into conflict with those markets. Even the fundamental right against indirect discrimination on grounds of sex or race is subject to justification on grounds of business necessity or cost. Fourthly, social rights lack effective procedures and mechanisms for their enforcement. Indeed, as we have seen throughout this book, increasing reliance on 'soft law' (such as voluntary corporate codes and guidelines laid down by regional and international bodies), the tendency towards privatisation of enforcement through management-controlled disputes resolution procedures rather than public tribunals, and restrictions on collective solidarity, reduce much rights talk to a rhetorical device—in Jeremy Bentham's famous phrase 'so much bawling on paper'.[38]

---

[37] Hepple (1998a) at 72–76.
[38] Bentham (1843) at 23; see generally on the law and politics of enforcement, Hepple (2002a) ch 10.

4. Seeking comparative institutional advantage

Competitivity and flexibility

Which of these economic and political models offers nation-states the optimum comparative institutional advantage? One approach puts 'competitivity' of the enterprise and 'flexibility' of work practices at the centre of the stage. This argument is familiar in the context of federal and transnational labour regulation. It is said that the liberalisation of trade and investment within a regional economic area or internationally, by removing barriers on the movement of goods, services and capital, throws the labour and welfare systems of the states into competition with each other. This leads to a process of market selection by which states adopt the most efficient form of regulation. Countries with low labour costs will attract investment; this in turn leads to greater demand for labour, higher wages and improved working and living conditions. On the other hand, it is said, regional or international labour regulations hamper this natural operation of the market and so lead to a loss in general welfare (chapter 1, above).

At EU-level this kind of argument has been used against harmonisation of employment laws or the setting of universal minimum standards (chapter 8, above). At national level, regulatory competition theory is increasingly used as a justification for limiting employment rights and their enforcement in developed countries. A recent example is the British Employment Act 2002 which limits access to employment tribunals. A justification put forward by the government was that this would 'strengthen UK competitiveness' by creating the 'right regulatory framework' with minimum standards 'to protect the most vulnerable workers.'[39] Similar arguments have been used in France, Germany, Italy and Spain to justify recent reforms of employment rights. A model of the employment relationship which concentrates on competitivity of the employer, not on the welfare of the human being at work, is readily used by the state to avoid costs for the employer and to protect public funds.[40]

There are several objections to the competitivity arguments. First, firms are not likely to relocate to another state with lower nominal labour costs if those lower costs simply reflect lower productivity of workers in that state. Empirical evidence, reviewed in chapter 1, shows just the reverse. TNCs tend to favour investment where skills of the labour force are high. Secondly, if labour costs do not reflect the relative productivity in a particular state and firms do

---

[39] Hepple and Morris (2002) at 246.
[40] Wedderburn (2002) at 27.

re-locate to those states, the result would be to create increased demand for labour with the likelihood of raising wage levels. This would soon cancel out the advantages of relocation which is simply based on low labour costs. Thirdly, firms which adopt low labour-cost strategies are likely to be trapped in a downward spiral of repeated cost-cutting rather than investment in technology and skill creation. This is a recipe for commercial failure.

Labour costs

Another popular approach is to call for reductions in differences in labour costs between countries. However, it is essential to distinguish the domestic implications of such differences from their use as an argument for blatant protectionism. For example German employers have understandably put pressure on German unions to accept greater flexibility in respect of working time on the grounds that hourly labour costs in the western part of Germany in 2002 were 28 percent above the average among its competitor countries.[41] But it is not sensible to make the liberalisation of trade conditional on convergence of labour costs. As Hoekman and Kostecki say, 'the gains from trade result precisely from differences in costs, which are due to differences in endowments, technological capacities, and output per worker.'[42] They add that 'as long as the labour standards in force reflect the desires of voters, the costs of implementation simply reflect the trade-off between monetary and non-monetary wealth that society has made.'[43]

Public choice, legal pluralism and localisation

A more profound analysis leads one to ask what are the nature and functions of labour laws within a particular nation-state? As argued earlier, the main economic function is to delimit managerial power within the employment relationship. This may be done in a variety of ways such as requiring direct benefits for workers, or introducing dynamic elements which increase skills and productivity, or spreading economic risks through forms of social insurance, or by empowerment rules. The nature of the resulting labour laws depends crucially on power relations within the nation-state and the outcomes differ depending on whether the dominant political formation is liberal constitutionalism, or social democracy, or neo-liberalism, or a rights-based

---

[41] *European Industrial Relations Review and Report* 360, January 2004, at 26.

[42] Hoekman and Kostecki (2001) at 449. One may add that currency fluctuations and general economic instability may also affect the comparative differences in labour costs.

[43] Hoekman and Kostecki (2001) at 450.

regulation. The question that globalisation raises for all these political models is whether the employment relationships remain governable within a political system whose central unit is the sovereign nation-state.[44]

Those—particularly public choice theorists—who give priority to the economic functions of labour laws tend to argue that that economic globalisation is leading to 'law without the state' because the state is a fetter on the free play of global market forces.[45] On the other hand, those who continue to see the state as essential to social cohesion and consensus stress the importance of state intervention to establish a normative order for labour relations. An intermediate group of social theorists have emphasised the 'pluralism' of legal orders. The state recognises or tolerates the autonomy of these orders. This is particularly relevant in the labour field, where 'law' is not necessarily coterminous with the state. A variety of actors make rules, enforced through non-state mechanisms or customs, within the workshop or office, enterprise or industry, and these rules may be even more important in practice than state-made laws. There are also transnational rules made by TNCs as well as international and regional institutions.

The pluralist perspective sees regulatory diversity and competition not so much as a conflict between state systems of labour law, but as a strategic or political process between different legal orders both within and beyond the state. Stone argues that globalisation 'not only breads a desire for localisation, it also breeds the means to achieve it.'[46] She points to the agglomeration of TNCs in particular places, such as the computer industry in Silicon Valley, partly because of the skills and knowledge of the locality's workforce and the networks they can establish. The attractions of such regions dissuades TNCs from moving offshore to avoid high labour costs, increases the leverage of local work and community groups, and the opportunities for local investment in human capital. If the centralised state is not able to provide the redistributive functions of labour laws, then struggles for social protection will become increasingly localised. This leads to some important conclusions. One is that local unions and community groups can act together to put pressure on TNCs to adopt best practices; another is that divisions between different employment statuses at local level (employees, contingent or atypical, and self-employed), and between working life and family life can be reduced; and a third is that solidarities can be developed with local groups employed by the same TNC in other countries.

The 'glocalisation' thesis can be criticised on the ground that it simply reinforces and aggravates inequalities between regions, those that are naturally

---

[44] Picciotto (1996) at 95.
[45] Piciotto (1996) at 93, 95.
[46] Stone (2004a).

endowed or have the appropriate workforces to attract transnational capital, and those that lack these factors of production. More generally, in the absence of supranational regulation, it is unlikely that local actors will succeed at the sharp end of regulation aimed at redistribution. This is because redistributive rules attempt to change the balance of economic and political power among different interest groups. Barenberg comments that 'interest groups threatened by such rules, of course, predictably exert pressure to weaken their enforcement or alter them in their favour. Interest groups aided by such rules will attempt the opposite.'[47]

Alternative strategies

What then, are the alternatives? The first would simply be to leave things to global market forces in the belief that the 'invisible hand' will in the long run result in equilibrium. This is an argument for widespread deregulation of the kind described as illusory in section 3 of this chapter. The second choice is to *help* markets work more effectively by correcting market failures and ensuring greater transparency, in particular by states and localities putting pressure on TNCs to follow best practices and requiring local non-export industries and services to adopt these practices as well in accordance with the principle of national treatment—a 'race to the top' as discussed in chapter 3 above. This is certainly a necessary step but insufficient in itself to guarantee comparative advantage. A third choice is to go further in encouraging best practices by offering *incentives* to firms that observe them or *punishments* on those who do not, for example through public procurement policies that favour socially responsible enterprises. This is an important method that falls outside the scope of this book.[48]

Finally, the most important lesson for states is the empirical evidence, reviewed in chapter 1, that high labour standards and investment in vocational education and training can lead to higher productivity, are good for business and in practice attract investment. The 'varieties of capitalism' approach outlined in section 1 of this chapter suggests that states should concentrate on their comparative strengths for particular kinds of trade and not attempt to impose convergence through unilateral actions. It is particularly ironic that some developed states now seek to impose on developing countries standards which they once themselves persistently violated on the path to development.[49]

---

[47] Barenberg (2000) at 315.
[48] Reference should be made to McCrudden (forthcoming).
[49] Charny (2000) at 300.

The advantages and effects of borrowing

The globalisation of legal cultures will greatly increase the process of legal transplants and borrowing from other systems, which has been a feature of labour laws since the very beginning. The adaptation of the model of 19th century British factory legislation by other countries was described by Stephan Bauer, first Director of the ILO, as being at least as important for humanity as the reception of the Roman law of property and obligations.[50] Although the claim was extravagant, it serves to emphasise the historical relationship between the labour laws of different countries. Many other examples can be found, including the extraordinary influence of the *Code Napoléon* in the development of contractual ideas of the employment relationship; the spread of Bismarckian-style schemes of compulsory social insurance in the first half of the 20th century; and the inspiration given by the Weimar Republic's Works Councils Act of 1920 to the concept of unjustified dismissal in the second half of that century. More recently, there have been transatlantic crossings, such as US union recognition laws to Britain, and Caribbean labour relations laws to some African countries. Comparative law has been a central feature in the development of labour laws within the EU and candidate states.[51] ILO experts who have helped to draft labour laws in many African and Asian countries have freely borrowed ideas and concepts, and even copied texts directly from other labour law systems.

It was said by Kahn-Freund that while rules directly regulating the individual employment relationship may be relatively easily transplanted, those related to collective labour relationships are usually too closely connected with the structure and organisation of political and social power in a particular environment to be successfully imported elsewhere.[52] However, recent experience with workers' participation measures in European countries[53] and with collective bargaining and strike law in South Africa,[54] suggest that there may be 'borrowing and bending'[55] even of collective institutions. So Watson's generalisation that 'borrowing (with adaptation) has been the usual way of legal development'[56] can be readily applied to nearly all aspects of labour law. There is an important qualification to this. He notes that 'a rule transplanted from one country to another . . . may equally operate to different effect in the two societies,even though it is expressed in apparently similar terms in the two

---

[50] Hepple (1986a) at 1–2.
[51] Malmberg (2003).
[52] Kahn-Freund (1978).
[53] Carley and Hall (2000).
[54] Hepple (1999c).
[55] Thompson (1993) at 109.
[56] Watson (1974) at 7.

countries.'[57] In Teubner's words, transplants may operate as a 'legal irritants'. They 'unleash an evolutionary dynamics in which the external rule's meaning will be reconstructed and the internal context will undergo fundamental change.'[58] This leads Teubner to reject both the convergence thesis, and the idea of 'functional equivalence'. The latter means that legal systems facing similar problems find different doctrinal solutions which serve the same functions.[59] Instead of this, argues Teubner, transplants produce new differences. Globalisation encourages difference not convergence.

The conclusion to which one is led is that legal convergence is not the likely outcome of globalisation. Differences between the labour laws of countries and localities will remain and may even increase. How far, then, can the adverse effects of regulatory competition be met by transnational labour regulation?

5. Re-inventing transnational labour regulation[60]

In this book it has been argued that if the benefits of growing trade and investment are to be spread to the poorest, this will not come from re-locating labour law within the sphere of international trade law (see chapters 4, 5, and 6). Instead the efforts of those who are committed to promoting social justice within the global market should re-directed to strengthening the many strands that are emerging of a new global labour law.[61]

Regional treaties

The first important strand is the social and employment dimensions of regional economic treaties. The most important example is the EU (chapters 8 and 9, above). Recent Directives are transforming the equality laws of the Member States and the candidate Members, broadening the scope of labour law to include excluded groups. The most important developments in the EU have been the open method of co-ordination and the social dialogue against the background of fundamental rights. The important lesson from the EU—in contrast to US labour federalism[62]—is that synchronised *co-ordination* (not

---

[57] Watson (1974) at 20.
[58] Teubner (2001) at 418.
[59] Zweigert and Kötz (1992).
[60] This section is based on Hepple (2002b).
[61] See in similar vein, Arthurs (2001) at 286–94; Stone (1999) at 127–30.
[62] Barenberg (2000) at 315.

convergence) of social and employment policies, through a social dialogue between the main interest groups, offers an important, even if not wholly adequate, means of overcoming competition for capital among national and regional workforces. Fundamental rights, based on a European consensus about the essential values shared by the governments and peoples of the region, provide the necessary basis of principle for these developments. There is, of course, a 'dark side' to European integration, in particular the absence of a collective labour law and the many tensions which still exist between competition and labour policies (chapter 8, above). Moreover, the EU treaties are essentially the product of bureaucratic elites whose drafts become diluted and distorted in the process of negotiations between governments pursuing their own national interests rather than any supra-national ideal. But this does not diminish the importance of these treaties as a framework for reconciling market freedoms with social and labour rights under the rule of law. What is lacking is democratic participation in this process.

Other regions may find it more difficult to move in this direction. But one should not undervalue the Labor Side Accord of the NAFTA, which has had modest successes in enforcing national labour laws and in helping to launch a new independent trade union movement in Mexico, and improved co-operation between Mexican, US and Canadian unions and NGOs.[63]

Transnational corporations

A second strand is the culture of corporate social responsibility developing within TNCs mainly in the form of voluntary codes of conduct and collective agreements but also through the informal dissemination of 'best practices' (chapter 3, above). These codes have the potential to harness processes within the market activities of TNCs that favour the raising of labour standards, that is a 'race to the top'. The essential point is that the internal labour markets of TNCs usually provide better wages, conditions of work and social security benefits than those prevailing in domestic firms, due to the fact that they tend to be concentrated in industries which utilise high skills, are capital intensive and have superior managerial and organisational techniques. These standards can have a spill-over effect in domestic firms. The many difficulties and obstacles to this approach were discussed in chapter 3, above. If the global commodity chains dominated by TNCs are to disseminate best practices, then international conventions and guidelines and national legislation will need to be strengthened and directed at TNCs. In particular, the codes should at least

---

[63] Arthurs (2001) at 287.

specify ILO core standards. National laws should place TNCs under legal obligations to observe their own codes. There needs to be independent monitoring; and effective national and international complaints mechanisms.

Empowering local actors

A third strand of the new labour law involves the empowerment of local actors. Unions and new social movements of women, consumers, students, and human rights activists are building alliances with groups in developing countries and awakening public awareness of abuses of labour rights. It is in this context, that the selective use of trade boycotts and disinvestment becomes relevant. A case in point is apartheid South Africa. Sanctions were imposed at the request of, and in order to support, the anti-apartheid forces within the country. Trade sanctions in the 1980s worsened an already serious economic situation under the apartheid regime. It was in fact financial sanctions which eventually gave a major impetus to regime change—the reduced access to foreign loans, obligatory debt repayments, and the repatriation abroad of the proceeds of disinvestment.[64]

ILO standards

A fourth strand is to secure the application of international labour standards. A real problem in this respect is whether or not the standards set in the ILO's 185 Conventions are the ones that are needed to counteract poverty and inequality suffered by the majority of the world's workers, and whether these standards are being effectively implemented (chapter 2, above). One indication that there is something seriously wrong is the failure of most developing countries to ratify ILO conventions and to implement them. From this the inference may be drawn that the standards are not appropriate to the real needs of those countries.

All these developments have put in question the legitimacy and even the survival of the ILO in its present universalised form. The ILO's response has been an attempt to revitalise international labour standards in three ways. First by promoting the 1998 Declaration on Fundamental Principles and Rights at Work, secondly by revising labour standards to make them more integrated and coherent. and thirdly by a campaign for 'decent work'. These efforts must be supported, but they need to be developed in new ways, along the lines suggested in chapter 2, above. First, the focus should be on all forms

---

[64] Jenkins (1993).

of productive work, not limited to paid employment, on the basis of minimum socio-economic rights. Secondly, the artificial distinction between conventions and recommendations should be replaced by a few framework conventions that set out principles, accompanied by codes of practice directed at specific groups of countries at a similar level of development. Thirdly, the core conventions should be enlarged and updated to include, for example, health and safety and labour inspection. Fourthly, a rights-based approach should be taken to the implementation of these, making compliance with them a condition of membership of the ILO, and providing for a complaints-based enforcement mechanism along the lines of the investigation of complaints on freedom of association by the CFA but with more effective follow-up. Fifthly, outside the area of core rights the ILO should adopt methods of co-ordination of national policies on employment promotion, training and the like similar to those of the EU's Open Method of Coordination (OMC). This would require the targeting of specific groups of countries at a similar stage of development so as to maximise peer pressure, with an effective surveillance system. This would be an essential part of expanded ILO technical assistance, and financial aid.

It has been argued that sanctions for breach of international labour standards imposed unilaterally are undesirable (chapter 4, above), and that WTO sanctions would be both undesirable in principle and unlikely to work in practice (chapter 6, above). This does not mean that sanctions should be absent from the system of transnational labour regulation. On the contrary, persuasion and conciliation will not work unless there is ultimately a sanction which can be invoked. First, it would not be unreasonable to insist that no country which is in flagrant breach of fundamental human rights should be admitted into the WTO and ILO. These pariah states (*hostis humani generis*) who wish to join the WTO or ILO should first have to demonstrate respect for democracy and human rights, as is the case for membership of the EU. They should also be forced to withdraw from the WTO and ILO if they are ruled by highly corrupt or dictatorial regimes which grossly abuse fundamental rights. The WTO-ILO linkage could be strengthened, so as to give the ILO prime responsibility in respect of the core labour standards. Once a state is a Member of the ILO on these conditions, it should also be able to enjoy the benefits of WTO membership. Another fruitful approach is to provide positive, as distinct from negative conditionality, in granting trade preferences along the lines of the EU's GSP (chapter 4, above). Apart from these measures, the ILO should show more willingness and urgency than it does at present in the application of Article 33, making it an obligation (not simply a request) for Member States to take 'action' within the permitted limits of the WTO agreements. The emphasis, however, needs to be on carrots rather than sticks.

Inter-jurisdictional dynamics

One of the most important consequences of modern globalisation is that there are multiple, overlapping layers of norm-creation and norm-application. This is familiar in federal systems, and is a feature of the EU legal order. Corporate codes of conduct operate within systems of corporate governance and are influenced by transnational guidelines, such as those of the OECD and ILO. None of this is surprising to labour lawyers who are familiar with the legal pluralism of employer regulation, collective bargaining, trade union rules and national laws. Labour lawyers are also aware that the boundaries between these orders can be vague, and that the prevalence of particular norms depends upon complex power relations that can change, sometimes rapidly.

It is within this dynamic relationship between multivalent legal orders that the ability of labour law to contribute to social justice within the global market will be determined. The supra-nationalising of labour law, through ILO standards, regional treaties and the codes of TNCs, gives trade unions, NGOs and national governments opportunities to emancipate themselves from the confines of national or local laws.[65]

An example of the way in which this can work is provided by the case of the BJ&B factory in the Dominican Republic (Box 10.1). This is a case where a combination of ILO standards and a corporate code, coupled with the active involvement of a human rights group collaborating with the government and local workers, is in the process of holding the contractor to a higher standard than could be enforced under national labour law.

None of these new strategies will be easy. They will face resistance and distortion. Yet the revolution in global trade opens enormous opportunities for economic growth and world-wide prosperity. The urgent task of labour and social law at local, national and international levels, is to provide the essential framework within which these benefits can be enjoyed by the poor, the weak and the dispossessed, as well as those who live in relative affluence.

---

[65] See Kilpatrick (2001) at 489, for an important discussion of this process in the field of gender equality.

Box 10.1

THE BJ & B CASE IN THE DOMINICAN REPUBLIC

The BJ & B factory, owned by a Korean parent company, produces Nike, Reebok and Adidas products. In October 2001, a group of 20 workers employed at the factory filed a petition under Dominican law for the recognition of their union. (The Dominican Republic has ratified 35 ILO Conventions including those on freedom of association and the right to organise.) In the course of the next two months all these workers were dismissed or resigned in circumstances that led to the allegation that they had been victimised for trade union activity. Over a five-year period there had been other allegations of forced overtime, physical and verbal abuse of workers and lack of proper grievance procedures. The Labour Code of the Dominican Republic leaves considerable discretion to management with respect to dismissal without cause, and this coupled with managerial practices at BJ&B led to unfair actions and the restriction of the right to organise. Nike and the other brands filed a complaint against their contractor with the Fair Labor Association based in Washington DC. The FLA investigated the complaint, with the support of the Dominican Department of Labour, put on a training course on freedom of association for all 1600 workers (in small groups) with supervisors, and negotiated the return to work of the dismissed trade unionists. The brands involved put pressure on the head office of BJ&B's Korean parent company to observe the brands' corporate codes which include freedom of association. Despite a threat from that company to relocate the facility in Bangladesh, as at October 2002, it was still operating in the Dominican Republic. The union has now secured support from a majority of workers and is seeking negotiations for a collective bargaining agreement. At the time of writing, the company's lawyers are trying to use the letter of Dominican law to avoid this.[66]

---

[66] Information supplied by Auret van Heerden, Fair Labor Association, Washington DC (http//www/fairlabor.org).

REFERENCES

Abrams, P (1982), *Historical Sociology* (Shepton Mallet, Open Books).

Adams, RJ and Singh, P (1997), 'Early experience with NAFTA's Labor Side Accord', 18 *Comparative Labor Law Journal* 161.

Adamy, W(1994), 'International Trade and Social Standards', 29 *Intereconomics* 269.

Alben, E (2001), 'Gatt and the Fair Wage: A Historical Perspective on the Labor-Trade link October' 101 *Columbia Law Review* 1410.

Alcock, A (1971), *History of the International Labour Organisation* (London, Macmillan).

Alston, P (1993), 'Labor Rights Provisions in US Trade Law: 'Aggressive Unilateralism?', 15 *Human Rights Quarterly 1*.

—— (2002), 'Resisting the Merger and Acquisition of Human Rights by Trade Law: a Reply to Petersmann', 13 *European Journal of International Law* 815.

—— (2004), '"Core Labour Standards" and the Transformation of the International Labour Regime', 15 *European Journal of International Law* 457.

Amin, A and Thrift, N (eds) (1994), *Globalisation, Institutions and Regional Development* (Oxford, OUP).

Anderson, K (1996), 'The Intrusion of Environmental and Labour Standards into Trade Policy', in W Martin and LA Winter (eds), *The Uruguay Round and the Developing Countries* (Cambridge, CUP) 435.

Arthurs, H (1996a), 'Labour Law without the State' 46 *University of Toronto Law Journal* 1.

—— (1996b), *The New Economy and the Demise of Industrial Citizenship*, The 1996 Don Wood Lecture (Kingston, Ont, Queen's University, Industrial Relations Centre).

—— (2001), 'Reinventing Labor Law for the Global Economy: The Benjamin Aaron Lecture', 22 *Berkeley Journal of Employment and Labor Law* 271.

—— (2002), 'Private Ordering and Workers' Rights in the Global Economy: Corporate Codes of Conduct as a Regime of Labour Market Regulation', in J Conaghan, M Fischl and K Klare (eds) *Labour Law in an Era of Globalization* (Oxford, OUP).

Atkinson, AB (2001), *Inequality, Poverty and the Welfare State: a European Perspective on the Globalisation Debate.* Available on http//www/nuff.ox.ac.uk/users/Atkinson.

Baker, MB (2001), 'Tightening the Toothless Vice: Codes of Conduct and the American Multinational Enterprise' 20 *Wisconsin International Law Journal* 89.

Bal, S (2001), 'International Free Trade Agreements and Human Rights: Reinterpreting Article XX of the GATT', 10 *Minnesota Journal of Global Trade* 62.

Ball, S (2001), 'The European Employment Strategy: the Will but not the Way', 30 *Industrial Law Journal* 353.

Barenberg, M (2000), 'Labor Federalism in the United States: Lessons for International Labor Rights' 3 *Journal of International Economic Law* 303.

Barnard, C (1997), 'P *v* S: Kite-Flying or a new Constitutional approach?' in A Dashwood and S O'Leary (eds), *The Principle of Equal Treatment in EC Law* (London, Sweet and Maxwell) 59.

—— (2000a), 'Social Dumping and the Race to the Bottom: Some Lessons for the European Union from Delaware?' 25 *European Law Review* 57.

—— (2000b), *EC Employment Law*, 2nd.ed. (Oxford, OUP).

—— (2000c), 'Flexibility and Social Policy', in G de Búrca and J Scott (eds), *Constitutional Change in the EU: From Uniformity to Flexibility?*' (Oxford, Hart Publishing).

—— (2004), *The Substantive Law of the EU: the Four Freedoms* (Oxford, OUP).

—— and Deakin, S (1996), 'Social policy in search of a role: integration, cohesion and citizenship', in A Caiger, M Andreas and D Floudas (eds), *1996 Onwards: Lowering the Barriers Further* (Chichester, Wiley).

—— and —— (2002), 'Corporate Governance, European Governance and Social Rights' in B Hepple (ed) *Social and Labour Rights in a Global Context: International and Comparative Perspectives* (Cambridge, CUP).

—— —— and Hobbs, R (2003), 'Opting-out of the 48-hour Week: Employer Necessity or Individual Choice?', 33 *Industrial Law Journal* 223.

Barnes, GN (1926), *History of the International Labour Office* (London, Williams and Norgate).

Basu, K (2001), 'Compacts, Conventions and Codes: Initiatives for Higher International Labor Standards', 34 *Cornell International Law Journal* 487.

Bell, M (2002), *Anti-Discrimination Law in the European Union* (Oxford, OUP).

Bentham, J (1843), 'Anarchical Fallacies' in J Bowring (ed) *Collected Works of Jeremy Bentham* (London, Simpkin & Marshall).

Bercusson, B (1992), 'Maastricht: a Fundamental Change in European Labour Law' 23 *Industrial Relations Journal* 177.

—— (1999), 'Democratic Legitimacy and European Labour Law', 28 *Industrial Law Journal* 153.

—— and van Dijk, J (1995), 'The Implementation of the Protocol and Agreement on Social Policy of the Treaty of European Union', 11 *International Journal of Comparative Labour Law and Industrial Relations* 3.

Bhagwati, J (1996), 'The Agenda of the WTO', in P van Dijk and G Faber (eds), *Challenges to the New World Trade Organisation* (London, Kluwer).

—— (2004), *In Defense of Globalization* (Oxford, OUP).

Biagi M, (1998) 'The Implementation of the Amsterdam Treaty with Regard to Employment Co-Ordination or Convergence', 14 *International Journal of Comparative Labour Law and Industrial Relations* 325.

Blackett, A (1999), 'Whither Social Clause? Human Rights, Trade Theory and Treaty Interpretation', 31 *Columbia Human Rights Review* 1.

—— (2001), 'Global Governance, Legal Pluralism and the Decentred State: A Labor Law Critique of Codes of Corporate Conduct' 8 *Indiana Journal of Global Legal Studies* 401.

—— (2002), 'Mapping the Equilibrium Line: Fundamental Principles and Rights at Work and the Interpretative Universe of the World Trade Organisation', 65 *Saskatchewan Law Review* 369.

Blank, R (1994), *Social Protection versus Economic Flexibility: Is there a trade-off?* (Chicago, University of Chicago Press).

Blanpain, R (2000), 'The OECD Guidelines for Multinational Enterprises' in *International Encyclopedia for Comparative Labour Law and Industrial Relations: Codex* (Deventer, Kluwer).

—— (ed) (2000), *Multinational Enterprises and the Social Challenges of the XXIst Century* (London, Kluwer).

—— and Engels, C (2003), *European Labour Law,* 9th rev ed (Deventer, Kluwer).

—— Hepple, B, Sciarra, S and Weiss, M (1996), *Fundamental Social Rights: Proposals for the European Union* (Leuven, Peeters).

Boyer, R and Drache, D (1996), *States against Markets: Limits of Globalisation* (London, Routledge).

Braithwaite J and Drahos P (2000), *Global Business Regulation* (Cambridge, CUP).

Brandtner, B and Rosas A (1999), 'Trade Preferences and Human Rights' in P Alston (ed), *The EU and Human Rights* (Oxford, OUP).

Brown, D and McColgan, A (1992), 'UK Employment Law and the International Labour Organisation: the Spirit of Co-operation?', 21 *Industrial Law Journal* 265.

—— Deardriff, DV and Stern RM (1996), 'International labor standards and trade: a theoretical analysis' in JN Bhagwati and RE Hudec (eds) *Fair Trade and Harmonisation: Prerequisites for Free Trade?* (Cambridge Mass., MIT).

Butler, H (1939), *The International Labour Organisation* (Oxford, OUP).

Caire, G (1994), 'Labour standards and international trade' in W Sengenberger and D Campbell (eds) *International Labour Standards and Economic Interdependence* (Geneva, International Institute for Labour Studies) 297.

Cappuyns, E (1998), 'Linking labor standards and trade sanctions: an analysis of their current relationship' 36 *Columbia Journal of Transnational Law* 659.

Carley, M and Hall, M (2000), 'The Implementation of the European Works Councils Directive', 29 *Industrial Law Journal* 103.

Castells, M (2000), *The Rise of the Network Society,* volume 1, 2nd ed (Oxford, Blackwell).

Cecchini, P (1988), *The European Challenge 1992: The Benefits of a Single Market* (Aldershot, Wildwood House).

Charnovitz, S (1987), 'The influence of international labour standards on the world trading system: a historical review', 126 *International Labour Review* 565.

—— (1992), 'Environmental and labour standards in trade', 15 *World Economy* 332.

—— (1994), 'The World Trade Organisation and Social Issues' 25 *Journal of World Trade* 17.

—— (1998), 'The Moral Exception in Trade Policy' 38 *Virginia Journal of International Law* 689.

—— (2002), 'Should the Teeth be Pulled? An Analysis of WTO Sanctions' in DLM Kennedy and JD Southwick (eds) *The Political Economy of International Trade Law* (Cambridge University Press, Cambridge).

Charny, D (2000), 'Regulatory Competition and the Global Co-ordination of Labour Standards' 3 *Journal of International Economic Law* 281.

Chau, N H and Kanbur, R (2001) 'The Adoption of International Labor Standards Conventions: Who, When and Why?' in SM Collins and D Rodrik, *Brookings Trade Forum 2001* (Brookings Institution, Washington).

Chin, D (1998) *A Social Clause for Labour's Cause: Global Trade and Labour Standards—a Challenge for the New Millennium* (London, Institute of Employment Rights).

Clarke, M, Feys T, and Kalula, E (1999), *Labour Standards and Regional Integration in Southern Africa: Prospects for Harmonisation* (Cape Town, Institute of Development and Labour Law, University of Cape Town).

Clay, L (2001), 'The Effectiveness of the Worker Rights Provisions of the Generalised System of Preferences: the Bangladesh Case Study', 11 *Transnational Law and Contemporary Problems* 175.

Clegg, HA (1975), 'Pluralism in Industrial Relations', 13 *British Journal of Industrial Relations* 309.

Cleveland, SH (1997), 'Global Labour Rights and the Alien Tort Claims Act' 76 *Texas Law Review* 1533.

—— (2002), 'Human Rights Sanctions and International Trade: a Theory of Compatibility' 5 *Journal of International Economic Law* 133.

Collier, J (2001), *Conflict of Laws*, 3rd ed (Cambridge, CUP).

Collins, H (2000), 'Justifications and Techniques of Legal Regulation of the Employment Relation', in H Collins, PL Davies and R Rideout (eds) *Legal Regulation of the Employment Relation* (London, Kluwer).

Commonwealth of Australia (1996), *Report on Labour Standards in the Asia-Pacific Region,* Tripartite Working Party on Labour Standards (Chair: Michael Duffy) (Canberra, AGPS).

Compa, L (1998), 'The Multilateral Agreement on Investment and International Labor Rights: a Failed Connection' 31 *Cornell International Law Journal* 683.

—— (2001), 'The North American Free Trade Agreement and the North American Agreement on Labor Co-operation', in R Blanpain (ed), *International Encyclopedia for Labour Law and Industrial Relations* (Deventer, Kluwer).

—— and Diamond, SF (eds) (1996), *Human Rights, Labor Rights and International Trade* (Philadelphia, University of Pennsylvania Press).

—— and Vogt, JS (2001) 'Labor rights in the generalized system of preferences: A 20 year review', 22 *Comparative Labor Law and Policy Journal* 199.

Conaghan, J, Fischl, M and Klare K (eds) (2001), *Labour Law in an Era of Globalization* (Oxford, OUP).

Cooney, S (1999), 'Testing Times for the ILO: Institutional Reform for the New International Political Economy', 20 *Comparative Labor Law and Policy Journal* 365.

Coppel, J and O'Neill, A (1992), 'The European Court of Justice: Taking Rights Seriously' 29 *Common Market Law Review* 669.

Córdova, E (1993), 'Some Reflections on the Overproduction of International Labor Standards', 14 *Comparative Labour Law Journal* 138.

Cowell, F (1977), M*easuring Inequality* (Oxford, P Allan), 2nd ed (London, Prentice Hall, 1995).

Creighton, WB (1974), *Working Women and the Law* (London, Mansell).

—— (1994), 'The ILO and Protection of Freedom of Association in the United Kingdom' in KD Ewing, C Gearty and B Hepple (eds), *Human Rights and Labour Law* (London, Mansell).

—— (1997), 'Combating Child Labour: the Role of International Labour Standards', 18 *Comparative Labour Law Journal* 362.

Davies, PL (1992), 'The Emergence of European Labour Law' in W McCarthy (ed), *Legal Intervention in Industrial Relations: Gains and Losses* (Oxford, OUP).

—— (1995), 'Market Integration and Social Policy in the Court of Justice', 24 *Industrial Law Journal* 49.

—— (1996), 'The European Court of Justice, National Courts and the Member States' in P Davies, S Sciarra, and S Simitis (eds), *European Community Labour Law* (Oxford, OUP).

—— (1997), 'Posted Workers: Single Market or Protection of National Labour Law Systems' 34 *Common Market Law Review* 571.

—— (2002), 'The Posted Workers Directive and the EC Treaty', 31 *Industrial Law Journal* 298.

—— (2003), 'Workers on the Board of the European Company', 32 *Industrial Law Journal* 75.

Deakin, S (1996), 'Labour law as Market Regulation: the Economic Foundations of European Social Policy' in P Davies, S Sciarra and S Simitis (eds), *European Community Labour Law* (Oxford, Clarendon Press).

—— (2004), *Renewing Labour Market Institutions,* International Institute for Labour Studies, ILO Policy Series (Budapest, Central European University).

—— and Reed H (2000), *The Contested Meaning of Labour Market Flexibility: Economic Theory and the Discourse on European Integration.* Working Paper 162 (Cambridge, ESRC Centre for Business Research).

—— and Wilkinson F (1994), 'Rights vs efficiency? The economic case for transnational labour standards' 23 *Industrial Law Journal* 289.

—— and —— (2000) 'Labour Law and Economic Theory' in H Collins, P Davies and R Rideout (eds), *Legal Regulation of the Employment Relation* (London, Kluwer).

—— and —— (forthcoming), *The Law of the Labour Market: Industrialisation, Employment and Legal Evolution* (Oxford, OUP).

De Búrca, G (1993), 'Fundamental Human Rights and the Reach of EC Law' 13 *Oxford Journal of Legal Studies* 283.

—— (2000), 'Differentiation within the Core: the Case of the Common Market', in G De Búrca and J Scott *Constitutional Change in the EU: from Uniformity to Flexibility* (Oxford, Hart Publishing) 133.

De la Porte, C (2002), 'Is the Open Method of Co-Ordination Appropriate for Organising Activities and European Level in Sensitive Policy Areas?' 8 *European Law Journal* 38.

Department of Employment (1985), *Employment: the Challenge to the Nation* Cmnd.9794 (London, HMSO).

Department for International Development (DFID) (2003), *Labour Standards and Poverty Reduction.* Consultation Paper (London, DFID).

Dicey, A and Morris J (2000) *On the Conflict of Laws* 13th ed (London, Sweet & Maxwell).

Dicken, P (1998), *Global Shift: Transforming the World Economy,* 3rd ed (London, Paul Chapman Publishing).

Dickerson, CM (2001), 'Transnational Codes of Conduct through Dialogue: Levelling the Playing field for Developing Country Workers' 53 *Florida Law Review* 611.

Diller, J (1999), 'A Social Conscience in the Global Marketplace? Labour Dimensions of Codes of Conduct, Social Labelling and Investor Initiatives', 38 *International Labour Review* 99.

Dillon, CH (1942), *International Labor Conventions: Their Interpretation and Revision* (Chapel Hill, University of North Carolina Press).

Docksey, C (1985), 'Employee Information and Consultation Rights in the EC', 7 *Comparative Labor Law Journal 32.*

Dworkin, R (1977) *Taking Rights Seriously* (London, Duckworth).

Elliott, KA and Freeman, RB(2003), *Can Labour Standards Improve Under Globalization?* (Washington DC, Institute for International Economics).

Ellis, E (1998) *EC Sex Equality Law,* 2nd ed (Oxford, OUP).

Engerman, S (2001), 'The History and Political Economy of International Labour Standards', Paper presented at the seminar on International Labour Standards, Stockholm, August 23–24, 2001.

Enderwick, P (ed) (1994), *Transnational Corporations and Human Resources* (London, Routledge)

Epstein, R (1984), 'In Defense of Contract at Will' 51 *University of Chicago Law Review* 947.

—— (1995), *Forbidden Grounds* (Cambridge, Mass, Harvard University Press).

Erikson, CL and Mitchell, DB (1998), 'Labor Standards and Trade Agreements: US Experience', 19 *Comparative Labor Law and Policy Journal* 145.

Estlund, C (2002), 'An American Perspective on Fundamental Labour Rights', in B Hepple (ed) *Social and Labour Rights in a Global Context: International and Comparative Perspectives* (Cambridge, CUP).

Esty, DC and Geradin, D (2000), 'Regulatory Competition' 3 *Journal of International Economic Law* 235.

European Commission (1990) *Explanatory Memorandum on the Proposals concerning certain employment relationships* COM (90) 228 - SYN 280 - SYN 281 (Brussels and Luxembourg, DGV, EC).

—— (1993), *European Social Policy: Options for the Union* [Green Paper] COM (93) 551 (Brussels and Luxembourg, DGV, EC).

—— (1994a), *European Social Policy: a Way Forward for the Union* [White Paper] COM 94 (333) (Brussels and Luxembourg, DGV, EC).

—— (1994b), *Growth, Competitiveness, Employment: The Challenges and Ways Forward into the 2ist Century,* White Paper (Brussels and Luxembourg, EC).

—— (1996), *For a Europe of Civic and Social Rights. Report of the Comité des Sages* [Chair: M de Lourdes Pintasilgo] (Brussels and Luxembourg, DGV, EC).

—— (1999), *Applying Fundamental Rights in the European Union. Report of the Expert Group on Fundamental Rights.*[Chair: S Simitis] (Brussels and Luxembourg, DGV, EC).

—— (2000), *Social Policy Agenda* (Brussels and Luxembourg, DGV, EC).

European Parliament (1999), *Report on EU Standards for European Enterprises Operating in Developing Countries: Towards a European Code of Conduct.* Committee on Development and Co-operation [Rapporteur: Richard Howitt] (Brussels, European Parliament).

Ewing, KD (1994), *Britain and the ILO,* 2nd ed (London, Institute of Employment Rights).

—— (2004), *Global Regulation of the Global Economy: the Role of Trade Unions.* Unpublished paper.

—— and Hendy J (2004), *Submission to the Joint Committee on Human Rights on the Right to Strike* (London, Institute of Employment Rights).

Fentiman, R (2000), 'Ousting Jurisdiction and the European Convention', 3 *Cambridge Yearbook of European Legal Studies,* 107.

Ferguson, C (1998), *A Review of UK Company Codes of Conduct* (London, Department for International Development, Social Development Division).

Follows, JW (1951), *Antecedents of the International Labour Organization* (Oxford, Clarendon Press).

Fox, A (1966), *History and Heritage: The Social Origins of the British Industrial Relations System* (London, George Allen and Unwin).

Fredman, S (1998), 'Social Law in the European Union: the Impact of the Law Making Process' in P Craig and C Harlow (eds) *Law Making in the European Union* (London, Kluwer).

Garcia, FJ (2001), 'Building a Just Trade Order for a New Millennium' 33 *George Washington International Law Review* 1015.

Germanotta, P (2002), *Protecting Worker Solidarity Action: a Critique of International Labour Law* (London, Institute of Employment Rights).

—— and Novitz, T (2002), 'Globalisation and the Right to Strike: the Case of European-Level Secondary Action', 18 *International Journal of Comparative labour Law and Industrial Relations* 67.

Ghebali, V (1989), *The ILO: a Case Study of a UN Specialised Agency* (The Hague, Nijhoff).

Ghoshal, S and Bartlett, C (1993) 'The Multinational Corporation as an Inter-organisational Network', in S Ghoshal and D Westney (eds) *Organisation Theory and Multinational Corporations* (Basingstoke, Macmillan).

Goldsmith, Lord (2001), 'A Charter of Rights, Freedoms and Principles' 38 *Common Market Law Review* 1201.

Gould, WB (2001), 'Labour Law for a Global Economy: The Uneasy Case for International Labor Standards' 80 *Nebraska Law Review* 715.

Greenway, D and Milner, C (1995), 'The world trade system and the Uruguay round: global employment implications', 134 *International Labour Review* 497.

Grimwade, N (1996), *International Trade Policy: a contemporary analysis* (London, Routledge).

Grossmann, H and Koopman, G (1996), 'Social Standards in International Trade' in H Sander and A Inotai (eds), *World Trade After the Uruguay Round* (London, Routledge).

Gunter, H and Bailey, P (1992), 'The ILO Tripartite Declaration of Principles concerning Multinational Enterprises and Social Policy', in R Blanpain (ed) *International Encyclopedia for Comparative Labour Law and Industrial Relations* (Deventer, Kluwer).

Hall, PA and Soskice, D (2001), *Varieties of Capitalism: The Institutional Foundations of Comparative Advantage* (Oxford, OUP).

Hanson, G (1983), *Social Clauses and International Trade: an Economic Analysis of Labor Standards in Trade Policy* (New York, St Martin's Press).

Hayek, F (1980), *Law, Legislation and Liberty* (London, Routledge).

Hayter, S, Kooijmans, J and Sparreboom T (1998) *Globalisation, Social Norms and Worker Protection* (Cape Town, University of Cape Town, Institute of Development and Labour Law).

Heintz, J (2003), 'Global Labour Standards: their Impact and Implementation' in J Michie (ed), *The Handbook of Globalisation* (Cheltenham, Edward Elgar) 216.

Held, D (2004), *Global Covenant: the Social Democratic Alternative to the Washington Consensus* (Cambridge, Polity Press).

—— McGregor A, Goldblatt, D and Perraton J (1999), *Global Transformations: Politics, Economics and Culture* (Stanford, Stanford University Press).

Hepple, B (1974), 'Conflict of Laws in Employment Relationships within the EEC' in K Lipstein (ed), *Harmonisation of Private International Law* (London, Institute of Advanced Legal Studies).

—— (1983), 'Harmonisation of Labour Law in the European Communities' in J Adams (ed) *Essays for Clive Schmitthoff* (Abingdon, Professional Books) 14.

—— (1986a), 'Introduction' in B Hepple (ed) *The Making of Labour Law in Europe: a Comparative Study of Nine Countries up to 1945* (London, Mansell).

—— (1986b), 'What About the Workers?', 39 *Current Legal Problems* 259.

—— (1987), 'The Crisis in EEC Labour Law', 16 *Industrial Law Journal* 77.

—— (1990a), 'The Implementation of the Community Charter of Fundamental Social Rights' 53 *Modern Law Review* 643.

—— (1990b), *The Transfer of Undertakings Directive*. Report for the Commission of the EC, DGV (unpublished).

—— (1993), *European Social Dialogue: Alibi or Opportunity?* (London, Institute of Employment Rights).

—— (1994) 'Trade Unions and Democracy in Transitional Societies: Reflections on Russia and South Africa', in KD Ewing, CA Gearty and B Hepple (eds) *Human Rights and Labour Law: Essays for Paul O'Higgins* (London, Mansell).

—— (1996), 'Equality and Discrimination' in P Davies, A Lyon-Caen, S Sciarra and S Simitis (eds) *European Community Labour Law: Principles and Perspectives. Liber Amicorum Lord Wedderburn* (Oxford, Clarendon Press).

—— (1997), 'New approaches to international labour regulation', 26 *Industrial Law Journal* 353.

—— (1998a), 'The Impact on Labour Law' in B Markesinis (ed) *The Impact of the Human Rights Act on English Law* (Oxford, Clarendon Press).

—— (1998b), *The Legal Consequences of Cross-Border Transfers of Undertakings within the European Union*. Report for the Commission of the EC, DGV (unpublished).

—— (1999a), 'Labour Regulation in Internationalised Markets' in S Picciotto and R Mayne (eds), *Regulating International Business: Beyond Liberalisation,* (London, Oxfam and Macmillan).

—— (1999b), 'A Race to the Top: International Investment Guidelines and Corporate Codes of Conduct' 20 *Comparative Labor Law and Policy Journal* 347.

—— (1999c), 'Can Collective Labour Law Transplants Work? The South African Example', 20 [*South African*] *Industrial Law Journal* 1.

—— (2001), 'Equality and Empowerment for Decent Work', 140 *International Labour Review* 5.

—— (2002a), 'Enforcement: the Law and Politics of Co-operation and Compliance' in B Hepple (ed), *Social and Labour Rights in a Global Context* (Cambridge, CUP).

—— (2002b), *Labour Law, Inequality and Global Trade* (Amsterdam, Hugo Sinzheimer Institute).

—— (2003), *Rights at Work.* Discussion Paper DP/147/2003 (Geneva, International Institute for Labour Studies).

—— (2004a), 'Race and Law in Fortress Europe 67 *Modern Law Review* 1.

—— (2004b) 'The Right to Strike: a Case Study in Constitutionalistion')University of Cape Town, Institute of Development and Labour Law, occasional paper 1 (2004).

Hepple, B and Morris G (2002), 'The Employment Act 2002 and the Crisis of Individual Employment Rights', 31 *Industrial Law Journal* 245.

Hervey, T K and Kenner, J (eds) (2003), *Economic and Social Rights under the EU Charter of Fundamental Rights—a Legal Perspective* (Oxford, Hart Publishing)

Héthy, L (1994), 'International labour standards in Central and Eastern Europe' in W Sengenberger and D Campbell, *International Labour Standards and Economic Interdependence* (Geneva, International Institute for Labour Studies).

Hilowitz, J(1997), *Labelling Child Labour Products: a preliminary study* (Geneva, ILO).

Hirst, P and Thompson G (1999), *Globalisation in Question: The International Economy and the Possibilities of Governance,* 2nd ed (Cambridge, Polity Press).

Hoekman, BM and Kostecki, MM (1999), *The Political Economy of the World Trading System,* 2nd ed (Oxford, OUP).

Honjosa-Ojeda, R and Robinson, S (1992), 'Labor issues in a North American Free Trade Area' in N Lustig et al (eds), *North American Free Trade: Assessing the Impact* (Washington DC, Brookings Institution).

Hufbauer, G C, Elliott K A and Schott JJ (1983), *Economic Sanctions in support of foreign policy goals,* (Washington DC, Institute for International Economics).

—— —— —— (1990), *Economic Sanctions reconsidered,* 2nd ed (Washington DC, Institute for International Economics).

—— and Mitrokostas, NK (2004), 'International Implications of the Alien Tort Statute' 7 *Journal of International Economic Law* 245.

Hunt, E H (1981), *British Labour History 1815–914* (London, Lawrence and Wishart).

Hutchins, B L and Harrison, A (1966), *A History of Factory Legislation,* 3rd ed (London, Frank Cass, 1966; original publication 1926).

Ietto-Gillies, G (2003), 'The Role of Transnational Corporations in the Globalisation Process' in J Michie (ed) *The Handbook of Globalisation* (Cheltenham, Edward Elgar).

International Confederation of Free Trade Unions (ICFTU) (1975), 'Charter of Trade Union Demands for the Legislative Control of Multinational Corporations adopted by the 8th World Congress' in ICFTU, *Multinational Charter* (Brussels, ICFTU).

International Confederation of Free Trade Unions (ICFTU) (1997), *Labour and Business in the Global Market.* Economic and Social Committee (Brussels, ICFTU).

International Labour Organisation (ILO) (1996), *Working Party on the Social Dimension of the Liberalisation of Trade* (Geneva, ILO Governing Body 267th session).

—— (1997a), *Working Party on the Social Dimension of the Liberalisation of Trade* (Geneva, ILO Governing Body 268th session).

—— (1997b), *Working Party on the Social Dimension of the Liberalisation of Trade* (Geneva, ILO Governing Body 269th session).

—— (1997c), *World Labour Report: Industrial Relations, Democracy and Social Stability, 1997–98,* (Geneva, ILO).

—— (1997d), *ILO Standard Setting and Globalisation*, Report of the Director-General, (Geneva, ILO, International Labour Conference 85th session).

—— (1998a), *Working Party on the Social Dimension of the Liberalisation of Trade* (Geneva, ILO Governing Body 270th session).

—— (1998b), The ILO Declaration on Fundamental Principles and Rights at Work (Geneva, ILO).

—— (1998c), *Report of the Committee on the Declaration of Principles* (Geneva, ILO, International Labour Conference 86th session).

—— (1998d), *Discussion in Plenary on the Report of the Committee on the Declaration of Principles* (Geneva, ILO, International Labour Conference, 86th session).

—— (1998e), *Overview of Global Developments and Office Activities concerning Codes of Conduct, Social labels and other Private Sector Initiatives,* (Geneva, ILO Governing Body 270th session).

—— (1999), *Decent Work: Report of the Director-General* (Geneva, ILO).

—— (2002a), *A Guide to the Tripartite Declaration of Principles concerning MNEs and Social Policy* (Geneva, ILO).

—— (2002b) *Decent Work.* ILO Decent Work Programme (Geneva, ILO).

—— (2003) *Report of the Committee of Experts on the Application of Conventions and Recommendations.* Report III. Part 1A (Geneva, ILO, International Labour Conference, 91st session).

—— (2004a), *A Fair Globalisation. The Role of the ILO* Report of the Director-General on the World Commission on the Social Dimension of Globalisation (Geneva, ILO).

—— (2004b), *Organising Social Justice.* Report of the Director-General under the Follow-Up to the ILO Declaration of Fundamental Principles and Rights at Work (Geneva, ILO).

Irwin, D (1996), *Against The Tide: an Intellectual History of Free Trade* (Princeton, Princeton University Press).

Jackson, JH (2000), *The World Trading System: Law and Policy of International Economic Relations,* 2nd ed. (Cambridge, Mass, MIT Press).

Jenkins, C (1993), *The Effects of Sanctions on the Formal Sector Employment in South Africa* (Sussex, Institute of Development Studies, Discussion Paper 320).

Jones, R (1998), 'The OECD Multilateral Agreement on Investment: key concepts and the trade union response', Discussion Paper (Brussels, TUAC).

Kahn-Freund, O (1960), 'Labour Law and Social Security' in E Stein (ed) *American Enterprise in the European Common Market: a Legal Profile* (Ann Arbor, Michigan University Press).

—— (1976), *Labour and the Law* (London, Stevens), 3rd ed (1983) (ed) P Davies and M Freedland.

—— (1978) 'Comparative Labour Law as an Academic Subject' in *Selected Writings* (London, Stevens) [reprinted from (1966) 82 *Modern Law Review* 40].

—— (1981), *Labour Law and Politics in the Weimar Republic,* (ed) R Lewis and J Clark (Oxford, Blackwell).

Kenner, J (2003), *EU Employment Law: From Rome to Amsterdam and Beyond* (Oxford, Hart Publishing).

Kidner, R (1998), 'Jurisdiction in European Contracts of Employment' 27 *Industrial Law Journal* 103.

Kilpatrick, C (2001), 'Gender Equality: a Fundamental Dialogue' in S Sciarra (ed), *Labour Law in the Courts: National Judges and the European Court of Justice* (Oxford, Hart Publishing).

Klare, K (2000), 'Countervailing Workers' Power as a Regulatory Strategy' in H Collins, P L Davies and R Rideout (eds), *Legal Regulation of the Employment Relation* (London, Kluwer).

Koh, HH (2004), 'Separating Myth from Reality about Corporate Responsibility Litigation', 7 *Journal of International Economic Law* 263.

Knowles, A (2000), 'The ILO: time for change', *New Zealand Law Review* 326.

Krebber, S (2000), 'Conflict of Laws in Employment in Europe' 21 *Comparative Labor Law and Policy Journal* 501.

Kucera, D (2004), 'Effects of Standards on Labor Costs and FDI Flows' in H Corbet and J Bhagwati (eds) *Labour Standards in an Integrating World Economy: Clarifying the Trade and Labor Issue* (London, Cameron May).

—— and Sarna, R (forthcoming), *International Trade and Freedom of Association and Collective Bargaining Rights* (Geneva, International Institute for Labour Studies).

Lall, S (1995), 'Employment and foreign investment: policy options for developing countries', 134 *International Labour Review* 521.

Landy, EA (1966), *The Effectiveness of International Supervision: Thirty Years of ILO Experience* (London, Stevens).

Langille, B (1996), 'Competing conceptions of regulatory competition in debates on trade liberalisation and labour standards' in W Bratton, J McCahery, S Picciotto and C Scott (eds), *International Regulatory Competition and Co-ordination: Perspectives on Economic Regulation in Europe and the United States* (Oxford, OUP).

—— (1997), 'Eight Ways to Think About International Labour Standards' 31 *Journal of World Trade* 27.

La Sala, B (2001), 'NAFTA and workers rights: an analysis of the labor side accord after five years of operation and suggested improvements', 16 *Labor Lawyer* 319.

Leary, V (1996a), 'Workers' Rights in International Trade: the Social Clause' in J Bhagwati and RE Hudec (eds), *Fair Trade and Harmonisation, vol.II* (Cambridge, Mass, MIT Press).

—— (1996b) 'The Paradox of Workers' Rights as Human Rights' in LA Compa and SF Diamond (eds), *Human Rights, Labor Rights and International Trade* (Philadelphia, University of Pennsylvania Press) 22.

Lee, E (1996), 'Globalisation and employment: is anxiety justified' 135 *International Labour Review* 485.

Linan Nogueras, DJ and Hinojosa Martinez, LM (2001), 'Human Rights Conditionality in the External Trade of the European Union: Legal and Legitimacy Problems' 7 *Columbia Journal of European Law* 307.

List, F (1885), *The National System of Political Economy,* trans by Sampson and Lloyd (London, Longman).

Lo Faro, A (2000), *Regulating Social Europe: Reality and Myth of Collective Bargaining in the EC Legal Order* (Oxford, Hart Publishing).

Lopez-Hurtado (2002), 'Social Labelling and WTO Law' 5 *Journal of International Economic Law* 719.

Luckhardt, K and Wall, B (1980), *Organise or Starve: The History of the South African Congress of Trade Unions* (London, Lawrence and Wishart).

Macklem, P (2002), 'Labour Law beyond Borders' 5 *Journal of International Economic Law* 605.

Mahnkopf, B and Altvater, E (1995) 'Transmission Belts of Transnational Competition? Trade Unions and Collective Bargaining in the Context of European Integration' 1 *European Journal of Industrial Relations* 101.

Malmberg, J (2003), *Effective Enforcement of EC Labour Law* (Deventer, Kluwer).

Marsden, D (1999), *A Theory of Employment Systems: Micro-Foundations of Societal Diversity* (Oxford, OUP).

Martenczuk, B (2000), 'From Lomé to Cotonou: the ACP-EC Partnership Agreement in a Legal Perspective', 5 *European Foreign Affairs Review* 461.

Marx, K (1864), 'Inaugural Address to the International Working Men's Association' reprinted in D Fernbach (ed), *The First International and After* (Harmondsworth, Pelican, 1974).

—— and Engels, F (1848), 'Manifesto of the Communist Party' reprinted in D Fernbach (ed) *The Revolutions of 1848* (Harmondsworth, Pelican, 1973).

Maupain, F (1996), 'Protection International des Traveilleura et la Libéralisation du Commerce Mondiale: Un Lien ou un Frein?', 100 *Revue Génerale de Droit International Public* 45.

—— (2000), 'International Labour Organisation Recommendations and Similar Instruments' in D Shelton (ed), *Commitment and Compliance: The Role of Non-Binding Norms in the International Legal System* (Oxford, OUP).

—— (forthcoming a), 'Is the ILO Effective in Upholding Workers' Rights?' in P Alston (ed) *Labour Rights and Human Rights* Vol. XIV/1, *Collected Courses for the Academy of European Law* (Oxford, OUP).

—— (forthcoming b), 'La "Valeur-Ajoutee" de la Declaration' in I Daugareith (ed) *Mondialisation, droits fondamentaux de l'homme* (Brussels, Bruylant).

Mayne, R and Le Quesne C (1998), 'Calls for a Social Trade' in A Taylor and C Thomas (eds), *Global Trade and the Rise of New Social Issues* (Southampton, University of Southampton).

—— (forthcoming) *Buying Social Justice* (Oxford, OUP).

McCrudden, C (1999a), 'Human Rights Codes for Transnational Corporations: What Can the Sullivan and MacBride Principles Tell Us?' 19 *Oxford Journal of Legal Studies* 167.

—— (1999b), 'International Economic Law and the Pursuit of Human Rights: a Framework for Discussion of the Legality of "Selective Purchasing" Laws under the WTO Procurement Agreement' 2 *Journal of International Economic Law* 3.

—— (forthcoming), *Buying Social Justice* (Oxford, OUP).

McCrudden, C and Davies A (2000), 'A New Perspective on Trade and Labor Rights' 3 *Journal of International Economic Law* 43.

Michie, J (2004) 'Globalisation: Introduction and Overview' in J Michie (ed) *The Handbook of Globalisation* (Cheltenham, Edward Elgar) 1.

Mitro, ML (2002), 'Outlawing the Trade in Child Labor Products: What the GATT Article XX Health Exception authorizes unilateral sanctions' 51 *American University Law Review* 1223.

Moorman, Y (2001), 'Integration of ILO Core Rights Labor Standards into the WTO' 39 *Columbia Journal of Transnational Law* 555.

Morgenstern, F (1984), *International Conflicts of Labour Law* (Geneva, ILO).

Muchlinski, P (1995), *Multinational Enterprises and the Law* (Oxford, Blackwell).

Murray, J (1998), 'Corporate Codes of Conduct and Labour Standards' in R Kyloh (ed), *Mastering the Challenge of Globalisation: Towards a Trade union Agenda*, (Geneva, ILO/ACTRAV).

—— (2001a), *Transnational Labour Regulation: the ILO and EC compared* (Dordrecht, Kluwer).

—— (2001b), 'A new phase in the regulation of multinational enterprises: the role of the OECD', 30 *Industrial Law Journal* 255.

—— (2001c), 'The Sound of One Hand Clapping? The "Ratcheting Labour Standards Proposal and International Labour Law"' 14 *Australian Journal of Labour Law* 306.

Myrdal, HG (1994), 'The ILO in the crossfire: would it survive a social clause?', in W Sengenberger and D Campbell (eds), *International Labour Standards and Economic Interdependence* (Geneva, International Institute for Labour Studies).

Novitz, T (2003), *International and European Protection of the Right to Strike* (Oxford, OUP).

O'Donovan, K and Szyszczak, E (1988), *Equality and Discrimination Law* (Oxford, Blackwell).

O'Higgins, P (2002), 'The Interaction of the ILO, the Council of Europe and European Union Labour Standards', in B Hepple (ed) *Social and Labour Rights in a Global Context: International and Comparative Perspectives.* (Cambridge, CUP).

Ohlin, B (1956), *Social Aspects of European Collaboration*, ILO Reports and Studies (New Series) No.46 (Geneva, ILO) [also in 74 *International Labour Review* 99].

—— (1992), *Foreign Direct Investment, Trade and Employment* (Paris, OECD).

Organisation for Economic Co-operation and Development (OECD) (1996, rev. 2000), *Trade, Employment and Labour Standards: a study of core workers' rights and international trade* (Paris, OECD).

—— (1997), *The OECD Guidelines for Multinational Enterprises* (Paris, OECD).

—— (1998), *The Multilateral Agreement on Investment: Negotiating Text* (Paris, OECD).

—— (1999), *Codes of Corporate Conduct. An Inventory.* Working Party of the Trade Committee (Paris, OECD).

—— (2002), *Managing Working Conditions in Supply Chains.* OECD Roundtable on Corporate Responsibility (Paris, OECD).

Owen, R (1813), *A New View of Society* (London).

—— (1818), *Two Memorials on Behalf of the Working Classes* (London, Longman).

Oxfam (2002), *Rigged Rules and Double Standards: Trade, Globalisation and the Fight Against Poverty* (Oxford, Oxfam).

Palley, T (2003), 'The Economic Case for International Labour Standards' 28 *Cambridge Journal of Economics* 21.

Pankert, A (1977), 'Some Legal Problems of Workers' International Solidarity', 116 *International Labour Review* 67.

Parkinson, J (1993), *Corporate Power and Responsibility: Issues in the Theory of Company Law* (Oxford, OUP).

Petersmann, E (2002), 'Time for a United Nations "Global Compact" for Integrating Human Rights into the Law of Worldwide Organisations: Lessons from European integration', 13 *European Journal of International Law* 621, 845.

Picciotto, S (1996), 'The Regulatory Criss-Cross: Interaction between Jurisdictions and the Construction of Global Regulatory Networks' in W Bratton et al (eds), *International Regulatory Competition: Competition and Coordination* (Oxford, Clarendon Press).

—— (1999), 'A Critical Assessment of the MAI' in S Picciotto and R Mayne (eds), *Regulating International Business: Beyond Liberalisation* (London, Oxfam and Macmillan).

Piore, M (1994), 'Labour standards and business strategies' in S Herzenberg and J Perez-Lopez (eds), *Labour Standards and Development in the Global Economy*, (Paris, OECD Employment Outlook).

Porter, M (1990), *The Competitive Advantage of Nations* (London, Macmillan).

Qureshi, A (1996), *The World Trade Organisation: Implementing International Trade Norms* (Manchester, MUP).

Ramm, T (1986), '*Laissez-Faire* and State Protection of Workers' and 'Epilogue, the New Ordering of Labour Law 1918–45' in B Hepple (ed), *The Making of Labour Law in Europe: a Comparative Study of Nine Countries up to 1945* (London, Mansell) 73, 277.

Rawls, J (1973), *A Theory of Justice* (Oxford, OUP).

Reed, A (2001) 'Multiparty Group Actions and Legal Aid' 151 *New Law Journal* 177.

Rhodes, M (1991), 'The Social Dimension of the Single European Market: National versus Transnational Regulation', 19 *European Journal of Political Research* 245.

Ricardo, D (1817) *On the Principles of Political Economy and Taxation*, republished 1971 (Harmondsworth, Penguin).

Ridenour, A (2001), 'Apples and Oranges: Why Courts Should use international standards to determine liability for violations of the law of nations under the Alien Tort Claims Act' 9 *Tulane Journal of International and Comparative Law* 581.

Riedel, E and Will, M (1999) 'Human Rights Clauses in External Agreements of the EC' in P Alston (ed), *The EU and Human Rights* (Oxford, OUP).

Rubin, N (1998), *International Labour Law and the New South Africa*. (Cape Town, University of Cape Town. Inaugural Lectures New Series No. 206).

—— (forthcoming), *Code of International Labour Law: Law, Practice, Jurisprudence*. (Cambridge, CUP).

Sapir, A (1996), 'Trade liberalisation and harmonisation of social policies: Lessons from European Integration' in J N Bhagwati and R E Hudec (eds), *Fair Trade and Harmonisation: Prerequisites for Free Trade?* (Cambridge, Mass., MIT).

Schlyter, C (2003), *International Labour Standards and the Informal Sector: Developments and Dilemmas,* Working Paper (Geneva, ILO).

Sciarra, S (1996), *How Global is Labour Law? The Perspective of Social Rights in the European Union,* EUI Working paper 96/6 (Florence, EUI).

—— (2002), 'Market Freedom and Fundamental Social Rights' in B Hepple (ed) *Social and Labour Rights in a Global Context: International and Comparative Perspectives* (Cambridge, CUP).

Sen, A (1999), *Development as Freedom* (New York, Knopf).

—— (2000) 'Work and Rights', 139 *International Labour Review* 139.

Sengenberger, W (1994a), 'Labour standards: an institutional framework for restructuring and development' in W Sengenberger and D Campbell (eds), *Creating Economic Opportunities: the Role of Labour Standards in Industrial Restructuring* (Geneva, International Institute for Labour Studies).

—— (1994b), 'International labour standards in a globalised economy: the issues' in W Sengenberger and D Campbell (eds), *International Labour Standards and Economic Interdependence* (Geneva, International Institute for Labour Studies).

Servais, J-M (1989), 'The Social Clause in Trade Agreements: Wishful Thinking or Instrument of Social Progress?, 128 *International Labour Review* 423.

—— (2004), *Normes Internationales du Travail* (Paris, LGDJ).

Seyfang, G (1999), *Private Sector Self-Regulation for Social Responsibility. Mapping Codes of Conduct* (Norwich, University of East Anglia Overseas Development Group).

Shaw, M (2003) *International Law,* 5th ed (Cambridge, CUP).

Shotwell, JT (1934), *The Origins of the International Labour Organisation* (New York, Columbia University Press).

Singh, A and Zammit, A (2004), 'Globalisation, Labour Standards and Economic Development' in J Michie (ed), *The Handbook of Globalisation* (Cheltenham, Edward Elgar) 191.

Snyder, F (1999), 'Governing Economic Globalisation: Global Legal Pluralism and European Law' 5 *European Law Journal* 334.

Standing, G (1999), *Global Labour Flexibility—seeking distributive justice* (Basingstoke, Macmillan).

Stiglitz, J (2002), *Globalization and its Discontents* (London, Penguin Books).

Stone, K (1996), 'Labor in the Global Economy: Four Approaches to Transnational Labour Regulation' in W Bratton, J McCahery, S Picciotto and C Scott (eds) *International Regulatory Competition and Coordination: Perspectives on Economic Regulation in Europe and the United States* (Oxford, OUP); and in 16 *Michigan Journal of International Law* 987.

—— (1999), 'To the Yukon and Beyond: Local Laborers in a Global Labor Market', 3 *Journal of Small and Emerging Business Law* 93.

—— (2004a), 'From Globalism to Regionalism: Protecting Labor Rights in a Post-National Era' (Unpublished paper).

—— (2004b), *From Widgets to Digits: Employment Regulation for the Changing Workplace* (Cambridge, CUP).

Streeck, W (1995), 'Neo-Voluntarism: a New European Social Policy Regime' 1 *European Law Journal* 31.

Supiot, A (2001), *Beyond Employment: Changes in Work and the Future of Labour Law in Europe* (Oxford, OUP).

Szyszczak, E (1997), 'Building a European Constitutional Order: Prospects for a General Non-Discrimination Standard' in A Dashwood and S O'Leary (eds) *The Principle of Equal Treatment in EC Law* (London, Sweet & Maxwell).

—— (2000a), *EC Labour Law* (London, Longman).

—— (2000b), 'The Evolving European Employment Strategy' in J Shaw (ed) *Social Law and Policy in the Evolving European Union* (Oxford, Hart Publishing).

—— (2001), 'The New Paradigm of Social Policy: a Virtuous Circle?' 38 *Common Market Law Review* 1125.

—— (2002), 'Social Policy in the Post-Nice Era', in A Arnull and D Wincott (eds), *Accountability and Legitimacy in the European Union* (Oxford, OUP).

—— (2004), 'Citizenship and Human Rights 53 *International and Comparative Law Quarterly* 493.

Tergeist, P, Clarke O, Evans J, Lanfranchi N and Pearson M (2000), 'The Organisation for Economic Co-operation and Development' in R Blanpain (ed), *International Encyclopaedia for Comparative Labour Law and Industrial Relations* (Deventer, Kluwer).

Teubner, G (2001), 'Legal Irritants: How Unifying Law ends up in New Divergences', in P Hall and D Soskice (eds) *Varieties of Capitalism: The Institutional Foundations of Comparative Advantage* (Oxford, OUP).

Thelen, K (2001), 'Varieties of Labour Politics in Developed Democracies) in P Hall and D Soskice (eds) *Varieties of Capitalism: The Institutional Foundations of Comparative Advantage* (Oxford, OUP).

Thomas, A (1948), *International Social Policy* (Geneva, ILO).

Thompson, C (1993), 'Borrowing and Bending: the Development of South Africa's Unfair Labour Practice Jurisprudence' in R Blanpain and M Weiss (eds), *The Changing Face of Labour Law and Industrial Relations. Liber Amicorum for Clyde W Summers* (Baden Baden, Nomos).

Trachtman, JP (2000), 'Regulatory Competition and Regulatory Jurisdiction' 3 *Journal of International Economic Law* 331.

Tsogas, G (2000), 'Labour Standards in the Generalised Systems of Preferences in the EU and the US', 6 *European Journal of Industrial Relations* 349.

—— (2001), *Labour Regulation in a Global Economy* (Armonk, NY and London, ME Sharpe).

Tuytshaever, F (1999), *Differentiation in European Union Law* (Oxford, Hart Publishing).

United Nations Conference on Trade and Development (UNCTAD) (1994), *World Investment Report 1994: Transnational Corporations, Employment and the Workplace* (New York, United Nations).

—— (1996), *International Investment Instruments: a Compendium*, 3 vols. (New York, United Nations).

—— (2000), *Employment*. UNCTAD series on International Investment Agreements (New York, United Nations) [based on an original paper by B Hepple].

Valticos, N and von Potobsky, G (1994), 'International Labour Law', in R Blanpain (ed), *International Encyclopaedia for Comparative Labour Law and Industrial Relations* (Deventer, Kluwer).

Van Liemt (2000), 'Codes of Conduct and International Subcontracting: a "private" road towards ensuring minimum labour standards in export industries' in R Blanpain (ed) *Multinational Enterprises and the Social Challenges of the XXIst Century* (London, Kluwer).

Van Roozendaal, G (2002), *Trade Unions and Global Governance: The Debate on a Social Clause* (London: Continuum).

Vázquez, CM (2003) 'Trade Sanctions and Human Rights- Past, Present, and Future', 6 *Journal of International Economic Law* 797.

Vousden, S (2000), '*Albany,* Market Law and Social Exclusion', 29 *Industrial Law Journal* 181.

Vranken, M (1986), 'Deregulating the Employment Relationship: Current Trends in Europe', 7 *Comparative Labor Law Journal* 143.

Ward, A (1998), 'Frameworks for Cooperation between European Union and Third States: a Viable Matrix for Uniform Human Rights Standards?' 3 *European Foreign Affairs Review* 505.

Ward, H (2001), 'Securing Transnational Corporate Accountability through National Courts: Implications and Policy Options' 24 *Hastings International and Comparative Law Review* 451.

Warner, J (1984), 'EC Social Policy in Practice: Community Action on behalf of Women and its Impact in the Member States' 23 *Journal of Common Market Studies* 141.

Watson, A (1974), *Legal Transplants: An Approach to Comparative Law* (Edinburgh, Scottish Academic Press).

Watson, P (1980), *Social Security Law of the European Communities* (London, Mansell).

Wedderburn, KW (1971), *The Worker and the Law*, 2nd ed, 3rd ed (1980) (Harmondsworth, Penguin).

—— (1972), 'Multinational Enterprise and National Labour Law', 1 *Industrial Law Journal* 12.

Wedderburn, Lord (1992), 'Inderogability, collective agreements and Community law', 21 *Industrial Law Journal* 245.

—— (1997), 'Consultation and Collective Bargaining in Europe: Success or Ideology?', 26 *Industrial Law Journal* 1.

—— (2002), 'Common Law, Labour Law, Global Law' in B Hepple (ed), *Social and Labour Rights in a Global Context: International and Comparative Perspectives* (Cambridge, CUP).

Weiler, JH (1995), 'Does Europe need a constitution? Reflections on Demos, Telos and the German Maastricht Decision' 1 *European Law Journal,* 219.

—— (2000), *EU, the WTO and the NAFTA: Towards a Common Law of International Trade* (Oxford, OUP).

—— and Lockhart NJS (1995), 'Taking Rights Seriously: the European Court and Fundamental Rights Jurisprudence' 30 *Common Market Law Review* 51.

Weiss, M[anfred] (2002), 'The Politics of the EU Charter of Fundamental Rights' in B Hepple (ed), *Social and Labour Rights in a Global Context: International and Comparative Perspectives* (Cambridge, CUP).

—— (2004), 'The Future of Workers' Participation in the EU' in C Barnard, S Deakin and G Morris (eds), *The Future of Labour Law. Liber Amicorum Sir Bob Hepple QC* (Oxford, Hart Publishing).

Weiss, M[arley] (2003), 'Two Steps Forward, One Step Back or Vice Versa: Labour Rights and Free Trade Agreements from NAFTA, Through Jordan via Chile to Latin America and Beyond', 37 *University of San Francisco Law Review* 689.

Wolf, M (2004) *Why Globalisation Works: The Case for the Global Market Economy* (New Haven, Yale University Press).

World Bank (1995), *World Development Report 1995: Workers in an Integrating World* (Oxford, OUP).

—— (2000), *Engendering Development through gender equality in rights, resources and voice* (Washington DC, World Bank).

—— (2001), *World Development Report 2000/1. Attacking Poverty* (Washington DC, World Bank).

World Commission on the Social Dimension of Globalisation (2004), *A Fair Globalisation: Creating Opportunities for All* (Geneva, ILO).

Zweigert, K and Kötz, H (1992), *An Introduction to Comparative Law* (Oxford, OUP).

INDEX